Mountain Guru

Mountain Guru

The Life of Doug Scott

Catherine Moorehead

BIRLINN

First published in 2023 by
Birlinn Limited
West Newington House
10 Newington Road
Edinburgh
EH9 1QS

www.birlinn.co.uk

ISBN: 978 1 78027 831 5

British Library Cataloguing-in-Publication Data
A catalogue record for this book is available from the British Library

Typeset by Initial Typesetting Services, Edinburgh

Papers used by Birlinn are from well-managed forests and
other responsible sources

Printed and bound by Clays Ltd, Elcograf S.p.A.

For
Trish

Doug Scott, 1941–2020,
by Hazel Morgan

Contents

Foreword   ix

Introduction   xiii

Notes on the Text   xv

Maps: sites of Doug Scott's Principal Climbs and Expeditions   xvi

1   A Nottingham Family   1

2   Childhood and Education   13

3   Starting Out: Climbs in the UK, 1955–60   25

4   Climbs in the UK, 1960–70   40

5   Climbs in the Alps, Spain and Dolomites, 1958–69   55

6   Expeditions beyond Europe, 1962–67   69

7   Growth of a Mountaineer (I), 1959–70   93

8   The Big Walls, 1968–78   106

9   The Road to Everest, 1972–75   126

10   The Hub, 1975–79   137

11   Growth of a Mountaineer (II), 1970–85   148

12   Classics Master, 1978–2000   164

13   Explorations, 1980–2005   185

14   Growth of a Mountaineer (III), 1985–2003   227

15   CAN and CAT   240

16   Non-retirement   268

17   'A Very Different Man'   284

Appendix: A Timeline of Doug Scott's Recorded Climbs   297
    and Expeditions

Notes   307

Bibliography   323

Acknowledgements   329

General Index   331

Index of Climbs and Expeditions   342

List of Maps

Great Britain and Ireland   xvi

Iceland, Baffin Island and South Greenland   xvii

Continental Europe   xviii

Africa and the Middle East   xix

Central Asia with Southern India and Sri Lanka   xx

Nepal with Uttarakhand (India), Bhutan and Arunachal Pradesh   xxi

Australasia   xxii

United States and British Columbia   xxiii

South America   xxiv

Antarctica   xxiv

Foreword

Doug Scott, like all the best people, was a jumble of paradoxes: tough guy rugby player fascinated by Buddhist mysticism; anarchic hippy with a deep sense of tradition; intensely ambitious one day, laid back the next. He was as egotistic as any climber, adroit at getting his own way, but was also demonstrably generous and compassionate, admired universally for his philanthropy. In his Himalayan heyday he resembled a beefed-up version of John Lennon; in latter years, presiding over his gorgeous Cumbrian garden in moleskins and tweed jacket, he looked more like the country squire.

I first met him in his John Lennon phase, although 'met' is an over-statement: I was far too young, shy and awestruck, that October evening in 1975, actually to talk to the hero of the day, standing at the Alpine Club lectern with Chris Bonington and Pete Boardman to deliver the first public account of their recent triumph on the south-west face of Everest. The room was packed, mainly with former Everest climbers like Michael Ward and John Hunt from the 1953 expedition, Charles Warren and Jack Longland from the thirties and Noel Odell, last surviving member of the 1924 expedition. There was a palpable sense of history as the tweeded and suited elders congratulated the denim-clad new generation.

Doug and Dougal Haston were the first British climbers to reach the world's highest summit. For all the meticulous logistics of their leader Chris Bonington, this final chapter of the climb was a bold push into the unknown, at times virtually swimming through deep powder snow on a long committing traverse across the upper south-west face. They reached the South Summit late in the afternoon; the sun was setting as they stood on the actual summit. Rather than risk descending in the dark they bivou-acked at the South Summit before returning to Camp VI in the morning.

Now here were those men in the flesh, right in front of me – including Doug Scott, who had survived a night in the open at 8750m, higher than any previous human being, with no sleeping bag – not even a down jacket

– and yet who had returned safely without even a bit of frostbite to show for it. He certainly *looked* tough – solid and powerful – but his story-telling was casual, modest, laconic and a touch rambling, with occasional meditative diversions. A few years later I did get to meet him properly and discovered that his conversation, like his lecturing – or indeed his expeditioning – could be enigmatic, discursive, elliptical, often veering off the beaten track into untrodden side valleys, but always with an undercurrent of humour. And never pulling rank: he was a humble, approachable man, happy to talk with anyone. That humility was impressive in someone who was unarguably one of the greatest Himalayan climbers of the late twentieth century. And not just a *Himalayan* climber. Long before he went anywhere near Everest, his prolific magazine articles and masterful photos were chronicling pioneering climbs – often on huge rock walls – in the Hebrides, the Dolomites, Yosemite, Baffin Island, the Tibesti Mountains in Chad, Turkey, Afghanistan . . .

It was only after Everest – realising that if he could survive a night in the open out at nearly 9000m then the possibilities were immense – that his high-altitude career really took off. And what a career it was. However, Himalayan ambition never dimmed his love of home turf. He had learned his climbing in the Peak District and never lost his enthusiasm for the crags of Britain.

I only climbed with him once, when we were both speaking at an Alpine Club symposium at Plas y Brenin in Snowdonia. We were not on until the afternoon and it was a beautiful sunny morning – far too good to be shut indoors – so we sneaked off over the Llanberis Pass for a quick jaunt up *Cenotaph Corner*. Doug said the first time he had done this classic rock climb was on his honeymoon. It was now 1989, so he must have been forty-eight – middle-aged, but definitely still in his prime. He led with powerful ease and then suggested we continue on the upper tier of the Cromlech, up that brutal creation of his old mentor Don Whillans – *Grond*. In the absence of large cams to protect the initial off-width, he grabbed a large lump of rhyolite – explaining cheerfully, 'This is how we used to do it, youth' – shoved it in the crack, hitched a sling round it and clipped in the rope. As soon as he moved up, the chockstone flew out of the crack, narrowly missing my head, but Doug carried on regardless – blithely calm, assured and fluent, supremely at ease with the rock.

The meeting that made the biggest impression on me was in 1987 in the village of Nyalam, in Tibet. It was the end of an expedition to Shishapangma. We had failed on that peak but had managed to put a new route up Pungpa Ri, which Doug had climbed five years earlier. Also staying at the Chinese hostel were members of Doug's current team, who had been attempting the *North-East Ridge* of Everest. Doug himself only turned up late that night, at the end of a gruelling road journey from Rongbuk, across the border to Nepal, then up to Solu Khumbu, then all the way back across the border to wind up the expedition in Tibet. The reason? A young Sherpa man who had been helping his expedition had been killed in an avalanche near base camp during a huge storm two weeks earlier. Doug had taken it on himself to travel all the way to the man's family in Nepal to tell them personally what had happened and to ensure that they received financial compensation.

That empathy with the people of Nepal came to fruition in his remarkable charity, Community Action Nepal (CAN). At an age when most people in his position would be happy to rest on their laurels, perhaps accepting the occasional lucrative guest appearance, Doug travelled the length and breadth of the country on gruelling lecture tours – often only just out of hospital, after yet another operation on old injuries from his first ascent of The Ogre – pouring all the proceeds into his charity. Lecture fees were topped up by sales of Nepalese crafts and auctions of Doug's most classic photographs. Doug the auctioneer was a force to behold, as he mesmerised and cajoled audience members into donating ever more astronomical sums for a signed photograph.

In addition to a hectic lecture programme, Doug managed in his seventies to pen hundreds of thousands of words, completing three new books, including volume one of the long-awaited autobiography for which he had first been paid an advance in 1975. Defying illness, he tried doggedly to complete the second volume but even he could not outdo the brain cancer which killed him at the end of 2020. With the autobiography incomplete, it was decided that a full biography was required. Catherine Morehead, who worked closely with Doug on his Ogre and Kangchenjunga monographs, has devoted two years to researching Doug's huge archive and interviewing his global network of friends and colleagues to produce this permanent record, celebrating the extraordinary life of one of the world's greatest mountaineers.

Stephen Venables
September 2023

Introduction

Before looking into Doug Scott's background, it is worth dwelling briefly on how the shape of his life can be understood. The man himself enjoyed a self-promoted destiny-myth: his birth in 1941, on the auspicious date of 29 May – the same day as Hillary and Tenzing's first ascent of Everest in 1953 – provides the first clue; Scott's redoubtable, long-lived and much-loved mother, Joyce, had been born within twenty-four hours of Hillary, thereby reinforcing the idea of a man of heroic mountain destiny. When still in adolescence, Scott made it clear to several friends that he wanted to be famous. 'Why' is harder to discern: certainly not for personal glory, but more likely as a way of earning his mother's love.

Yet his character was formed from clashing opposites – Scott's ethical ideals often conflicted with a grim everyday reality. When not reading esoterica, such as Buddhist tracts or works by Gurdjieff or Castaneda, or the *I Ching*, consulted at many a base camp, Scott's greatest intellectual interest otherwise lay in history, both human and natural, inspired not just by a good teacher but by Nottingham's own rich heritage. *The Ogre*, Scott's second-last book, comprises about one-third history and two-thirds climbing; in *Kangchenjunga*, his final book, that proportion is reversed. For climbing books, both contain an unusual amount of often excellent historical background research. This very widely read climber spent a lifetime with history and myth contending endlessly for his mind and soul. Such a conflict may be illustrated by Scott's fellow Nottingham alumni: Torvill and Dean's disciplined, athletic fantasies are the polar opposite to the inebriated, brutal escape from working-class reality described by Alan Sillitoe in *Saturday Night and Sunday Morning* (1958).

A war between self-myth and sourced history, however, is scarcely sufficient to account for the most unusual energy and drive of one of the world's greatest climbers, who became one of its outstanding humanitarians. The shape of Scott's life might helpfully be pictured as a Catherine wheel, fizzing and spinning, with bright flashes: his decidedly Freudian upbringing; leading climbs in the UK and the Alps; early explorations of little-known territory in Africa, the Middle East and Central Asia and encounters with their peoples; wide reading after an uncertain education; an early, tumultuous marriage; global fame as a climber of 'big walls'. These flashing strands burnt through to the vortex, that extraordinary period between 1975 and 1979 when Scott climbed Everest then survived one of the most testing epic descents in mountaineering history, followed by arguably his finest achievement in climbing Kangchenjunga (8611m), the world's third-highest mountain, lightweight, without supplementary oxygen. Scott acquired a global, historical stature. Flung out from the belief that such experiences permitted him to climb anywhere and survive anything, the strands of his life followed twenty more years of climbs and explorations at the highest level, one turbulent and one highly successful marriage and thirty years of coming to terms with semi-divine status in Nepal as an effective provider of health, shelter and education in some of its remotest areas.

Notes on the Text

Heights and distances are expressed in the metric system. Vertical height is marked by 'm' after a number, eg, 'Everest is 8848m high.' Horizontal distance is written as 'metres' or 'kilometres', as in, 'The river was ten metres wide.' Where a conversion has been made, the calculation is based on one metre equalling 3.28 feet.

Climbing grades are included in brackets after route names. Different countries use different grading systems, but the UK system is most commonly used in this book.[1]

Doug Scott is referred to as 'Doug', 'Douglas', 'Scott' and very occasionally as 'Dougie' or 'Scotty', sometimes within the same chapter. This is deliberate. He is referred to as 'Douglas' in specific family situations, as 'Doug' in the chapters dealing with his personal growth and development, and as 'Scott' when describing him on expeditions.

Because Doug's climbing life was so diverse, I have arranged this book according to the kind of climb he was undertaking, whether British, Alpine, big wall, on high-altitude routes on familiar mountains, or explorations of lesser-known routes, mountains and ranges. Chapters within each of these areas are presented in chronological sequence but the kinds of climbs themselves can be understood to have taken place roughly parallel with each other. For example, the climbs in the Classics Master chapter (new routes on familiar mountains) and the Explorations chapter (expeditions to new or less familiar areas) all took place in the same twenty-year period. In any given year, it could be the case that Doug would have undertaken a combination of different types of climbs.

1. Old Man of Hoy
2. Am Buachaille
3. Old Man of Stoer
4. Suilven
5. Stac Pollaidh
6. Seana Braigh
7. Ben Wyvis
8. Liathach
9. Beinn Bhan
10. Five Sisters
11. Cuillin
12. Strone Ulladale
13. Ben Nevis
14. Mamores
15. Bidean nam Bian
16. Ben More
17. Cairngorm
18. Ben Macdhui
19. Cir Mhor
20. Grey Mare's Tail
21. Borrowdale
22. Scafell Pike
23. Old Man of Coniston
24. Gordale Scar

25. Malham Cove
26. High Peak
27. Kinder Scout
28. Derwent Valley
29. High Tor
30. Gogarth
31. Tryfan
32. Snowdon
33. Mount Errigal
34. Slieve League

• Rock-climbing area
▲ Peak

0   50   100 km

0   50 miles

Great Britain and Ireland

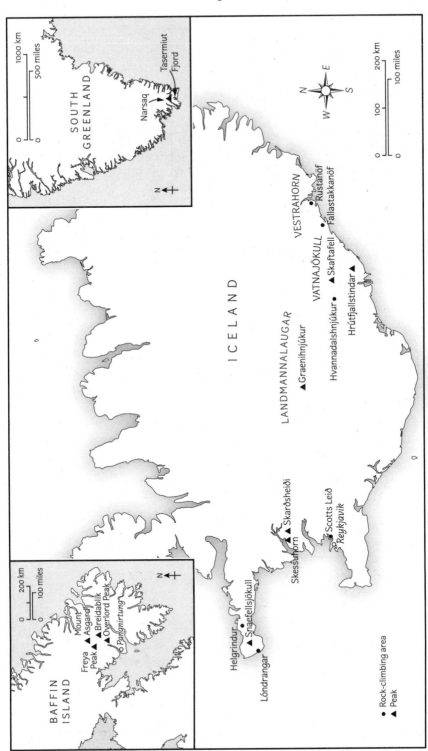

1000 km
500 miles

SOUTH GREENLAND

Tasermiut Fjord

Narsaq

N

200 km
100 miles

N
W E
S

VESTRAHORN
Rustanöf
Fallastakkanöf

VATNAJÖKULL
Skaftafell ▲
Hrútfjallstindar ▲

Hvannadalshnjúkur ●

LANDMANNALAUGAR

ICELAND

▲Graenihnjúkur

Skarðsheiði ▲
Skessuhorn ▲

Scotts Leið ●
Reykjavik ○

Snaefellsjökull
Helgrindur ●
Lóndrangar ●

BAFFIN ISLAND

200 km
100 miles

N

Mount Asgard ▲
Freya Peak ▲
Breidablik ▲
Overlord Peak ▲
Ó Panginirtung

● Rock-climbing area
▲ Peak

Iceland, Baffin Island and South Greenland

Mountain Guru

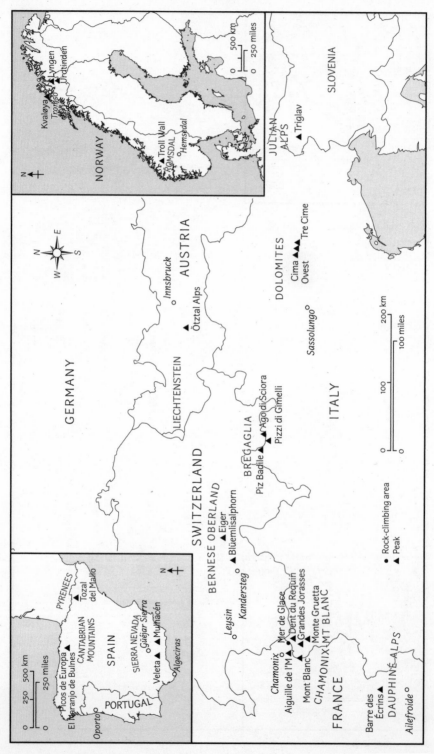

Continental Europe

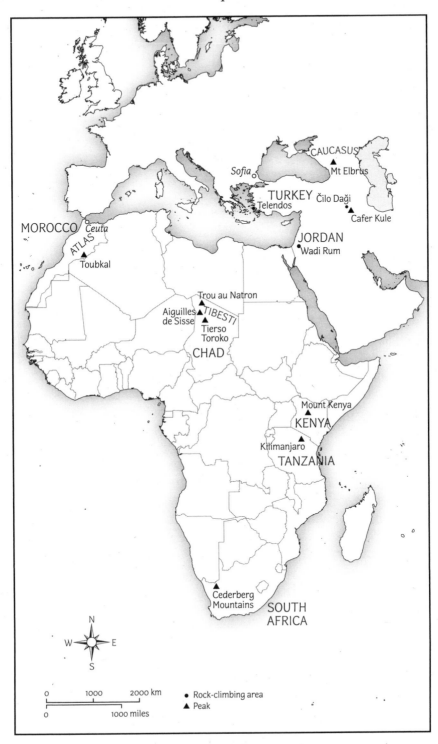

Africa and the Middle East

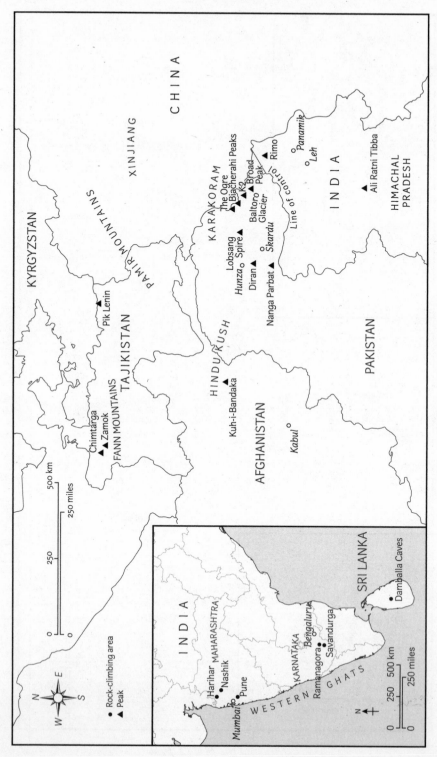

Central Asia with Southern India and Sri Lanka

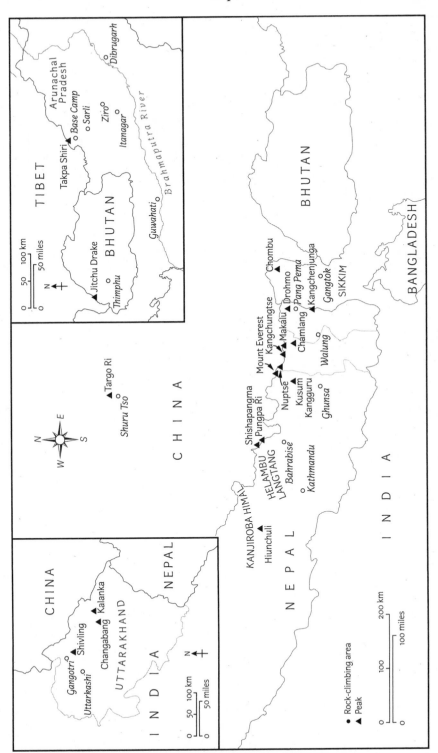

Nepal with Uttarakhand (India), Bhutan and Arunachal Pradesh

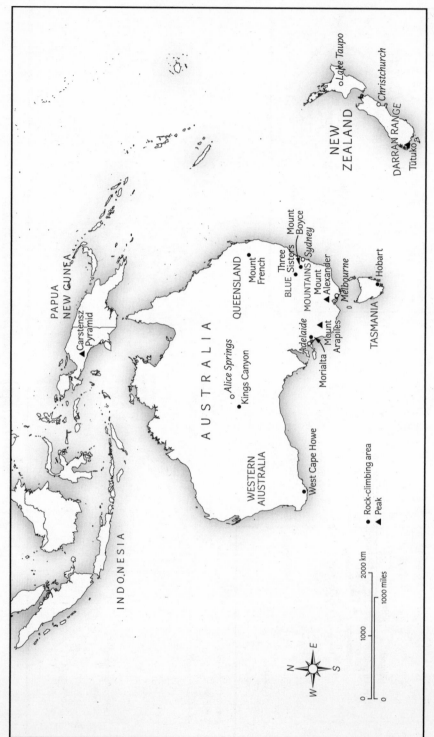

Australasia

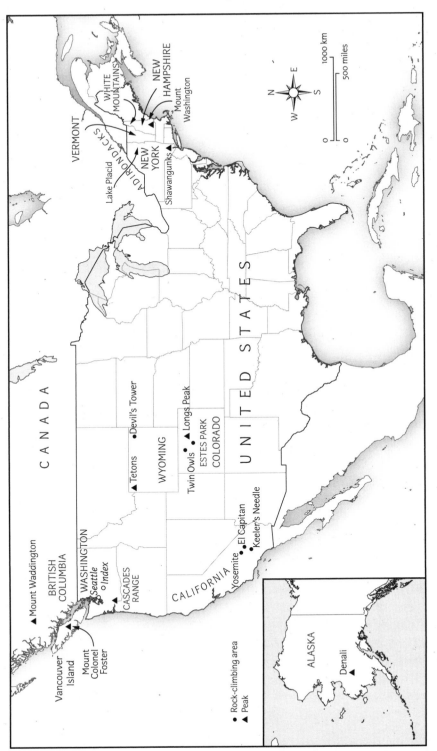

United States and British Columbia

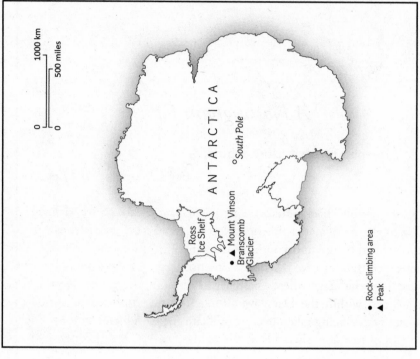

Antarctica

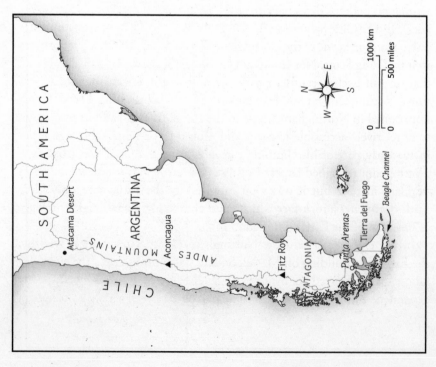

South America

I

A Nottingham Family

'The past is always close behind.'

— Doug Scott, *Up and About*

Scott's family background and upbringing were partly defined by Nottingham's own rich history. Nottingham began as a Mercian settlement ruled by the unbecomingly named King Snot of the Saxons. Earlier references talk of cave dwellers, housed in the local sandstone. It weathered into the crags where Scott began his climbing career. Nottingham remained within the Danelaw, although it was captured by Alfred the Great before being taken over by William the Conqueror in 1067. Such a 'waves of invasion' theme is developed by Scott in the historical sections of several of his books.

Nottingham prospered. Possibly England's oldest pub, Ye Olde Trip to Jerusalem, perhaps dates back to 1189 (but probably three or four centuries later), and Ye Olde Salutation Inn allegedly dates from circa 1240 – this latter pub becoming home to the Nottingham Climbers' Club (NCC), founded in 1961 by Doug Scott. Nor could anyone there not know about Robin Hood, that icon of twelfth-century crypto-socialist wealth re-distribution. At this time, Nottingham endured incursions by the Scots; King David II was imprisoned in Nottingham Castle in the 1340s. Scotland and its mountains were relatively accessible to Scott and proved to be remarkably significant in the early part of his climbing career. During the Civil War (1642–49), Nottingham remained largely Royalist. The castle garrison flew Charles I's standard in 1642 but it was soon captured by the Parliamentarians. This castle dominates a rock-face which Scott climbed by exercising his privilege as Freeman of the City, conferred in 1976.

In the eighteenth century, Nottingham became increasingly wealthy: the Exchange Building on Market Square was built in 1742. The eight-day Goose Fair (referred to by D.H. Lawrence in *Sons and Lovers*) greatly expanded; the textile trade, particularly in lace, for which Nottingham continues to be famous, burgeoned. A German traveller, C.P. Moritz, whom Scott read as a schoolboy, remarked, 'Of all the towns I have seen outside London, Nottingham is the loveliest and neatest. Everything had a modern look, and a large space in the centre was hardly less handsome than a London square. A charming footpath leads over the fields to the highway, where a bridge spans the Trent . . . Nottingham . . . with its high houses, red roofs and church steeples, looks excellent from a distance.'[1]

In the nineteenth century, Nottingham's new suburbs, some no better than slums, contained the flood of workers who staffed the new cottage industries and factories. In 1877, the parishes of Radford, where Scott's paternal grand-mother lived during Scott's childhood, and Lenton, where Scott attended secondary school and lived for a time, were added, as was West Bridgford, where Scott's father, George, was born in 1915. City status was awarded as part of Queen Victoria's Diamond Jubilee celebrations in 1897. Nottingham was extended in 1933 by adding Wollaton, where Scott was brought up.

Among the better-known of Nottingham's new factories, the Raleigh Bicycle Company began production in 1886 in Raleigh Street, Radford, about two kilometres from where Scott grew up. John Player's cigarette company, where Doug's mother, Joyce, worked as a supervisor, opened in 1877 in Radford; in the 1960s Player's sponsored several of her son's early expeditions.

Scott's immediate environment also directly influenced the formation of his character. Wollaton, then a resolutely lower middle-class district, contained the newly built Charlbury Road, where at number 174 Scott grew up in a rented, unremarkable but thoughtfully designed semi in a long road of similar houses. He was conceived there during the Battle of Britain. He was born only a fortnight after the terrifying Luftwaffe raid of 8–9 May, in which 159 people were killed and 274 injured.

In Scott's over-detailed autobiography, *Up and About*, he describes himself with an eye to posterity as a 'warchild', thus self-dramatising his first four or five years. He claims, for example, to remember his father coming home on leave in 1943 – when Scott would have been only about two, well before such memories are possible. Other wartime events in this chapter are slyly described as though from direct personal memory rather than what must have been indirect retrospective description. As he himself concedes, creating an attractively dramatic persona might have been a cry for attention which never left him.

Aside from self-mythmaking and historical ideas vying for dominance in his psyche, Scott's physical environment influenced him in other ways.

Wollaton suburb was named after Wollaton Park, a 202-hectare deer park and lake surrounding Wollaton Hall, an Elizabethan country mansion from the 1580s which houses Nottingham's Natural History Museum, a likely early stimulus to Scott's later environmental interests (although he was specifically interested in trees and plants). The park, which lay only about 500 metres from Scott's house, was used to billet American soldiers during the run-up to D-Day. Later, German and Italian prisoners-of-war were housed there; Scott's paternal grandparents lived there. The park provided an ideal pram walk for Joyce while bringing up Scott's brothers Brian, born in 1944, and Garry, born in 1952. This extraordinary site also contained a cross-country running route and athletics track, both of which figured in Scott's outstanding adolescent sporting achievements.

Even closer to home lay the canal and railway line. The main line from Nottingham to Eastwood (D.H. Lawrence's birthplace) and Alfreton, or to Kirkby-in-Ashfield and beyond, ran past the north side of Charlbury Road. Its sandy embankment offered ideal soil for sprawling blackberry thickets and building tunnels, although one attempt to tunnel under the line itself led to police intervention. The canal, completed in 1796 for transporting coal and other industrial materials, lay immediately to the south of Charlbury Road: a meeting place and an adventure playground. Climbing on the lock- and sluice-gates, rafting on the water, fishing or getting involved in gang confrontations developed physical strength and an interest in ecology (though it would not have been thought of in that way at the time), especially in summer when the low water-level made the sight of small creatures and insects more obvious. These activities helped Scott to understand how others thought and behaved (particularly when they fell in). In *Up and About*, Scott implies the canal might be a kind of metaphor for the course of a life based on honesty, reliability, lack of jealousy or self-importance – qualities which, in his self-contradictory way, he adhered to in some respects while completely disregarding them in others.

By going as far as the mining centre at Wollaton Pit, where some of the earliest rail transportation was developed, a lifelong interest in technology, particularly engines – enhanced by his father's workshop at home – began. Such knowledge would prove particularly useful throughout the 1960s, when war surplus lorries were used to transport Scott's expeditions to Tibesti, Turkey and the Hindu Kush and later, up to 1975, when fiddling with truculent oxygen equipment at high altitude.

Thanks to prevailing parental laissez-faire, as well as family cycling excursions, Scott's childhood geographical horizon extended some way beyond Wollaton and its neighbouring suburbs. Although only a few kilometres away, the steep-sided Stapleford Hill (101m), near Bramcote, west-south-west of Wollaton, attracted Scott's early attention, principally because of its quarry and cave, and the Hemlock Stone, an unusual 8.5m monolith on its south-east side. (The origins of the name are uncertain, possibly Druidic.) Composed of two types of differently ageing red sandstone, the upper part black with pollution, it presents itself as a waisted tower. This was Scott's first climb. It required several visits for him to reach the top, with a harder descent over slightly overhanging layers of bedding rock. The year of the climb is not recorded but would most likely have been around the very late 1940s. Another climb, where Scott records his first feeling of exposure, involved negotiating an enormous ancient oak near the canal. It 'stretched the muscles' and, when spending time high up among its scented leaves, produced his first mention of a mystical and sensual association with nature, a rapport Scott enjoyed to the end of his life.

∽

Knowledge of Scott's family background is quite detailed. Several strands emerge: predominant on the female side is a love of pernickety, controlling organising of others and home, while on the male side lie business acumen and an exceptional physical, athletic prowess. Some sense of risk-taking adventure also prevails, across both male and female ancestors. Kindness and consideration for others cascade through both sides of the family.

Scott's family tree can be traced in part as far as a Samuel Green, born in the hamlet of Oxton, Nottinghamshire, in 1784. Samuel, Scott's great-great-great-great grandfather, married a Sarah Green, who was born in Halam, only about five kilometres from Oxton. The speculative conclusion is that Samuel and Sarah came from the same extended family with an agricultural background.

Although also born in Halam, Samuel's son George (1818–97) became a successful businessman in Nottingham, where the trade directories are littered with addresses for George's business ventures as coal merchant, maltster, brick-maker, builder – an occupation which fascinated Doug Scott throughout his life and for a time provided his only income – and pub landlord, an occupation for several generations of this family, first at the Duke of Newcastle Arms then at the Sir Isaac Newton. In the 1871 Census he is recorded as 'maltster and farmer'. George married three times, like his famous descendant. He appears to have died wealthy. George's sister Mary, born 1822, married twice. On her death she left £2,883 3s 1d (equivalent to £335,000 today). Her first husband, Charles, was an inn-keeper, thus establishing what would become a recurring employment strand. He died in January 1877. Her second husband, Edmund Tatham, whom she married within eighteen months of her first husband's death, appears to have been a factory worker. Mary died in Yorkshire in 1891. Scott's great-great grandfather, Edwin Stafford Browne (1843–1904), who married George the businessman's daughter, Lucy, in 1865, introduced the 'sporting prowess' gene into the family. He was the first secretary of Nottingham County Football Club, from 1883 to 1893, and assistant secretary to the Nottingham County Cricket Club. Little else is known about him outside his sporting interests, though they link nicely in both sporting and administrative ability to his great-great grandson's presidency of the Alpine Club in 1999.

A wilder card, the introducer of the Scott branch on the family tree, is Albert Edward Scott (1863–1940). He married Georgina, Edwin and Lucy's eldest daughter, although when is not known. 'Scott' might not, ironically enough, have been his original surname. He was probably an orphan, born in High Holborn in London, but by the age of eight was living in Nottingham, at the home of Henry and Harriet Savidge. On all Census records up to 1911 he is described as 'warehouseman, lace'. His son's recently discovered marriage certificate, however, lists Albert in 1915 as a 'commercial traveller'. A probable younger sister, Josephine Scott, born 1870, appears in the 1881 Census, residing at the same place. By the 1911 Census, Albert is domiciled in West Bridgford, for a time in the middle class-sounding Chestnut Grove, so he may have gone up in the world.

Up to this point, births and marriages, where known, almost all occur in Nottinghamshire. During the latter part of the nineteenth century, however, several of Georgina's siblings began to take risks: Hilda (born around 1873), married a Cecil Kerry and emigrated to New Zealand, as Doug's son Michael did rather more than a hundred years later. Georgina's youngest sibling, George (born around 1878) emigrated, unusually, to France. Georgina and Albert's daughter Mary (birth date not known but presumably around 1885) married John Cliney then emigrated to Canada. Cliney worked as a lumberjack and was killed by a falling tree. The Greens and Brownes, therefore, were not averse to risking their futures in the lottery of emigration.

More typically of his generation, Douglas (1896–1917), Scott's great-uncle and Georgina and Albert's fourth child, was recorded by the *Nottingham Evening News* as a casualty on the Western Front (either at

Festubert or on the Somme) during the First World War. He had to return home where, several months later, he died. He too was a lace factory warehouseman but joined the military and served in the King's Royal Rifle Corps. He was unmarried. The first Douglas in the family records, this name was taken up by Scott's parents for their eldest's first name (though it was also one of Scott's father's middle names).

After these more distant characters, we move to the generations whom Doug Scott mostly knew and remembered. On the maternal side, we can begin with Great-Grandma Sansom (1862–1953). She is referred to inaccurately in *Up and About*: her name is misspelled as 'Sanson'; Scott claims, furthermore, that when he visited her with his parents in 1948, she was 'well into her nineties' – in 1948, she would have been eighty-six. Scott recalls her Edwardian dress, her excellence as a pastry cook and her generosity in sending the young man away with half a crown, a generous tip. Scott also alludes to her 'great age' and suggests she might have known people born in the eighteenth century. In Beeston, a suburb just south of Wollaton, she lived with her daughter Edie in a townhouse which was large enough to contain a garden with a mature plum tree. This house offered curtained steps leading to a cellar, giving Scott one of his earliest opportunities for exploration. As he descended the steps, Great-Grandma's exclamation, 'Joe Lob lives down there, Douglas!' occasioned Scott's hasty retreat.[2]

Great-Grandma Sansom's daughter Catherine (1897–1973) is also described in *Up and About*. She, her husband and three children, the eldest of whom was Doug Scott's mother, lived in a terraced house in The Meadows, near Nottingham city centre. Catherine was very houseproud, spending much time on scrubbing and polishing and keeping one room for 'best'. Doug recalls her sugar butties (in 1979, a 'butty-bag' accompanied him for the final 600m climb to the summit of Kangchenjunga). She also enjoyed Shipstone's Nut Brown Ale, which she would fetch in a jug every evening and at lunchtime on Saturdays from the Queen's Grove Tavern opposite her home. Doug admired her skill in bringing up three children on very little money, a thought which might have motivated him while fundraising for CAN several decades later. Her husband, Roland, was born in 1894; he married Catherine in 1915, presumably when he was on leave. Scott mentions his wheezing and coughing, brought about by excessive smoking and gas attacks while at the Front. He appears to have worked as a delivery driver. He died in 1952 of pneumonia, aged only fifty-eight.

Catherine's two sons, Keith (1928?–2005) and Roy (1936–2015) both contributed to family life in ways already seen. Keith did his National

Service with the RAF. He was, like so many others already mentioned, a pub and property landlord and ran the Plough Inn in Wysall, a village about halfway between Nottingham and Loughborough, for many years. He married twice and was racy enough to drive Jaguars and Daimlers. Roy was an engineer and lab technician, known as a keen sportsman. He swam for the county, played a lot of tennis, took up golf in later life and played water polo for Nottingham. He was a keen DIY man and gardener, traits which his great-nephew inherited. Scott recalls their lively, gregarious household.

Grandma Gregory's sister Edie seems to be the only family member since the family emigrations in the late nineteenth century to have moved long distance: first to Bournemouth then to Poole. While still in Nottingham with her husband Walter, however, she spent several years helping to bring up Doug's mother, Edith Joyce, in order to relieve the financial burden on Grandma Gregory, who earned probably no more than £4 a week working in a factory which made cardboard boxes. Edie worked as an insurance agent for the Liverpool Victoria Friendly Society; she maintained contact with the family until her death in 1977.

Turning to Scott's paternal side, we encounter Sarah Brookes (1889–1971), who in 1915 married Scott's grandfather, George Green Scott (1893–1937 or 1938), another war marriage of passion, optimism, desperation or all three. After George's death, Sarah was systematically defrauded by a female companion and was obliged to move from her 'comfortable bungalow' in Wollaton Park to a condemned house in Radford, where she lived in penury. In the 1950s, Scott visited her once a week, mainly to carry out chores. She in turn visited the Scotts every Tuesday, for tea, and tested Brian on his homework, Douglas being inexplicably absent. Scott mentions an unexplained 'tension' between Sarah and her son, Scott's father, possibly because he considered her to be foolish for having been defrauded of her husband's many sporting trophies and anything George might otherwise have inherited. She did, however, look after Douglas and Brian during parental absences. Evidently a kindly person who would walk once a week to Charlbury Road to see her family and bring chocolate, and who watered the vegetables when the family was on holiday, Sarah's otherwise unhappy life was compounded by a compulsory move from her slum-clearance dwelling to a new estate of high-rise flats at Balloon Woods, near Wollaton, in the late 1950s. This badly constructed estate lasted a mere twenty years, only just beyond the time of Sarah's death in a nearby old people's home.

Sarah's husband, George Green Scott (1893–1937), Scott's paternal grandfather, died four years before Scott was born. Another native of Nottingham, probably having been raised in West Bridgford and dying in nearby Beeston, he did depart to run a pub in Newmarket for a few years, probably in the 1920s, before returning to his home city. In the 1911 Census, his profession is unsurprisingly noted as lace warehouseman. He is remembered as a fine sportsman, 'winning many trophies'. His youngest sister, Hilda (1901 or 1902–1980), known as 'Aunt Fo', is recalled as a 'thoughtful' person: worth linking to Doug's capacity for careful reflection, a quality which saved him from death on several occasions.

Scott's parents, Harold (known as George) and Joyce, influenced Scott's life fundamentally. George was born in West Bridgford, Nottingham in 1915, married Joyce in 1940 and died in 1995, a lifespan of only twenty-one days fewer than his distinguished eldest son. He left Lenton (a suburb adjoining Wollaton and Radford) Secondary School as head boy. George served in Nottingham Police from 1934 to 1965. During the Second World War he served first in the Royal Artillery then from 1942 onwards as a Sergeant Instructor in the Army Physical Training Corps. His police service testifies to his incorruptibility and his gentlemanliness. After retirement from the police, he became a social worker.

What distinguishes him above all is his sporting qualities and record. In 1938, he became European Police light-heavyweight boxing champion, defeating the reigning German champion in Stuttgart in front of senior Nazis, an echo of Jesse Owens in the 1936 Berlin Olympics. The following year he repeated the feat, this time in London, once more against a German opponent. As the *Nottingham Post* remarked, 'We have nothing to fear from Hitler with men like George Scott in our midst.' At the end of the war, he became ABA (Amateur Boxing Association) heavyweight champion, as well as British Army heavyweight boxing champion and inter-services champion. Naturally, the 1948 Olympics became a possibility, although after heated arguments with Joyce relating to diet and injury worries (the National Health Service began only in 1948), this plan was abandoned. He also competed in charitable exhibition matches, against top-class opponents. George's prowess extended far beyond boxing, however: while still at school, he played football for Nottingham Boys, completed the annual Town Swim from Wilford Bridge to Trent Bridge and later became an official for the Notts Amateur Athletics Association. The parallels with his eldest son's adolescent sporting and charitable career are striking.

George Scott (1915–95), with one of his many boxing trophies.
(Scott family collection)

After the war, George edited the Nottingham City *Police Bulletin*, despite problems with literacy inherited, as Scott explicitly states, by his eldest son. (Scott's spelling was often wayward.) George was consistently described as outgoing and helpful, a powerful source of the resolute altruism displayed by Scott throughout his thirty years of running CAN.

Scott's mother, the redoubtable Joyce (1919–2015), lived to be ninety-five. Scott on several occasions refers to breast-feeding as the happy outcome to him screaming literally and metaphorically for attention when a baby. If emulating then outperforming his father motivated Scott in the physical or athletic world, being lovingly recognised for his achievements and granted his mother's affection, with the pleasures of female company generally – George was often absent for longish periods for work – became the strongest motive imaginable for seeking an often hurried journey home from climbing high peaks, particularly on dangerous new routes which satisfied his longing to be away from the city.

Joyce worked for about six years in the Player's cigarette factory, becoming a supervisor, an office job and therefore a cut above the shop-floor workers, until she married George in 1940.[3] A measure of George's solicitousness is that he and Joyce met when she had had an argument with her then boyfriend. As she crossed the road, away from the boyfriend, George happened to be on traffic duty and asked her what was wrong . . . Joyce gave up the Player's job on marriage as it was thought unsuitable, in the stratified attitudes of the day, for a policeman to be married to a non-professional person.

Continuing the family tradition of caring for others, Joyce looked after her younger brothers when her mother was obliged to seek work because of her husband's poor health. She remained a family woman, keeping people together and supporting them. Her domestic skills extended to good cooking: she would cook for others well into her eighties. Scott's expedition diaries frequently mention tea, stews, butties and pancakes, a reflection of what he had learnt from Joyce. Not just a cooking apprenticeship, though: on asking one day for processed, powder-derived potato mash such as he ate at school, Joyce reproved Scott for this request when their own home-grown potatoes were available – the beginning, perhaps, of Scott's lifelong interest in the cultivation of organic vegetables.

Most of all, however, Joyce evinced determination. She was irrepressible.

These kindly, upright, hard-working parents, along with a weight of domestic, family, municipal and national history pressing in the

Joyce (1919–2015), Doug's mother; portrait believed to be in the late 1930s.
(Scott family collection)

background, shaped and brought up their young tearaway. Scott embodied an aversion to education – at least until his academic work epiphany at the age of fifteen – yet embraced the disciplines required of the outstanding sportsman, until, on a summit ridge in the Mamore mountain range in Scotland, he decided, at Easter 1960, where his true calling lay.

2

Childhood and Education

'. . . at my birth
The frame and huge foundation of the earth
Shaked like a coward.'

— Glendower, in Shakespeare's *Henry the Fourth,
Part I*, Act 3, Scene 1

Doug Scott's birth was imbued with a 'man of destiny' significance. Joyce had been born within twenty-four hours of Sir Edmund Hillary, on 20 July 1919 (although she was born on 21 July). Scott's birth date, 29 May 1941, coincided with the day that Everest was first climbed by Hillary and Tenzing, 29 May 1953. The superstitious Joyce recalled that as an adolescent she had consulted a gypsy fortune-teller who predicted she would marry a man in uniform with shiny buttons and have three sons, the eldest of whom would be in trouble in a shelter very high up, and that the whole world would be watching. Joyce duly married her policeman with shiny buttons; their eldest son was born almost a year to the day thereafter. Scott's brother Brian, however, cannot recall this story. He comments, 'When aged about nineteen, Joyce visited a fortune-teller with a friend, perhaps while courting our father. She was told she would meet a lady with white hair. Soon after, she met our dad's mother, who had white hair. She must have thought that significant, otherwise she would not have related it.'[1]

What is important is Joyce's conviction that her eldest son was starcrossed. By introducing himself with the first fortune-teller story in *Up and About*, Scott suggests he shared his mother's opinion. The clashing effects of laissez-faire, absentee parenting – perfectly typical of that time – and an intensity of contact when his parents were present shaped Scott's upbringing.

Although Joyce was usually very busy with time-consuming domestic chores, she also acted as the more overt moral guardian; nonetheless, she was happy for the over-active Douglas (the family's name for Doug, then and now) to play outside on the embankment, along the canal and at Wollaton Pit. When he was seven, he was given a bicycle, thus extending his range to nearby building sites. Thoughtlessness, inexperience and a gang's herd mentality reverberating with excess of energy led to trouble. Apart from the police visit after his tunnelling beneath the railway, Scott and his gang were chased by the local bobby when he spotted them stealing apples and pears. The bobby's word with Scott's parents embarrassed his father, the bobby's sergeant. Scott concedes that if charges had been pressed for that or similar misdemeanours, his father might have lost his job, something George pointed out to him before occasionally administering the cane. Several of Scott's brushes with the law occurred despite George's warnings, suggesting that even as an adolescent, Scott was moving beyond imitation of his father to outdoing him. An obvious Freudian interpretation of Scott's strong wish for his mother's love and approval by athletically outperforming his father, possibly by 'killing' him professionally, is clear.

The boy's freedom to roam was enhanced by George's lengthy absences. He was away on active service, bar occasional leave, from 1942 to 1945; then from 1948 to 1950 he worked as an instructor at King's Mill Police Training School in Sutton-in-Ashfield.[2] (Although George was resident there, it was possible to phone him and to visit occasionally, to enjoy the school's opulent training facilities.) Along with police shift work, George spent some years with the CID; he worked as an instructor and examiner in lifesaving; he was involved in self-defence and physical education with Nottingham Police, the tallest force in the country according to one of Scott's earliest friends, Clive Davies, who also says that George's grip was reputedly the strongest of any man in it. George became, furthermore, secretary to the police athletic club for many years and organised their sports days. When Scott was nine, George, with a Norman Watson, formed the Nottingham Attendance Centre for Juvenile Offenders, which he supervised on Saturdays. He was engaged in administrative tasks when at home. Thus, he was largely absent for at least half of Scott's first ten years.

George's absences fostered a compensatory bonding between mother and son. Douglas would creep into his mother's bed when his father was away, for consolation and comfort. We can link the boy's happiness through achieving maternal love and approval (when his father was absent) to his later comments on breast-feeding providing relief from the pain of attention-seeking. After his first real climb ('I was smitten'), the language of youthful passion shows how Scott's early relationship with his mother motivated his desire to climb and explore, and to be approved of for so doing, while the athleticism and manly achievements inherited from his father gave him the means to do it.

Scott thus developed a capacity for self-reliance and a love of adventure on the edge of the law. He showed a dismissive attitude while pursuing his own interests as leader of a gang which co-existed with other gangs – not always peacefully. It is not surprising that fifty or sixty years later, CAN staff could find Scott as intolerant and infuriating as he was dedicated, charming and lovable.

Both parents undoubtedly adored their son. When he was fifteen months old, he was entered for a 'Bonniest Baby' competition which, in his class, he won. Not so surprising: Joyce was pretty and George was handsome. Scott proved physically very attractive to women once he had left behind the awkwardness of adolescence.

A durably productive parental interest into which Douglas was introduced – if only to imitate his father – was gardening. George's nearby allotment, which he had used to 'dig for victory', had been bombed into extinction in 1940, but the front and back gardens of the Scotts' house remained. The seemingly banal work of tending to vegetables, tomatoes and soft fruit began what for Scott would become a lifelong pleasure, not just in promoting the vegetarianism he espoused for more than thirty years, but in inspiring his near-obsessive tending of his strictly organic vegetable gardens at Stewart Hill Cottage in Cumbria.

When George was at home, father and son engaged in an array of sports. Douglas would accompany his father to the Raleigh factory gym, where George would train for boxing matches. Sometimes, they would attend exhibition bouts, where George would box against such luminaries as Freddie Mills.[3] Once, they watched the Harlem Globetrotters perform at the local ice rink. Apparently randomly, the star player hauled Douglas out of the crowd and helped him to throw a basket. Or was it random? By the way in which Scott describes the event in *Up and About*, the reader is again made to wonder if Scott thought he was some form of 'chosen one'. A visit to a local football match, however, induced only boredom and was never repeated. Then, in the severe winter of 1947, George had a local blacksmith build an unusually fast sledge for Douglas, who exploited its power by knocking over others until a larger boy proved one too many. Douglas, however, learnt from this experience not to push advantages over others too far. Too late for that incident, George taught self-defence to

Douglas and Brian, a skill which Scott used effectively when he started at his fairly rough secondary school, Cottesmore. George also taught his eldest son to swim: Scott loved a dip during a day's walk-in on his expeditions; he taught his own children to swim.

George, moreover, was manually creative. In his workshop, Douglas and his friends made catapults, swords, shields, arrows and even a crossbow, along with lesser weapons such as peashooters and popguns. Airguns for making further mischief could be obtained. Fireworks caused quite a lot of damage in the neighbourhood, literally and figuratively. The emphasis, because there wasn't much money, was on make-do-and-mend creativity, a skill which Scott brought to many an expedition, whether in repairing vehicles or equipment such as oxygen sets or crampons. These 'toys' also taught Scott practical skills which were to assist him during his time as a builder with brother Garry. Indeed, they proved valuable for his many building projects with CAN, or when helping to construct the stupa at the Samye Ling lamasery (see chapter fourteen), or when renovating his own homes.

George also meticulously recorded family events. His scrapbook of Scott's achievements, comprising mainly newspaper cuttings, invitations, photos and the like, stretches to two hefty folios. Family holidays on the Lincolnshire coast between Ingoldmells and Skegness (to which Scott once cycled), for every one of Douglas's first twelve years, were carefully recorded in the family photo album – perhaps the beginning of Scott's lifelong interest in photography.

When attending to Douglas, Joyce acted as nurse, administering brandy for stomach troubles or a Friar's Balsam infusion (breathed in over a basin) for chest colds. She ensured Douglas was well treated by the nascent NHS. The results were variable: vaccinations against killer diseases such as diphtheria or polio were successful, but ear-syringing left Scott with permanent ear perforations, while sinus draining led to a long-term reduced sense of smell.

Joyce was, of course, the cook of the family. Scott recalls her ability, in the frugal management of resources, to blanch, salt and store George's runner beans, or to make butter and cottage cheese – activities Scott enjoyed observing in Tibet (and elsewhere) fifty years later. When Douglas decided to cycle the 100 kilometres from Wollaton to Skegness when he was twelve, Joyce was ready with Tizer, sandwiches and cake. He admired her treacle flapjacks, as well as stew and dumplings, baked bread, rice and milk, foods he replicated on his apprentice expeditions throughout the

1960s. On some expeditions he and the other members seemed to eat very little else.

Despite the heavy food, the Scotts enjoyed a healthy family lifestyle, 'often' cycling six kilometres each way to visit Great-Grandma Sansom at Beeston. Until he was seven, Scott sat on George's handlebars; after that, he used his own bike. Brian sat on Joyce's bike.

The Scotts, although not churchgoers, were Conservative voters and royalists, unusual in predominantly Labour-voting Nottingham (at least until one moves to the suburbs). They were children of Empire and believed strongly in Churchill's capacity to lead the nation to war victory. They bought *Empire* magazine, which surveyed its exotic territories and turbulent histories. Unquestionably, this magazine stimulated the young Scott's fascination for exploration and travel. The outcome was remarkable: by the end of his mountaineering career in 2000, Scott had travelled to at least forty countries and climbed seriously in at least thirty-seven, on all seven continents.

While she herself felt ill at ease with those obviously wealthier than herself, Joyce entertained quite forceful social ambitions for her son. (These ambitions are best viewed as developing in her son an ability to carry himself socially in a way that she could not.) While disquieted by Scott's speed and lack of social ambition in marrying Jan when only twenty, she was rather bemused, though still welcoming, given the racist attitudes of her own upbringing and lack of advanced education, when Scott married Indian climber Sharu Prabhu, from the Brahmin caste, in 1993. Joyce was delighted that after the Everest triumph in 1975 her eldest son was presented to the Queen and attended a party at 10 Downing Street, as well as being awarded the Freedom of Nottingham in 1976.[4] She was more than happy when Scott married Trish, with her relatively elevated social connections, in 2007.

Joyce and George were no snobs, though. Scott frequently refers to neighbourly solidarity, sharing and support during the war years and the austerity which followed. He praises the neighbourliness before civic clearance and poor-quality housing set in, because it kept crime and vandalism in check. It is no accident that Scott's charity in Nepal, based on helping the Nepalis to help themselves, begins with 'Community'.

∽

Scott's character was, of course, also formed by his education. Until he was fifteen, he was bored and truculent at school, except during outdoor and athletic activities. Like many pupils averse to authority and discipline, he experienced a kind of epiphany when on the cusp of leaving his secondary modern and entering Mundella Grammar School for his sixth form.

When he was five, Scott's education began at what he mistakenly calls (in *Up and About*) Harrow Road Primary School. In fact, he attended Middleton Primary School, confusingly located on Harrow Road, near Wollaton Park. By his own admission, Scott was never among the brightest nor more attentive pupils, preferring hyper-energetic gang activity to classroom focus. The only exception was a daily half-hour reading of Hans Christian Andersen. The sole event of any significance occurred just before departing Middleton in 1950: an all-school running race led to stardom when Douglas finished second behind a smaller and slighter boy. Scott's reflective analysis told him that competitors, however they appeared, should never be underestimated. Scott claims in *Up and About* that such adulation meant he no longer needed to perform attention-seeking activities at this school, though he conceded that it remained a necessity for the rest of his life.

After four years at Middleton, Scott was transferred in July 1950 to the newly built Robert Shaw Primary School, off the Western Boulevard about two kilometres from his Charlbury Road home.[5]

Here, Douglas's short-sightedness was quickly diagnosed and led eventually to his famous John Lennon circular glasses. Douglas then discovered some success in singing and acting, mostly inspired by good teachers. (Several unpleasant teachers are also recalled.) Classes were extremely large; the belt was frequently used. There were, however, constructive moments: Brian recalls Douglas making a fort out of hardboard and managing to get hold of a magnet strong enough to extract ball-bearings. Apart from falling in love and being rejected for the first time (at age eight or nine), little of note seems otherwise to have occurred until Scott's final year, when the 11+ exam, to determine one's future educational level, had to be faced. Although Scott had not worked hard, with below-average academic performance, he had been made a prefect and was motivated by not wanting to go to Cottesmore Secondary Modern, a relatively tough school, rather than grammar school.[6] Despite harder work and promotion, Scott failed the 11+, probably through lack of interest rather than lack of ability. George and Joyce were deeply disappointed, partly because George had by then (1952) given up most of his athletic life and wanted a successful son to fill the vacuum, while for Joyce the failure limited her social aspirations for Douglas.

Cottesmore's motto was *tenax propositi*: 'tenacious in purpose'. On the school shield, a mountain figures as one of the quarters, presumably to symbolise aspiration realised through effort. Scott was placed in Mallory House.[7] The apprehensive new boy (as one of his earliest climbing partners and fellow Cottesmorians, Richard Stroud, has confirmed) managed to avoid the Cottesmore initiation rite of being thrown into a prickly bush, because of a sheath-knife cut to the thumb, requiring stitches. Little else went well. He was physically punished regularly. An attempt at bullying Scott was met with an unarmed combat move which he had been taught by George; after that, the bullying stopped. What should have been a memorable event, when the whole school went on an outing to the Albert Hall to hear John Hunt talking about the Everest success, seems to have been met with Scott's indifference and inattentiveness. Inevitably, a particularly detested teacher surfaced. Scott's impertinence to him was rewarded with blows of the strap on each hand; further insolence resulted in the teacher slapping him across the face. However, Scott says that most of his teachers were 'good men'.

Most notable, perhaps, was one of Scott's English teachers, Mick Graham, who also played rugby for Nottingham RFC's First XV: Mick's coaching led to Scott taking a greater interest in English literature.

On the rugby field, he was a very strong back row forward who, on occasions, would run twice as far as anybody on the field without touching the ball. When he did get it, he liked to show off his exaggerated dummy. Once, in the third team, Doug arrived at a maul, burrowed in, ripped the ball out and raced away upfield. Unfortunately, because of his poor eyesight, he was running the wrong way.

Often, if the firsts had kicked off early to watch an international, Doug would race to one of the other sides to play a second match. Tigers' coach 'Chalkie' White reckoned that Doug's press-ups were 100 per cent better than any he had seen. He could climb a rope with his legs parallel to the floor and do many pull-ups on his fingertips underneath a door frame. In hospital after he had broken his legs on The Ogre, a friend asked him why he was out of breath. He replied that he had eaten a packet of chocolate digestives and, as he didn't want to get fat, had just done a hundred pull-ups.

In playing for Notts Moderns, Scott first met one of his earliest friends and climbing partners, Dez Hadlum, from the John Player school, the first secondary modern in Nottingham to take up rugby. According to Dez, Douglas was powerfully built even then: 'Being tackled by Scott was like being hit by a train.' Scott was selected for the Three Counties:

Nottinghamshire, Lincolnshire and Derbyshire. Rugby was a fixture every Saturday morning; Scott followed this sport enthusiastically until the end of his life. When in the Cairngorms in the 1980s, he turned up suddenly at Glenmore Lodge, the Scottish National Outdoor Sports Centre, thrust a bag of 'magic' mushrooms 'fresh picked from the Peak District' into the clutch of surprised instructor Allen Fyffe and asked to watch a big rugby match on television.

Further athletic success followed, probably in 1954: compelled, after yet another disciplinary incident involving drawing attention to himself, to enter the 440- and 880-yard races, Scott broke the school records. George spotted his potential. On the nearby Wollaton Park running track, he used his expertise as an AAA coach to develop this athletic talent in his wayward son. Scott represented the school, then Nottingham. In the Cottesmore Prize List for 1956–57, in the 'Other Special Successes' section, 'D.K. Scott' is congratulated for breaking the city records for the quarter- and half-mile races in the under-fifteen category: he clocked 57.3 seconds for the former and 2 minutes, 11.05 seconds for the latter. Encouraged and trained by George, Scott went forward to the AAA National Youth Championships, where he was convincingly beaten into second place by the future British team captain in the 1964 Olympics, John Whetton. After this, Scott realised he could not run competitively at higher than county level; he began to lose interest. A motorbike accident in 1961, resulting in a broken patella, extinguished any remaining running ambitions. Scott retained a long-term interest in cross-country and fell-running, however.

Thanks to the English teacher Mick Graham, some academic achievements began to appear. Scott began to read, seriously. He mentions Fielding, George Eliot, John Buchan (who better for adventures?), Edgar Allan Poe, John Wyndham, Hemingway and, inevitably, George Orwell and Aldous Huxley.[8] But what really excited him were tales of Roman and Greek myths and Norse mythology. He would later add the ancient Indian epics to this list. Range, however, does need to be accompanied by the kind of critical training which sifts good from bad. Perversely, when he was told that Lobsang Rampa's best-selling *The Third Eye* was a hoax – the author was no lama, but Cyril Henry Hoskin, from Plympton in Devon – Scott obstinately declared that he would continue to read it. Scott retained an uncomfortable relationship with works of rather muddy pseudo-philosophy.

When Scott was fifteen, he realised that unless he read more, he was unlikely to pass his O-Levels. Failure to get a sixth form place at a grammar school might lead to a life of financial, social and imaginative limitations. He aimed, therefore, for O-Levels in English, history, general science and geography. Scott's only two 'top of the form' appearances were in Mick Graham's English class and Maurice Davidson's history class. The history of Empire, only recently converted into the Commonwealth, inspired him in a romantic, escapist way. Davidson fired Scott's imagination; as in English, Scott began to read avidly, if somewhat uncritically. Of egregious interest was the story of Asiatic explorer Francis Younghusband, although the appalling British conduct against defenceless Tibetans in Younghusband's 1904 Tibet incursion left its mark. This was probably Scott's first contact with the Himalayas (other than the ascent of Everest talk in 1954, which he had largely ignored). When British imperial pride was shocked by the Suez Crisis in 1956, Scott was on Kinder at the time.

Scott was similarly absent on Arran, completing his first major new climbing route, when his O-Level results came through. He had passed in all but English. Four O-Levels, however, were sufficient to enter Mundella Grammar School, which came with the bonus of being co-educational. Scott left Cottesmore in 1957, little realising that – to the shock of his future colleagues – he would return as a teacher there in only a few years' time.

Scott's life at Mundella (motto: 'Go Forward'), which closed in 1985, was much more organised and purposeful than at Cottesmore.[9] He had to work hard to gain sufficient A-Levels to enter higher education; he had to re-sit his English O-Level; he kept up athletics training in the evenings; there were Scouting activities – he became a Queen's Scout, an achievement of which he always remained proud. He played rugby on Saturday mornings, often went to jazz clubs on Saturday evenings and was away climbing for the remainder of the weekend. In sixth form, he met several of his earliest climbing partners and friends, though not all were fellow pupils. Some of those were female; the most durable of Scott's female friendships was with Janice Brook, whom he married in 1962. (Their relationship did not begin until Scott had established himself at Loughborough College, some months after he left Mundella.)

A schoolfriend, Mick Poppleston, tells us that Doug was now diligent. He liked and respected Thomas Robinson, their history teacher, an inspiration in nineteenth-century European history with a first from Manchester to back it up. Robinson instilled in Scott a love of learning for its own sake, even to the extent of after-school work at the Mechanics' Institute Library; as a result, Scott acquired an intellectual curiosity which never left him.

Despite (perhaps because of) some rather desultory coaching, Scott failed English O-Level for a second time. While a much stronger reader than hitherto, a limited ability to write discursively and critically let him down. Time he was now spending on climbing and rugby also worked against him, as did his pursuit of climbing manuals and mountaineering history. He passed, however, at his third attempt, thanks to a fascination for the topic of leadership serendipitously appearing. He had recently discovered the contrasting styles of Scott and Shackleton; Scott gave much thought throughout his mountaineering life to this topic.

Scott's Mundella athletic career ended well. On 21 April 1959, he was presented with a tie, as *Victor Ludorum*, at the Albert Hall in Nottingham.

What remained at Mundella was planning his next educational stage: with two A-Levels (history and geography, passed in 1959), Scott could now enter further education. He elected to apply for the teacher training certificate in PE and geography at the excellent Loughborough College, as many climbers have done, in order to take advantage of teachers' relatively long holidays.

In parallel to his academic and sporting career at Mundella was Scott's rising interest in females. On his paper round while still at Cottesmore, almost certainly aged fourteen, Scott fell for a new neighbour, Jill. They became friendly, then rather inept (by his own admission) lovers. Perhaps after being discovered *in flagrante delicto* by a 'disgusted' Joyce, Scott was shattered on his next visit to discover Jill in the arms of another. Impressed by his devastated reaction, Jill offered a renewal of the relationship, but advice from a male climbing friend recommended rejection of all troublesome females and the relationship stopped.

During his first term at Mundella, however, Wes Hayden, another important early climbing partner, and Scott took two girls to Nottingham's renowned Goose Fair. Scott's partner was Susan Webster; her brother, Mick (Michael), became a fine amateur climber under Scott's tutelage, and accompanied him to the Baffin Island big walls in 1973. Scott recognised that the raven-haired Susan was far brighter than he. Nor was she interested in sport or mountaineering. While Scott soon lost out to an older youth who became her husband, he and Susan remained friends, with perhaps more affection on Doug's side than on Susan's. However, as Susan remarks about her relationship with Scott, with a lifetime's perspective:

Today, the usual large envelope arrived addressed to Mrs Sue Webster (although I have been Mrs Sue Holland now for 60 years). I knew it must be the usual Community Action for Nepal (sic) newsletter. Sadly it was this time in memory of Doug Scott CBE. I have always put it down to Doug's egocentrism that he has always assumed that I must be interested in Nepal, although I never replied or donated, my interests being with social action therapy with working class, black & minority ethnic communities here in England. When I received the massive tome of his biography along with an appreciative card inside I was surprised that in retrospect he saw himself as a suitor that lost to my husband Ray. To me, he was one of many co-ed Grammar School buddies.

But my most vivid memory of Doug was when he persuaded me to go out on our own in freezing cold to an isolated rock in some wilderness somewhere, where he hauled me up on a rope. That was my most vivid but not fondest memory of Doug. My fondest memory was long ago, in 1993, after my father's death when Dougie came to help me clear some of the furniture in his big old battered Volvo. That was the last time we met and I remember him with affection as big, good-natured bear-like Dougie.[10]

*The christening of Doug's youngest brother, Garry,
in October 1952. (Scott family collection)*

Of even greater significance in Scott's life was a fifth-form pupil at the time Scott left Mundella in 1959: Janice Brook. Their unruly yet sometimes brilliant marriage lasted for twenty-seven years.

Other newcomers had appeared during Scott's time in secondary education. The most important was his brother Garry, born in 1952. Despite being eleven years Douglas's junior, they bonded successfully, for example spending time together on cycling excursions along the canal in the Wollaton and Bramcote districts. They climbed the Hemlock Stone freestyle and rewarded themselves with ginger beer, in true Enid Blyton fashion, from glass bottles. Later, while Scott was moving from teaching to becoming a professional climber in 1972, the brothers entered into a building partnership. Garry, like Brian, who studied medicine in London, went on to Nottingham University to study civil engineering, and at the time of writing is still working for Leicester City Council as Project Director, Major Transport Schemes.

Although Loughborough formed the final part of Scott's education, his life there was consumed by climbing and developing climbing connections.

3

Starting Out: Climbs in the UK, 1955–60

'I don't object to people going to the mountains. I just don't
want to meet them.'

– Doug Scott

Scott's formative climbing period lasted from 1955 to 1960. During this
exciting time, the ethical and technical foundations of the Scott edifice
were laid. He consolidated his local reputation; he first led on a new route
and in 1958 began his Alpine climbing career. At Easter 1960, Scott visited
Ben Nevis (1344m) and the Mamores for the first time. Here, he experienced the epiphany which decided him to commit his life to climbing.[1]

When did Scott start climbing? The biographical pages on the 'Doug
Scott' website declare he was twelve. In *Up and About*, however, he tells
us that his first, introductory, summer camp with the Scouts took place –
without any climbing – on Exmoor in 1953. Then Scott informs us in some
detail about his first visit to the Black Rocks on a Scout hike at 'Easter
1955', when he would have been almost fourteen. Here, he observed 'men
climbing the rocks', and calls it, 'something completely new'.[2] This year
seems by far the most likely as it fits better with dates we can objectively
confirm.

Many outstanding climbers began their careers in the 1950s, thanks to
changed educational practices and economic conditions. The founding
and development of such organisations as the Public Schools Exploring
Society (1932), Outward Bound (1941) and the Duke of Edinburgh's Award
Scheme (1956) were encouraged. (George Scott served on the Nottingham
Co-ordinating Committee for the Duke of Edinburgh's Award.) Reforms
also stimulated competitive change in older organisations such as the
Boy Scouts. Organisers and founders sought to improve mental and
physical wellbeing in young people through Outdoor Education, though
a wide variety of emphases from 'character-building' to the acquisition
of useful life skills was exercised. Happily for Scott, the outstanding

*On the way to Scout camp at Retford, 28 May 1955, the day before Doug's
fourteenth birthday. Doug is third from the left. Photo courtesy of the
Nottingham Evening News.*

pre-war climber and Everester, Sir Jack Longland, had become Director of
Education for Derbyshire (where Scott's first climbs took place) in 1949.[3]
In 1951, he brought about – in the face of considerable opposition – the
opening of White Hall, the UK's first 'outdoor pursuits' centre, on the
western periphery of the Peak District. As Longland declared in a letter to
Mountain magazine, then renowned for its controversies, 'Some of us have
been trying to further the beliefs of Geoffrey Young and of Kurt Hahn,[4]
the inspirer of those Outward Bound schools which, amongst others, nur-
tured Doug Scott.'[5]

With these changes came the end of petrol rationing in May 1950. Its
immediate consequence was to encourage greater geographical mobility:
most pre-war climbers had tended to walk or cycle to their climbing
destinations. Travelling by car meant that expenses could be pooled, so
greater distances could be travelled. From there, only one step led to the
formation of climbing and walking clubs, with their members transported
by bus. If a club wasn't available, or the climber was not a 'clubable' sort,

hitch-hiking then became a preferred mode of transport for the impecunious and the solitary.

Transport had improved; so had access. The Mass Trespass on Kinder Scout in 1932 led to improvements (in England) in the laws governing access to hill country. The creation of the UK's first national park, the Peak District (which includes Kinder Scout), coincided usefully in 1950 with the end of petrol rationing. Many young people became interested in escaping from the city to explore our upland areas – one of the themes of Scott's writings, not least because of the city's lack of affordable entertainment and the filthy air conditions, only alleviated by the Clean Air Act, 1956. The 1950s thus held considerable outdoor promise.

Scott was no exception in becoming a member of some of these post-war organisations. In May 1950, he had joined the Cubs, but was expelled after only two years: the Cub leader had offended Douglas with his sarcasm, despite Douglas's success in earning more than any other Cubs during Bob-A-Job week; a well-placed punch to the leader's groin brought Douglas's immediate departure. (The story also carries a rather concerning implication of Scott's aversion to the leader's effeminacy.)

Scott nonetheless joined the Scouts in 1953. The father of one of his earliest climbing partners and school friends, Mick Garside, ran the local YMCA Scout Group in Nottingham city centre. Introduced to Scott in a coffee bar in Canal Street, Nottingham – according to the approved manner of the time – Mick persuaded Scott to join the troop. It was a momentous decision.

Scott's first summer camp took place on Exmoor in 1953. Here, he was joined by Wes Hayden, another long-standing early climbing partner. Scott learned to smoke, although unsuccessfully: it made him vomit; on later expeditions, he mostly smoked *bidis*.[6] Despite this setback, another of his earliest Scout climbing partners, Dez Hadlum, recalls that Scott even then was 'fitter and stronger' than the other Scouts. Scott became proficient in first aid, one of several humanitarian skills he would practise during his expeditions.

Learning first aid and camping chimed well with his father's *curriculum vitae*: in 1961, George became a 'Serving Brother of the most Venerable Order of St John of Jerusalem'.[7] 'Preventing and relieving sickness and injury', the St John's ideal, would prove useful: after he retired from the police in 1965, George joined the former Nottinghamshire Children's Department. A *This Is Your Life* booklet, in fine calligraphy, presented to him on his final retirement refers to his giving 'many evenings and week-ends to take groups of young people walking and climbing in the Peak District and further afield'. It is not hard to make the leap from George's Peak District activities to his eldest son's Scouting first aid knowledge being applied at 'clinics' for locals on expedition walk-ins, or to the founding of CAN itself.

Scout camps developed further skills and interests across the seasons: in summer, Scott broadened his familiarity with trees and their ancient, mystical (when referring to the Celts' reverence for them) qualities.[8] Winter camps were particularly exciting when, for example, negotiating the slippery, ice-covered boulders of the King's Brook down to the River Soar, the start of the route leading to many arduous, perilous trudges along some of the world's greatest glaciers.

The first pivotal moment in Scott's climbing career occurred at Easter 1955. On a hike from a Scout camp near Wirksworth, just west of Derbyshire's beautiful Derwent Valley, he spotted men with ropes on the Black Rocks above the town of Cromford. This activity surpassed even the excitement of tree-climbing! The siren's call was answered: Douglas and his friends were soon clambering about on the rocks at the base and gullies at the side: 'I was more than curious; I was smitten,' he says in *Up and About*.

Only a fortnight later, with two more of his earliest climbing companions, Clive Smith and Terence 'Stengun' Sterney, Scott cycled the eighty-kilometre round trip from Nottingham up the Derwent Valley to Cromford. Their first climb, *Fat Man's Chimney*, an 18m Diff described unappetisingly as a 'squeezy green rift' was followed by *Central Buttress* and *Lone Tree Gully*. Their equipment has become the stuff of legend: for a rope, Scott used his mother's washing-line (umbilical cord?) while Stengun used his father's car's tow-rope. Thus began what Scott declared to the end of his life to be his favourite kind of climbing: an afternoon's cragging.

Cragging became the primary weekend activity. Outside the rugby season, Scott would spend the weekend camping and climbing with his friends. He acquired, through birthday presents – his birthday occurring conveniently near the start of the summer season – a tent, Primus stove and personal gear such as Tricouni-nailed boots and karabiners. His group graduated from the Black Rocks to gritstone crags such as Birchen Edge, east of Baslow, described by UKClimbing as having 'a friendly atmosphere and a good collection of low grade routes'. Birchen Edge had the bonus of the nearby Robin Hood pub, with a base camp just behind it, at what was then called Moorside Farm. The pro-climbing farmer, who loved the company of the new wave of climbers, was Ben Froggatt; he would offer a berth in his sweet-smelling hay barn for one shilling a night. He was also a one-man information exchange for the predominantly young climbing community. Fellow-expeditioner Dez Hadlum recalls a typical weekend:

> On Saturday morning we had rugby; then the X2 bus to Bakewell; Hulley's bus to the Robin Hood Inn; walk up to Birchen's Edge. [Doug] thought he could build a snow cave but there was not enough snow, so we built a three-walled wind protection instead. We shared our sleeping bags naked but lasted only two hours. Later, we tried string underwear but that didn't last much longer.
>
> In summer, out of the rugby season, we got one extra night, but what we dreaded was Doug saying, 'Let's just . . .' 'Let's just . . .' meant a weekend camp at Edale; a hike over Kinder Scout to the Downfall[9] and 'pull in' Bleaklow as well. We complained but got nowhere: Doug was our leader and inspiration.[10]

In 1956, probably at Easter, an important step forward occurred when Scott and friends (we are not given their names, apart from Mick Garside) were sent on the initiative of Mr Happer, the 'strict but humane' Cottesmore Head Teacher who encouraged outdoor activities, to White Hall on an Outdoor Education course. Instead of learning by trial and error, they would receive tuition from some of the finest climbers in the country, such as Harold Drasdo, Joe Brown and Gordon Mansell.[11]

The White Hall warden from 1955 to 1959 was the outstanding climber and polymath, Geoffrey Sutton, another formative if more distant influence.[12] Sutton had already climbed with Don Whillans and Joe Brown; by getting to know Sutton, not only did Scott establish his connection to these exceptional climbers, but they, with others, formed the élite Alpine Climbing Group in 1952. Scott joined in 1961 and was president from 1975 to 1977. Scott recalls the hospitality shown to him by Sutton and his wife, Ann, when he would arrive at White Hall on a Friday evening: 'The Warden, Geoff Sutton, tall, broad-shouldered and usually wearing thigh-length sealskin boots from a Greenland expedition, was there to greet us and invite us into the kitchen. His charming wife Anne [sic] would cook us delicious, garlic-flavoured omelettes for supper as we sat listening to stories told by permanent staff members Harold Drasdo and Andrew Maxfield.'[13]

Encouraging spontaneity, rather than stifling initiative through excessive instruction, was emphasised. Climbing and belaying were practised on nearby crags such as Windgather and Castle Naze, situated between Chapel-en-le-Frith and Macclesfield. Students were given the lead once the instructors thought they were ready. Hill-walking skills, particularly the use of map and compass, figured on the course as well. The underlying idea was to increase personal responsibility with a minimum of pressure.

Thanks to school, White Hall and the Scouts, Scott's social circle was expanding. He and Mick Garside, with Clive Smith, all signed up for a weekly Mountaineering Association course at Lenton Boulevard school. Fortune allocated to them the effervescently lively, roguish instructor Bob Pettigrew, later MBE. Bob and Scott became lifelong friends. Scott and Mick Garside rose a notch in the climbing world by becoming rescue technique demonstrators. Bob's students exercised on the school's wallbars and learnt navigation while going through a whole mountain rescue syllabus. He encouraged and stimulated his students with books and films from his own extraordinary Alpine and Himalayan experience.

Geographical horizons were expanding, also. Bob Pettigrew ran Scout expeditions to the Beddgelert Forest in North Wales at that time. Funding for these trips was made available from Nottingham City Education Authority through the good offices of Ken Wall, Inspector of Education, who was an early pioneer and enthusiast for Outdoor Education in the Longland tradition. Scott participated on at least one of these in 1954 or 1955, and the idea for forming the NCC (founded 1961) may have originated here.

Interest in North Wales grew. Mick Garside, who had recently completed a course run by Olympian athlete and outstanding mountaineer John Disley, at Snowdonia's Plas-y-Brenin, enthusiastically persuaded Scott to join him in North Wales at Whitsun, 1956. The pair took the bus from Nottingham to Llandudno, then hiked over the Carneddau to the Ogwen Valley. Inexperience told: their tent caught fire and was reduced to its frame; they had to seek farmhouse accommodation, on tick. From the farmhouse they climbed, first unsuccessfully, on Tryfan's *Milestone Buttress*, then on Little Tryfan, where their first multi-pitch routes were completed. The pair then walked over the Glyderau to the Conwy Valley and so, blistered and weary, to Llandudno and the long bus journey home.

Horizons were stretching in other directions in 1956. Following an imagination-stimulant from Bob Pettigrew concerning the legend of the Madwoman's Stones on the Kinder plateau, Scott and Mick, this time accompanied by John Hudson and Pete Newbold, caught a bus to Bakewell, from where they first walked to Ashford. (Scott claims that this hillwalk took place at 'half-term', but as the Suez Crisis, which forms the external context to this expedition, had occurred in August, the Scott memory must again be rather wayward.) After a wet night, the foursome set off up Kinder, to cross its then mostly trackless plateau through twisting, deep, muddy groughs. The party arrived at the top of Grindsbrook Clough after two days of failing to find Kinder's 'summit'; they then turned east along the scarp edge to the Stones. A food-replenishing trip down to Edale brought jingoistic news of the Suez Crisis. The route was concluded by a descent to Ladybower reservoir then along the gritstone edges – and some blister-making roads – to Bakewell. Scott says this expedition left an indelible impression on him; he often returned.

∽

On Arran, in 1957, on a White Hall expedition in August, Scott led his first multi-pitch route. This lead was the Hard VS *Rosa Pinnacle South Ridge Direct*. This grey granite pinnacle lies just off the summit of Cir Mhor (A' Chir Mhòr, 799m), Arran's 'Matterhorn', to the west of Goat Fell. Maureen Mansell tells us that to undertake such a lead suggests Scott must have been unusually strong (it's a 160m route) and mature for his age – he would have been sixteen at the time: he was there, after all, as a guest instructor, so had clearly made very rapid progress during his two-year acquaintanceship with White Hall. Gordon Mansell, who had arrived as Instructor at White Hall only in January 1957, spoke with pride about Scott being 'a student of mine'. Another member of the trip to Arran was Harold Drasdo, then a full-time instructor at White Hall. While Drasdo would have had nominal charge of the climb before handing over to Scott, the overall trip leader would have been Geoffrey Sutton, the warden, with his wife, Ann.

The journey to Arran was made by Land Rover, full of camping gear and provisions. The students, perhaps a dozen or so, travelled by hired minivan driven by either White Hall's boilerman or handyman. Accommodation was under canvas close to the Glen Sannox Youth Hostel, within easy walking distance of Cir Mhor. The warden and the permanent instructors took duty turns to do all the cooking for the course's duration.

In the early evening, Scott led Harold, Maureen, Gordon and probably Mick Garside up Glen Sannox and over The Saddle to Cir Mhor for the climb. On the first of the two ropes, Scott led Mick Garside, with Harold Drasdo as third member or soloing just behind. The second rope

comprised Gordon Mansell leading his future wife, Maureen. Because of
the danger of rockfall, the first rope would climb, belay all members and
await the second rope, both ropes climbing fast between belays. Scott was,
it seems, 'cheered on' by the others. This was a free climb: pegs and pitons
were not issued to White Hall at that time. The only technical equipment
used, other than nylon rope, was slings and karabiners. Scott recalls, 'We
set off to climb . . . a splendid symmetrical peak in the centre of the island.
It was the longest route I'd yet done. I was pushed into the lead, spurred
on by these luminaries watching from below, feeding my ego as I made
short work of the layback crux. The rock was just wonderful, the setting
superb and the company always inspiring.'[14]

Back in Nottingham, Geoff Stroud came on the scene shortly after the
Arran success. Geoff lived only a mile from Charlbury Road but attended
a different school. He recalls, however, the indefatigable Sergeant Scott
coming to his primary school to give road safety lessons. Geoff became
friendly at Mundella with Wes Hayden, who mentioned Doug and his
unusual climbing abilities, with the result that Geoff and Doug first met at
the Scout Jubilee Jamboree in Sutton Coldfield in August 1957, just before
Doug transferred to Mundella. Geoff then joined the 1st Nottingham
YMCA Scout Troop, with Doug and Wes. Wes and Geoff were a year
above Scott at Mundella, suggesting Scott's relative maturity. They
enjoyed regular Rover Scout weekend outings to the various millstone
grit edges where Scott had begun his climbing career. They also kept fit
and earned some trip-money working at Car Colston farm, taking in the
harvest, despite it being a fifty-kilometre round trip, sometimes by bike,
at other times by hitching. Even the seasoned farmhands were impressed
by Scott's strength – the farmer did ask Brian what Douglas had had for
breakfast that he (Brian) hadn't, the difference in the two lads' physiques
being obvious.

Scott's social and geographical horizons expanded further at Easter
1958 when, on the recommendation of the Mundella headmaster, he
was selected for a course lasting a month at the Eskdale Outward Bound
Centre in the Lake District, where the new warden, John Lagoe, had only
recently taken over from one of Scott's boyhood heroes, Eric Shipton. For
this course, Scott discarded his nailed boots in favour of Vibram-soled
Arvons: with increasing numbers, the market for improved technology in
climbing clothing and equipment was expanding.

The course itself was wide-ranging: not just the obvious technical skills of
navigation and first aid, but also mountain rescue, athletics, rock-climbing,

fell-walking and bivouacking. To these was added natural history, a subject which immediately fascinated Scott, provoking a lifelong interest in geology and how human intervention through farming and forestry altered the landscape; he wrote extensively about the geology and landscaping of Nepal in his final, posthumously published book, *Kangchenjunga*. After the first week's assessment, Scott was put in charge of a patrol of twelve young climbers, mostly older than himself (he being not quite seventeen). Scott revelled in every aspect of the course, which included his first ascent of Scafell Pike, Skiddaw and, nearly, Helvellyn, with several rock-climbs on Yewbarrow. His social acquaintanceship on the course extended to meeting his first Etonian, with whom he enjoyed a friendly relationship. In *Up and About*, Scott declares that he found the Lake District 'lovelier' and 'more inviting' than Wales, a view reinforced by his settling there, in the tourist-free northern part, with all three of his wives.

In autumn 1958, Geoff Stroud, Wes Hayden and Scott, now showing fresh enthusiasm for the Lake District, returned there on a Duke of Edinburgh's Silver Award hike organised by the Education Department of Nottingham City Council. They explored the Great Gable and Styhead Pass areas. In late December, they returned under their own auspices. After an inadvertent camp in the dark on the lawn of a 'grand mansion' near Windermere, a wet and freezing night's camp at Sprinkling Tarn (some sources say Angle Tarn) put them in position to be the first arrivals on England's highest point, Scafell Pike (978m), on 1 January 1959. They descended to dry off at the Wasdale Barn, where Scott first met Don Whillans. Although Scott's friendship with Whillans did not develop at this point, it eventually led (among other climbs at home and abroad) to Everest in 1972 and Shivling in 1981, until Whillans's not unpredictable death in 1985. Scott evidently returned to Wasdale the following winter.

Even further afield, the following extraordinary expedition to Torridon and Kintail took place thanks to another influential figure in Scott's life, Geoff Hayes. He had replaced Bob Pettigrew on the Lenton Boulevard school course. In the Oread Mountaineering Club's *A Commentary on Geoff Hayes*, in honour of Hayes, who died on Dow Crag in the Lake District in 1971, Scott describes his adventure as follows:

The 1960 Christmas holidays were for me divided between a life of debauchery at Wasdale Head and adventurous mountaineering in the north of Scotland. Wasdale Hotel was traditionally the Christmas home of the Rock and Ice (Cock and Spice) club, their camp followers and impressionable hangers-on such as Dez Hadlum, Wes Hayden and me. For us three aspiring Oreads it was a time to challenge our heroes – not at climbing but at barn rugby, feats of strength and continuous drinking without falling over. In between these festive events, I made enquiries about the chap who had invited me to go up north with him to Torridon.

'Hard bloke, Geoff Hayes.' 'Walk you off your feet.' 'You'd best stay off the liquor if you want to keep up with that one.' I left in a hurry to meet him at Ambleside bus station. I walked over Sty Head and up Langdale, hoping the exercise would remove concentrations of Black Velvet from my system. Geoff arrived at midnight on 27 December with Margaret Lowe and Ray Gillies. Lean in build, short-cropped hair, the features of an aesthete, Geoff peered through the sleet, driving hour after hour while talking incessantly about the mountains. The hours passed by winding around road works to Glasgow then by Loch Lomond, with Geoff still yarning away. But he was more than that, for he was just as interested in our modest accomplishments on gritstone and bog trotting in the Peak. We drove straight up to Glen Torridon, had a few hours' sleep and set off across the heather to Liathach. The mountains were uniformly covered with a dusting of snow above 2,000 feet. Geoff strode out in front: even on the rough tussocks he moved with great certainty in his bounce, never tripping and stumbling. We walked the whole ridge from East to West, finishing at Sgurr a'Chadail before descending to the car and our camp.

We were roused to an Alpine start with a brew by Geoff. Ray, Margaret and I staggered after the bounding Hayes to the eastern end of Beinn Eighe. By the time the sun was shining on our backs we had reached the ridge at Sgurr Ban. We crossed innumerable saddles before being taken on a conducted tour of the 'finest corrie in Scotland, Coire Mhic Fhearchair'. No sooner seen than off again down to Loch nan Cabar and up Beinn Dearg. It was getting to be 'quite a day out for a lady'. On the northern promontory of Beinn Dearg we stopped to rest and spot peaks that were unfolding in every direction. Margaret decided to go on down to the car. Ray and I were keen to join her, especially with our blistered feet from Arvon Jones's 'Tiger' boots.

'Try Alligin,' urged Geoff.

'It's too steep, it'll take too long,' we said hopefully.

'It'll flatten out when you get to it, that's how ridges look head on.'

We clambered down to the Allt a'Bhealaich and scrambled up to Beinn Alligin's summit, shattered after an eight-hour day, then revived with the setting sun shining over a placid Loch Torridon. One more bump over Tom na Gruagaich and off down to Geoff, thoughtlessly shouting our young heads off about the sunset and how the last peak had finished the day off nicely. He praised our efforts with just a touch of envy. He never let on – just accepted his responsibility to Margaret. That was the sort of bloke he was.

It was raining next day so we set off south to the Five Sisters of Kintail. We made a leisurely camp and set off early next morning in a light snowfall up the eastern end of the ridge. The wind blew increasingly hard from the south-west; the snowfall became a blizzard.

'Keep the wind on your left cheek!' yelled Geoff, who had followed up with Margaret. This was our Everest that day. We kept on, over all five summits in the full fury of the blizzard. As we descended into a forest, we temporarily lost each other. Ray and I came across a Nissen hut set in the middle of a clearing with no sign of a track leading to or from it. The door was on the latch and opened to reveal a double bed made up with clean sheets and damp blankets. Apart from two coat hangers on the wall and a 'home sweet home' message, there was no other furniture. Being so tired, we naturally hung our sodden trousers and anoraks on the coat hangers, put our boots on the bedpost and jumped into bed. Twenty minutes later there was a clatter at the door and peals of laughter as Geoff and Margaret, amused at the incongruity of the scene, arrived. Whose it was we will never know, but they can be thankful that we gave their blankets a good airing.

The snow lay thick and deep the next day as we continued south to Glencoe. 'We'll just make it,' declared Geoff as we left the Queen's Cairn and stormed the fortress of Bidean. We did make it, but after dark and in sleet that steamed off our clothes all the way back to Nottingham. It was climbers like Geoff, with their infectious enthusiasm, who pointed the way.

Other excursions followed to the Lake District and North Wales. Freed from school by the spring of 1959, Scott, Geoff and others headed for Ben Nevis and the Mamores, an elegant range of ten Munros lying immediately south of 'the Ben', on the far side of the upper reaches of the River Nevis.[15]

The Mamores (Gaelic for 'big breasts') follow a sometimes narrow, undulating ridge which is nowhere difficult in summer. To complete this range, starting and finishing in Glen Nevis, requires a strenuous total ascent of approximately 3100m.

Scott's epic walk began at Polldubh, the furthest point attainable up Glen Nevis by buses. The friends camped out in the barn next to the (very noisy) cattle grid. (Scott occupied many barns and derelict buildings in the UK and elsewhere, usually without permission, in his younger, more impecunious years.) An ascent of the westernmost Munro, Mullach nan Coirean (939m), led to a taxing but exhilarating traverse of the remaining nine Munros which conclude at the ridge's eastern end on Binnein Beag (943m), although Scott unaccountably substitutes that with its neighbour, Sgurr Eilde Mor (1010m). The aim was to descend to the River Nevis and follow it back to Polldubh. Scott, however, was enjoying himself so much that he left his companions at this halfway point. He had decided to climb the length of the Grey Corries, the quartzite-covered range of three Munros, plus its outlier, Stob Ban (977m), followed by the very high Aonach Beag (1234m), leading to the Nevis horseshoe's eastern high point, Carn Mor Dearg (1220m).[16] Here, he recognised that he was too tired to continue to Nevis itself. This is hardly surprising: he had covered much of the higher ground in soft spring snow! He scrambled down the long, awkward and dangerous south face of Ben Nevis back to Polldubh, having completed a fourteen-hour day. Scott does not provide very precise details of his route, but it must have required a total climb of something in excess of 5500m and an ascent of somewhere between twelve and seventeen Munros. The statistics were impressive, but the important matter was the effect: 'It had been the best day I had ever had in the hills and the feeling of contentment I had experienced persisted for days . . . No other activity bore comparison. Those fourteen hours [were] a turning-point in my life.'

On many future occasions, Scott returned to this kind of transcendent experience after a really hard day in the mountains, particularly when combined with a summit where conditions permitted a pause for contemplation.

∽

With his A-Levels completed, Scott was ready in the summer of 1959 to progress to further education. Bob Pettigrew, with his Loughborough College background, influential as his rugby coach at Nottingham Moderns, leader of the climbing course at Lenton Boulevard school and leader of Scout expeditions to North Wales of which Scott was a member, advised taking a Social Science degree there; Scott, however, chose to follow the easier teacher training course for a certificate in PE and geography, with a view to the long holidays being used to expand his climbing experience.

While planning his future, Scott was gathering certificates: apart from formal qualifications in first aid, he obtained his Duke of Edinburgh's Silver Award in December 1958. Although the Gold Award duly followed in 1959, Scott refused to collect it at the ceremony at Buckingham Palace, thus beginning a lifelong aversion to formal occasions and of certificate-gathering at the expense of lived experience (a principle re-examined after the Cairngorms Disaster in November 1971). Remarkably, a meeting was arranged at Nottingham City Hall with Sir John Hunt; Scott justified himself to the Award leader. Brian, who had no such qualms, duly collected his certificate and Douglas's from the Palace. Scott's 'ethical' stance, as he calls it – but perhaps not much more than a rationalisation of discomfort in unfamiliar formal situations – extended to avoiding hobnobbing with the many high-achieving athletes at Loughborough, in his words, 'all hungry for gold and glory'. Instead, he remained hungry for praise, a niggling psychological craving from which he never escaped. At Loughborough, for example, the college newspaper satisfyingly praised him for his climb of Joe Brown's classic *Cenotaph Corner* in Llanberis Pass, Snowdonia.[17]

Since the Loughborough course did not begin until September, Scott had time on his hands. The previous summer, he and his Rover Scout friends had already visited Kandersteg in Switzerland at an international Scout jamboree, followed by a hitch-hiking tour to Yugoslavia. He repeated this in summer 1960, taking in Chamonix, Mont Blanc and various other Alpine peaks (see chapter five). Later that summer, when Wes and Dez had returned to work, Scott headed with Geoff Stroud and Mick Poppleston for the Julian Alps, the Dalmatian coast, Venice, Vienna, Innsbruck and Paris. It was a natural progression from Scott's explorations in the UK.

By his own admission, Scott did not spend much time in college during his first year there. His long weekends were occupied in climbing and he worked at Car Colston farm on Wednesdays. Lectures, some of which he found interesting, as well as teaching practice and essay-writing passed in little more than a blur – Scott and deadlines never sat very comfortably together. Indeed, he arrived late at the beginning of his first term. Lyn Noble describes the event: 'Our geography group was attending its first seminar of the autumn term when in walked Doug, late, looking as if he'd just come off the hill. The tutor looked up, "Ah, Mr Scott, honoured that you have deigned to join us." (Or words to that effect.) "Would you like to tell us where you've been?" Doug: "Yugoslavia, and we met a bunch of nudes [pronounced 'noods'] on a beach." I've no idea what happened in the rest of the seminar!'[18]

Scott's first teaching practice, during the summer term of 1960, took place at the William Crane school in Nottingham, situated conveniently near Charlbury Road at only about two kilometres north of Wollaton Park. There, he learnt to understand his pupils through their backgrounds, very often of a severely disadvantaged kind. Scott tells us that he ended this practice with a good report and that his pupils were genuinely sorry to see him leave. He otherwise attributes his successful bonding with his pupils to taking them walking in Derbyshire. Passing on what he himself had only recently but very successfully learnt marks part of Scott's transition into adulthood. Many expeditions with pupils followed over the succeeding ten years, although he found the twenty Cottesmore and other Nottingham schoolboys he led on expedition to Turkish Kurdistan's Čilo Daği in 1966 to be as far as he was prepared to go down that exotic foreign road.

While not attending lectures during what had effectively become a two-day week, Scott spent his time climbing. Lyn Noble, an early Alpine climbing partner, describes some of their non-academic activities:

> We first met as students at Loughborough College. He was training to be a PE teacher. I was a 'chippy' [trainee craft teacher]. We did the usual sort of stuff, bivvying in the heather above Gardoms and waking (if we ever slept) covered in frost before going on to the old classics. Most of the time Doug climbed with his Nottingham mates while I teamed up with Colin Mortlock and other college pals. However, once a year we joined forces for a bit of indoor aid climbing.
>
> The Victory Hall at Loughborough was a massive, grim building with steel rafters in the roof . . . Forty feet above the desks and chairs were the rafters, perfect nesting places and ideal for bombing exam papers. Although most of the college staff and students had little idea what climbers got up to, Doug and I were seen as a convenient and cheap way of evicting the birds. We had great fun and cleared out one or two nests but never met anything with feathers.[19]

At the end of the summer holidays, another late return by a week from his first non-European excursion, the Atlas Mountains in Morocco, led to Loughborough's vice-principal questioning Scott's commitment to teaching, a question to which Scott could not provide a wholly credible answer. Scott was testing authority: he was frequently late back from holidays during his teaching career, whether from Strone Ulladale in Harris, one of his earliest major big wall challenges, or from more distant parts such as Tibesti or the tumultuous conclusion to Turkey's Čilo Dağı expedition; conniving with sympathetic school secretaries helped to placate disgruntled head teachers and colleagues who had to cover for Scott's self-indulgent absences.

Such alienation from his colleagues is underscored by Scott when he describes his second teaching practice at 'a huge new comprehensive in Leicester'. Having perhaps judiciously not named the school, which was in fact Rushey Mead, still a successful comprehensive on Leicester's north-eastern fringes, he admits that his colleagues found him a 'nuisance', without elaborating further: unjustifiable absences requiring extra cover would be the most likely cause.[20] However, he did make the acquaintance there of Peter Biven, who had pioneered new gritstone routes but was primarily known for his climbing in Cornwall, particularly with Trevor Peck.[21] Biven was able to give Scott advice about new routes on High Tor and other gritstone areas. New routes interested Scott a lot.

Geoff Stroud sums up his view of Scott as this time:

I don't think anyone who met Doug could not be affected or influenced by him. From the times we spent together, my lasting memories are of him having boundless energy, being full of ideas and never being stuck for a solution to problems. I remember on his runs, he would go on until he was absolutely exhausted and then turn round and run home again.

Our school was an ancient Victorian pile covered with brick ornamentation; Doug spent time devising a traverse around the building, fortunately, as far as I know, not attempted. He had the same plans for the Castle Rock in Nottingham, the sandstone outcrop on which Nottingham Castle was built. [Steve Read recalls climbing on it with Scott, probably in 1976.] Although he was a really big, strong guy, he was truly a gentle giant and I can never recall him losing his temper or being unkind to anyone. Technically, he was extremely competent and resourceful. Doug was very well read and aware of current world affairs. We spent happy evenings while away devising quizzes and discussing books and world politics.[22]

From his increasingly wide reading and his expanding acquisition of equipment, skills and experience, we know that Scott was, for a nineteen-year-old, remarkably purposeful and ambitious. His 'insatiable urge' was to visit 'more mountains, everywhere'.

As he declared to Geoff Stroud, 'I've got plans.'

4

Climbs in the UK, 1960–70

'When Doug Scott squared up to you, you took a step
back.'

– Allen Fyffe, Everester and Glenmore Lodge instructor

Scott's friendships now extended through the Scouts, Cottesmore,
Mundella, White Hall, Eskdale Outward Bound and Mountain Heritage,
as well as through sports. He had become friends with climbers he met at
Loughborough, notably Lyn Noble and David 'Ben' Sykes. These friends
began to introduce their own friends; the next step was, in 1961, to found
the NCC, one of Scott's proudest achievements.

Club life was beneficial: transport was cheaper and conviviality greater.
A weekend's therapy on the crags would lead to a feeling of rebirth after
the deadening routines of the working week. Thursday meetings at The
Spread Eagle or the Salutation decided on the weekend's venue. Outings
often coincided with other clubs, notably the Rock and Ice and the Oread.
Scott and several friends attended Oread meets, as aspirants, as early
as 1959.

Scott covered up his aspirant membership of the Oread because he
would have been seen (according to the prejudices of the time) to be
moving beyond his established social class. Scott's mother had already tried
to improve social opportunities for her sons. Scott's social circle, however,
grew with his fame, because he was meeting more widely educated people,
of different social character from his own origins. His own interests were
also expanding beyond mountaineering.

This early attempt at social betterment via the Oread went wrong.
The incident of Dave Penlington's socks occurred in the Glan Dena hut
below Tryfan during an Oread joint meet with the Midland Association
of Mountaineers. Scott, Dez Hadlum and Dennis Gray had climbed *Great
Gully* on Craig Yr Ysfa and had received a soaking. It was winter. Socks,
with other clothes, hung in the hut drying room. Rightly or wrongly, Scott

assumed they had been abandoned. The owner, however, had intended to return for his property. Scott's purloining of the socks was discovered: his aspirant candidacy for the Oread was abruptly ended, as it was for several of his friends. (Penlington, an Oread founder member, had a reputation as a disciplinarian.) Thereafter, Scott tended publicly to disparage the Oread for excessive formality. The riposte came during an Oread dinner when Scott was referred to as 'the bandit of Sherwood Forest'!

The NCC was modelled, Guy Lee says, on the Rock and Ice Club as well as, according to a more waspish commentator, Scott's own image.[1] The NCC reputation was for hard climbing and harder celebrating. Entry was informal: an 'interview' over Thursday evening drinks at 'The Sal' would lead to a brief discussion about acceptability. No particular standards were required, though the ability to climb Severe to Hard VS became a benchmark; candidates mostly just had to be 'good people'. Other clubs employed a more formal entrance procedure.

The Thursday evening arrangement before the advent of the NCC coach followed a pattern: members would meet at, say, the Dinas Cromlech boulders at lunchtime on Saturday, or 6 p.m. for latecomers. Such an arrangement underpinned the club's ethos of trust and loyalty, the willingness to get your friend out of a fix, and a resolute intolerance of dishonesty. One of Scott's earliest companions, Steve 'Sid' Smith, comments, 'Hitching was common; Doug hitched a lot and was good at it. That's what made the NCC bus trips so popular to places like Wales or the Lake District; they were great affordable outings for the Nottingham climbers . . . And if anyone in the Club had a car and was going to Wales, Scotland or the Lake District, they always had a full car when they left!'[2]

The first NCC meet took place at Easter 1961. The eight founding members, some with their girlfriends, climbed on Dow Crag on the Old Man of Coniston (799m) in the Lake District. Numbers grew; within two years, a fifty-two-seat bus was required for the weekend outing.

Through the Oread, Scott got to know Dennis Gray, one of the most influential people in UK and European mountaineering. Dennis had moved to Derby from his native Leeds; he was part of a loose group of climbers known as the Bradford Lads. Dennis's astringent wit did not always sit well with the NCC's more thin-skinned members, but it was outweighed by his generosity in giving fundraising lectures and speeches for the club. He was perhaps the first to question Scott's (sparing) use of bolts, for example on *Kilnsey Main Overhang*. Gray, in his pithy 1970 memoir, *Rope Boy*, was among the first to identify the sea-change evolving in British climbing from amateurism to professionalism in thrall to sponsorship and other financial sources, a subject which vexed Scott throughout his climbing life. Dennis became and remained a lifelong friend.

In the main, NCC meets centred on new routes on the limestone crags of the Derwent Valley, such as High Tor, Wildcat and Willersley Castle. (Scott put up thirty-four first ascents on Wildcat Crag.) Climbing was a mix of aid and free. Generally speaking, pegs (pitons) were used only on the most difficult pitches or on overhangs. Scott's first new route was the *Traverse* of Raven Tor, in October 1961, with Ray Gillies. He followed this with *M1*, just left of the main gully of High Tor, then by *Flaky Wall* (E4 6a) with Clive Davies, during which the climbers experienced a testing snowfall. Sometimes access problems intervened: the path to Willersley Castle rock was used by churchgoing locals, so cragging could only begin in the afternoon.

Club life also entailed sociability. The NCC loved nicknames: 'Yoff', 'Mash' and 'Sherpa'. Dennis Gray enjoyed referring to them as the Nottingham Cricket Club. (This might have been more than just a jibe – Scott never took up cricket because of his short-sightedness.) Their cry of 'Milko!' when hollered across various routes on a crag, called them to assembly. (The cry originates from the milk deliveries in those parts of Nottingham where many club members resided.) Girls were not much mentioned; most girlfriends generally had to suffer cold and boredom at the foot of the crag, weighing up whether their young man was worth it.

Evening celebrations were often lively. The outstanding club legend is commemorated as The Battle of the Dog and Partridge. Early in 1965, a typically raucous NCC evening turned to chaos when the landlord of this fine pub, a few kilometres north-east of Ashbourne, decided to close early. A mêlée ensued: Steve Read was clattered by a banjo from behind by the publican; the publican's wife called the police. The club members piled into an expedition truck then roared off with a panda car in pursuit. Driver Ray Gillies thoughtfully powered through a ford of the River Dove, in spate, at Clifton. The police decided not to risk it. Cheering (jeering?) club members drove on, their defiant finger gestures scarcely visible in the darkness, until they secured their getaway by sleeping under Baslow bridge, a good twenty-five kilometres north-east, with the lorry hidden behind a cricket pavilion.

The NCC's sociability extended to folk-singing. Several members were quite accomplished singers; at least four could play the banjo, double-bass, guitar and accordion. Non-climbers sought out the NCC for their music.

Inevitably, this led to trouble. One evening, at the Prince of Wales in Baslow, in early 1963, a fight broke out between Scott and a combative lad from Chesterfield over the possession of someone's hat. The fight took place outside the pub, in the local graveyard. The police intervened. Scott was discovered hiding in a bunkhouse and was charged with disturbing the peace. In court, the case was dropped because his opponent had given a false name and address. Scott's absolute discharge was fortunate: being found guilty would have severely embarrassed his father and would not have done Scott's reputation as a young professional much good either.

∞

After starting as a teacher at Cottesmore in 1961, Scott's year took on a new pattern: the Lake District was visited in the New Year, although Scotland, particularly the Cairngorms, became preferred as the decade progressed. NCC outings to the Peak District, Wales and the Lakes shared the weekends with rugby. The Easter, autumn and summer holidays mixed Cottesmore trips to the Peak and other parts of the UK with trips to Donegal, mainly to the sea-cliffs on Ireland's north-west coast. Other holiday activities saw Scott in the Alps, either leading Mountaineering Association courses usually based in Chamonix or putting up new routes of his own with his friends.

Within this yearly arrangement, the Dovedale Dash occupied a fixed place. This eight-kilometre race, begun in 1951 by the Derby Mercury Cycling Club, traced a circular route beginning at Ilam Hall then followed the River Dove to the Stepping Stones before returning to Ilam along the base of Bunster Hill. The race was made open in 1959; it was held on the nearest Sunday to Guy Fawkes night. After the race, up to 600 members of local clubs (by the mid 1970s) would converge on a mighty bonfire in the grounds of Ilam Hall, to be followed by a pantomime, organised by Tinsel Allen. Dennis Gray wrote some of the scripts, one notably entitled 'William T'Hell'. Memorable performances came from Eric 'Beardie' Beard in his Al Jolson routine; more recently, Guy Lee completed the course handicapped by a well-filled bra. As the *Climber and Rambler* reporter Gordon Gadsby recounts, however, 'One of the finest performances ever by a climber was by Doug Scott of the NCC who, in 1975, had only just returned from Everest yet managed to finish in the first ten. According to Nat Allen, most climbers would have been happy to put their feet up, but not Doug. He just ran better than ever before against first-class opposition from athletics clubs, thus helping to put climbers back on the map.'

En route to the Dash in 1960, Scott called in to see Nat Allen and his wife, Tinsel, in Derby. Here, he chanced to meet Don Whillans on his way back from his six-week motorbike ride from the Karakoram, having been a member of the expedition led by Wilf Noyce which made the first ascent of Trivor (7577m). Scott's connections to the 'greats' of the climbing world were widening: Noyce, a member of the 1953 Everest expedition, gave advice to Scott in preparation for his Atlas expedition in 1962.

Scott's climbing hours outside school were predominantly spent until 1965 in or near the Derwent Valley. Just before leaving for Tibesti, his *Climbs on Derwent Valley Limestone* publication appeared. It cost 5s (approximately £5 at today's prices). Richard Stroud had its eighty-one pages duplicated and bound, with all profits going to the club.

In his introduction, Scott hopes that 'other clubs will find it useful'. He acknowledges Graham West's *Rock Climbs on Mountain Limestone* but says it needs revision, especially since routes change as they are cleaned up. The book covers eighty routes on Wood Bank Tor and Upper Tor. Scott's case for limestone is that it offers routes of a more 'mountaineering' nature which require route-finding. Limestone, he says, is harder than gritstone to climb on because the grain is finer in the wet. Steve Read, Paul Nunn and Dave Woolcock are also acknowledged.

The route grades go from V Diff to Hard VS. Problems of grading are recognised, however. Artificial routes based on a first ascent are not graded. A discussion follows on the use of 'golos' (an engineering bolt with two pieces of aluminium forming a split sleeve). These needed to be drilled into the place, the beginning of a long and complicated relationship with bolting, to which in general Scott remained strongly averse. Scott defines his grades of A1, A2 and A3 (there are no grade A4 routes) but rejects the relevance of exposure on artificial routes. He advises tackling easier routes first.

Also included – often seen in his future books and articles – Scott gives the history of High Tor, as well as its location, and discusses its likely future. He describes access routes and concerns and identifies features with crag diagram-drawings by Brian Evans.[3] Each climb is given a name, length, pegging requirements and number of pitches (rarely more than three). The climbs and first ascents, in which Scott figures on three out of fourteen on High Tor, are listed. Upper Tor is similarly described, as is Wood Bank Tor. Willersley Castle (probably Scott's favourite Derwent

Doug in 1966 on Windhover at Stoney Middleton.
Photo by and courtesy of Peter Thompson.

crag) has thirty routes listed, with Scott claiming six as first ascents. He mentions *Lone Tree Groove* (VS 5a) and *Gangue Grooves* (HVS 5b) in particular. This list is also notable for the first mention in print by Scott of Don Whillans.

A further interesting feature of *Derwent Valley* is its advertisements, from such diverse sources as Timpson's boots, the Austrian Alpine Club, Jackson & Warr of Sheffield and Timberg Climbing Wear of Derby. These perhaps mark the beginning of Scott's long and complex relationship with sponsorship and how money funded climbing.

Scott's guide could be seen as about self-promotion as much as anything else. At least two climbing friends have attested to Scott's ambition by the time he was seventeen. We know he enjoyed a part-ironic sense of self as a 'man of destiny'; his excellently presented *Expedition Reports* for the four 1960s 'apprentice' expeditions all suggest not just the altruistic wish expressed at the beginning of *Derwent Valley*, but that their compiler, D.K. Scott, was a climbing, organisational and exploratory force to be reckoned with.

Graham West's important guidebook to the Peak District, published by Manchester Gritstone Climbing Club in 1961, records Scott's now established reputation for aid climbing. When Scott first met a long-term climbing partner and friend, Guy Lee, in 1963, they climbed using pitons and cheaters on such routes as *Mecca* (8b+), at Raven Tor, or *The Big Plum* (E6 6c).[4] (The limestone crags of the Derbyshire Dales were great places for experimenting with placing pitons, often on overhangs and dangling from *étriers* – two- or three-rung ladders that were clipped to the pitons. This allowed climbing on previously unclimbed rock that had no natural hand or footholds. As skills progressed, climbers searched out the biggest overhangs like Kilnsey Crag and Malham Cove in Yorkshire and *The Big Plum* in Chee Dale, Derbyshire.)[5]

Scott at this time was not known as 'a delicate climber' – 'he's no Ron Fawcett', as someone put it. But he was very strong and could power his way up a climb. He was probably happier on limestone than on gritstone, especially as the limestone of the Derwent Valley was largely unexplored in the early 1960s, thus giving Scott the chance to promote his first ascents through publishing his guidebook. (British climbing had been competitively finding new routes since the 1930s.)

Of course, Scott was climbing elsewhere in England, mainly in the Lake District, as the decade progressed. Not long before the founding of the NCC, Scott, Rod Hewing, Steve 'Feech' Bowes, George 'Yoff' Jones,

Tony 'Mouse' Watts, Clive 'Claude' Davies and Dan Meadows spent the night at Stickle Tarn. It was bitingly cold – the tarn was frozen over – and it was the first time that most of the lads had been away from home at Christmas. On Christmas Day they climbed Scafell. After this excursion, Scott became more interested in winter climbing in Scotland.

Among other noteworthy climbs, in 1963, Steve Read and Scott put up the first ascent on Derbyshire's High Crag of *Cataclysm* (HVS 5a), followed by *Catastrophe Grooves* (HVS 5a) on Coyote Buttress.

By 1964, Scott had extended his climbing repertoire to Malham Cove and Gordale Scar, in the Yorkshire Dales. He recalls a fractured limestone overhang, named *Grot*, which he opines was so difficult that climbing in the Dolomites seemed quite easy. At this time, on *Twilight* on High Tor, Scott used his first bolt, as well as thirty-five pegs: Scott has been criticised by some for over-pegging. By his own admission, Scott was a cautious and safe climber, not least because he suffered from nervousness at the exposure on big walls. His excuse was that 'lots of other people had bolted High Tor'.

Another notable climb for which we have a personal record occurred in 1967, when Scott and a new companion, Peter Thompson, climbed *Thirlmere Eliminate* (E2 5b) on the Castle Rock of Triermain in Cumbria. Thompson describes the event:

I led the final pitch, as Doug had struggled. But at the time, this was a climb above my skills. I climbed to the top of the final groove and at the crux hung around a bit trying to work out the final moves. Doug said, 'Go for it! I will take the strain if you pop off!' I did go for it, but my runners all pulled off and slid down the groove to Doug. I was certainly now on my own but luckily found the key hold to allow me to reach the top. Any error in that groove would have resulted in a major fall. On top, a climber from the Rock and Ice passed by with the remark that he'd enjoyed seeing two old men making a pig's ear of the route![6]

This climb chimes remarkably with an account by Bob Holmes, who joined the NCC in 1962: 'On my first visit to the Roaches, a gritstone edge in Staffordshire, I asked Doug to suggest something for me to climb. "Try this, youth; you'll like it." I barely made it to the top. There was almost no protection and I was pushed to my limits. The climb was graded HVS, way out of my skill range at the time. Not only did Doug push himself to the limits, he expected others to do the same.'[7]

Steve Read comments on Scott's rock-climbing abilities at this time: 'He was never a top rock gymnast, but a very competent rock climber with great strength, stamina and determination. He was very good at sorting out problems and avoiding difficulties. I remember Doug as someone who gave me and many others some experiences that have lasted a lifetime.'[8]

When Scott rejoined Cottesmore as a member of staff in 1961, he was obliged to juggle his interest in his pupils with fulfilling his own climbing ambitions. Scott's pupils were frequently unruly. Scott, however, realised quite quickly, after the repercussions from kicking a miscreant in the backside, that corporal punishment was wrong; he stopped using it. Instead, he discovered that by coaching rugby and taking his pupils for walks in the Derbyshire uplands, a relationship more conducive to learning could be formed.

By the mid 1960s (dates are sketchy, but most probably from 1966) with the help of colleagues, Scott was leading school expeditions to Donegal. Pupils and teachers stayed in youth hostels; they were joined by friends from the NCC, such as Terry Wells, George Jones, David Nicol and Bob Shaw, all happy to leave behind a bad-weather season in the Alps. Donegal probably derived from Scott's time at White Hall: Geoffrey Sutton and Harold Drasdo were the first English climbers properly to explore Donegal's Poisoned Glen.

This 1967 trip was not without incident. At Stranraer, Scott planned to exchange the school minibus for a hired vehicle in Larne. The Larne minibus could not accommodate all the students, however, so a chat-up on the ferry resulted in Bob Wark and a friend being driven by two young ladies to a closed border post near Londonderry, where the two students spent an uncomfortable night. In the morning, a Customs officer took sufficient pity on the pair to give them breakfast. He provided a lift in a truck carrying pigs, so that on reaching Errigal the pair could be smelled before being seen. The party went on to climb Mount Errigal (751m), the highest peak of the Derryveagh Mountains. They looked at the 601m-high sea-cliffs of Slieve League, probably the second highest in Ireland. On a boat trip from Teelin, they discovered a vast slab called Sail Rock. Later that year, Scott and Ray Gillies returned to put up several routes on it, notably *Roaring Forties* (VS 4c). They returned the following year, in April, for more. School outings made consistently stronger impressions than classwork. Hardly surprising, as Bob Wark (who started at Cottesmore in 1961) dispiritingly remarked, 'The academic level was never going to be very high; the idea was to produce factory fodder.'[9]

A typical field trip would involve travelling by Camm's coach to the Cottesmore Field Centre at the disused railway station in Tissington, where Scott might describe Derwent village, now visible thanks to low reservoir levels caused by drought. On the way back, Scott would stop at Birchen Edge to comment on the local geology. Some of the climbing trips involved rather greater excitement. At half-term in February 1964, he decided to go to Scotland. Cold weather gear was bought at the local Army Surplus store (a source for many future occasions). Unfortunately, when approaching Carlisle, the rearside wheel of the hired minibus fell off in a shower of sparks. After a night at Jan's parents, the repaired minibus reached the Cairngorm area in the small hours: a local bothy was shared with 'a bunch of snoring Glaswegians'.[10] Cairngorm (1245m) was climbed next day in deep snow and worsening weather. The party passed along the top of the Northern Corries before descending into the depths of the Lairig Ghru (high point 835m). On reaching the Lairig Ghru path, the younger members got lost, having followed the wrong footprints through the snow. They were building a snow-shelter when Scott turned up shortly after, 'cursing and muttering about us not following him'. Wark's pithy response was that if following Scott was so fucking important, then he ought to have 'fucking well waited for us'. The remainder of the walk was frosty.

Next day, the party left for the far north-west, to clamber over the sandstone pinnacles of Stac Polly (Stac Pollaidh, 612m) followed by a very long day out on spectacular Suilven (731m). The tired party commandeered an unoccupied house near Lochinver, but the police challenged their illegal occupancy, so the party packed up and headed for Britain's most north-westerly point, Cape Wrath, to camp on the beach. Somehow a night-dip in the sea was then called for to test the waterproof flashlights. Thus ended an expedition which in every aspect would now be unimaginable. Wark, tellingly, thought that 'every effort we had made had been worth it'.

Numerous other near-misses occurred, such as a near-fatal crash one Christmas on the hairpins leading down from Cairngorm car park. (One boy, aged only thirteen, remembers spending freezing nights in midwinter at Glenmore, the pain mitigated by the ceilidhs in Carrbridge.) Or on Skye, Scott reached Glen Brittle before realising that two pupils had been left an hour's drive away at Kyle of Lochalsh, in those days separated from Skye by ferry. On another occasion, the school one-tonner lost control crossing the Pennines, broke through a bridge parapet and landed end-up in the river below. Remarkably, there were no serious injuries despite children being propelled horizontally out of the truck; repairs were completed after a night in the cells and the journey continued.

What is best is the confidence Scott gave his students, although sometimes in unorthodox ways. For example, on *Lavaredo Wall* (HVS 5a) on Carreg Alltrem in Gwynedd, Bob Wark set off up the steep second pitch, Scott having led the first. About halfway up the pitch, Scott could be heard from above, shouting, 'Hold there, youth!' Scott had untied then soloed to the top by another route to get a better angle for the photograph he wanted! Wark was soloing without knowing it.

It is not entirely surprising, given Scott's discomfort in submitting to conventional disciplines, that what happened in the classroom during his ten years as a teacher is hardly mentioned in *Up and About*: a few paragraphs deal with disciplinary events, but learning is hardly described. Scott's biggest success appears to have occurred in 1968 after climbing the *Bonatti Pillar* on the Petit Dru, when the consequent invitation to write a book on artificial climbing provided topic material for a social studies course Scott was obliged to teach that autumn. For that time, slightly unconventional methods were employed: visual aids, films, visits and guest speakers. They helped to engage pupils who would rather not have been at school. Scott even mentions a more personal initiative: teaching yoga to a class of forty. Scott's popularity was never in doubt: a Facebook site about 'Old Nottingham' brings out spontaneous memories of an engaging teacher.

∽

Not all excursions were school-based, however: serious climbs in Scotland and Wales after the 1965 publication of *Derwent Valley* included some of the greatest mountaineering achievements in Scott's life.

In Scotland, winter tended to be his favoured time for climbing. Ever mindful of his growing reputation, Scott cunningly visited the Cairngorms when most other climbers were putting up new routes on Ben Nevis and in Glencoe. As early as January 1959, Scott had hitched to Aberdeen and then on to the village of Garve, about an hour north-west of Inverness, where he met Ray Gillies. They climbed Ben Wyvis (1046m), a whaleback Munro of no particular distinction: an odd choice.

Fresh from his 1960 epiphany on the Mamores, Scott returned at Christmas 1961 with Mick Garside to Glencoe. Foolishly setting off late, they reached the highest summit in the area, Bidean nam Bian (1150m);

in winter conditions it is an Alpine climb. Scott's own description, even allowing for his self-dramatisation, is worth repeating:

> We set off impulsively, in the afternoon, knowing there was only three hours of daylight. We rushed off in light sweaters and light anoraks. We got to the top of Bidean in a hurricane, looked for the easy way off. Missed it and couldn't find a way. Soon, it was totally dark with visibility down to nil, the blizzard blowing horizontal snow straight into our faces. I knew we had to get out of the wind. We started heaping snow up. The wind was blowing the snow off the mountain, so there wasn't much depth but we managed to pile it up and dig into it. With bare hands, we piled snowballs up spirally. We got inside and began digging out the interior, putting the snow above our heads, eventually sealing the gap so we were out of the wind and in for a fourteen-hour shivering with no sleeping bags, just a rope to lie on. That same night on Ben Nevis, four lads died in the same storm.[11]

Had Scott and Garside not been unusually resilient, they might well not have survived. In the morning, the pair struggled down through 'huge crags' until the inhabitants of a 'large house' in Glen Etive (about five kilometres from the summit) received an unexpected Christmas present when Scott and Garside turned up to ask if they could phone the Mountain Rescue. Hamish MacInnes and his team had been at the ready. (Scott and MacInnes later became friends for several decades until MacInnes's death preceded Scott's by only a fortnight, in 2020.)

Despite this setback, Scott returned to the Cairngorms many times. Bob Shaw tells us, 'I had my first winter climbing trip to the Cairngorms in 1967 with Doug and Martin Harris and spent a freezing week in atrocious weather at Jean's Hut in Coire an Lochain, where we did probably a very early, if not the first, winter ascent of *Savage Slit* (V6) and also a new route called *Milky Way* (Scottish Grade III).'[12]

A similar experience took place in the winter of 1968–69. Allen Fyffe, a fellow member with Scott on the 1975 Bonington Everest south-west face expedition, tells us that Scott found a derelict estate cottage in the Rothiemurchus Forest between Aviemore and Cairngorm, and remained there until thrown out. (This accommodation was shared with Guy Lee, Tom Morrell, Rob Wood and Tom Patey: it gave rise to the idea of going to Baffin Island, in 1972.) Scott nonetheless put up the new *Chute Route* (V5) on Coire an Lochain on 24 December 1968, with Martin Harris and Bob Shaw.

At New Year 1969, Scott was back in the Cairngorms, this time with the legendary Eric 'Beardie' Beard. Beardie had just prevented Scott from getting involved in a Hogmanay brawl provoked by Jan spending too long dancing with another man. To distract him, Scott was persuaded to spend New Year's Day ski-ing: they ascended 900m from Loch Morlich to Cairngorm, skied over the plateau to the UK's second-highest mountain, Ben Macdhui (1300m), then descended to the Lairig Ghru and so to Loch Morlich. While Beardie sang, Scott struggled along in his tracks. Beard was killed in November 1969 in a car accident, one of the great losses of Scott's life.

The Cairngorms consolidated Scott's reputation for unusual climbs, for extraordinary stamina, for a willingness to live outside conventional rules and for the ability to survive in extreme conditions. As Allen Fyffe remarked, 'Scott was a kind of mountains' main man.'

If winter tended to be spent in Scotland, Scott claimed that in the summer of 1966 he spent thirteen weekends in a row in North Wales. Inspired by Joe Brown and Don Whillans's astonishing achievements, he was climbing all the classic routes at Dinas Cromlech (Llanberis Pass), such as the *Girdle* (E2 5b) and *The Thing* (E2 5c). He appears to have been particularly interested in repeating Joe Brown's routes on Clogwyn Du'r Arddu ('Cloggy'), such as *The Corner* (HVS 5b), comparable to *Cenotaph Corner*, and *The Boulder* (E1 5a). Scott's interest lay in developing a detailed understanding of a crag. He passionately enjoyed the newness of each climb. He liked nothing more than warm, dry rock, a theme he returned to in Yosemite in the 1970s. And true to the conflicting co-existence of opposites in his character, the feeling of engagement with every imperfection and handhold was set against the mental detachment generated by looking back on a demanding climb.

The magnificent sea-cliffs of Gogarth, on the west side of Anglesey, however, at the time a relatively undiscovered climbing area, also attracted Scott's attention. Its *Big Overhang* became most significant for Scott's future. His first Gogarth success was *Crowbar* (E1 5b), with Bill Cheverst. A better variant was climbed by Scott, with Ray Gillies. Scott was criticised by editor, journalist and controversialist Ken Wilson, a kind of mountaineers' Kenneth Tynan, for over-pegging: seven pegs on *Crowbar* and 'several' pegs to protect a hanging belay on loose rock on the variant.

On 11 June, Scott and Gillies made the first ascent of *Syringe* (E4 6a). Peter Thompson describes the name's convoluted history: 'Wittily called *Crewcut* when first climbed by Doug Scott and Ray Gillies. This was a route eyed up by Pete Crew but he was beaten to it by Doug and Ray. Les Farrah and I were on the approach to the climb when Crew and his rope buddy appeared and saw Doug and Ray already well up the route. "Fucking Scott!" he shouted. In answer to Doug's naming the route when the official guide, edited by Crew, came out, the route was renamed to expunge the slight to himself.'[13]

A rivalry lasting several years evolved between Scott and Peter Crew. Scott did not care for Crew personally, it is said, because he believed him to be a 'public school toff', not a convincing reason as Scott had a strong tendency to take fellow climbers on their merits.[14] Crew named this route *Syringe* in the official guide in recognition of the competitive needle around in Wales at that time. Scott modestly concedes that Brown, Whillans or Crew would have made a better job of *Syringe* than he did, but also sensibly adds that such debate was becoming irrelevant as the use of chocks on wires ('friends') was spreading rapidly at that time and thus changing the nature of the experience.

Of perhaps longer-lasting significance was *The Big Overhang*, a thirty-metre projection near the fog warning tower on Gogarth's North Stack. Over three weekends in 1967, Scott and Brian 'Henry' Palmer attacked this monstrosity, not least because it represented an escape from a foot-and-mouth outbreak in Derbyshire. Henry has been able to provide a first-hand recollection of that momentous climb:

Terry Wells and I had found the *Overhang* at the beginning of 1967. Doug got to hear of it, but the Hindu Kush expedition (1967) put our plans on hold. *The Roof*, as it was known, is situated in Parliament House cave. The profile resembles a saw blade, with constant pegging up and down. Doug and I took turns leading, although on more than one occasion I had to tell Doug to stop fucking about with his cameras and hold the belay ropes! On the sixth and final day, Doug led through to the top of the crag, which left me with the job of clearing the route of gear. Doug and I worked out a drag rope system, whereby when gear around my waist amounted to a third of my body weight I would clip it to the drag rope, Doug would haul it to the top of the crag, when I would pull the drag rope back ready for the next haul. The fog warning station master, John Carey, kindly let us stay with him. In May 1968, Doug and I put up a new route, *Whip* (HVS) on the outer left wall of Parliament House, a very clean and pleasant climb.[15]

While Scott had acquired a taste for overhangs in the Dolomites, the sustained, highly exposed nature of this climb activated his interest in the UK's biggest wall at remote Strone Ulladale, on Harris. Several attempts on it, despite being of limited success, showed Scott was now ready to tackle some of the world's most demanding big wall routes, beginning in 1971 with the Salathé Wall in Yosemite, the climb which established Scott's international reputation and changed his life forever.

5

Climbs in the Alps, Spain and Dolomites, 1958–69

'In order to climb properly on a big peak, one must free oneself of fear. This means you must say to yourself: "I may die here."'

– Doug Scott

Scott visited the Alps eight times, the Dolomites three times and Spain twice between 1958 and 1969. When not guiding clients on Mountaineering Association courses, he followed only a small number of classic routes – difficult enough, but not innovative or exploratory. He came close to death several times: youthful errors of judgment, perhaps, but also a recognition that no amount of pegging can protect against objective dangers.

The first trip, in late July 1958, lasted five weeks, three of them in the Alps then two weeks behind the Iron Curtain, in Yugoslavia. George and Joyce's laissez-faire parenting allowed their seventeen-year-old son with two friends to cross Western Europe and penetrate the Communist zone unsupervised. This 1958 Rover Scout outing comprised Scott, Geoff Stroud and Wes Hayden. An expedition on a shoestring: Geoff Stroud recalls that in preparation, as they could not afford rucksacks, they bought an ancient sewing machine for £2 10s at the local market and sewed sheets of canvas together to make Yukon-style backpacks.

Transport was equally basic: a bus to London, where they stayed in the Scout hostel in the East End; boat-train to Calais; then train to the International Scout Centre at Kandersteg, in the Bernese Oberland. They were 'staggered by the scale and grandeur of the Alps'.

The first aim of ascending the Blumlisalphorn (3663m) via the Oeschinensee was highly ambitious, although their route is now graded at only PD+: their failure owed to 'heat, height and inexperience'. Scott reflected that a vast readjustment of times was required to accommodate the change of scale. Wisely, they explored passes instead. Their longest day led over the Gemmi Pass (2270m) for almost forty kilometres to Leuk (Leukerbad). From there, they hitched to Chamonix: such was their skill that they all arrived within a few hours of each other.

Here, the British contingent would gather at Snell's Field. The *Rock and Ice* magazine description can hardly be bettered: 'Snell's Field, the climbers' camp outside Chamonix, was for 20-odd years a squalid conglomeration of makeshift rain shelters, tents and rolling wrecks typically populated by British, American and German alpinists, none of whom especially liked the others. When it rained in the Alps, which was often, the football-field-sized campground became a fetid bog.'[1]

On the Mer de Glace they were lucky to survive as they wove their way unprotected round crevasses and past *séracs* (blocks of glacial ice). Stroud found it 'terrifying'. The second day's walk, to Mont Blanc (4807m) via the Aiguille du Midi (3842m), was even more foolhardy.[2] Not only did route-finding fail: they found (later) that they were climbing Severe pitches in the Boeuf Couloir of the Aiguille du Peigne (3192m); bad timing meant being doused in snowmelt. Scott fell 20m; Stroud sustained rope burns in holding him – another narrow escape and a judicious retreat.

Suddenly, hitching to Yugoslavia seemed more enticing. After crossing the Saint Bernard pass, a romantic adventure awaited: in Peschiera and Venice they revelled in northern Italy's sensuality; sleeping on the beach at the Lido was wish-fulfilment. From Venice, they hitched to Trieste then took a ferry down the Adriatic to the beach-island of Rab, now in Croatia, where they lodged in a local monastery in exchange for helping to tidy up storm damage.

Scott's luck deserted him while trying to reach Chamonix in 1959: it took four days. He had worked on postal deliveries and in a pork pie factory to earn sufficient cash; he also worked on weekends as a farm labourer at Car Colston. These jobs gave him further experience of adult life and show how strongly motivated he was to fund six weeks in the Alps and beyond.

Hadlum joined Scott (Hayden was delayed); they camped at Chamonix's Biolay and treated themselves to new ice-axes and crampons. They were helped with advice on routes by Derek Burgess, a friend of Bob Pettigrew, whom they would soon encounter in a new role.

First objective was the Dent du Requin (3422m). When the rain cleared near their Requin Hut campsite, Scott experienced another Wordsworthian 'spot of time' moment, where he felt his senses heightened and elevated by the magnificence of his surroundings. Wearing crampons for the first time, they walked to the start of the *Voie des Plaques* (AD) route up the Requin.³ The climb began well on easy, warm granite. Soon, however, a lightning storm and blizzard developed; retreat was reluctantly agreed around two hours from the top. Their lightweight rope was unsuited to abseiling, so long delays ensued and camp was not reached until 11 p.m. Another powerful learning experience for Scott and friend.

A rest day at Chamonix was spent meeting Wes and hiding from the 'taxman' (campsite fees collector). The three then returned to the Requin, to start their route at 6 a.m. The climb was successful, after chimneys and an overhang had been negotiated. The descent again proved problematic: an abseil down the wrong side required a re-ascent. A storm hit them, forcing another route-finding error. The final thirty-metre abseil to the Envers du Plan hung on a very fragile support peg. Meanwhile, the snow bridge over the bergschrund was melting: crossing it put a strain on rope and muscles; another long delay. The glacier was followed, hair-raisingly, in the dark: leaps across crevasses were of uncertain outcome, especially when launching from slippery water-ice. The lightning continued and the party reached the Requin Hut at midnight, to meet a disgruntled *gardien*. They had only just avoided a night on the hill, but they had now achieved their first Alpine summit.

Back in Chamonix, Scott found Bob Pettigrew was leading a Mountaineering Association course. This Alpine training body had been formed in 1947 by J.E.B. Wright, who wrote *The Technique of Mountaineering*. Wright was, controversially, a commercial Lakeland guide. He used established but often youthful mountaineers, such as Bob Pettigrew and, from 1961, Doug Scott, as Alpine tutors. It provided, according to Ken Wilson, Alpine training for thousands of aspirant climbers in a modest but highly effective way. The establishment – the Alpine Club and, later, the British Mountaineering Council (BMC) – regarded Wright with some suspicion because of his commercial and socialist – though 'evangelical' might be nearer the mark – interests and his association with Nazi climbers. (When Wright retired, the Mountaineering Association was absorbed into the Youth Hostels Association.)

With Wilks, a friend of Pettigrew from Derby, the three friends climbed the Aiguille de l'M (2816m; the *voie normale* is graded PD+). A good climb on excellent rock was compromised by slow Chamonix guides with slower clients.

The final climb of the 1959 season was, somewhat uninspiringly, Mont Blanc (4807m). A camp at a hut above the *Tramway du Mont Blanc* led to a climb to the Goûter Hut for a second breakfast. The Dôme du Goûter was then crossed to the Vallot Hut in time for lunch. The Bosses Ridge was followed to the summit, which they reached at 4 p.m. In his autobiography, Scott quotes Wordsworth in response to his heightened emotion on reaching the summit and appraising the view; similar sublime experiences on distant summits followed. The descent was blemished by some unacclimatised Austrians' nocturnal retching at the Vallot Hut. The descent continued down Mont Blanc's north side from the Col du Dôme, past the Grands Mulets hut to the Plan de l'Aiguille. They lost their way in the forest but nonetheless reached their campsite at Chamonix-Biolay by noon; here, they could celebrate with 'red wine, as long as there was a lump of sugar in it'. With typical ambition and enthusiasm, Scott declared that he was now ready to tackle new ranges, but more sensibly added that he was happy to begin his mountaineering apprenticeship.

Having been accepted for Loughborough College, he had a month on his hands. Scott was, remarkably, able to fund a second visit to Yugoslavia that summer. Geoff Stroud and Mick Poppleston were free to join in. Near Venice, they stopped to visit a family Scott had stayed with the previous year, and for whom he brought presents of Nottingham lace. The friends then headed for the Julian Alps in what is now Slovenia, to spend a week at the Kranjska Gora ski resort, near Slovenia's highest point, Triglav (2863m). Emulating Whillans, some sort of altercation occurred with the Yugoslav border guards, equipped only with ox-carts, worn-out boots and ancient rifles, as the group crossed too freely between Yugoslavia and Austria.

Scott proceeded homewards via Innsbruck and Paris, to reach Nottingham for his first term at Loughborough. Heading first for Vienna, he was given a lift and accommodation from a set of rather 'dark' characters engaged in promoting Moral Rearmament, an organisation some have described as a cult. No lasting damage occurred, it seems. Afterwards, he visited the Vienna Opera House, thus initiating an interest in a perhaps surprising future passion.

∽

A new range was chosen for the summer of 1960: the Dauphiné, a forced choice because of poor weather around Chamonix. Scott suddenly popped up at La Bérarde to meet Lyn Noble and Mark Hewlett: many people have remarked on Scott's ability suddenly to materialise from apparently nowhere. The three attempted Les Bans (3669m) but were stopped by poor weather. A 'strenuous circuit of peak-bagging', however, followed:

on the first day, Pic Coolidge (3774m, F) was reached from the Col de la Temple (3322m); they descended to the Glacier Noir and so to the Glacier Blanc refuge. From there, a demanding day led over the Dôme de Neige des Écrins (4015m, F), then the harder Barre des Écrins (4101m, TD) with a long descent down the Glacier Blanc to Ailefroide.[4] The return to La Bérarde was effected via the pleasant Sélé hut and the Col du Sélé (3278m, F).[5] At La Bérarde, they met an American tourist who, on hearing Doug's Nottingham accent, started speaking in German.

The rest of Scott's summer was occupied by a mad dash to Morocco, his first venture beyond Europe. He hitched to Arles, then to the Camargue, having arranged to meet Brian and a friend on the coast at Le Grau du Roi. Brian and Boris accompanied Scott as far as Barcelona. They then returned, while Scott hitch-hopped his way via Valencia to Gibraltar. Being short of money, Scott succeeded in getting a job helping to refit an old ship, the MV *Saint Ernest*, which would then (he hoped) convey him to the Channel Islands. The plan, however, had been to climb Toubkal (4167m), the highest peak in North Africa. Scott caught the ferry to Ceuta, but nothing was achieved and he returned to Gibraltar. Delays caused by the ship's poor state of repair meant that Scott had to leave. Using his wages, he took the train across Spain (still carrying a heavy load of climbing gear) then hitched to Calais. He reached Loughborough a week late. Eighteen months later, Scott read that the ship had been lost with all hands while crossing the Channel.

One year later, Scott returned for a distinctly more ambitious season: he ran his first course as a Mountaineering Association guide. On this trip, his companions were drawn from the newly formed NCC. In July, Dez Hadlum and Scott left for the Bregaglia, on the Swiss-Italian border. Their aim was to attempt another classic, the *Cassin route* on the Piz Badile, this choice confirmed by Geoff Sutton's assurance that it was within their abilities and by an earlier parental Christmas present of Gaston Rébuffat's *Starlight and Storm*, in which he describes his experience on the north-east face of the Badile.

Hitching did not go particularly well: one day brought Scott to a potato field outside Paris, the next to a park in Basel. On the fifth day, he reached Promontogno and slept in a builder's hut. A 'four-hour slog' up the Val Bondasca reunited Scott with his NCC friends, Lyn Noble and David 'Ben' Sykes, as well as others from Loughborough. Several accidents followed. On the first day out, the three climbed the granite wedge of the *North Ridge* of the Ago di Sciora (3200m), with its considerable exposure towards the summit. At the base, Scott slipped and fell 30m sideways into a boulder before disappearing into a hole. Both hip and pride were badly bruised.

After Dez had arrived, he and Scott set out to climb the *Ferro da Stiro* (3206m, TD-), on the Pizzi Gemelli (3262m). The climb was accomplished in less than guidebook time, despite big boots being used on open slabs. It was followed by the *North Ridge* of the Piz Badile (3308m, D), a 1000m classic route which gave little trouble. They descended to examine Riccardo Cassin's equipment shop at Lecco.

They now judged themselves ready to climb the Piz Badile by the long *Cassin route* (TD; 25 pitches). The climb proved enjoyable, on perfect granite. They reached the summit eight hours after starting, a fast time. In a burst of ethical purity, old pitons were removed, during which Scott discovered a gold wristwatch deep in a crack. The descent was made by abseiling the *North Ridge*. Unfortunately, tiredness had set in: crossing a greasy slab, Scott slipped and slid, on his back then front, to the edge of an abyss. He was bruised and shaken, had lost his glasses and was soaked: they decided to bivvy out, not realising until morning came after a shivering night that they were near a path and only half an hour from their tent.

A few days' recovery followed, occupied in reading letters from home and sewing up clothes. Colin Mortlock arrived suddenly to report that Lyn had taken a bad fall, resulting in a broken femur, on a new route on the Ago di Sciora; Colin himself had sustained severe rope burns. Lyn was stretchered to a hut and then to a point accessible to a helicopter, from where he was flown to the Samedan (now the Oberengadine) hospital. Lyn recalls the aftermath: 'Visitors were few and far between, so I was pleased to see Doug stroll in. However, I soon realised that he was more interested in the hospital's laundry than me. His fall on the Badile had had a predictable effect on his bowels. Nurses found an unsavoury bag of underclothes in my locker.' Not for the first time, an apparently altruistic act by Scott actually masked self-interest. Scott was not unaware of this trait.

Chamonix beckoned: Geoff Sutton had offered Scott work as a Mountaineering Association guide. The casualness of the appointment reflects the spirit of the time, where trust in an individual's capabilities prevailed over certification. En route for Chamonix, Scott had the pleasure of meeting Gwen Moffat, barefoot climber, explorer, poet, crime writer and radio broadcaster. Moffat was born in 1924; at the time of writing, she remains exuberant and communicative.

In Chamonix, Scott teamed up with an Old Etonian referred to only as Mick. (Scott's unusual ability to team up with virtually anyone he found worthy of his interest remained a lifelong practice.) They walked up to the Chalet Austria, then to the Couvercle Hut, attempted the Aiguille du Moine (3412m) by a route on the east face but were prevented from summitting by plastered ice; an ascent by the south ridge was their consolation prize.

While Scott's clients rested, Scott departed with Jerry Lovatt, future Honorary Secretary of the Alpine Club (1997) and Honorary Librarian. They tackled the Pointe Albert (2816m, French grade VI), a 200m rock climb on the Aiguille de l'M (2844m). A vigorous free climb resulted in reaching the summit after only five hours, followed by a speedy descent to Chamonix then a re-ascent by cable car to the Albert Premier Hut to meet the clients.

Their first day of the course was ideal: perfect weather and snow conditions made for an enjoyable ascent of the classic *Forbes Arête* (AD) of the Aiguille du Chardonnet (3824m); they finished by mid-morning (helped by a guide's trail cut in front of them). One of the group's members was Shirley Angell, subsequently one of the most distinguished women in British climbing. With Angell leading one rope of three and Scott leading the other four, they climbed La Nonne (3341m, AD), L'Évêque (2687m; AD) and Le Moine (3412m, PD) from the Couvercle Hut on successive days.

While the rest of the group recovered, Scott and Angell went off to climb something technically harder on the Aiguilles Mummery and Ravanel. Angell was fit and well-acclimatised and could equal Scott's remarkable pace. As she appreciatively remarked, 'The shape of Doug Scott's calves is imprinted on my memory.' Inevitably, the rest of the group were keen to climb Mont Blanc, accomplished over two days. At the summit, a helicopter arrived; a French journalist with wine and purple flares jumped out.[6] He had arrived to celebrate the first ascent of the Central Pillar of Frêney. Instead of a French success, however, he faced Whillans and Bonington. Scott endeared himself by cooking them a meal at the Vallot Hut. Whillans and Scott chatted while Bonington ate. This first encounter with Bonington led to a friendship, interspersed with some spectacular rows, for the rest of Scott's life.

Characteristically, Scott carefully weighed up his first experience as a Mountaineering Association guide: useful pay and instructing satisfaction on the one hand; time which might have been spent on better routes on the other. All that remained was to hitch-hike back to Nottingham and his blossoming relationship with Jan.

In July 1962, now recently married, Scott hitched to Chamonix to meet his wife and the NCC.[7] On the Nantillons Glacier, Jan's first Alpine experience, after being hit by a rock, provoked a tempestuous confrontation, fortunately quickly over. Lyn Noble's broken leg had mended: he and Scott headed for the *Bonatti Route* (TD+) on the Grand Capucin (3838m), a pinnacle near Mont Blanc du Tacul. On a 40m wall, they resolved to clean it of gear abandoned there by gathering it on a sling. While being passed from one to the other, however, the collected hardware slipped and fell, fortunately becoming hooked over Scott's boot. Thanks to a storm, the route was not completed: they reached the Torino Hut only at midnight.

Next day, they headed for the Dent du Géant (4013m), one of the later Alpine peaks to be climbed (first ascent, 1882). Having successfully climbed the south face, a lightning storm hit them on the double summit. Pitons sparked; hair stood on end; the air stank of sulphur; Scott feared for his life and had to master himself to overcome the danger, a technique later applied on The Ogre and elsewhere. By the time Noble had coiled the rope, Scott had raced down the fixed ropes and was running across the glacier![8]

The season continued: Scott climbed the Aiguille du Plan (3673m) with Brian Chase, followed by the awkward ledges of the Aiguille du Fou (3501m). Here, another near miss occurred when Scott dislodged a boulder during a mantelshelf move: the boulder only just missed the rope.

Ray Gillies had turned up, so he and Scott set out to attempt the Grépon from the Mer de Glace. Unfortunately, another map-reading error occurred, resulting in a hard new route being put up on the neighbouring Cornes du Chamois (2562m). Success had to be balanced against the embarrassment of having climbed the wrong mountain.

Another Mountaineering Association course was approaching, and Jan and Doug hitched to Austria's Ötztal Alps. After meeting the clients at Innsbruck, some easy but unmemorable climbs followed. Jan then returned to Nottingham by train while Scott set out for the Sierra Nevada before tackling the Moroccan Atlas.

To the NCC cry of 'Milko!' Scott, Ray Gillies, Clive Davies and Steve Bowes converged on Granada. The aim was to climb as many of the 3000m peaks in the range as possible. Local information and a map came from the Granada Tourist Information Office. A mountain tramway following the Rio Genil brought the party to the roadhead at Güéjar Sierra: here, they were looked after by the hospitable stationmaster's family.[9] A baking hot ascent followed, through harvested fields and olive groves to rockier country. The first peak reached was Veleta (3398m), uninspiringly accessed by a metalled road. The group slept in a disused military installation, having ascended 2000m and walked for twenty kilometres.

An empty shepherd's hut was then discovered on the Veleta–Tajos de la Virgen col; it was (of course) immediately commandeered as base camp. The grassy moorland reminded them of Snowdonia. A relatively hard ascent followed next day: a narrow ridge of crumbling gendarmes, one of them offering VS pitches, to the summit of Tajo de los Machos (3088m). Despite going off their map, they descended to the Rio Lanjarón. Lunch comprised almonds and apricots; the river was ascended to a lake at its source from where their hut was reached. At night, the lights of Granada could be seen. Scott expatiated on how happy and peaceful he felt, away from city life.

Another similar ridge followed: the colourful Laguna del Caballo, contrasting with the blackish surrounding rocks, was appreciated. A short scramble led to the summit of Caballo (3011m), the westernmost 3000m peak of the Sierra. A hurried descent encouraged by worsening weather got the party back to the hut for an evening banquet of pancakes and stew. (This menu was repeated *ad nauseam* on several expeditions.)

The shepherd's hut was abandoned (after repairing the roof) the following day. Re-crossing Veleta, an awkward climb down to the Lagunillo del Veleta led to the ridge between Veleta and Mulhacén (3479m), the highest peak on the Iberian Peninsula. A broken ridge followed to Cerro de los Machos (3327m) before dropping to the corrie lake of Laguna de la Caldera. Here, the lads met a young climber from Barcelona – their only human encounter during this stay – who shared his food with them and accompanied them to Mulhacén, from where the coast of North Africa could be seen.

Lack of food necessitated a return to Güéjar Sierra. Some awkward steps covered in debris had to be negotiated before reaching farmland again. The group passed yodelling, salt-strewing shepherds, mule parties and 'primitive' dwellings, all a source of fascination to Scott, whose interest in ethnic life was germinating. After a day enjoying a village fiesta, the party said farewell to the kindly stationmaster and his family and headed off towards Gibraltar and the Atlas.

A taste for Spain combined with a wish to explore a relatively unvisited area may account for Scott's choice at Easter 1963 of the Cantabrian

Mountains. Despite returning to this area and the Pyrenees on at least two other occasions, these mountains are barely mentioned in Scott's writings, although it is unclear why. Doubly odd because, unusually, this laddish jaunt is recorded on a well-made if silent twenty-minute film. The expedition members were NCC stalwarts: Mick Garside, Ray Gillies, Brian Manton, Tony Henson and Geoff Stroud. (One other expedition member remains unidentified.)

The film begins with a Nottingham send-off. Scott is clowning with local children and quite a large group of mothers, including Joyce. His thick glasses and broad shoulders are immediately striking. A cut to Paris focuses on tourist clichés (*bouquinistes*, *bateaux-mouches*, etc.), with close-ups of *gendarmes*, replicated in shots of the Guardia Civil in Spain. (With shots of mothers on departure and of policemen in France and Spain, the parental influences on the twenty-one-year-old Scott are striking.) More endearingly, buying provisions at a farmers' market is filmed, with oxen, milking and shoeing and Scott in a donkey-cart. Local beauties and mischievous schoolkids are also dwelt on.

From there, we are led up country; we are shown Brian Manton's heavily laden minibus, the *de rigueur* transport of the era. Several minutes are devoted to local life: a lady peasant with a rake; a bucket bridge; local architecture with mighty crags behind; local men drinking wine. The village became base camp; equipment is shown. The camera surveys 'A' pole tents and jerrycans, billy-cans, ropes and long-shafted wooden ice-axes, along with more technical equipment such as *étriers*. The provisions are all neatly laid out: this is a well-equipped, well-organised expedition.

The expedition proceeded to an advance base at the deserted Refugio de Áliva (1660m), which they broke into (though no one seemed to mind). The party, with large, heavy packs in evidently hot weather, is filmed toiling up a track to it. Scott leads the way: his walking style combines evenness of pace with a kind of gliding thrust. The camera dwells on eating at the *refugio* then on snowy crags and tracks. The party is seen setting off up a snow-slope. Steep ground over avalanche debris follows, then thigh-deep snow; despite a clear sky, the wind bends the ropes. A roped and belay section then follows. The peak appears to have been the Tiro Alfonso XIII. No summit views are shown. Descent follows a controlled ice-axe run, complete with avalanche-clowning. The film closes with a descent to base camp, past a local with his donkey carrying wood, then a final pan at sunset from the coast to the mountains. The group travelled on to the Pyrenees, though what they climbed there, if anything, is not recorded.

Later that year, a mere ten days after the birth of his first child, Michael, Scott departed in search of the NCC, supposedly in the Dolomites. Hitching via Dover and Calais, he reached Innsbruck the same day where he accidentally met 'Sid' Smith. There being no sign of the NCC, they decided to climb together.

What struck both climbers immediately was the exposure and length of the routes. They began on the Cima Picolissima (2700m), another Cassin first ascent, then tried the north face of the Punta di Frida (2792m), all parts of the Tre Cime de Lavaredo. The pair learned to keep their heads and take each pitch carefully. Their next route, the sensationally exposed and long *Spigolo Gallo* (VI+) of the Cima Piccola (2857m), Scott calculated as eight times longer than the longest route on High Tor: one pitch at a time, they succeeded.

Following this climb, the NCC was located. Scott had arranged to climb with Birmingham lecturer Bill Cheverst, with whom he had previously climbed, for example on *Jericho Wall* of the Cromlech. From the Lavaredo hut, they tackled the *Comici Route* (VII/E3 5c) on the Cima Grande's north face, having overcome concerns about lack of retreat. Their rest was interrupted by a call for help with a rescue on the south face of the Cima Ovest (2999m). Cheverst and Scott were first to reach the badly mangled body of the climber, who had fallen a long way. They placed the casualty in a body bag which could then be transported quickly to base. Scott comments during this process on the dispassionate attitudes of the two Englishmen contrasting with the Italians' physical revulsion and recourse to prayer.

⁓

For the following season, 1964, three one-ton ex-Army trucks had been bought in preparation for the Tibesti expedition. Seats to Chamonix were sold at £10 per person for climbers and friends, to recoup costs and fundraise for Tibesti, the beginning of a long and interesting life of creative fundraising for Scott's many projects in mountaineering, for CAN and for good causes in the Lake District.

Thanks to comparatively fine weather, the climbing went well. Will McLoughlin and Scott climbed the *North Ridge* (TD) of the Aiguille du Peigne (3192m) without incident. Scott then consulted their campsite neighbours, Joe Brown and Don Whillans, about their route on the west face of the Aiguille de Blaitière (3522m): Scott, aged only twenty-three, could now count himself among the foremost British climbers.[10]

McLoughlin and Scott accomplished the climb in under guidebook time. Their partnership ended with a thoroughly enjoyable ascent of one of the finest classic routes in the Chamonix area, the *Frendo Spur* (D+) on the Aiguille du Midi (3842m). Time remained to climb with the NCC, some of whom were former pupils. A large group climbed Mont Blanc by the Goûter-Bosses ridge, although Brian Palmer recalls that Doug, like the Duke of Plaza-Toro, led from behind so that others broke trail through the snow.

Palmer tells us that 'a brilliant mountain day' followed, in completing the Midi-Plan Traverse, a complicated route beginning at the Aiguille du Midi *téléphérique* station before winding its way via the Col du Plan to the Rognon du Plan and on to the Aiguille du Plan. From its summit, the descent was made via the Requin Hut then the Envers du Plan Glacier. The next day, the descent was concluded by reaching Chamonix via the Vallée Blanche, the Mer de Glace and the Montenvers Hotel.[11]

Scott's plan was to proceed to the Dolomites on 'Sid' Smith's BSA 650cc Super Rocket motorbike. The bike broke down in Chamonix but parts were not available in France, so Mick Garside, who was supposedly driving the passengers back to England, hitch-hiked to Folkestone, bought a copy of *Exchange and Mart*, then hitched onwards to Northamptonshire where gypsies seemed to have the requisite parts for sale. Garside hitched back to Chamonix; repairs were effected; Smith and Scott set off for Lavaredo. The passengers arrived home three days late. In the Dolomites, Smith, despite only being a casual acquaintance, helped Scott with his Mountaineering Association course. They spent their nights in a tent near the chairlift station. Scott managed to wangle free chairlift passes. (The students were staying in a hut higher up the mountain.) Climbs took place mostly in the Sassolungo, but left Scott resolved to guide no longer: the variations in ability, the inability to relax, the time spent away from serious climbing all counted against the extra money available.

When the course was complete, Smith and Scott headed for the Sella Pass (2218m), where some 'good routes' were followed. Time for another near miss: on a final abseil (we are not told on which route), Smith dislodged a large rock. Despite a new fibreglass helmet, the rock hit Scott and smashed it. Scott was able, despite near-unconsciousness, to abseil down and proceed to the local cottage hospital, where he was stitched and bandaged. One more climb rather heroically followed. As usual, Scott felt homesick as soon as the climbing was over, particularly as Jan was again pregnant. On the BSA, they followed the autobahns, a tedious, dangerous and frustrating process because of several high-speed rear tyre punctures. Smith comments about his companion: 'Doug was a very genuine and friendly person. Climbing meant everything to him. He was good company and always helpful, which was fortunate when climbing a difficult route with him!'[12]

In 1967, transport to Chamonix differed from all other previous approaches, as Scott and his NCC party arrived from the east, on their way home from Afghanistan. Two lorries of eleven NCC members and a dozen fee-paying passengers plus a variety of exotic goods, such as antique flintlocks, Afghan coats and lapis lazuli jewellery were crammed into the lorries when they appeared at the Biolay campsite, to be traded in at Chamonix's boutiques. Funds were further boosted by English climbers paying for a lift home. Before departure, Cheverst and Scott walked up through the forest to the Plan de l'Aiguille. Next day, they attempted the *North Face Direct* (TD) of the Aiguille du Plan (3673m). Progress was speedy: they reached a bivouac before the harder final section in only three hours. Difficult and badly protected steps were obliterated by an avalanche, with only moments to spare: death had been bypassed once again. They reached the summit, followed by a descent without further incident to Chamonix via Montenvers.

One of the most notorious events in Scott's career had occurred on this climb. Shortly before the avalanche, Scott had noticed a frozen body, probably of a Czech climber, seated awkwardly in the ice. Scott took a number of black and white photos. In Chamonix, Scott was asked for these by a reporter from *Le Dauphiné*, the principal Haute-Savoie newspaper. Scott was heavily criticised by his companions: the controversy surrounding the photographing of Mallory's body on Everest thirty-two years later comes to mind. Fortunately, the photo was never published but, as Scott himself wrote, it was not his first punishment for being greedy (and tasteless).[13] Scott's jejune rationale was that many Continental climbers photographed bodies, for example on the Eiger. He had, however, previously made a similar excuse for his ethical slipperiness in relation to bolting.

One of the Afghanistan expedition lorries unsurprisingly gave up on the way home. Near Geneva, a baffling breakdown had occurred, resolved by Ray Gillies who turned up in the second lorry four days later. (Scott had planned the first lorry to leave early for a quick return to Jan, who was sounding unwelcoming.) A repair involving the use of condoms proved short-lived; the second lorry towed the first all the way to Paris, where proper repairs were carried out, and the return to Nottingham was completed without further difficulties.

Scott arrived for his penultimate season in the Alps during this period in a new mode of transport: the family minivan. Scott, Jan and Michael joined the NCC in the Bernina, in south-east Switzerland. These predominantly snow and ice peaks contrast with the nearby granite spires of the Bregaglia. NCC members tended to live out of their minivans. Illegal layby parking resulted in a confrontation with the local police near Pontresina and an on-the-spot fine. Next day, the NCC grouped themselves into several ropes and enjoyed the sustained high-level traverse of Piz Palü's three summits (3900m) from the Pers Glacier. Inevitably, thereafter, the party headed for Chamonix.

Dave Nicol teamed up with Scott: they, with two other NCC ropes, climbed the *Bonatti Pillar* (TD) route on the Aiguille du Petit Dru (3733m). The pillar was climbed with just one bivouac. Scott's confident description of their climb suggests that his Alpine apprenticeship was coming to an end and his apprenticeship on big walls was beginning. As a result of this climb, Scott contributed an article to Ken Wilson's influential *Mountain* magazine, then was invited to update Geoff Sutton's work on artificial climbing. He thus established himself not only as an authority but one in the tradition of an earlier technical expert, Geoffrey Winthrop Young (1876–1958).

Scott and Upton's 1969 climb on the Cima Ovest at Lavaredo, in the Dolomites, is dealt with in the chapter on big walls. Only one other notable event occurred at Lavaredo: Dave 'Wink' Wilkinson (Climbers' Club) came across Scott in his tent and enquired about a climbing partner for an attempt on the north face of the Cima Grande. Scott suggested 'an Irish guy', who turned out to be slow, refused to bivouac on ledges and preferred to abseil in the dark. Wilkinson wondered if Scott had played a dangerous trick on him but concluded that the recommendation was probably genuine. Nonetheless, he chastised Scott, whose response was to shrug his shoulders.[14]

Scott's Alpine apprenticeship comprised mainly classic climbs. We do not see the adventurous, innovative Scott of future years: instead, he is climbing conservatively while learning to refine the famous instinct which got him out of trouble during the following thirty years. His approach was carefully progressive, with a sense of strategy related to his ambition, not just to become well known but to have his fame recorded in print (and later, on film). Those exploratory and innovative aspects missing from his Alpine seasons were developed in parallel to them, with remarkable success, in his four expeditions outside Europe between 1962 and 1967.

6

Expeditions beyond Europe, 1962–67

'Doug Scott was a force of nature.'

– John Tasker (brother of Joe)

Scott extended his experience by leading four expeditions to Islamic lands in two continents. He visited the Moroccan Atlas in autumn 1962, followed by the Tibesti mountains of Chad in spring 1965. In August, September and October of 1966 Scott shifted his attention to the Kurdish part of Turkey, focusing on the Čilo Dağı. From May to July in 1967, he explored part of the Hindu Kush in eastern Afghanistan.

Four excellent *Expedition Reports* were produced: systematic, detailed and as well presented as funds and technology permitted. (Scott's first published article appeared in 1963 in *Mountain Craft*.) The *Reports* are designed to inform future expeditions but also to promote Scott's name, which figures prominently in all of them, consistent with his desire for acclamation. He even refers to himself as a member of the prestigious Alpine Climbing Group rather than as a member of NCC, despite having founded the latter only a year before the Atlas expedition. His ambition also shows in the *Reports*' progressive character. They move from home typing on cyclostyled paper to professional printing. The covers are arresting, beginning with amateur drawing and rather bizarre Gothic script to black and white to full colour. Photographs are introduced, albeit in black and white. Maps improve successively in quality. Detail is increased, particularly when describing finances, equipment and food.

The *Reports* all include a strong involvement with human geography: how the indigenous peoples' lives are shaped by their environment. Considerable space is given to describing dress, customs, food and architecture. While Scott had earlier shown an interest in how mountain people lived in say Ireland, Yugoslavia or Spain, his *Reports* declare not just the dispassionate curiosity of the human geographer but a personal, sympathetic interest, no doubt in part derived from the locals' generosity towards an impecunious young man and his friends without expectation of return, but also a Romantic interest in the 'noble savage'. To the end of his life, Scott maintained his admiration for those who led the simpler life beyond the city, free to enjoy a creative, uncluttered *modus vivendi*.

The Moroccan Atlas and the Tibesti Mountains of Chad

Why begin with Africa? A question of money, of course. And the Eastern Bloc would have placed too many constraints on Scott the rule-breaker. North Africa was known to be inexpensive. Most of all, however, Scott was attracted by Africa's remoteness, that beguiling interest in a range of mountains, including North Africa's highest, about which relatively little was known at that time.

The aim was simple: as for the Sierra Nevada, to climb as many peaks above 3000m as possible and any others which offered 'interesting possibilities'. This expedition differed from the others in being dependent on hitching and public transport, unlike the others' use of ex-War Department trucks. The route was consequently less complicated than the three other expeditions; it was based on advice from Everester Wilf Noyce, who had been there the year before, as well as a Club Alpin Français guidebook and a 1/25,000 map of the Toubkal area, plus research in geography textbooks.

From Gibraltar, the party (Scott, Ray Gillies, Clive Davies, Steve Bowes, Steve Read) boarded the ferry to Ceuta. From there, they split up and hitched to Marrakesh. The city proved fascinating; they spent a few days there. Then on by bus to Asni, a small market town about thirty kilometres north of Toubkal. Here, they hired mules but rejected a guide. Leaving injudiciously at midday, they progressed south to Imlil while passing through terraced millet fields backed by mud-brick houses. They bivvied out in a deserted shepherd's hut at Chamrouch, beyond Imlil. Next day, after some progress, the muleteers' services were relinquished when they arrived at the well-appointed Neltner Hut. It was shut, but that was no barrier to Scott. One night there was followed by a walk to a bivouac which would act as base camp. There, the party divided between bivouac-improvers (Davies and Bowes), and climbers, who ascended to the very high pass of Tizi n'Ouagane (3745m) from where a short scramble led to the twin summits of Ouanoukrim, named Timzguida (4089m) and Ras Ouanoukrim (4083m), the second- and third-highest summits of the Atlas.[1] No acclimatisation difficulties are mentioned.

No question as to the following day's climb: a steep path led to Tizi Ouanoums (3630m) and from there they climbed the *Beetham Route* (VD) up the west-south-west arête via a pillar, then round rock towers and a snow scramble to the summit of Toubkal (4167m), where they enjoyed the view back to Marrakesh and endless ridges to the south. A 300-metre scree run brought them back to base camp. Being October, the weather was changing to storms and bitter cold. Delayed by a day owing to gastric illness (perhaps due to unwashed fruit?), Scott and Read climbed Tadaft n'bou Imrhaz (3899m), a rock-climb all the way on good granite and a new route. They returned by the Col de l'Amguird.

Doug holding a First Aid clinic in the Atlas Mountains, Morocco, 1962.
Photo by and courtesy of Clive Davies.

Satisfied with their high climbs, the group travelled 130 kilometres south to their second objective: the Volcan du Siroua (Jebel Siroua, 3304m), reached by a rocky valley 'full of quartzes and amethyst'. At the Lac d'Ifni, an aged Berber mentioned that fish were to be caught, though as Scott wryly remarked, their only fish came from tins. That night, they reached Tizgui, a pleasant mountain resort, with waterfalls, lying at 983m. Here, they carried out a five-day field study of the valley. Because of the stormy weather, the *makaden*, or headman, invited the party to stay in his home, thus providing the human geographers with first-hand material.

After five days, the group headed further south, to Asserag, where they were invited to stay with the local teacher. From there, they walked all day to Askouan, gaining fine views of the Atlas as they crossed a low plateau while receiving hospitality as they proceeded. At Askouan, they were invited to stay with the *kedhive,* a regional administrator, who fed them generously. The southward journey continued: heading east after Azimer they reached a shoulder of the volcano. The countryside resembled Utah. They walked to the head of a valley before establishing a bivouac. On the way, they gathered seven kilos of mushrooms, turned into a stomach-churning stew with maize and Oxo. The ascent of Siroua, a mild scramble at worst, followed next day.

From Siroua, having appraised the rock-climbing possibilities, they moved east to Anzel and the main road north. Hospitality continued, mainly with mint tea, eggs, a kind of local chapati and honey. After Anzel, the hitch-hiking began again. We are not told the route, only that the party arrived home on 24 October.

In Gibraltar, however, Steve Bowes was taken to hospital with suspected dysentery. Scott was invited by a nurse to stay over in the hospital, rather than sleep on the beach. Unfortunately, Scott was put into the isolation ward. On his return he was immediately diagnosed with hepatitis A and found himself in a Nottingham hospital for ten days, with a punitive three-month ban on fish 'n' chips and alcohol.[2]

In his report on the 'human geography' of the expedition area, Scott describes the erosion, local architecture and local crafts – milling, cobbling, bread-making. Perhaps his greatest fascination concerned the relationship between men and women. Women work in the fields and at home, while the men idle around, smoking their curious pipes, drinking mint tea, managing the finances or occasionally going to the bazaar for conversation. This apparent imbalance between work and leisure in the Islamic countries which he visited is a strong theme of this and later *Reports*. Given Scott's own furlough from his recent marriage, his fascination for the relative ease of male life is unsurprising. He summarises, 'Indeed, their robes and slip-on shoes did not allow for manual work, and why should they work when three or four willing wives could do it?' Irony or sexism? Both. Otherwise, the observations on local life tend to describe the food, much of which they lived off during such a low-budget expedition.

A brief summary of their Alpine equipment is provided, but it is Scott's concluding remarks which are most thought-provoking. Scott is rightly proud of the whole expedition, from the Alps to the Sierra Nevada and back to England, costing each individual no more than £22 (about £330 at today's prices). He adds, tellingly, 'We had no sponsors to tie us down to a pre-arranged route.' The aversion to the constraints of sponsorship, and pride in self-reliance, are thus apparent from this first opportunity. He is blunt about several aspects of the expedition: 'The easy nature of the terrain was perhaps disappointing . . . [but] the lack of tourists and other mountaineers led to a very easy acceptance of us by the natives . . .'

This 'easy acceptance' is then contrasted with the 'extraction of every last penny' by the 'natives' at Chamonix, Zermatt and Courmayeur. Scott expresses his satisfaction at travelling through relatively unknown country, through adverse weather and over rough terrain as a 'self-contained unit'. They overcame 'tiredness, ill-health, hunger and temper'. They did, more-over, obtain some material which would be useful in the classroom.

The Doug Scott of later years makes his appearance in the final para-graph. It is virtually his manifesto: 'For six weeks, we went our way, unfettered, wherever we felt we could practise our mountaineering skills, see new country, visit new people – in fact, taste some of the delights of mountain exploration and enjoy good physical adventuring to the full.'

℘

The idea for the Tibesti (in the local Toubou language, 'the place where the mountain people live') expedition had hit Scott towards the end of the Atlas expedition. He evidently viewed it as a source of income and fame: after all, his article for *Mountain Craft* had earned him about £80–£100 at today's prices. Clive Davies, Ray Gillies and Steve Bowes were interested, as was trainee geography teacher Mick Garside. They were later joined by Peter Warrington, Dan Meadows and Tony Watts. Scott's hepatitis, however, meant a delay of six months, so it was not until February 1965 that the expedition set out.

The *Report* looks smart: the front cover is in colour; the back cover is an arresting photo of a local tribeswoman in full fig. The text is professionally typed. The narrative comment is more extensive than the Atlas *Report*. Comments on equipment, food, the study programme and finance are much more detailed than hitherto. Scott's concerns about financial support have been banished in favour of support from many local businesses, indi-viduals and institutions – for example, his grant from the Mount Everest

Foundation (MEF). Such support, however, was mostly contracted for publicity returns without compromising the route and aims. Fundraising otherwise depended on self-help. Mick Garside organised dances. Lectures were arranged: it is a measure of Scott's European stature by this time that he was able to persuade his boyhood hero, Lionel Terray, to give a lecture to over 450 people.[3] Gaston Rébuffat also lectured, but constant trouble with the projector led to Rébuffat's rage, some walkouts and cool applause.[4] Funding was augmented by Dennis Gray and Don Whillans, both very popular speakers. Bonington was supposed to appear but sent Ian Clough in his place.

Even the exploratory background was better researched. Roger Akester, a Cambridge academic who had previously visited the Tibesti, was consulted. He was enthusiastic but discouraging about likely costs and bureaucratic challenges – Chad had only recently become independent. The positive counterbalances were Scott's own interest in traversing the Sahara, stimulated by the sight of it from the Atlas: he was strongly attracted by this remote, isolated wilderness. The Cambridge Expedition, led by Peter Steele, of which Akester had been a member, helped with maps. References to previous Austrian and Belgian expeditions also occasionally crop up. Finally, Wilfred Thesiger's comment that Tarso Tieroko (2935m) was 'possibly the most beautiful mountain in Tibesti' clinched their involvement. Tieroko was also unclimbed: the aim was clear. During preparations, Scott went to see *Lawrence of Arabia* (1962), which suggested that his exploratory interests, while comprehending geographical objectivity, were also Romantic. Not entirely, however: during his convalescence in 1964, Scott had successfully studied for an A-Level in geology, an interest he followed for the rest of his life. He had also studied leadership, which helped him to an O-Level in English: he unselfconsciously identifies with Columbus, Cook, Shackleton, Robert Falcon Scott, Wally Herbert and others.

The travel was as important as the destination, unlike most of Scott's later mountain explorations. The route was rather more complicated than for the Atlas expedition, not least because it would traverse five African countries, all bureaucratically and socially unstable as they emerged from French and Italian rule.

Three ex-War Department lorries had been bought, for £70 and £50, two for transport and one for cannibalising its parts. The send-off from the Salutation Inn was 'rousing'. International driving licences were obtained with minutes to spare at Dover; at Calais everything was examined then, most inconveniently, sealed; the listing of items had to be repeated, twelve times, at the Spanish border (the Customs there also requiring a bond of £111). With hitch-hikers clinging to the lorries' sides, the convoy passed through Madrid then Seville to Algeciras. A diversion for cheaper petrol to Tangiers from Ceuta ended badly in added insurance costs.

Determined driving brought the party to the Algerian border in twelve hours. To cross the border, the surveying equipment was carefully hidden. Rain after Oran made for slippery roads and a minor crash which traumatised an accompanying Algerian hitch-hiker. An apparently pleasant coastal road gave way to relentless hairpins, inducing boredom and carsickness.

After sightseeing at Algiers, they continued east, soon to reach fiercely cold, snow-covered mountains. At the Tunisian border, exit was forbidden until their last Algerian dinars were spent and two hours of form-filling had been completed. Tunisia did not take long to cross. Oranges and fried dough for breakfast at Gafsa led on to the border with Libya, where an overnight stay was enforced to satisfy visa omissions. Visiting the magnificent Roman ruins at Sabratha provided a welcome diversion. By a chance encounter there, the whole party came to be accommodated in the Medenine Barracks, an opportunity to clean up and be properly fed.

Tripoli was soon reached; they admired the king's palace and the Catholic cathedral. Signs of Italian colonisation were ubiquitous, although the Italians had left in 1943. Tripoli, as an oil capital, was also useful for obtaining a very substantial petrol discount from Shell. It was time to load up: spare parts, fruit and vegetables were all obtained for the great journey into the interior.

They turned south to cover 800 kilometres efficiently as far as the regional capital of Sebhā. The road, however, had been washed away in short sections, a sign of trouble to come. Although some distance from the border with Chad, Immigration was run from here, largely because what remained was desert. They headed off with 2,600 litres of petrol to see them through. A friendly policeman gave them food and water as well as some handy vocabulary in Toubou.

The real desert began. Stony wastes gave way to the Mourzouk Sand Sea. Bearings wore away, repaired by the ingenious Ray Gillies. Lowering tyre pressure also helped, as did laying out specially constructed sand-tracks, backbreaking work in such heat. These devices helped progress enormously: they covered a much faster 100 kilometres and spent the night in an old Italian fort. Near the border, at El Gatroun, progress was further enhanced by a bottle of whisky each for Immigration and Customs.

Many Bedouin were assembled at the border: with their colourful dress and camels, they fascinated Scott.

The next 650 kilometres through Chad were uninhabited and little visited. A Toubou guide proved useless. After seventy perplexing kilometres across a plain covered with fossil wood, the convoy arrived at Sarazac, located by a reflector on a pylon. Nissen huts provided makeshift accommodation. The next section was worse: chaotic boulders over which the lorries somehow had to drive, repeated the next day; lumps of shale, sand and rock to be negotiated at dead slow speed; result, only 100 kilometres completed by nightfall, after a melodramatic sunset of violet merging into yellows and reds.

Next day, the convoy crossed the Korizo Pass, first traversed by vehicle in 1941 by General Leclerc. Despite their first puncture, they continued across barren land until the Tibesti mountains could at last be discerned through the dust haze. Their route circled the range's western end before veering north-east into the heart of the mountains. They camped near the soaring sandstone Aiguilles de Sisse, rising cathedral-like for 600m from the desert floor. Thorn bushes and grasses were now visible.

After encountering some gazelle, then a lone Berber, the convoy continued north-east over undulating ground to an astonishing sight: the rim of the extinct volcano, the Trou au Natron (2450m); the crater is twelve kilometres across and 600m deep, with a soda lake at the bottom. After some rock-collecting, they pressed on to Bardai, where there was a German research centre, a welcome place for a clean-up, servicing the lorries and having visas validated, fortunately without further difficulties. They had now reached the penultimate stage, lasting 200 kilometres, heading west to Yebbi Bou. Progress was slowed by incessant ups and downs over dried *wadis*. A night under the stars was followed by further steep-sided *wadis*. They reached Yebbi Bou, where the local Toubou welcomed them with ready smiles and scrounging. They lodged at the local fort.

The party split: Tony, Dan and Steve were heading for Tarso Toon, while the rest were moving to Modra. Camels were awaited and failed to appear. The Tarso Toon party was driven to a nearby oasis to obtain camels. Meanwhile, the Modra team was plagued by insects. Next day, two camels appeared, their snorting, grumpiness and foul breath making a convincingly bad impression. The camel-drivers had put up their fees by 400 per cent, however, so it was decided to travel by lorry – something Scott regretted as, by using camels, he had hoped to identify with the locals. Foolishly, it was decided to take a walk of apparently about five kilometres to a point where Tieroko might be seen. The walkers returned severely dehydrated. They pressed on to Modra despite a poor track with many boulders. They camped outside Modra; Clive Davies, releasing long pent-up energy, led the way on a vigorous run into the village.

Once there, two principal problems had to be confronted: route-finding and water supplies. They had to fit into the daily routine at Modra (disparagingly described as 'not as good as Gordale Scar'), which started early. A servant boy, in exchange for barley sugars, would fetch water and wood; coffee and porridge usually followed as the villagers woke. Plane-table work came after breakfast, followed by a return to the huts before the unbearable heat of midday. In late afternoon, a medical session for the locals' benefit often took place. Thereafter came the evening meal of relentless (often vegetarian) stews and pancakes, sometimes with dates, before an early night.

With two donkeys, the Modra group began a reconnaissance. The aim was to reach the rim of the crater, about sixteen kilometres away, of which Tieroko was the highest part. The second excursion from Modra led them to slabs and a gully where they camped at just under 3000m – it was hard work since all the water had to be hauled up to it. It was decided to try the west side of Tieroko to avoid long abseils down extensive steps on the return. Warrington and Gillies tried the south ridge and reached Tieroko summit after a climb of only V Diff grade. Davies and Scott tried the top part of the north side which, with its steep walls and overhangs, resembled the Dolomites. They reached the summit after a 'good VS' climb. On top, bearings for a sketch map were taken.

With surprising vagueness, Scott reports two more days of rock-climbing, followed by several more days of interesting mountaineering. Further bearings were taken to improve the map. A plan to descend to the Tieroko crater was rejected, mainly because of water supply difficulties. The *Report*'s 'Climbing' section concludes that enthusiasm waned after having climbed Tieroko, despite the sense of 'neverendingness' which the summit prospect of so many unclimbed peaks produced. Clive Davies remarks that after Tieroko, Scott seemed to become more negative about further climbing and exploration.

During the return journey home, Davies, Gillies and Warrington risked a walk of 140 kilometres to Bardai. Scott and Garside concluded the field-work, consisting mainly of theodolite measurements and plant-collecting. The walkers ran out of water, attempted to kill a goat for its milk, only to be told where to find (muddy) water by its bemused herdsman. The arduous walk to Bardai took a further two and a half days. Reloading the donkeys at Modra was chaotic. En route to Bardai, Scott and Garside met four vehicles staffed by French geographers – their first Europeans for several weeks. A very tiresome, jolting journey followed to Bardai, over boulders and steep-sided *wadis*; nonetheless, they met the three walkers just outside Bardai. The Taro Toon team had already arrived. The German researchers treated them to a fine (tinned) German meal, with much beer.

At Bardai, the vehicles were serviced for the journey home. Photos were taken of nearby Neolithic rock carvings, mostly depicting animals. The journey had no sooner started than a fire broke out in one of the lorries, acutely dangerous as a lot of petrol stored in jerrycans remained. Having reached the Trou au Natron, they descended, again, foolishly without water, to the crater floor. At the Aiguilles de Sisse, richer by a goat acquired cheaply along the way, the group made some minor climbs on small pinnacles while the goat was being slaughtered.

A hundred kilometres beyond Mourizidi, after the *roches chaotiques*, having pursued a more navigable westerly line, one of the lorries was left to its fate, cannibalised as far as possible, in order to save £85 on the Tunis–Palermo ferry. A three-day delay ensued at the border when the party was mistakenly identified as Lebanese. Nonetheless, return time had improved greatly on the outward journey, because the lorries were much more lightly laden and desert driving techniques had been learnt. From Sabhā, the beginning of civilisation, the convoy proceeded without further major incidents to Tunis via Carthage, Palermo, then through Italy via Pompeii and across the Alps – revelling in its greenery – and so to Nottingham by the end of March. Scott's greatest regret was that they did not travel by camel for greater distances, partly to identify with the Saharan way of living, partly to escape the lorries' incessant roar.

The *Report* meticulously records the expedition's finances, totalling £1,447 17s, or about £20,000 now. Expedition members contributed almost half the total. The MEF contributed a generous £400, a sign of Scott's careful preparation and his reputation. Otherwise, it is noticeable that of the twelve institutions and companies supporting the expedition financially, all had given donations rather than, strictly speaking, sponsorship. Twenty-four individuals contributed, as did the NCC collectively. Fifty-one companies donated or gave concessions on food, clothing and equipment (including photographic), a figure which reveals just how passionately Scott must have worked to generate sufficient begging letters for that degree of response.

The *Report* provides a few pages of helpful hints for future travellers, followed by a detailed summary of the route, with petrol consumption. A short section then describes the 'special problems' of guides, surveying equipment, fundraising and visas. The *Report* concludes with some detailed comments on the geographical programme.

This expedition spent a disproportionate time on the road instead of on climbing, much in line with R.L. Stevenson's dictum about it being better to travel hopefully than to arrive. The geographical programme was carried out seriously, but also at the expense of time spent climbing and exploring.

Scott must have wondered if all the fundraising, the arduous driving, getting round the jobsworth Customs officials, the crushing heat, the hunger, the constant worry of maintaining the schedule, even the damage to his marriage were worth it. Clive Davies echoes this: '[I]n the years since Tibesti I have hiked and trekked through many different countries, but none have come anywhere near the difficulty we had in Tibesti.'

Yet there were compensations. Scott evidently found the Toubou fascinating. He contrasts their modest lifestyle with 'our own complicated homes 5000 miles away'. On several occasions, Scott held a clinic for ailing villagers: even allowing for placebo medicines, helping to cure the sick or at least alleviating their pain gave him great satisfaction. Was this the germination of CAN? Once the *Report* came out, his reputation rose, greatly enhanced, both in civic Nottingham and among the wider band of mountaineers.

Having reflected in characteristic fashion on the joys and sorrows of this expedition, Scott believed he was ready to explore somewhere ethnically and geographically very different; or so he thought.

The Čilo Dağı and the Hindu Kush[5]

'Many expeditions have been born in public houses and this one was no exception.'

This opening line from Scott's *The Cilo Dağ Mountains, S.E. Turkey: Expedition Report* tells us that the Čilo Dağı venture had a laddish character yet was the brainchild of an experienced expeditioner. The *Report*'s author nonchalantly dismisses the problem of a 'minor' Kurdish rebellion in the area as 'largely over' and asserts, 'since 1965 foreigners have been encouraged to tour the area'.[6] Scott was acquiring a persona of outward insouciance to mask an inner obsession.

According to the *Expedition Report*'s preface, the principal aims were 'to climb unclimbed mountains and to study the Kurdish communities that live there'. Scott's interest in ethnic peoples had become a theme of his expeditions' aims. The secondary aim was to produce a 16mm film of the venture; in this they failed as, 'some unkind person stole the camera and film'.

Although a large undertaking, it was anything but a siege-style expedition: ten 'organisers' (the term 'leader' is avoided) joined twenty 'lads', aged fifteen to nineteen, drawn from Cottesmore boys' school and the Meadows Boys' Club Climbing Group. Many came from deprived backgrounds, and only two had previously travelled abroad. Responsibility for training the lads and organising equipment fell to Richard Bell (who withdrew shortly before the expedition left). Training was thorough: with the help of the Cottesmore school lorry, expeditions were mounted to the Cairngorms, Ben Nevis, the Lake District and North Wales. The adults were teachers, youth leaders, carpenters, engineers, mechanics and a medical student. Two one-tonners were acquired; the Nottingham Association of Boys' Clubs lent their Land Rover.

This corner of Turkey near the Iraqi border was chosen by Scott the geography teacher because its distance from a maritime climate would encourage settled weather conditions, a hopeful opinion duly fulfilled. South-east Turkey's numerous unclimbed peaks and a native population living as they had for generations would, moreover, provide an interesting geographical study, Scott claimed. One could hear him rehearsing this before asking his headmaster, Mr Happer, for the time off work. Happer approved, having asked himself: would I let my own child go on an expedition run by Scott? He would, and he went on to lend the school's own lorry to the expedition. While these educational opportunities were being piously presented, the trip also gave Scott himself a wonderful chance to climb in an area little visited by Westerners.

Was Happer being irresponsible? There was, of course, no risk assessment; the only insurance cover was for the expedition's Land Rover and two lorries. We are told that Happer did not wholly trust certificates since they could be 'learnt up': they did not necessarily reflect the experience required for leading young people into dangerous areas. Yet if a young expedition member had suffered permanent brain damage in a fall, how would he have received enduring medical and other care without insurance?

Preparations began with prodigious attempts to generate funds. Seven organisations, such as banks and charitable trusts, responded: nineteen companies including Marks and Spencer and Mansfield Brewery, and nine individuals, including Sir John Hunt, who sent three guineas (around £60 at today's prices) made cash donations. Thirty-nine companies, national and local, donated food and drink products; five organisations helped with photographic concessions; ten companies provided camping, clothing and climbing equipment. Many of these individuals and companies had already contributed to the Tibesti expedition; Scott claims he sent out over 1,100 letters, with at least 500 hand-written. That he achieved such productivity while continuing his teaching job, carrying out his obligations as a husband and father of a young son, wrapping up the Tibesti expedition, producing a climbing guide to the Derwent Valley and carrying out his usual programme of climbs in the UK and beyond testify to his prodigious drive and remarkable organisational skills.

Alderman Percy Holland, the Lord Mayor of Nottingham, gave the expedition a formal send-off from the steps of the Council House on 7 August. Thereafter, dates become hazier, a fault which Scott noticed and rectified in the Hindu Kush *Expedition Report.*

In the rain at Dover, Scott picked up a package of Kodak colour film from HM Customs: 'that way, you avoid paying duty on it'. He was learning fast. They followed endless autobahns as far as Innsbruck for an equipment pick-up. Over the Grossglockner pass (2504m) they trundled, then into Yugoslavia. Crossing the Sava plains through dreary Zagreb, Belgrade and Nis was voted easily the most boring part of the whole journey. They ate windfall from roadside fruit trees, probably a source of future stomach upsets. Nearing Istanbul, however, Scott's excitement rose as they began to rub shoulders with 'Iraqis, Lebanese, Syrians, Persians', one of whom advised on the best local café for advantageous if illegal currency exchanges. Previous problems with borders had largely been left behind. Mike Webster notes that 'what I remember most about that trip was how confident and capable Doug was in dealing with all the red tape at the borders'.[7]

The expedition paused in Istanbul. Most members visited the Grand Bazaar, one of the largest in Asia, and marvelled at the craftsmanship of the goods and the colourful mix of peoples. They ate Black Sea pollock and Turkish Delight, washed down with raki and strong coffee.

From Istanbul, they pressed on bleary-eyed through the night to reach the Black Sea coast – a greener land, of oxen wallowing in muddy pools while the air smelt of tobacco leaves drying in the sun. Sometimes, though, the vehicles would halt, for all to gaze in horror at the wreckage of lorries and coaches which had fallen hundreds of feet from cliff-edge roads . . .

Near Ordu, on the Black Sea coast, a shackle pin broke on the trailer lorry. Swerving violently to avoid other traffic, the trailer shot into the air and overturned, yet without losing its connection to its parent lorry. Three lads were thrown clear, bags of flour spilled everywhere and, in true 1960s style, several guitars were smashed. No bones were broken or stitches needed, but a visit to Ordu hospital followed for anti-tetanus injections. (Few preparatory inoculations seem to have been administered.) The party was gratefully assisted by the Turkish military, who found them a camping place while one rather groggy lad remained in hospital for observation. Scott was allegedly required to remain in jail until the boy was discharged from hospital.

Their journey continued to exotic Trabzon, where they loaded up with freshly baked bread, then headed south over the Zigana Pass (2032m) hairpins and into the glare on the Anatolian Plateau. At the pass, a celebratory sheep was converted into kebabs – Scott explains in his *Report* what kebabs were, a minor piece of cultural history. Scott lost his spectacles after a plunge into the Euphrates. From the pass, a long run led down to turquoise Lake Van. Curiously, Scott does not mention seeing Mount Ararat (5137m), Turkey's highest mountain.

A rickety road of crushed rock along the Great Zab river valley led to base camp. Greenery gave way to contorted rock formations and scrub. The road 'twisted like a silver eel in the moonlight'.[8] Base camp was pitched opposite the Diz Valley, near a police post, where the police put themselves under lock and key overnight; one night, shots were heard, as the police mistakenly believed they were under attack from Kurdish rebels. The journey had taken twelve days. The climbing period was scheduled to last ten days.

Planning for the climbs had been based on Dr Hans Bobek's 1937 geological map.[9] Fortuitously, during the planning, an article on the area by Robin Fedden had appeared in *Geographical* magazine.[10] Scott immediately wrote to Fedden and received a detailed reply about access, maps and suitable areas for climbing.

After three days' reconnaissance, a higher advance base was established at 2150m on an alpine flower meadow at the confluence of glacier-outlet streams about twenty kilometres up the Diz Valley. From there, climbs were made on the Čilo Dağ's northern sides while supplies were sent up regularly from base camp. The peaks, mostly rocky, but with snow patches on the higher summits and corries, rose from 3000m to 4170m. Study excursions were also made to visit the local Kurds.

A typical climbing day began at 3 a.m. with curses. Boys cursed because equipment which should have been packed the night before had to be packed by torchlight. Adults cursed because of the avoidable delay. The lads left the high camp in small groups, each accompanied by one or more NCC members. Techniques of moving together over snow and loose rock were taught *in situ.* The groups would cross dirty glacier snouts covered in moraine before reaching the pristine snows above. The disorganised late starts meant that the snow was usually very soft: plodding wearily through it was alleviated by frequent photography stops. Climbers and pupils quickly realised they were not as fit as they thought they were (despite having beaten the Turkish military in a press-ups competition); the scope of the climbs had to be reduced. But there was the satisfaction of reaching high cols, to gaze at distant, mostly unclimbed peaks.

The lack of guidebooks or scratch-marks left by previous climbers made route-finding hard work, with progress dependent on intuition and experience. The leader, of course, had to give himself completely to the challenge. For Scott, this commitment was the main source of pleasure in rock-climbing.

The highest peak above advance base was Reşko Tepe (4170m on Scott's map; now 4134m). To reach the summit, a bivouac was necessary part way up a 300m rock face. Scott declared his aversion to bivouacs, finding them, 'invariably uncomfortable, however well-equipped and planned they may be', ironic in view of him making the highest bivouac in history only nine years later. He and the lads found their exposed ledge, about 200m below Reşko's sharp summit, exciting: '[The ledge] slopes to the void below. We knock in several pitons and tie ourselves in to them . . . The stars are never seen so clearly as from a perch at 13,000 [feet] in the clear mountain air. The moon gives an unreal, if not sinister touch to the surrounding peaks and deepens the depth of the valleys in shadow and widens the gulf between friends far below.'[11]

Reşko's summit eluded them, the top 200m being steep, holdless rock. They settled for another unclimbed, slightly lower summit west of Reşko before descending easier slopes, then crossing several passes to reach the stream which led back to Base Camp.

Altogether, thirteen routes were attempted. Several resembled the kind of exposed climbing found in the Bregaglia. The most spectacular achievement was Scott's and Brian Palmer's ascent of Cafer Kule, a 250m pillar. From a col three kilometres north of High Camp, a gully led to a shoulder; an exposed (very!) traverse then led up to a 75m chimney, from where easy rock led to the top. Most of the lads made it up Sirt Tepe (Pinnacle Ridge, 3460m). The ridge was deeply serrated, with one gendarme after another. The ascent provided 1500m of continuous climbing at Grade IV, with the occasional pitch at Grade V. They descended the west ridge, to reach High Camp after a sixteen-hour day. Scott and Tony Watts also put up a route via the buttresses and a gully on the east face of this mountain, with an overall grade of TD-.

Further attempts were made on Reşko but all failed, since, according to Scott, the upper sections of the routes would have required 'bolting and pegging all the way', a prescient assessment.

Some minor routes were also attempted. A 175m buttress almost fell to Bob Wark but he was stopped only a few feet from an easy summit ridge by rock which was too steep and unsuited to pitons. Dave Palmer tried another buttress, but his party was forced off the steep limestone by difficult rock. They moved to the side of the buttress and scrambled up the remaining few metres to their summit.

Scott's growing interest in indigenous peoples can be measured by almost half of the *Expedition Report*'s main section being devoted to describing the Kurds. The *Report* offers a brief history of the area from Nestorian times.[12] He summarises the Kurds' uneasy relationship with the Turkish government and quotes a Turkish naval captain who asserted that there were 'no Kurds in Turkey, only Turks', an opinion reiterated by the Provincial Governor at Hakkiari, who entertained them on their return journey. Scott stoutly if undiplomatically informed the governor that the locals had told him that they were Kurds, asserting in the *Expedition Report*, 'It is natural for Englishmen to wish to preserve the minority peoples from central government attempts to absorb them.'[13]

Scott remarks on how the new road into the Čilo area from Van extends government 'colonisation'; he compares the Kurds' situation to the 'Lapps and Eskimos', despite having never visited their territories.

The *Report* describes in some detail the Kurds' dress, settlements, food, agriculture and religion. The distribution of the Kurdish settlements along the valley is backed by sketch-maps, village plans and photographs. Several accounts of meals with the Kurds are dwelt on, and distinctions of dress and habit between the males and the females are recorded, though more as an enthusiastic amateur than a professional ethnographer. The Kurds are sympathetically compared with the Berber peoples Scott had met in the Southern Atlas. However, he is sharp enough to notice that one old Kurd sported a cap made in Bradford and rubber shoes made in Hong

Kong, concluding that cultural character no longer remains untainted by the outside world.

The return journey was uneventful as far as Ankara, where a great surprise awaited the party: a major earthquake had occurred in Eastern Anatolia.[14] The UK's national and Nottingham press had reported this handy disaster and garbled the story nicely, generating considerable worry at home. One newspaper had even suggested the party had been assisting in the rescue attempts! 'City Boys in Earthquake' had appeared on billboards across Nottingham. One distraught mother berated Mr Happer for charging her £25 to send her son to his death! Scott chides the press for causing unnecessary anxiety, then somewhat caustically remarks that 'if this is the kind of reporting the public wants, this is the kind they will get'.[15] From then on, Scott treated the press 'with great caution'.

No date is given, but the party (having spent a fortnight rather than the ten planned days at or above base camp) would have returned to Nottingham around 12 September. Not for the first time in Scott's career – but on this occasion officially sanctioned – he arrived unhelpfully late for the start of term.

After returning, the *Report* was finished quickly. Its photos are excellent: remarkably sharp and informative, whether of mountain features or the Kurds' way of life. Close-up photos of Kurdish women testify to Scott's charm in persuading them to be photographed. Bob Holmes, a member of the Hindu Kush expedition, tells us that Doug first owned an Exa, an entry level single lens reflex camera made by the East German company Exakta.[16] Since we know Scott used this camera in 1967, it is probable that he used it on this expedition also.

For the most part, the *Expedition Report* is commendably thorough: food, for example, is meticulously listed, although the statistic that each expedition member was allocated nine kilograms of sugar for the five-week trip is somewhat alarming. Local meals, such as 'goat's cheese flavoured with onions in copper bowls', are also recorded with relish. Dates are hazy, however, and next to no interest is expressed in local botany, zoology or ornithology. The sketch-maps are accurate, if crude. The *Report* reflects on the expedition's value for the young people, by encouraging them to explore their world further. As Scott perceptively observes, 'Problems seem sharper when stripped of the comfort and security of a familiar city life.'[17]

The lads discovered stoicism, resilience, co-operativeness and courage in overcoming the demands of travel, the strangeness of their environment and the dangers of the climbing. Scott produced the *Report* within thirty days of returning to Nottingham.

✐

The final expedition of Scott's 'apprenticeship' period – to the Hindu Kush, between May and August 1967 – included his first ascent above 6000m and the first loss of a member of an expedition he was leading. Scott's *Alpine Journal* article states that Scott was the leader and Bill Cheverst the deputy leader. Scott was making his first foray into the Greater Ranges, where he would spend most of his mountaineering time over the following thirty-three years.

The *Expedition Report* sold for 16s 6d (about £12 at today's prices) and it improved on previous reports: a colour cover; dates were more precise; maps were more detailed and nuanced. It was advertised as having '40 full plate photographs and stiff cover', although the stiff cover never materialised. Unusually, in addition, Scott sent out a document running to several pages of 'Pre-Expedition Arrangements', covering news about permits, money, possible film contracts, members' experience, etc., plus a route map. His aim was clearly to draw the team members together and establish a common purpose. The *Report* itself is very neatly printed, with ten sections, six appendices, six maps and a diagram. Its smartness and thoroughness make it salesworthy. Douglas K. Scott's name is prominent throughout; he states that the *Report* is for the expedition members' benefit as a permanent record of their trip. He also makes no bones about hoping that the expense of producing such a report will be recouped through high sales.

The expedition comprised twelve members, all adults and mostly from NCC – the official title, however, was 'The Midlands Hindu Kush Expedition' – and several members had been on the Tibesti and Čilo Daği expeditions. Expedition patrons were the Bishop of Leicester and the Lord Mayor of Nottingham, Sir Jack Longland, connections which must have gladdened Joyce's heart. (Longland also helped by leaning on Rolls-Royce to give Brian Palmer time off.) The group travelled in two Austin one-ton lorries, named very much of their time as Zebedee and Dougal, after *The Magic Roundabout* TV programme.

Funding once again required an enormous effort. Scott's climbing achievements, though, made him a good bet for the MEF, which granted £600 (about £8,500 at today's prices). Another £200 was raised in donations. Expedition members contributed £75 each. What remained came in

sponsorship and donations of food, equipment and other supplies, plus
the sale of Afghani wares in Chamonix and the fees paid by twelve independent travellers returning from Kabul. Because the *Report* was produced
so briskly, the financial statement is incomplete, although all donors were
promised a full, detailed statement in due course.

Leaving on 30 May 1967, they followed what was for several members
a well-worn route through Belgium, Germany, Austria and Yugoslavia,
to Bulgaria then across Turkey via Istanbul, Ankara and Erzurum to Iran
(then, of course, pro-Western under the Shah). They navigated along
the fringes of the Great Salt Desert to the holy city of Mashad, to enter
Afghanistan near Herat, then proceeded by Kandahar to Kabul. Scott
writes on how much more accessible distant ranges now are, because of
improved roads and the ability to share expenses.

On reaching Kabul, they split into two groups, an unsatisfactory
arrangement as some expedition members did not see or talk to others for
the greater part of their time in Afghanistan. Such a division also impaired
communications when John Fleming was lost. One group, comprising
Bill Cheverst, Brian Palmer, Dick Stroud, George Jones, Bob Holmes and
John Fleming left for the Panjshir Valley to climb Mir Samir (6059m),
an unsuccessful attempt on which had been described by Eric Newby in
A Short Walk in the Hindu Kush. Scott, Guy Lee, Mick Terry, Ken Vickers,
Ray Gillies and Tony Watts headed north via Faizabad to the Kuh-e-
Bandaka (6812m) region.

Pages devoted to the nature of the territory and a very detailed history
of climbing in the region mark Scott's future, scholarly style. Another
detailed page describes every climb (the hardest route was AD), up to the
time of summiting.

Beyond the roadhead, and after much haggling, transport with
ponies and donkeys continued to the Sakhi Valley just west of Bandaka.
Negotiations were compromised by the liberality of a recent Japanese
expedition which Scott implicitly criticises for setting a higher spending
bar for its successors. A porter strike until they received gifts similar to
those provided by the Japanese was, however, called off, after a Nuristani
porter was spectacularly overthrown by a judo move from Ray Gillies.

Climbing Bandaka by its south face proved hard work. Slow acclimatisation in thick cloud on the south glacier led to a laborious establishing of
Camp I. A historical moment then occurred as Scott announced his plan
to climb the south face Alpine-style, 'carrying all our food and gear for a
continuous assault without the necessity for more build-ups'.[18] Scott was

way ahead of fashion. The Austrians had demonstrated an Alpine-style approach in the Karakoram on their successful Broad Peak expedition in 1957. Wojciech Kurtyka had made an early Alpine-style climbing attempt at high altitude in 1972 on Akher Tsagh (7017m) and Koh-e-Tez (7015m), in the Hindu Kush. Messner and Habeler's ascent of Gasherbrum (8080m) did not occur until 1975. Scott's 1967 climb on Bandaka, therefore, if not as high a summit as these others, nevertheless represented one of the very earliest high-altitude Alpine-style successes. It earns him his place in mountaineering history as a prescient visionary of good climbing style.

The old misnomer of Alpine-style expeditions being 'lightweight' was again proven next day when the climbers had to shoulder thirty-six-kilogram packs while ascending Bandaka's South Glacier at about 5500m under a line of fortunately stable *séracs*. Cameras were extensively used, as 'a good excuse for stopping'. Lee and Watts carried food up while Scott and Gillies reached the col between Bandaka and its south peak, Tawiki. An igloo was built at almost 6000m. All were suffering from headaches and nausea. Lee and Watts gave up and offered to bring superfluous equipment down, but Scott and Gillies continued, intending to descend by the west ridge. With heavy loads, they reached a snow-hole at 6500m where a brew and a tin of ravioli sent both contentedly to sleep for eight hours. The painful ascent continued: a rock buttress was turned by a snowy gully. Wind-scoured ice at forty degrees led to a second rock band. By evening, yet another bivvy was required; Scott states that bringing a snow-shovel rather than a tent was the key to success.

A frozen stove and disintegrating crampon straps meant a late start on summit day. The second rock step required five 'strenuous' pitches. The summit arrived as an anti-climax as the mist obscured the view, while congratulations were made in the knowledge that the descent of the west ridge would be difficult, especially as fuel supplies were low. Gillies lost a crampon and slipped on the ridge but was fortunately stopped by some boulders before his weight came on the rope: Scott described both climbers as 'white with fear'. Proceeding only ten paces at a time down what resembled the Rochefort Ridge above Courmayeur, the pair eventually gained a sight of the glacier and a safe way down to advance base by following cairns built on the upward route. Scott's hands suffered for weeks after as he had been using them to clear snow. Both climbers had frostbitten toes. Scott was experiencing another of those recurring near-misses throughout his climbing life. But he cheerfully remarks, 'It seemed that our horizons had widened.'[19]

The remainder of the northern group's time in this area was spent in the upper reaches of the Sakhi Valley. Bagging of first ascents began: eight peaks between 5500m and 6110m were climbed, a testimony to the party's fitness, skill and commitment. They then departed for their second exploratory area, the Sharan Valley.

They set out for this new area on 15 July. After a halt at the police post, a pony and four donkeys helped to transport a fortnight's worth of supplies to the Sharan Valley, from where Scott would eventually leave to join the southern party at Anjoman; the lorries would then be recovered at Kokcha and driven to Kabul. Along the way, they encountered many Nuristani villagers, several of whom took pity on their emaciated state and fed them. (Scott writes for several pages about the life of the local Nuristanis and Badakhshanis.) Hospitality went too far, however, when a local offered some shepherdesses to them for an agreed sum to satisfy their manly desires! (They had mistakenly thought that the pimp required first aid assistance.)

In the Sharan Valley, a number of granite peaks all around 5500m were climbed. Scott named some of them, properly, according to local topography, for example Koh-i-Quarch. Almost all were first ascents. The warm granite was found pleasant to climb on, although it damaged their leather boots (their Aquascutum trousers, however, were pronounced 'excellent in every way'). Watts and Scott attempted one 6000m peak. As Scott lyrically remarks, 'We were intruders beyond the frontiers of nature.' A survey was carried out from a high col, after which a glacier couloir became the chosen route. The ground gradually steepened to seventy degrees; ice-screws looked as though they might not hold; it was an anxious section. Jamming cracks were climbed between sweeping slabs, up several pitches graded IV and V followed by a snow arête leading to a steep wall and a summit cornice. The view to the north, towards Tirich Mir and the Russian Pamirs, was rewarding. Hair-raising rappels followed to reach deep ridges of drifted snow on the Suigal Glacier. When they met, Lee and Mick Terry described their successful, enjoyable ascent of a neighbouring peak, which they named Sharan Kuh.

The end of July was approaching; the rendezvous with the other team had been set for 10 August. On the way back, Scott assessed the climbing potential in 'that one valley having more scope for climbing in it than all the peaks in the Mont Blanc massif'.

The southern group were able to describe their ascent of Mir Samir. After ascending scree above the nomads' tents, they reached a valley of flowers, perfect for a base camp. Each member brought exceptional talents: Brian 'Henry' Palmer's outstanding rock-climbing ability; Dick Stroud's unusual capacity for carrying heavy loads at altitude uncomplainingly; 'Yoff's' (George Jones) selflessness, and so on. On 17 July, everyone carried thirty-kilogram loads up to Camp I, at the edge of a glacier below the junction of Mir Samir's south and north ridges. After a rest day, they crossed the south ridge at the Nuristan Gap to establish a camp on the west glacier at about 5200m. Exhausting equipment haulage through the Gap then followed. The glacier camp was hot, being tucked away between two high ridges. The summit ridge was reached by a 'pleasantly' steep gully between vertical rock walls. A bivvy had to be endured, followed by the inevitable haulage of food and equipment.

Unfortunately, the weather changed, necessitating a day at the bivvy. On 1 August, however, a magnificent, unforgettable sunrise heralded a freezing 5 a.m. start. Cornices led to a VS chimney just before the summit snowfield. Both ropes were united on the summit just after noon. The descent down the length of the west glacier was accomplished without incident. The whole climb had been 'wonderful beyond words'.

Much earlier, however, on 27 June, the southern party had reached a camp below the Andoman Pass. At 3 p.m. John Fleming said he was going for a walk to take photographs from a nearby ridge. He was never seen again. Search parties were dispatched: some of Fleming's footprints were found, along with his rucksack, intact, on the riverbank, suggesting that he had crossed the main stream descending from the pass when the water level was low but had fallen into it when the level had risen on his return. Prayers were said. Questions were asked about whether it was right for Fleming to have gone off alone. A fortnight's bureaucratic interactions were required in Kabul to resolve the matter administratively. Newspapers, suggesting that Fleming had gone swimming, were criticised. Some agonising about continuing with the southern expedition then followed. In the end, it was decided to continue out of respect for Fleming's love of the mountains and that while ascending Mir Samir 'he was in all our thoughts'. In the *Report*, Bill Cheverst wrote a poem commemorating Fleming's life. Fleming was one of only a very small number of people to die on a Scott expedition.

In this abridged account from *Up and About*, Scott suffered the kind of near miss which for Fleming probably proved fatal: 'We arrived at a point where the river was fifty yards wide, fast flowing and seemingly deep. We needed to get someone over to belay the horses so on an impulse I stripped off, handed my spectacles to Guy, tied on, ran down the bank, took a deep breath and dived in. Then I realised I was tight on the rope thirty yards downstream and being bashed around by a strong current. I had overestimated my powers as a Nottingham city swimming champion and completely underestimated the power of a youthful mountain river.'

The return journey followed the outward route. Three major incidents occurred. First, to lighten the loads on the lorries, as much superfluous equipment as possible was dumped. Ken Vickers poured the expedition's remaining washing powder into Kabul's central fountain. The ensuing froth upset the locals, who had used the fountain for washing and cleaning. The police 'went berserk'. Vickers, with his packets of powder, was arrested. The British embassy had to intervene to secure his release.

To help funds, up to twelve (accounts vary) independent travellers were offered places at £25 each on the lorries for the journey back to Europe. On the way back, one lorry flipped in the middle of the night in eastern Turkey and landed on its side. One of the travellers, a Dutchman, had fallen asleep at the wheel. Bob Holmes was thrown out 'like a slingshot' but, miraculously, no one was hurt. Scott's lorry was some way behind and was able to get the other lorry back on four wheels.

Finally, a typical mechanical problem occurred, also in Turkey, where a water-pump bearing on one lorry went 'belly up'. Spotting a nearby abandoned American engineering workshop, Scott talked his way into using an engineering lathe. Brian Palmer manufactured a new bearing; he and Ray Gillies fitted it. It worked sufficiently well for the convoy to reach Ankara, 1,600 kilometres to the west, where a spare part could be purchased.

Rather than return directly to Nottingham, the lorries stopped off at Chamonix, where Afghani exotica – fashionable sheepskin coats, lapis lazuli jewellery and the like – were sold to mitigate expedition costs. Scott and Cheverst had time for some climbing before continuing, with a new cargo of paying clients, to Nottingham.

For Scott, the Hindu Kush expedition represented a great step forward in his development. The view from high ground inspired him to consider the peaks of Nepal and the Karakoram. He wanted to return to Afghanistan but never did: the Russians invaded in 1979. He did, however, reach the Fann mountains in Tajikistan in 1992, from where the Hindu Kush's higher peaks are just visible.

When he returned from the Hindu Kush, Scott was twenty-six. He had acquired considerable climbing experience and had lived through extremes of heat, cold and altitude. He had gained much administrative experience.

He had become fascinated by the lives of the ethnic inhabitants of the places he had visited, with a particular concern for their medical well-being. Gathering such experience, of course, took up a great deal of his time, yet by 1967 he had been married for five years. Most of the preceding chapters have largely concerned themselves with Scott the climber. It is now time to look at Scott the husband, father and thinker.

7

Growth of a Mountaineer (I): 1959–70

'By caring for each other, we are relieved of the burden of our own self-importance.'

– Doug Scott

By the late 1960s, Doug was on the cusp of international renown. He was married to Jan, a physically attractive flower-child with an assertive practicality who in childhood was something of a rebel.[1] He also had a son, a steady job and a house. Yet he remained conflicted between his compulsion to seek out ever more demanding climbing challenges and a longing to be at home with Jan and Michael, to look after them through routine work.

Doug was tall, 1.88m, with a big upper body. As a young man he discovered he was physically attractive to many women. When not climbing, he still enjoyed playing rugby and swimming. He found it difficult to sit still and, like his father, expended surplus energy in gardening. Photos of Doug in the 1960s illustrate his geeky Bill Gates look with 'short back and sides' hair, tweed or flannel jackets, shirt and tie and near-rectangular glasses, with all of these exchanged for a rugby strip or cord breeches and woolly jerseys on the crag. The alteration in appearance and persona to John Lennon (or guru?) lookalike had to wait until the 1970s.

Doug's ambition to become famous has already been mentioned. Geoff Stroud, however, recalls his self-deprecating humour, his modesty and his fair-mindedness when credit had to be shared, at least as far as climbs and climbing companions were concerned. These three virtues did not extend to his marriage.

The marriage began inauspiciously. While both young people were passionately fond of each other, their surprise wedding, when aged only twenty and eighteen – Doug was among the first of the NCC members to get married – in April 1962 resulted from a false pregnancy scare.[2] The Scotts and the Brooks were both alarmed by the couple's haste: they had met only a year before. The families decided to meet, but the meeting was inconsequential and the wedding went ahead. In Doug's flippant phrase, which reveals some disquieting underlying attitudes, 'We decided to get married because we were fed up with having to say good-bye at the bus stop.' This apparently banal remark nonetheless illustrates the insouciant Scott persona necessary to the development of his own myth.

Doug's wedding party, 1962. From left to right: Dennis Gray, Clive Davies, John Stenson, Ray Gillies, Brian Scott, Doug, Mick Garside, Dez Hadlum, Geoff Stroud, Mick Poppleston. Photo by and courtesy of Tena Walton.

The course of the wedding day did not run smooth. An attempt to drag Doug into a pub adjacent to St Leonard's Parish Church, Wollaton for some Dutch courage was only just thwarted. Dennis Gray's wedding present was a pair of PAs, the de rigueur rock-boot of the day, thus ignoring the bride. Dennis made up for his faux pas by driving the couple to North Wales for their honeymoon and giving Doug £10 when the happy couple realised that neither had any money.[3] This sum paid for a night at the Pen y Pass hotel (now a hostel), after which, to Jan's discomfiture, the remainder of the honeymoon was spent, once the rubbish and rats had been cleared out, in a cave under the Cromlech Boulders, an egotistical choice of venue which set the tone for much of the marriage.

Marriage to Jan could be tempestuous: quarrels sometimes involved her forcefully dispatching items of cooking equipment at Doug's head.[4] They spent long periods apart, some as separations, others because of Doug's absence on expeditions. There were infidelities on both sides: not so much an open marriage of the kind that was fashionable in the 1960s but one involving encounters of mutual physical and (sometimes) emotional benefit. The imbalanced nature of the relationship is symbolised in *Up and About*, which describes the marriage to about its halfway point in 1975: the chapter titled 'Jan', which occupies eighteen pages of text, allocates a mere four paragraphs and a line to Jan.

The Scotts' first flat was situated on Lenton Boulevard, not far from where Doug taught, although they lived there for only a few months before moving to Derby Road. They had no car, so visiting climbing venues became a matter of hitching – a now largely forgotten art at which Doug excelled, having once hitched from Nottingham to Innsbruck within twenty-four hours. During their first married summer they visited Chamonix with the NCC. Jan was introduced to the Nantillons Glacier, her first time on Alpine ice. Unfortunately, an NCC member dislodged a rock which hit Jan on the arm and chipped a bone, an extremely painful injury. A screaming match ensued: Jan demanded to go home while Doug smashed his ice-axe against a rock, melodramatically declaring that it wouldn't be needed again. Passions had cooled by evening, however, and the holiday resumed, although Jan appears to have been left to her own devices.

Jan and Doug had been married for less than five months when Doug set out for the Sierra Nevada and Atlas. He was away for almost two months. Almost as soon as he returned, he was taken to hospital with hepatitis A, caught in Spain; he spent several weeks recovering. Absence was bad enough, but Jan found Doug, altered by his expedition experience, to be a trial on his return: the enthusiastic lover who suddenly re-entered her life was hard to recognise: as a self-reliant woman she had got used to her own company. Doug, with his wilful lifestyle, upset her well-organised routine; it was not unusual for fellow climbers to be invited back to the house for a 'doss' and breakfast without Jan hearing anything about it first. A variation on this theme occurred in 1968, when Professor Itakura, who had helped Doug at base camp on the Hindu Kush expedition, accepted his open invitation and appeared in Nottingham. Jan and Doug both liked the professor. A neighbour, however, who had served in the Royal Army Medical Corps and been appallingly maltreated by the Japanese in Singapore's fearsome Changi jail, strongly objected to the kindly professor's presence.

Despite these challenges to domestic harmony, Jan could never tell Doug that he should not go to the mountains because she recognised that 'feeding the rat', in Mo Anthoine's inimitable phrase – subsequently taken up by Al Alvarez – could not be stopped. When Doug first absented himself on expeditions, Jan said she was 'sick with worry'; she literally took to her bed. Not just emotional anxieties, either: on at least one occasion, Doug was absent for three months without paying the phone bill. The compensation was that Doug would come back from a big trip happier. After a time, the main recourse for Jan was denial: 'I completely oblite-rated my thoughts that Doug was going to get killed. I just wouldn't have it. I would have gone barmy otherwise.'[5] And life with Doug was always exciting!

By the winter of 1962–63, Jan had become pregnant. She decided to spend the weeks before her confinement with her parents, a decision showing her vulnerability and lack of adjustment to marriage. As the birth approached, Doug hitch-hiked to Carlisle every weekend. With Doug being somewhat accident-prone (he had already spilled paint on the Brooks' hall carpet), Jan's father Tom realised that his son-in-law's prodigious energies were best expended outside, preferably away from the house: he obtained a racing cycle on which Doug proceeded to crash, lacerating his hand. Tom then managed to persuade a Territorial Army soldier to go kayaking with Doug on the Solway Firth, notorious for its dangerous sands and tides. The excursion turned into an emergency, with the risk-takers returning to the Brooks' house at 1 a.m., to be confronted by an uncharacteristically but justifiably angry Tom. Scott nonchalantly recounts these successive upsets as if he was part of a kind of extended 'in-law' joke.[6]

Michael arrived safely in July 1963. Doug, however, rationalising himself as 'superfluous to requirements for all practical purposes' departed for the Dolomites ten days later: parental bonding did not suggest itself or was repressed. However, after five weeks in the Dolomites, and the climbing completed, he felt overcome with homesickness for Jan and Michael. Doug states he felt 'conscience-stricken' for having been away for so long, although this feeling does not appear to have withstood the lively reality of home life for very long.

Other signs of Doug's immaturity appeared. When Jan was heavily pregnant with Michael, she had appeared in court to support her wayward husband, arrested for breach of the peace after a punch-up at the Prince of Wales in Baslow. Fortunately, Doug's co-pugilist never showed up and left a false name and address: Doug was given an absolute discharge. Still, Jan and her parents must have wondered what sort of character she had married. Nor did Doug learn from his mistake: The Battle of the Dog and Partridge took place only eighteen months or so later (see chapter four).

The outcome of such rumbustious evenings was not Doug's only kind of brush with illegality. Drug consumption followed from smoking 'small cigarettes' while abroad in the 1960s. LSD and other drugs, the sale of which helped to pay for the trip, returned with Doug from Afghanistan in 1967. However, all the evidence points to hard drugs never having been consumed despite his interest in mind-altering substances developing during the 1970s.

In November 1963, to accommodate the new baby, the Scotts moved from Derby Road to The Park, a quiet residential area not too far from work. The move was not a success: a boorish Irish neighbour, prone to shouting and swearing, 'terrorised' baby Michael (and his own children). They moved again, this time to Oakdale Road in Chilwell, just beyond Beeston, an area of solidly respectable middle-class suburban brick houses.

Meanwhile, tensions arose between Jan and the Scotts. These surfaced during Doug's absence in the Sahara for two and a half months, when Michael was aged almost two. Jan expressed her unhappiness at being left alone to Joyce, who was not entirely sympathetic, having experienced a husband away at war while Doug was a toddler. Jan's solution, as a resourceful and practical person, was to leave her employment in a tax office to follow a three-year primary school teacher training course at the local college. Joyce looked after Michael, and Doug agreed to support Jan: he worked overtime – he never shirked hard work – and supplemented his income as a bouncer, something he did not enjoy and did little good to his already damaged ears. He also acquired a driving licence and then a minivan, thus giving him and his family a little more freedom, even if it meant a rather frantic early morning arrangement of dropping off Michael at pre-school then Jan at college before proceeding to his own work.

By his own admission, Doug's lengthy school holiday absences abroad – and for that matter at weekends divided between climbing and rugby – put an ever-greater strain on the marriage. His serial infidelities, few of any real importance, exacerbated the problem, although Jan tended to 'look the other way' in any case. Matters came to a head in 1968. Doug had left the family at New Year for climbing in Scotland. A fling with 'a young lass'

made him feel unusually guilty. At home in early summer, however, Jan
confessed to her own affairs – one with an unnamed climbing friend – and
declared that a doctor had asked to marry her. She was considering asking
for a divorce. While Doug declares in *Up and About* that this situation
had arisen because of his selfish behaviour, he seems to have done little
to correct matters other than to spend more time with Jan during the
holidays. A new marital existence developed, with Jan teaching and Doug
climbing and lecturing. Mutual support survived, however: Jan typed
Doug's manuscript for *Big Wall Climbing* and helped with lectures; both
thought carefully about how to ensure Michael's wellbeing. It was not an
ideal arrangement, however, and inevitably led in 1987 to separation then
divorce.

∞

Despite such domestic turbulence, Doug the intellectual, the reader and
thinker began to surface in the 1960s. Doug was one of the most widely
read mountaineers in history, particularly on subjects which interested
him: these were, apart from mountaineering and adventure books and
articles, largely concerned with philosophical, ethical and literary works.
He was also starting to write articles, guides and expedition reports.

Doug's reading was largely of its time. Early encouragement came from
his parents, who presented him with *The Mountain World*, edited by the
Swiss Foundation for Alpine Research, with the inscription, 'For Douglas,
With best wishes for your future mountaineering endeavours, Dad and
Mum, March 1966.'[7]

His early texts, to meet the demands of the English O-Level syllabus,
have been noted. His mountaineering literary heroes appear to have begun
with Shipton – he refers to *Upon that Mountain* on several occasions. While
Shipton was generally happier seeing what was round the next corner than
in aiming for summits, his 'back of the envelope' expedition planning,
with its emphasis on travelling lightweight and living off the land, might
reasonably claim to be an ancestor of those lightweight, Alpine-style
expeditions for which Doug became a historically important advocate.

Hermann Buhl was another hero, for his 1956 account of his ascent
of Nanga Parbat, in which he talks of a 'pilgrimage', perhaps the first
occasion for Doug of understanding mountaineering as a spiritual quest.
Lionel Terray, particularly in *Les Conquérants de l'Inutile* (*Conquistadors
of the Useless*, 1961), which had been translated by Geoff Sutton, Doug's
mentor at White Hall, was also a formative influence, although that was

qualified when Terray came to give a Tibesti expedition fundraising lecture in Nottingham and kissed Jan's hand in a way which suggested to the possessive Doug that his hero and his wife would be better kept apart. Maurice Herzog's international bestseller, *Annapurna* (1952), made a similar impact to Terray's work. Doug's other main mountaineering influence appears to have been the French novelist and historian Roger Frison-Roche, in his *Premier de Cordée* (*First on the Rope*, 1942) and his various works in the 1960s on the Mont Blanc area and the Sahara.

During his O-Level re-take, Doug had made a study of leadership, particularly the contrasting styles of Scott and Shackleton. It is clear from subsequent writing and experience that he preferred the *primus inter pares* approach by Shackleton to the more hierarchical style of Scott, not least because when an authoritarian leader makes a mistake there is less room for manoeuvre in rectifying it.

As a child of the 1960s, Doug readily took up with esoterica. One of Doug's difficulties was a lack of critical training in appreciating others' writing, thanks to a late start at school and only a very limited amount of time when young spent on developing reading skills. The *I Ching* played to his sense of his own apparently unusual destiny; he certainly used it for divination at a number of base camps and at home, despite it meriting the obvious criticism of abrogating personal responsibility.

The hokum offered by Carlos Castaneda, whom Doug admired for far too long, was perhaps fascinating, but it led nowhere constructive. Doug had a copy of *The Teachings of Don Juan* with him on Shivling in 1981; he had become familiar with Castaneda's works well before his discussions with Molly Higgins about them after 1974. The works offered escape, and colourful risk, based, however, on falsehoods.

The other principal 'philosophical' author to interest Doug was George Gurdjieff (1866–1949), whom Guy Lee suggests was introduced to Doug by a guru of the time, Frank Goldthorpe, who lived in a tepee in Sherwood Forest and was a teacher and acupuncturist before moving to a remote valley in Wales. Gurdjieff's oxymoronic idea of 'waking sleep' to describe our fragmented consciousness gained many followers, not least Doug, for whom such a self-opposing image was immediately attractive. Gurdjieff believed that by uniting the work of the fakir, the monk and the yogi, one could rise to a unified state of consciousness (with its obvious parallels with Buddhism) to achieve full human potential. Such a process attracted sentimental fantasists (or those pressed for time) for whom serious Buddhism was too much like hard work. Gurdjieff was one of Doug's earliest spiritual or philosophical mentors: indeed, he tried to convert Bob Pettigrew to Gurdjieff's teaching, unsuccessfully. A name often linked to Gurdjieff, the Russian explorer and philosopher P.D. Ouspensky, for a time a disciple of Gurdjieff, is also referred to by Doug on occasion.

What is noticeable about so many of Doug's literary interests is his search for a guru – a teacher or leader who could impart certainties, even a father figure to replicate his own father, whom he much admired but with whom he was always subconsciously competing. Eventually, of course, Doug himself became a kind of guru, through his John Lennon lookalike appearance and his propensity to play up to this image as part of his self-myth, while uttering gnomic phrases such as 'The more one goes into mountains, the more one realises they are but a medium for exploration into oneself.'

Doug also refers to The Beatles becoming involved with the Maharishi Mahesh Yogi from February 1968, though he was reluctant to concede that their relationship with the Maharishi had ended badly. A quest for wisdom offered by gurus was a feature of Doug's spiritual life for the next forty years.

Three other authors, in vogue at the time and who interested Doug, are worth mentioning. Jack Kerouac's *On The Road*, the Bible of the 'beat' or 'counterculture' generation, was a work which Doug was able to live through when travelling around the US from 1970 onwards. Herman Hesse's *Steppenwolf* (1927), *Siddhartha* (1922), *The Glass Bead Game* (1943), *Strange News from Another Star* (1919) and *Narcissus and Goldmund* (1930) are all referred to. They define not just his growing interest in the East long before he set foot there, but reflect these works' growing popularity throughout the 1960s. Those who believed in Hesse's supposed manifesto of interest in drug culture and Eastern mysticism were mistaken, however: Hesse was clean-living, preferring Jungian psychoanalysis to the extent of undergoing a few sessions with the great man himself. In *Steppenwolf*, the supposed heroic rebel, consumed by self-loathing, actually learns not to be a rebel. In *Siddhartha*, Hesse attempted to synthesise Eastern and Western thought but in such mannered language as to make the attempt at religious insight scarcely worth the effort. (The works above, however, led to Doug reading the *Upanishads*, from which he quoted extensively in *Kangchenjunga*, as well as *The Egyptian Book of the Dead* and the Ancient Mesopotamian *Epic of Gilgamesh*.) The third fashionable author was Antoine de Saint-Exupéry, whose *The Little Prince* (1943) was read to Michael as a bed-time story, although its supposed adult message about

how relationships with people whom one knows help one's understanding
of the world in general is of dubious value.

More earthily, as a Nottingham lad, Doug encountered Sillitoe's gritty
realism in *Saturday Night and Sunday Morning* (1958). He and Brian saw
the film version together in the cinema nearest to where Sillitoe lived. No
record exists of him reading D.H. Lawrence, however. His general literary
propensity was for the romantic and esoteric.

Doug's musical tastes ran on unsurprisingly parallel lines, although
Dennis Gray, who came from a sophisticated musical background, suggests Doug's tastes were fairly middle-of-the-road. An early liking for
Bob Dylan continued for most of the rest of Doug's climbing life: Dylan
surfaced on Baffin in 1971 and on Kangchenjunga in 1979 and on several
climbs thereafter. He was, according to Scott, a genius, 'a prophet without
the preaching'. Not far behind in interest were Jimi Hendrix, particularly
the rhythm and blues ballad 'Little Wing', as well as Crosby, Stills, Nash
and Young (*4 Way Street*), Pink Floyd, Meatloaf, Dr Hook, Joni Mitchell
and Leonard Cohen. Melanie Safka's 'Look What They've Done to My
Song' resonated when expeditions did not proceed to plan. His interest
in The Beatles' *Sergeant Pepper's Lonely Hearts Club Band* again demonstrated that Doug remained a child of the musical 1960s, for many years.
More unusually, Mick Poppleston recounts that in the late 1950s and early
1960s, he, Doug and others would go together to Saturday jazz clubs,
often after a rugby match, and listen to traditional jazz, such as that of
Chris Barber, Ken Colyer or Humphrey Lyttelton. These musicians were
regarded as superior to the Beatles (especially if you attended Nottingham
High School). Doug's interest in opera and ballet came very much later.

Doug was well aware that his reputation could be enhanced by writing:
'I was blinded by my own ambition to be in print.'[8]

The high, very studied quality of his four 1960s *Expedition Reports* has
already been mentioned. Doug's first contribution in commercial print
came in *Mountain Craft* magazine in 1963: Douglas Scott's article on his
expedition to the Atlas Mountains. He contributed further occasional articles then joined the ever-controversial Ken Wilson as a regular contributor
when *Mountain Craft* mutated into *Mountain* magazine, in which many
of his notable early climbs are reported, then throughout its published life
until 1992.

Doug's memory has again deserted him when in *Up and About* he tells
us that his first article in the *Alpine Journal* appeared in 1968. In fact, a
concise report on the Čilo Daği expedition appeared in the 1967 edition.

The Hindu Kush report – a rather shorter piece, for which Doug claims
he asked for the usual fee, only to be sent away with a flea in his ear by the
assistant editor, Tom Blakeney – appeared in the 1968 edition. His other
Alpine Club work consisted of his editorship of the Alpine Climbing
Group *Bulletin* from 1969.

Doug's remaining early publication was his 1965 guidebook, *Climbs on
Derwent Valley Limestone*. Doug's first book, *Big Wall Climbing*, appeared
in 1974, with a foreword by Chris Bonington, they having known each
other since the 1960s. Doug did, however, claim, largely on the back of his
experiences at Gogarth and Strone that his writing on it was 'well advanced'
in 1970; Doug and deadlines never sat very comfortably together.

With articles and reports came fundraising lectures. These were to play
a large and exhausting part in Doug's life, partly just as a way of earning
his living when he turned professional from the spring of 1971 and partly
to raise funds for CAN. Lectures at this stage of his life, however, meant
those which he hosted. Those which he delivered came later, after his
big wall and Yosemite climbs in the early 1970s. Doug had noticed that
Dennis Gray was supplementing his income from lecturing to climbing
clubs, schools and so on. He therefore invited the prominent climber-
photographer John Cleare to speak in Nottingham, during the winter
1964–65 season, as a fundraising lecture for the Tibesti expedition. Doug
and John met in a public library to set up, about forty-five minutes before
the lecture was due to start. Cleare takes up the story:

> Doug . . . turned up in classic schoolmaster tweed jacket with leather
> elbow-patches, pens and pencils in top pocket, etc. By zero hour, the
> hall was empty, save only for a pair of OAPs. Thirty minutes later, the
> OAPs upped and left. Doug was beside himself. My fee was I believe
> £30 plus £5 for petrol. 'I can't pay you,' he said. I told him I must have
> my petrol money. Very reluctantly, he slipped me a fiver. In the foyer,
> we passed a small library noticeboard. Pinned to it, on a page torn from
> an exercise book, was a handwritten note advertising my lecture – the
> only item of publicity he'd arranged! Although rather miffed, I offered
> to buy Doug a pint at the pub round the corner.
>
> It was full of Oread fellows. ''Ello, John. Whad are yoo doin' oop
> 'ere?'
>
> 'I came up to lecture for Doug.'
>
> 'Bloody 'ell, Scott, why'd yer not tell oos?!'[9]

One can be very confident, however, that Doug, always good at reflecting on experiences, especially when they had gone wrong, never made a similar error again. Indeed, Chris Bonington says that Doug in his early lectures arranged for the NCC, which maybe made £20 a time, was 'good at organisation' and cared for his speakers very well. Soon, Doug would be giving the lectures himself and find himself in demand across several continents.

∽

When not at home, school or in the lecture hall, Doug developed a life-long passion for driving. His mantra endures: 'Drive faster!' Near-misses and accidents, on bikes or motorbikes to cars or lorries or helicopters, are recalled by numerous friends.

Doug bought a motorbike when he was nineteen. In his second year at college, thanks to an 'away from home' grant, he upgraded to a 250cc Excelsior Talisman Twin motorbike. While advantageous in transporting him to Car Colston for extra work, and to Stanage Edge for longer hours to be spent climbing, his first accident soon occurred. Rushing to Stanage as usual, he lost control on a bend, slid across the road into an oncoming car and was catapulted over a wall into a field. The bike lay jammed, with the engine still at full throttle, under the car's front bumper. A woman was shouting, 'He's in the engine!' 'No, I'm not!' Doug shouted back, 'I'm here.' Doug then hopped over the wall to try to extricate the bike. The woman fainted. Once she had been revived and Doug had bashed the rear mudguard into shape with his peg hammer, the participants continued on their respective ways.[10] After this accident, Doug came round to Geoff Stroud's to return his motorbike overtrousers, now in a rather sorry state. He commented that it was fortunate that he was wearing them, as otherwise he could have been badly injured!

A more serious accident occurred soon after. In the winter of 1961, heading to Matlock after a tiring day, a routine piece of overtaking in foggy conditions led to Doug hitting and being thrown over an oncoming car. His knee was 'full of glass' from the car's headlamp. He had his broken kneecap set in plaster in hospital.

In July 1961, Doug and Geoff Stroud travelled on Geoff's Matchless motorbike to Snowdonia: the passenger, characteristically frustrated by the numerous bends of the A5 as they neared the end of the long journey from Nottingham, whispered in Stroud's ear, 'That is the last bend; it is now straight on to Betwys-y-Coed.' A rather terrifying bend followed, which Stroud failed to negotiate correctly: his handlebar touched the door handle of an oncoming car, fortunately driven by a doctor. Following the crash, Stroud was carried off to Llandudno Hospital, where he was visited that evening by Doug, though not thereafter. In *Up and About*, Doug recalls the story differently and shifts the responsibility onto Geoff: 'In 1966 . . . possibly because of the rucksack sitting on the petrol tank between his arms, (Geoff) miscalculated one of the terrifying bends near Betws-y-Coed and hit a telegraph pole.'[11] Stroud's version is the more accurate; the moulding of Doug's persona is at work in his version.

Doug's passion for speed and its damaging consequences contrasts with the care with which he climbed in the UK. On one occasion, he ended up in court.[12] Near Corwen, an attempt to overtake (a by-product of Doug's speed fetish, which generated consternation and anger among future friends and spouses) led to a near-miss with an oncoming car. Doug was charged with dangerous driving. He twice postponed his subsequent court summonses, thereby unfairly penalising his plaintiff's witnesses, who had had to come from Stirling. Court costs equivalent to three months' salary arose. The prosecution, however, when the case finally took place, carelessly failed to prove that Doug was the driver and the case collapsed.

Acquiring a vehicle had its advantages, however: Doug gained a strong technical understanding of how a wide variety of vehicles worked, a useful skill when driving long distances in extreme conditions on rough, far-away roads. A minivan helped with finances, in that expenses could be shared, and it gave the Scott family rather more freedom than they had hitherto enjoyed. Freedom from hitch-hiking, with its uncertainties and risks, was a bonus, but was also liberating for Jan in joining Doug on some of his travels, for example visiting the Ordesa National Park, high in the Pyrenees, in 1971.

The 1960s saw the beginning of another of Doug's lifelong passions: photography. Under Bob Holmes's influence, a serious interest began on the Hindu Kush expedition in 1967. Doug's first camera was an Exa. He owned two of them, although by 1975 he had graduated to a Rollei 35. Holmes comments, 'Doug was never preoccupied with the techniques of photography. He had a natural eye but claimed his photos worked because he could reach places others couldn't. His photographs provided material for books and lectures. In 1970, as a town planner for Leicestershire County Council I had access to the Council's darkroom. After work, I would often go down with Doug, ostensibly to make prints for the office, but in reality to produce huge poster-sized prints to be sold at lectures. Sometimes the prints were traded for climbing gear at Black's outdoor equipment shop in Nottingham, for use in window displays.'[13]

Doug's photographic expertise developed great sophistication. The sale of photos and posters became one of the mainstays of his income, both personally and for CAN. A measure of his reputation surfaced in March 2021, at a memorial event for Doug at the Royal Geographical Society (RGS), when an auction of some of his photos, compered by Rebecca Stephens, raised £26,000 in about twenty minutes.

When all else failed, Doug still had his favourite walking companion in the hills (as he stated in a UKClimbing interview), his dog Strider. As usual, however, the family picked up the pieces when Doug was absent: 'Douglas had a very nice and friendly cross labrador, Strider, which we often looked after when he was away. Douglas took him with him to London in his Ford Cortina Estate Mark 2 and left him in the car while at an appointment. Unfortunately, when he got back Strider was gone, having squeezed out through one of the windows. We thought that was the end of Strider. On Boxing Day, however, we got a phone call from Battersea Dogs Home saying Strider had been handed in! Douglas was away climbing so I had the job of once again going to London, this time to pick Strider up on Boxing Day. Needless to say, he was really pleased to see us!'[14]

As we approach the next phase of Doug's life, his breakthrough climbs on the big walls in the late 1960s and early 1970s, Doug's actively humanitarian side begins to appear, as he takes on an expedition doctor role, particularly using homeopathic medicine. Allied to that interest is his re-evaluation of his own diet as he espoused vegetarianism before his first visit, in 1970, to the US.

By 1970, Doug was at that pivotal point in his life when international recognition was soon to follow. His domestic behaviour varied from the responsible to the selfish, a better father than a husband. On climbs, if he wished to make a point it was generally with humour and calm insistence. It was hard to get angry with him. But he could be exasperating. He maintained the approach to leadership (and to marriage?) that things worked out best if everyone agreed with *his* plan.[15] Such an outlook was challenged through an extraordinary variety of tests over the following decade.

8

The Big Walls, 1968–78

'All true wisdom is only to be found far from the dwellings
of men, in the great solitudes; and it can only be obtained
through suffering and privation.'

– Igjugdrjuk, a Caribou Eskimo

Scott developed an interest in big walls in the late 1960s: in his first book,
Big Wall Climbing, he covers the Alps, Dolomites, Romsdal, Yosemite,
Baffin and Patagonia, although his interest probably began at Gogarth. As
many of Scott's other major climbs involved ridge routes, I have chosen
to broaden the understanding of a big wall from *Big Wall Climbing* to
include long, steeply angled mixed snow, ice and rock faces situated in
Scotland, the Himalaya, Alaska, Kenya and Canada, which Scott climbed
between 1968 and 1978. These were not his only climbs during that period,
of course: he attempted many new routes on familiar mountains such
as Everest or K2, as well as a small number of exploratory expeditions.
Common to all was a passionate desire for adventure and the heightened
emotions resulting from a suitably demanding climb.

Strone Ulladale, Cima Ovest, Yosemite, Romsdal, Baffin and The 'Gunks

Scotland's soaring 200m prow of Lewissian gneiss, Strone Ulladale
(Sròn Uladail), on Harris, came to Scott's notice from Guy Lee and Pete
Thompson, who had visited it in 1967 and been strongly impressed by
the UK's highest overhang.[1] This sounded like suitable preparation for
attempting a new route on the north face of Cima Ovest in the Dolomites,
planned for 1969. In 1968, moreover, Scott and Dave Nicol had climbed
the *Bonatti Pillar* (TD) on the Aiguille du Petit Dru, finding it not too
difficult (few pegs and only one bivouac) while enjoying overtaking the
prominent French alpinist Yannick Seigneur.[2]

Reaching Strone at Easter 1969, Jeff Upton, Mick Terry, Steve Read and Scott started out on a wrong route and quickly called it a day. Scott, Upton, Lee and Terry returned at Whitsun, accompanied by Ken Wilson, knowing that there was strong competition for the first ascent. A tough climb ensued: the overhang extended fifty metres from the vertical. Cracks for pegs and belay stances were not obvious. The difficulties justified inserting a bolt (which Scott had tapered in the school metal workshop). It took his weight. Bongs and small-angle pitons in deepening cracks lifted Scott beyond the great 'scoop', the face's central feature. *The Scoop* (E7 6b; 205m; eight pitches between 'terrifying overhangs') was the most demanding rock-climb Scott had done; he was unhappy that the climb had to be completed using a bolt and such a quantity of hardware, even if the situation was upliftingly beautiful. As he contritely declared in *Up and About*, 'To my eternal shame, I started a trend that cannot now be reversed. I decided that I would never again use a drill.'

Scott's success reached the press: James Gibbins of the *Scottish Daily Express* wrote a conspicuously inaccurate article for which Scott was paid £25, enough to cover his travel costs. Peter Gillman then wrote a more accurate account for the *Sunday Times*. Gillman comments, 'I think this was my first encounter with Doug. The *Sunday Times* used one of his photographs. When it came to fixing a price, I asked him how much he wanted. He said something like two thousand pounds. That was out of all proportion and I think that the ST paid him a standard rate, more like £200. Doug was clearly testing the market and named a ridiculous sum as a way of doing so. I admired his self-confidence and negotiating prowess.'[3]

Scott returned to Strone at February half-term 1970, this time with Ray Gillies and Tony Wilmott. Leo Dickinson joined them as photographer. They attempted *The Nose* (A5), with another prominent overhang but, compromised by frequent snowstorms, they could manage only a well-pegged 60m before time ran out. Scott returned late for the start of term once again. At Whitsun, Scott and Guy Lee returned. *The Nose* was attempted; the pair reached the ledge but turned back on the roof. In June 1971, before heading for Baffin Island, Scott and Guy Lee once more visited Strone, to climb *Sidewinder* (A5), without bolts, to the right of *The Scoop*. It took three days but was more enjoyable because of the greater amount of free climbing. Another attempt, this time unsuccessful, was made on *The Nose*. The final visit to Strone took place after the return from Baffin Island, in September 1971. Scott, Lee and Dennis Hennek arrived

with a film crew from the BBC, consisting of Leo Dickinson and a pro-
ducer, with the intention of making a thirty-minute documentary about
climbing *The Nose*. Dennis Hennek and a selection of new gear ('cop-
perheads and bashees') proved useful. Scott inched his way up, trusting
to skyhooks to hold him. After ten hours, he reached a ledge. Fortified
by sardines and marmalade butties, Scott spent a rainy night reasonably
happily on the ledge before he, Lee and Hennek completed the climb the
next day. Having their tyres slashed by overprotective local gamekeepers
proved unhelpful, however. The resulting film, *Rock Island Climb*, was
screened on Boxing Day 1971.

By 1969, Scott and Jeff Upton had acquired the experience to tackle the
Rudolf-Baur route (ED) on the north face of Cima Ovest (west summit of
the Three Peaks of the Lavaredo, 2973m). Upton and Scott were joined by
Ted Wells and Mick Terry, with a British first ascent in prospect.

Doug on the Rudolf-Baur route, first British ascent. Cima Ovest,
Dolomites, 1969. (Doug Scott collection)

The route is tremendously exposed. While extensive pegging was necessary, bolts were already in place: Scott declared that he was not averse to
using them if they were already there. Scott's misplaced reliance on a peg

resulted in a twenty-metre fall. Terry's burnt hands required treatment. On the re-attempt, Scott came across a note scratched into the rock: 'Fuck off Scott, this is too hard for you, Leo.' They had apparently been beaten to the first British ascent by Leo Dickinson, Jeff Morgan and Brian Molyneux.[4] As the note suggests, this kind of competition was friendly.[5] Photographic discussions kept Scott's mind off the vast drop below them. In an article for the *Alpine Journal*, 1970, Scott comments, 'After about 600 ft we reached the crux – the huge dominating roof. The second arrives, confident, to take over the stance, but wave after wave of fearful thoughts crowd into his mind as he has the time to appreciate the exposure . . . The leader sorts himself out, keeping the ropes running free, taking the strain off his arms and back with an economy of effort and thinking, not fumbling with clips and slings . . . Retreat (if it were possible) is rejected and strangulation (quite possible!) avoided.'

There are no valley noises high up on the Cima Ovest, but there are the inner sounds of throbbing blood vessels and hard breathing.

Once Scott realised there was no going back, he gained a new burst of mental energy; they all reached the Kasparek Ledge, to join the Cassin route to the summit.

⁓∾

Scott now began to travel abroad on two or three expeditions every year. At Easter 1970, he flew, for the first time, to the US, accompanied by Jan, who had been awarded a £50 research grant for studying primary schooling in the San Francisco area, and Tony Wilmott. Scott wanted to visit Yosemite after reading about its exceedingly testing new routes. His curiosity about how Americans tackled their climbing had also been aroused by the *Vulgarian Digest*, a sometimes lewd periodical compiled by notorious acid-droppers, boozers and rabble-rousers who nonetheless climbed hard. Much of its writing was focused (when not on topless females) on New York state's Shawangunk range.[6]

On arrival at Modesto, about 100 kilometres from San Francisco, the party stayed with Royal Robbins and his wife, Liz.[7] Next day, in Yosemite, Scott was 'struck with awe and wonder'. They began, after some cragging, on the *Steck-Salathé route* (V. 5.10 a/b; 16 pitches; 290m) on the west face of Sentinel Rock. Their route was kept aid-free apart from a short, bolted ladder near the top. Scott admired Robbins's speed and rhythm. He also reflected on how one-pitch routes in Derbyshire, such as *Tower Chimney*, helped him to enjoy multi-pitch routes in Yosemite.

Some minor climbs followed at the base of El Capitan. Scott climbed *Braille Book* (5.8+; 212m; six pitches) on Cathedral Spire with Dennis Hennek, Don Lauria and the extravagant yarner T.M. Herbert. Even better was their climb on the dome-like crag, BHOS, a five-pitch route.[8] The climb, graded III, 5.7, A3, took one and a half days. Don Lauria reported, 'The crux of the climb was trying to sleep through a Herbert tirade on the bivouac. It began about midnight during some snow flurries. "Wake up! Hey, you guys, wake up! Hennek, kick that damn Limey! Is everybody awake? I've actually been sleeping. This is the first time I've ever slept on [sic] a bivouac. Hennek, kick that rotten Limey!"'[9]

The Scotts left Yosemite briefly during a snowfall. On their return, Scott put up a number of shorter climbs, such as *Lost Arrow Spire* (III 5.5 A3 or 5.10 A2) with Andy Embick, 'various roof climbs' with Paul Sibley and *Reed's Pinnacle* (5.9) with George Homer.

At this point, Chouinard introduced Scott to Peter Habeler, a young Austrian guide with a magnificent climbing career ahead of him. He and Scott became lifelong friends. After joining forces to climb *Leaning Tower*, a strenuous three-day, 210m compatibility test, they decided on climbing the *Salathé Wall* of El Capitan, one of the hardest climbs in the world at the time.[10] Habeler recalls:

> Doug and I were on fire; there was nothing else on our minds. We got the special gear, hardware made by Yvon Chouinard in Ventura, food and water for three to four days and started. Very soon I realized what an incredibly strong and competent climber Doug was. (We had worked out I would lead the hard free climb pitches and Doug would do the artificial, nailing parts on the face.)
>
> On the Salathé route I remember Doug was a bit slow. The hauling bag was a real hassle, making things so much harder. It got stuck again and again. Of course, we had to use our hardware; there were almost no pitons on the face. Being very light (57 kg!), I drove our pegs in really lightly. They were safe on my weight . . . Doug, a heavier guy (85kg?) was complaining about that, yelling at me, 'Bloody Austrian! Get the pegs in better! You are going to kill us!' Of course, there was humour in his words as well.
>
> As we got higher on the face, we became happier and finally we really got to like each other. The Salathé was one of my real highlights.[11]

The *Salathé Wall* (VI, 5.13 or 5.9 C2; 884m; 35 pitches) is long and arduous.[12] Scott confirms that it began with the participants not getting on: 'He wouldn't stop moaning – about the haul moving too slowly, about my hitting the pegs too hard, and then about my moving too slowly up the free climbing, all of which was true enough . . . Then he was very fastidious: he would take boiled eggs out of a plastic container and slices of bread and butter from his snap tin.[13] And then I found he had put salt into the four gallons of water to stop us getting cramp!'

On the second day, their relationship improved as their fears diminished. An exchange on the use of cameras ('to rest is not to rust') helped. By the second evening, at their bivouac on top of El Capitan Spire, they enjoyed each other's company 'in true communion': Scott's religious expression shows a new emotional state developing. The haul-weight was diminishing while the friction, as the ground steepened, became less tiresome. On the third day, Scott's anxieties having greatly diminished, he had time to observe a frog hopping down a crack at the back of a belay ledge: 'It set me wondering how it could survive in this vertical desert . . . I felt good up there because of that frog; he seemed to know that we were all in it together – not just the El Cap scene but the whole business of being alive. I looked around with a new intensity . . . I was thinking and experiencing all the elements of joy and peace to such a degree that tears welled up . . .'[14]

This ecstatic moment evinced a kind of crypto-Gaia outlook: Scott could sense that concerns about our environment would perforce lead to global rather than national solutions.

Their painful hands were now bleeding horribly. They reached their final bivouac on the Sous le Toit ('Under the Roof') ledge. The final day's climb involved gazing vertically almost 900m to the forest below. Having traversed the overhang, Habeler led 'in good style' through wide cracks in the head-wall. By evening, they had succeeded in being the first non-American rope to climb this fearsome route.

Scott experienced on the top another of those Wordsworthian 'spots of time' moments of complete contentment and detachment from personal concerns: 'I saw for the first time the full range of subtle, mellow colours in that evening light. The wind-scalloped surface of lingering snow-patches twinkled like jewels in the fading light and all to the east the peaks of the High Sierra were pink above a purple haze [!] of forested valleys. Something enabled me to discern colours where before I had only seen one. I stood . . . hoping this beautiful experience would never end.'[15]

Scott goes on to contrast these feelings with those of the 'day trippers' in the valley, many of whom relied on artificial stimuli and were ignorant of the emotional and perceptual intensification arising from hard climbing.

Nor was it just the frog which had set Scott thinking. Jan and he had looked at the giant sequoias in Yosemite's Mariposa Grove; their magnificence impressed him greatly. While he had enjoyed climbing on trees as a child, the awesome beauty of these redwoods, which even Governor Ronald Reagan had prevented from being despoiled by a proposed motorway, compounded his lifelong interest in trees. He recognised the immense importance of the environmental pioneer John Muir (1838–1914), one of the earliest advocates for the preservation of wilderness (including a quasi-religious appreciation of it). Scott consequently returned to the UK 'relaxed, with a new zest and enthusiasm'.[16] He had 'arrived' as a climber of international renown.

Only a couple of months later, Scott headed for Norway, to Europe's highest cliffs at Romsdal, to try *Høibakk's Chimney* on the Søndre Trolltind (1788m). On their way, Guy Lee was delayed in Newcastle; Scott and Ted Wells had gone ahead and scrounged a lift from Bergen from Ned Newton. Scott pestered Newton to let him drive; they hit a bus head-on. Newton's Austin consequently needed a new radiator. When Lee caught up with Scott and Ted Wells, Scott gave Lee the defensively cheery assurance, 'Good as new!' after having panel-beaten the car's crumpled wings with a piton-hammer.

The Troll Wall rises in three steep sections above the scree which slides into the valley floor. (The routes are now much altered because of erosion and rockfall.) Tony Howard, Bill Tweedale and John Amatt had made the first British ascent of the Troll Wall only six years before. Scott and Ted Wells began, between storms, on the Adelsfjell, *South-East Cracks* (VI -), a 500m first ascent on 13 August 1970: they completed the route in nine hours. The route followed the left buttress of a shallow couloir near the top of the south-east side of the peak. The crack offered good VS free climbing with only 3m of aid at the base of the wall. On Søndre Trolltinden (The Other Troll Wall), Niall Lockwood and Lee made the second ascent of *Høibakk's Kamin (Chimney)* (A3) in thirteen hours on 24 August; they went on to the Søndre summit, thus ascending the whole peak. They were followed next day by Scott and Terry Bolger, in eleven hours. The route, a highly varied (grass, amphitheatres, chockstones, cracks) natural drain for melting snow, was descended in eight abseils of 150m. At the top, the pair had bivouacked miserably in a storm, with only two anoraks for protection; Bolger was suffering from exposure and had to be lowered, an extremely arduous task.

Scott and Jeff Upton, with Guy Lee and Ted Wells, then completed the *Rimmon Route* of the Troll Wall in an astonishing seventeen hours on 20–21 August. Scott describes the route as 'wonderfully varied', with cracks, walls and slabs. Much of the route was climbed free, thanks to the party's fitness and experience.

Again, Scott reflected on environmental concerns, for example on landscape changes wrought by nearby hydro-electricity construction. When writing up the climb, Scott stressed (quoting the Norwegian mountaineer Carl Rubenson) the human need to feel at home in nature, the need which drives city people out to sea, into the forest and up mountains.

⁓

Writing for journals at this time led to local contacts who could open up exciting new places. An article on Baffin in an old edition of *Mountain World* caught his attention. A further stimulus for the Baffin trip came in winter, 1969: Scott had commandeered a derelict house in Rothiemurchus, in the Cairngorms (until the estate evicted him). While climbing there – he put up the new *Chute Route* (V5) on Cairn Lochan on 24 December – he met Rob Wood in a pub after Wood's lecture on the first British ascent of *The Nose* on El Capitan. Wood's sister attended Montreal's McGill University. She and her brother contacted Pat Baird, probably the greatest living expert on Baffin Island, who was the director of the Canadian Arctic Institute at Montreal. Preparations began for the first of four visits between 1971 and 1976 to the vast 'sawn off chimney stacks' of Baffin Island.

To prepare, a minivan of NCC members, plus Jan and Michael, reached the Pyrenees in spring, 1971. The object was to climb routes on the little-visited, at least by British climbers, south face of Tozal del Mallo (2280m), although only one first ascent, requiring a snowy ledge bivouac, was completed. In the climbers' absence, bears ravaged their campsite and scattered granola bars, perhaps attracted by the honey.

For Scott, Baffin represented two steps into the unknown. His application for two months' leave from teaching was rejected. He therefore decided to leave teaching, which he did with Jan's support, to become a professional mountaineer, an adventurous decision. To raise income more immediately, however, he and his youngest brother Garry, at the time studying civil engineering at Nottingham University, joined forces as S & S Builders: Scott loved building, whether at his homes, at Samye Ling or in Nepal.

The intention on Baffin was to replicate the relatively intimate, spontaneous conditions of the Čilo Daği or Hindu Kush expeditions, in contrast to the media-friendly siege-style expeditions then prevalent. Raising funds

was hard work. While the MEF contributed £100, Scott managed to persuade his local John Player's cigarette factory to part with £500, unlimited
cigarettes and the money for a film, to be made by Mick Burke. The seven
members (Scott, Wood, Gillies, Lee, Steve 'Sid' Smith, Hennek and Phil
Koch) contributed £500 each (about £5,400 at today's prices).

They set off in July 1971. From Montreal, where Scott met Baird, Hennek
and Koch, they flew to Frobisher Bay (now Iqualit), on Baffin Island's
southern extremity. A Twin Otter then flew them north to Pangnirtung
Fjord, the starting point for Mount Asgard (2015m). To Scott's disappointment, the Inuit appeared thoroughly Westernised, although they eventually
made a profound impression on him.[17] He admired their hospitality, their
good humour in the face of trying environmental conditions and the simplicity of their everyday lives. He refers to his preference for the Inuit
returning to their 'old ways', particularly their extended family support
system, rather than rely on government welfare, a conservative-Romantic
position not untypical of Scott's hope for many indigenous peoples.

The party proceeded up the fjord by canoe and on foot. The canoeists
were forced by ice to land. Their packs now weighed a punitive forty-five
kilograms. (A helicopter organised by Pat Baird had already flown in heavy
equipment to Base Camp.) Eventually, on this highly punishing, marshy
trek, where they averaged less than two kilometres an hour, they reached
base camp at the head of Weasel Valley, near Crater Lake, about seventy
kilometres from Pangnirtung. Everyone was strongly impressed by the
variety of local plant, bird and animal life and by the towering mountains,
shaped like spires and cylinders, many named after the gods of Norse
mythology.

During their first week, Baird, Wood and Smith climbed twin summits overlooking base camp. Hennek and Scott climbed two 2000m
peaks south of Mount Asgard. Scott was evolving his own acclimatisation
method of ascending lower peaks near base camp. A violent storm prevented further exploration, and so a long period of reading, boredom and
overanimated discussion, mainly about matters political and ecological,
set in. When the sun returned, after a fortnight, so did the mosquitos.
They then focused on the vast red granite faces of Asgard. Wood reports
that Scott had become rather restless and 'ratty', as the expedition had
been sponsored to climb Asgard but had been prevented by the bad
weather. While Lee and Koch disappeared to attempt the 600m north
face of Breidablik (1650m), on which they succeeded in making its first
ascent, Scott and the others tackled the east face of Freya Peak (1831m), a

1000m mix of slabs and a headwall to a point they named Killabuk. The slabs were graded 5.7; these and the headwall turned out to be harder than expected. Food and equipment were in short supply. Debate followed; Hennek memorably declared, to general agreement, 'Why don't we just go up and have ourselves an adventure?!'

By evening, the headwall would not 'give' without a pendulum move to better cracks on about fifty metres of rope. A miserably cold bivouac followed. Next morning, they found themselves on an overhang. Scott tried not to notice the void beneath him. With persistence, they made their way up red granite chimneys, occasionally in the sun. A wide terrace led to a final wall of two pitches, then the summit, twenty hours after setting out. They dropped on long abseils to the Caribou Glacier and so to base camp. Shortly after, Lee and Koch returned. They too had succeeded, but only after eighteen pitches of 'pegging and hard free climbing'.

Ten days remained. Mick Burke's film, thanks to a brief weather window and Scott, Wood and Hennek repeating Lee and Koch's ascent of Breidablik, was in the can.[18] All that remained was an ascent of Asgard. Fiercely bad weather arrived during preparations. Frustrations grew; they moved up to Summit Lake, to eat 'a large quantity of chocolate bars'. Wood points out that it was Scott who consumed much of the chocolate when the others were absent. (Scott notoriously gobbled Mars Bars destined for others while climbing at Stanage.) Koch, Wood and Lee headed for King's Parade Glacier and climbed Asgard's south peak, a new route and first ascent. They endured an 'epic' descent in a full-blown blizzard, this same bad weather preventing Scott and the others from reaching Asgard's north peak.

The helicopter was still stationed at Pangnirtung. Scott and Wood decided to run the seventy kilometres there to get it to fly out the remaining kit. A food cache on the way had been rifled (innocently) by a trekker: all that remained was a tin of corned beef. Wood decided to cut the can into three, but Scott tried to bag the extra slice for himself. 'Wood was incensed,' says Scott, but eventually forgave him.

Return to the UK was made via the Shawangunks – the 'Gunks. A happy rendezvous with Lee and Hennek became a long, alcoholic evening listening to a bluegrass band in Burlington, Vermont. They slept, uninvited, in a derelict house. The owner caught Scott cooking chips on the verandah. When he challenged Scott, the answer came, 'That's what we do in England.' Next day, in unaccustomed heat on the crag, they made friends with some of the Vulgarians. Dick Williams allowed Scott to camp in his back yard for a few nights. Elaine Matthews recalls one climb: '*Broken Sling*, which has a very slippery start. I led it and was starting to belay Doug but he wouldn't do the start without tension because he was afraid of hurting an ankle and jeopardizing his next adventure.'[19] (*Broken Sling* is 5.8, in two pitches totalling 42m.) American hospitality and outgoingness, with Jim McCarthy and John Stannard turning up to point out routes of interest, made a strong impression on the impecunious Scott.

A few weeks after the unhappy Herligkoffer 'European' expedition to Everest in the spring of 1972, Scott returned to Baffin in June, this time with Hennek, Paul Nunn and Tut Braithwaite. Hennek was praised for his outstanding organisation of food and equipment. A sled-boat carried them for thirty kilometres to the head of the frozen fjord. Their sacks were even heavier this time, weighing in at sixty kilograms each. It took two days to cover the forty kilometres to the 1971 base camp because, as Scott explains, 'We reached Summit Lake after two awful days, falling into slushy snow, bogs and cold, turbulent side-streams, after doing considerable damage to our Achilles tendons and knee-joints.'[20]

The team, which had bonded well, then proceeded to an advance base at a glacial lake below Asgard, after two carries of food and equipment. Braithwaite and Nunn led the way strongly up the west face, on unconsolidated snow where protection was difficult to find. Hennek and Scott took over but were defeated quite high up by 20m of blank rock. They then tried the east side, up a 1200m pillar then headwall to the strangely flat summit of Asgard's north peak. The granite was 'the finest a climber could wish for'. Again, Braithwaite and Nunn led their 50 per cent of the route. The crux pitch on the headwall is now graded 5.11. Scott climbed the final pitch and reached the summit after thirty hours of climbing. Unfortunately, the view included a sight of their tents surrounded by meltwater. The descent took a whole day before they reached their snowshoes cached on the King's Parade Glacier. The return to Pangnirtung was spread over five days, most of it without food.

This long-distance husband collected Jan and Michael at Montreal, with the intention of driving to California with Dennis Hennek. The road journey included a stopover in Wyoming at the magnificent Tetons, where Hennek and Scott climbed the Devil's Tower, a large, truncated pillar, now a National Monument, with an approximate climbing difficulty of 5.7. Scott does not explain why they 'ran the gauntlet of the park rangers'; perhaps they were climbing during statutory seasonal closures designed to show respect for Native American cultural sensibilities. During the trip, when visiting the home of Dez and Ann Hadlum in Colorado, Jan discovered she was pregnant. Celebrating this event was scarcely possible as Scott had to leave very soon for his second Everest expedition that year.

March 1973 had been spent in Nottingham, where Jan had given birth, with some difficulty, to Martha. A month later, however, Scott had relinquished nappy-changing for Yosemite, this time accompanied by the irrepressible Ken Wilson.

Here, Scott first teamed up with Rick White, a top Australian climber who had recently put up some extremely hard new routes. (Scott often climbed with whoever he deemed suitable on the spot.) With thirty-five litres of water, a hammer, a few pegs and a large rack of nuts, they set off up *The Nose* (Grade VI, 880m) on El Capitan. They climbed mostly aid-free for 300m, hands often deep in cracks, on warm, sunny rock. They extracted water from cacti growing in the cracks. They placed altogether only fifteen pegs, although they did use the ladders and bolts already in place. Using nuts only for protection or aid, they climbed more than half the route free, thus making a useful contribution towards establishing 'clean' climbing.

This American trip continued with a visit to Estes Park, in Colorado, and the first meeting with Steve Komito, the charming, hospitable bootmaker. Here, he was introduced to Michael Covington, a highly gifted musician who eventually became a recluse. While at Estes Park, Scott climbed several routes on the Twin Owls with Doug Snively and Billy Westbay, two outstanding climbers who were in the process, like many others, of throwing away their hammers. From Estes Park, Wilson and Scott proceeded to Boulder then to Seattle, where Scott was to lecture to the American Alpine Club, a confirmation of his international reputation. In the nearby Cascades range, he climbed the steep granite cracks of the Index crags (highest point: 390m) and enjoyed bouldering on the edge of the forest. The trip ended with Scott and Wilson parting in rather bad-tempered circumstances: the ego-friction from spending too much time in each other's company led to a temporary rift.

Scott's enthusiasm for the fantastical Baffin Island was undiminished: he returned for a third time in 1973, indeed only five weeks after the end of his American odyssey. The expedition appears to have been sponsored by a company making paper Y-fronts, although complimentary supplies of these were lost during a river-crossing. Snowmobiles made shorter and much easier work of the journey up the fjord. A productive but quietly unpublicised time followed: Scott, Clive Davies, Tut Braithwaite and

Dr Mike Webster headed for the Mount Turnweather (1765m) area: here, they walked and scrambled over a dozen (unnamed) peaks. Scott, Webster and Hennek then attempted the central pillar of Overlord Peak (1480m) where Scott managed to pull out a rock which hit Mike Webster squarely on his crash helmet, causing considerable damage to his skull. The doctor, however, effected repairs. After this event, Scott, Braithwaite and Davies took a look at the 700m buttresses of the north face of Mount Turnweather but decided, because of loose flakes at critical positions, to avoid them. Otherwise, the trip was enlivened first by Scott disappearing into a crevasse while peeing; a cry of 'Help!' revealed only a pair of hands at the crevasse's lip; his disappearance was prevented by his snowshoes. The party also met a mysterious lone trekker who later wrote about his encounter with Scott and his party. He is known only by his pen name, given to him by the Scott party, of *En Solitaire*.[21]

In 1976, Scott, with Guy Lee, Dennis Hennek and Geoff and Elaine Brook, visited Baffin Island for the fourth and final time. Scott does not write about it in his books or in the usual journals or magazines. The party aimed for Mount Turnweather, using skidoos and kayaks, but found mostly bad weather and bad rock. Scott and Hennek climbed Baffin Fjord peak. Snowshoes were used extensively. Scott was following up on his 1973 policy of leaving only a few cairns and no publicity. As he had somewhat flirtatiously noted in the *Alpine Journal* for 1974, 'Anyone going to this area is guaranteed a good time with the possibility of making many first ascents, but the peak may have been climbed before!' However, a good time could still be had by one and all now and in the future, providing no sign is left by previous parties. Scott's 'good times' on big walls were about to be extended across three continents.

Changabang, Yosemite, Denali, East Africa and Mount Waddington

'Doug was a star but didn't behave like one.'
– Anonymous

Scott's next 'great wall', Changabang (6864m), the 'Shining Mountain', in the Garhwal, India, has been written about extensively. Well-illustrated and -written accounts of this 1974 climb came from Chris Bonington in *Changabang* and *The Everest Years*, by Martin Boysen in *Hanging On* and by Scott himself in *Up and About* and *Himalayan Climber*.[22]

To get behind the Indian 'inner line', a defence mechanism set up after the 1962 Chinese incursions, Bonington had agreed to a joint Anglo-Indian expedition. From the UK, he invited Scott, Dougal Haston and Martin Boysen. Scott had already been enthused before Bonington's invitation through reading lyrical descriptions of Changabang's 1500m spire of pale granite by Tom Longstaff and W.H. Murray in *The Evidence of Things Not Seen*: 'A vast eye tooth of milk-white granite . . . seemingly as fragile as an icicle; a product of earth and air and sky rare and fantastic, and of liveliness unparalleled . . .'

From ITN, they were joined by Alan Hankinson. The Indian party was led by Colonel Balwant 'Balu' Sandhu (1934–2010). He and Tashi Chewang Sherpa also reached the summit in this startlingly successful expedition. Sandhu's second, Captain Kiran Kumar, became the expedition's only casualty when, on losing his ice-axe while trying to cross the Shipton Col, he attempted a simulated parachute jump landing technique but rolled a considerable distance and put his shoulder out. The final member was Ujagar Singh, whom Scott did not get to know well, largely through lack of a common language. One of the Sherpas, Norbu, caught Scott's interest through his connections with pre-war expedition greats such as Dyhrenfurth, Ruttledge and Tilman. The participants concurred that this was an unusually happy expedition, perhaps because of its size and lack of sponsorship pressure. Other constructive factors were having to co-operate with the Indians (if future permissions were to be obtained), although Scott and others all write about how much they enjoyed the Indians' company; most of the climbers, moreover, already knew each other; perhaps even the unusual beauty of the Nanda Devi Sanctuary surroundings affected morale positively.

The party assembled in Delhi. The usual bureaucratic problems and a departure misunderstanding followed. Using an expedition lorry instead of their missed bus, they trundled through Haridwar to the Alpine scenery of Rishikesh, to reach the pilgrim centre at Joshimath. Problems arose in finding sufficient porters: 100 goats were hired, generating more difficulties than anything else. An early tussle did occur between Scott and Bonington concerning Bonington's man-management methods, but it was quite quickly resolved, though it was not the last growl between these two during their long friendship. Some of the porters were poorly clad road-workers who suffered during an early snowfall. With characteristic generosity, Scott lent his sleeping-bag to one of them, only to discover too late on its return that it was infested with lice. From Joshimath, the party trekked through flower-filled meadows and over rock bands to the Ramani Glacier.

The original plan had been to climb the west face. However, it was assessed as too difficult, so the party crossed from the Ramani Glacier via the awkward Shipton Col (fixed ropes by Scott and Boysen) just south of Changabang to a camp below the south-east face at 5300m, at the head of the Changabang Glacier.

Scott climbed for much of the time with Dougal Haston, a partnership which would bring lasting fame on Everest the following year. They understood each other through grunted shared intuitions. Their characters were more complementary than similar. Bonington shrewdly observed, 'Doug: undisciplined, warm-hearted and emotional, full of a vast, restless energy. Dougal: cool, analytical and taciturn. Yet both had in common a huge appetite for hard climbing and exceptional endurance and a love for the mountains.'

At their base above the Changabang Glacier they endured a few days of bad weather before the summit party started by moonlight on 2 June. After several ice-walls, a higher camp was established at about 6400m, followed by a rest day. On 4 June, they reached the East Ridge between Changabang and Kalanka. The ridge was long, corniced and exposed. After twenty rope-lengths, however, they arrived at the first summit, around 4 p.m. The mist cleared to reveal a slightly higher summit. Straws were drawn and the topmost summit was soon reached by Scott and Haston. From there, they could see the others abseiling on the descent, with Bonington taking photos. The weather changed; Scott was overcome by the mystery of a patchwork of sun and dark blue cloud over the unknown land of Tibet.

Scott needed to leave rather hurriedly, however, as he was heading for the Russian Pamirs to join the ill-fated Soviet International Camp at the base of Pik Lenin. On the way out, he managed to talk his way into the forbidden area of Badrinath. Here, he was taken off by the secret service (he says) to the local jail for questioning but was soon released (despite having been asked by the British Embassy to note military installations). Of much greater significance was the time he spent with a porter on the walk-out. He ate the porters' food, smoked their *bidis* (his first cigarette since he was twelve, he claims) and lived for a few days in their village. He enjoyed his time out of the company of Westerners. It was a pivotal moment in the development of Scott's long relationship with indigenous peoples.

After Changabang, further climbing and lecture trips to the United States ensued in 1975. From early to mid-March, Scott lectured in the

Boston area; on 26 March he arrived in Denver for more lectures; here, he met Molly Higgins – they had already begun an affair in England after first meeting in the Pamirs in 1974. Leaving Higgins rather unchivalrously (albeit temporarily), Scott then met Mike Covington. They travelled to Estes Park. After being defeated on the *Diamond* on Long's Peak by high winds – an ambitious 270m face climb all above 4000m – he opted for Taylor Peak (4012m) in the Front Range, in north central Colorado. He tackled the east face with Covington and Doug Snively. This turned out to be quite a complex though finally successful climb up ramps and snowfields in deep spring snow. From there, he moved to the Eastern Sierra with Dennis Hennek and Rick Ridgeway; they attempted a new route on the *Keeler Needle* (4346m), cut short after Ridgeway fell the length of several pegs then over an overhang, fortunately without the ropes severing. As Ridgeway points out, this attempt was on a new route in winter.

Ridgeway did not climb again with Scott. He remembers, however, stopping at a locals' bar in Lone Pine, the last town on the way to Keeler Needle: 'Doug was seated between Dennis and me at the bar, each of us having a beer. Behind the bar stood a life-sized, very realistic wood carving of an Indian chief. After a few minutes Doug nodded his head toward the wooden Indian and said, "Stoic buggers, aren't they?"'

The climbing continued in Yosemite: *Meat Grinder* (E2 5c), an unusually tough, hand-tearing gritstone route finishing on a 30m corner crack was completed with John Long. Scott then led *Little Wing* (5.11, possibly the technically hardest route he ever climbed, though he does not say who he climbed it with: the route had been suggested by Jim Bridwell). From there, Scott moved to San Francisco, where he was reunited with Higgins: they returned to Yosemite to climb, among other routes, *Outer Limits* (5.10c) and *Midterm* (5.10b, 39m) on Arch Rock, and *Anathema* (5.10a) on Cookie Cliff, as well as *Plumkin* on Last Resort Cliff. None of these climbs constituted a big wall, but they were very testing and should probably be seen in association with Scott's genuine, long big-wall climbs as a means of maintaining fitness and improving technical competence.

Scott's lengthy stay continued: he lectured at Modesto, Fresno, Los Angeles and Ventura. From Arizona, he continued to Utah, Idaho, Vancouver and Portland. In Vancouver, Scott met Rob Wood, with whom he hatched a plan to climb Mount Waddington, arguably the last of Scott's big walls, which they carried out in 1978. Scott then returned via Minneapolis to New York and home in early May, to conclude a very demanding tour, equally tough on Jan, who was having to hold down a tiring job and bring up two very bright young children.

∞

Scott left Nottingham very soon after his return for The Ogre 'recce' on Sosbun Brakk (6413m), in the Karakoram, which failed in bad weather. He returned to Nottingham in early July, to spend only about three weeks with Jan and his children before leaving for Everest and the first of the three defining moments of his mountaineering life. This colossal expedition was time-consuming at every stage.

Meanwhile, Scott and Haston planned to put a new route up the massive south face of Alaska's Mount McKinley (6190m), as it was then known. (President Barack Obama officially designated it Denali in 2016, coincident with the American National Parks' Service 100th anniversary.) The idea of climbing this face might have originated with the great American climber Arlene Blum, whom Scott had met in the Pamirs and stayed with while on his 1975 US lecture tour: in 1970, Blum had been deputy then leader of the first all-female ascent of Denali. In *Mountain*, however, Scott, wrote in his wry way that he chose Alaska because he was tired of Himalayan bureaucracy, expensive South American flights and New Guinea jungle logistics.[23]

Having taken advice and looked at photos from Denali's *éminence grise*, Bradford Washburn, they planned a line between the *Cassin* and *Direct Routes* of the 3000m south face. There would be no fixed ropes. Denali is one of the coldest high mountains on Earth, but its unenviable reputation was forgotten when Scott and Haston landed in a light ski-plane from Anchorage on 29 April. They trekked up the Kahiltna Glacier for about twenty-seven kilometres, with Haston on skis and Scott wearing snow-shoes, to the base of the south face. Other British and Japanese teams had already arrived. They were soon hit by one of Denali's notoriously sudden, violent storms.

Scott and Haston followed the *Direct Route* to about half its height before striking out on their own. The ascent plan was to allow the leader to climb freely (usually on a fifty-five-degree slope of powder snow covering hard ice), then haul up their heavy sack on a separate rope while the second jumared up the first rope. Their first night on a ledge was interrupted by snowslides and large avalanches roaring down the main couloir, uneasily traversed on the second day. In their second freezing bivouac, in swirling snow, thoughts of descent (they were less than halfway up) were dismissed because, despite everything, they had enjoyed the climbing: 'physically and mentally team form was high'. Haston asked Scott, 'Are you frost-bitten yet?' Scott's answer – 'No' – gave them their reason to continue.

On the third day, a vast icefield had to be arduously traversed, with constant windslab avalanche danger and many hidden crevasses. Then, the weather suddenly changed to clear skies, allowing views of a vast wilderness. Yet another miserable night in a snow-cave followed. High expectations of reaching the summit were dashed by having to negotiate a seemingly endless fifty-five-degree ice-slope. Then the storms returned; all their Himalayan experience was necessary to survive. They reached a snow-hole near the summit: the night was uncomfortable because they had climbed too fast. Next morning, 12 May, they scuttled up to the summit, in the hope of a quick descent.

The downward route led to Archdeacon's Tower, where, to their horror, they met two hypothermic young climbers. Their eight companions could not be found where they were said to be, at the Denali Pass at 5550m. Four members of this party were discovered 300m below the Pass. Two left to rescue their hypothermic companions. Scott and Haston only met the remaining four lower down the mountain, by evening. A Park Service helicopter was summoned but could not attain the necessary altitude. After eight hours' sleep, Scott and Haston, with superhuman strength, re-ascended to above 5000m to assist in the rescue. There, all the climbers were found, one badly frostbitten. Next morning, after Scott and Haston had accompanied the climbers down to about 4250m, four were evacuated by helicopter. The two original climbers lost most of their extremities, the awful effect of 'summit fever' clouding proper judgment. The party was composed of Christians, testing their faith. They said that their rescue was the result of divine providence. Scott's understandable response was, 'We just told them they had been bloody lucky.' Scott suggested that the well-equipped Park Service lulls climbers into a false sense of security. As ever, Scott believed most strongly in self-reliance and thoughtfully acquired experience.

Summer 1976 saw Scott, ever eager for a change of scene, back in Africa for the first time in eleven years. He was accompanied by Tut Braithwaite, a friendship which went back to meeting in a pub in Grassington, near Kilnsey, in 1966. The official account of this four-week trip is plain enough. They achieved 'a new direct route up the north-east face of the *Grey Pillar* (ED) (North face of Mount Kenya) in fifteen hours with one bivouac. They later climbed the *Diamond Couloir* via the head wall and continued to the Gate of Mists, then on to Batian, descending by Nelion and the Shipton Route in fourteen hours.'[24]

With local 'hard man' (as Scott calls him) Ian Howell, they climbed the classic route on Hell's Gate, *Olympian* (E1, 190m). Scott free-climbed it. After these climbs, Scott met Iain Allan, one of Kenya's climbing pioneers. In a *Memoir* of his life and times, Allan says, 'I had never before met a climber so famous, and I was terrified . . . He turned out to be the gentlest, most approachable climber I had ever met. Although Scott and Braithwaite's principal objective was the *Diamond Couloir*, I was lucky enough to put up two new routes on the *Main Wall* at Hell's Gate with them. They both then went on to climb a major new route on Mount Kenya, as well as the *Diamond Couloir* by way of Chouinard's direct Headwall. These achievements were gloriously written up in *Mountain . . .*'

During this expedition, Scott and Braithwaite also climbed the lava-based *Breach Wall*, not a long route, on Kilimanjaro.

In 1975, Scott had met his old climbing companion Rob Wood in Vancouver, where they had discussed a plan to climb Mount Waddington (4019m), once known as the 'Mystery Mountain'.[25] However, Everest and its aftermath, followed by The Ogre and the long recovery period after the famous descent, intervened, so it was not until 1978 that they were ready to set out.

Scott arrived in April 1978 at the Woods' home. At a bar in nearby Squamish, Scott distinguished himself in a game called 'boat racing', as Rob Wood relates: 'Beer was served in half pint glasses. The contest started each with one full glass in hand on the table. At "Go", the first to swig the beer down and stomp the empty glass back on the table wins. When the local champion leaned his head back for maximum flow he failed to notice that Doug had quickly taken his full glass out of sight on his knee while his other hand grabbed an empty glass and plonked it down on the table instead. The young macho dude was so surprised he ignominiously choked and spurted the last half of his beer all down his jacket, the table and floor.'

Even reaching the foot of the 2100m north-east face of Mount Waddington was an adventure. In the Woods' boat they reached the top of Bute Inlet, where they were hospitably received ('roast venison, home baking and all the booze we could handle') by some hand-loggers. They then proceeded by motorboat to Homathko Estuary. From there, they hitched for forty kilometres on an empty logging truck to Scar Creek, a logging camp where they were again wined and dined. A shorter road journey then led into a granite gorge. This obstacle required 'a tough bush-whack' to reach its far end; the party was perhaps the first to explore it since pioneering times in the nineteenth century. A band of cliffs, 600m high, had to be negotiated. Five days of stumbling over boulders, past clifflets and through lush virgin forest were needed to reach base camp near the head of the long Tiedemann Glacier at about 1900m.

The plan was to make another Alpine-style ascent in three days. The snow proved wet and deep, however, so two snow-caves were needed. On the third day, despite jettisoning most of their gear, they had reached only the foot of the final tower by nightfall. They had to dig into a crevasse, without much food and no stoves or sleeping bags. A storm broke. Scott kept the party's spirits up with tales of dreadful hardship in the Himalaya. In the morning, the others descended; Scott and Wood continued. Wood climbed an icy rock-chimney towards a patch of blue. He felt increasingly uncertain of his strength and perceptions and found his dream-like state compromised by piercing pain, agonised breathing and a desperate wish to rest. The exposure near the summit was formidable. At the summit, they hugged. They could see their friends (there were nine in the party) as dots, making their way down to base. Descent was motivated by a sym-bolic ritual from their youth: 'Let's make a brew.'

From 1968 for ten years, Scott had put up some of the longest, hardest routes on some of the biggest mountain walls and faces anywhere. These achievements alone would be enough to guarantee his pre-eminence. At the same time, he had been climbing some of the highest mountains in the world, notably in the Himalaya and the Karakoram. He also continued to put up new routes in the UK, often in Scottish winter conditions, as well as in the US and the Alps. Some of his ascents were compromised by the demands of the siege-style expedition, although Alpine-style ascents occu-pied more and more of his time and interest. With his belief that he could survive pretty much anywhere, so did his interest in mountain explor-ation. The path to Everest, begun in 1972 and thus running in parallel with the climbs described above, led to twenty-five years of new routes and explorations of the highest order.

9

The Road to Everest, 1972–75

'Why don't we just go up and have ourselves an adventure?'

– Dennis Hennek

While climbing his big walls during the 1970s, Scott was also starting to experience the Earth's highest peaks. His three expeditions to Everest and to Pik Lenin, moreover, were generally in the siege style. From his thoughts in the Hindu Kush in 1967, Scott was already evolving his own brand of Alpine-style climbing; Everest and Pik Lenin confirmed his aversion to sieges and encouraged his plans for more collectively organised Alpine-style expeditions.

Scott did not spend much time at home. In late November 1968, for example, he and Brian 'Henry' Palmer drove to North Wales on three successive weekends. Rugby was played in Nottingham on Saturday mornings during the season, with South Wales in addition for rugby tours. Christmas was spent at home, but New Year usually led Scott to Scotland. In summer, when not away with the NCC, he was climbing hard routes with the Alpine Climbing Group. From 1971 onwards he would spend weeks away on lecture tours. He climbed occasionally in the Alps. The major expeditions meant weeks or months away from home. By the summer of 1968, Scott's marriage to Jan had run into real difficulties. But what was the alternative? Separation was punitively expensive; in any case, both mother and father tried and succeeded in being good parents to their children. Besides, in 1971, the Scotts had invested in their future by buying a house in Raleigh Street, Nottingham, which required an immense amount of work to do it up.

Garry worked on the renovation more or less full time with Douglas regularly being interrupted by planning his climbing exploits:

We often had to listen to Douglas's favourite song, 'American Pie', by Don McLean, which he played on a vinyl record player with the mechanical repeat function, much to some people's annoyance!

I remember American visitors at the time planning future climbing trips as we discussed the Watergate scandal and President Nixon's impeachment.

Douglas wasn't a big fan of ladders so when we were renovating the roof, I operated from the top while Douglas had ropes wrapped round the chimney stack, working his way down the roof towards me. Douglas very much picked up skills on the job.

Another job concerned a concrete garage base for the *Nottingham Evening Post* reporter David Lowe, when he moved to his new house. The ready mix was delivered; we started to barrow it in place when Douglas decided to go somewhere and left me for an indefinite period (before mobile phones of course!). I had to work very hard to get the concrete placed before it started to set! He just got back in time to help me level it off as that's a two-man job.

The house became a centre for many parties and 'happenings', sometimes involving some of the world's finest climbers. Life *chez* Scott was never dull.

In February 1972, Don Whillans phoned to ask if Scott wanted to join Dr Karl Herrligkoffer's mostly German(ic) expedition to Everest's south-west face. History suggested it was not a good idea to accept. A large, well-equipped Japanese expedition had recently failed on the face. Whillans had just gone through the acrimonious shambles of Norman Dyhrenfurth's 1970 'international' expedition, wrecked by nationalism, poor leadership and uncertain strategy. Whillans was wary of Herrligkoffer, who had litigiously fallen out with Hermann Buhl after Buhl's extraordinary 1953 solo ascent (the only 8000m peak first ascended solo) of Nanga Parbat. Herligkoffer, moreover, was now at loggerheads in the courts with Reinhold Messner after the 1970 Nanga Parbat expedition on which Messner's brother died. Finally, when Whillans visited Herrligkoffer for a briefing in late February, the leader was mostly too busy to see him. Scott collected much important equipment (oxygen sets, tents, sleeping bags, etc.) and drove them to Munich, where the Germans appeared uninterested. Scott says, 'They turned up for Everest dressed for the Alps.'

Scott's membership was considered for his likely ability in dealing with the Rock Band at around 8000m, the crux of the climb, although he had not previously thought about joining a large expedition. The prospect of him becoming an Everester, however, undoubtedly stimulated his wish for fame and motivated him. This expedition, followed by Bonington's two Everest attempts and the International Pamirs Meet in 1974, gave Scott much experience of high-altitude expeditions to assimilate.

Later in February, Herrligkoffer responded superficially to Scott, believing him a 'hippy': having left teaching the year before, Scott had thrown off his geeky, bespectacled youthful persona in favour of the John Lennon look by which he is perhaps best remembered. Whillans, however, responded that Scott's membership was a *sine qua non*: 'No Doug, no Don'. Herrligkoffer then tried to buy out both Whillans and Scott by offering Hamish MacInnes a 'special deal', to which the predictable answer was, 'No Don, no Doug, no Hamish'. Endless arguments and threats followed relating to personal financial contributions and to film/ TV rights (which MacInnes had organised); membership and expedition title disputes continued beyond departure in March.

A demanding scientific programme was included; the British contingent tended to ignore it in favour of climbing. In late March, when the three Britons arrived at base camp, the Germans thought they looked off-putting and scruffy. Clearing the Khumbu Icefall had already begun. Scott took some time to get over dysentery and headaches; MacInnes was preoccupied with the film equipment, while Whillans came up with the interesting complaint of vertigo (probably related to longstanding ear trouble). The British were consequently considered lazy. An Iranian member of the team, previously crossed off Herrligkoffer's list, then appeared and threatened to physically attack Herrligkoffer with his ice-axe: he had to be restrained. The base camp manager was obliged to retire with altitude sickness. His replacement from the German embassy died near base camp from pulmonary oedema: little systematic acclimatisation appears to have been planned.

Wider problems of acclimatisation occurred, reinforcing the British suspicion that Herrligkoffer had not understood the scale of the face. A lack of equipment for the Sherpas then provoked a strike, resolved by Whillans and Mr Pandy, the liaison officer. Herrligkoffer, however, took the extraordinary step of leaving by helicopter then flying to Munich to obtain the necessary Sherpa equipment.

The personal splits became worse. One of the Austrians, Felix Kuen, had taken a dislike to Whillans after their experiences on the Dyhrenfurth International Expedition. Kuen spent too much time leading in the hope of being a summiteer, to Scott's and Whillans's irritation. Problems arose with food distribution: it was sent up to the Western Cwm ad hoc, rather than organised as daily personal rations. Some sort of buffer zone of German climbers and Sherpas appeared to have been set up between the British and the Austrian lead climbers, who were, however, now tiring. The casualties mounted. International difficulties were exacerbated by a famous exchange: when Whillans was challenged by Kuen about a World Cup score, he reminded Kuen that Britain had beaten Germany twice at *its* national 'game'. Whillans also caused more personal outrage when Scott, who had done all the cooking for the pair, reminded Whillans that he wasn't his mother, eliciting the sarky reply, 'You're not one of these people who moans about a bit of cooking, are you?'

The British, now coming into their own, forged their way up to the high Camp V, helped by previously placed ropes. Disputes then arose about summiteers and supporters. The Austrians made a half-hearted attempt but were defeated by the cold. The expedition was called off.

Scott, abetted by Ken Wilson, analysed the failure in his lively article in *Mountain 23*: personality problems, weak leadership and poor organisation.[1] Bonington's mastery of such difficulties is praised (the article appeared after the Bonington autumn expedition). At this stage, Scott also conceded that a gigantic face like Everest south-west is logistically no place for a small expedition. He also realised that he was good at acclimatising and standing up to extreme cold at high altitude.

Scott's chance to join another large Everest expedition occurred in June, when Chris Bonington invited him to join his attempt on the south-west face in the autumn of 1972. Whillans, however, was excluded. Scott was upset by Bonington's decision, as were others, not least an embittered Whillans. Scott could understand the decision, however: Whillans was just too prickly and self-indulgent to be part of Bonington's kind of team.

The expedition met in Kathmandu in the last week of August. Scott rendered himself semi-paralysed by eating a hash cake at the Garden of Eden restaurant. Barney Rosedale, expedition doctor, and nurse Beth Burke ('quiet and efficient') stayed with him until joining the others a few days later. On the approach to base camp, Scott adopted the local habit of walking barefoot, a bad idea given the rough terrain. The thick skin thus acquired slewed off at base camp after a carry to Camp I, costing Scott climbing time.

At base camp, Scott recognised several Sherpas from the previous expedition. He did not care much for the 'officers and other ranks' treatment they received (something for which Hunt had been criticised in 1953); combined with his happy experience of briefly living the Sherpa life after Changabang in 1974, it set Scott thinking about the Sherpas' wellbeing, thoughts leading to Community Action Treks (CAT) being founded seventeen years later.

October saw the party established in the Western Cwm, the subject of many of Scott's magnificent photos. Attempts on the face were rebuffed by the wind and cold. Graham Tiso and Ang Dawa were injured (though they recovered quickly thanks to Rosedale's skill). Eventually, Camp V, the springboard for the Rock Band, was established by Scott and Mick Burke. Here, Scott slipped and fell but stopped himself with his bare hands. Burke wondered where he'd been. A dispute then arose with Bonington, who wanted the exhausted pair to establish Camp VI. Dave Bathgate and Nick Estcourt arrived in support. Scott set off with Estcourt to the Rock Band. They fixed 400 metres of rope to the Rock Band's base at around 8100m. Scott, disgruntled at being told what to do by his leader, then descended to Camp II. A row followed, during which Scott compared Bonington to Herrligkoffer, an intemperate, unfair jibe. Bonington suggested Scott should leave. Rosedale displayed his sunny disposition and diplomatic skills; everyone, with guilty feelings on both sides, calmed down. At Camp VI, where Scott and Burke, in support, caught up with Haston, an unclear discussion (because of the wind and altitude) followed about the merits of climbing the Rock Band by the left-hand gully. The outcome was a decision to go down. The knowledge gained of the terrain and weather was to prove valuable in 1975, as was the consolidating of relationships. Tales did surface, however, of punch-ups in the Western Cwm, in which Scott was not involved, while Rosedale's gently purposeful misdiagnosis of Chris Brasher's pins and needles as phlebitis instigated the rather intrusive Brasher's sudden departure.

The expedition concluded unhappily: a young Australian friend of Haston, Tony Tighe, had helped Beth Burke and Roberts at base camp. He had intended to walk through the Icefall to the Western Cwm. There, just below Camp I, a large *sérac* collapsed; he was buried under tons of ice.

The walkout to Lukla was relaxing and enjoyable. There, thanks to a Nottingham poultry farmer's generosity, Scott was met by Michael, who was already displaying an interest in climbing. Jan, at home and pregnant with Rosie, had to make do with Chris Brasher's reports.

Scott scribbled a poem about the expedition:

Hard-headed anti-heroes

Loving it, Hating it, Passing time

Snowing, blowing, growing cold

Too scared to holler, to speak, to whine

Heroes no longer at the end – covered

Heroes no longer at the end – overpowered.[2]

Afterwards, mutterings began in the climbing world about the expense and publicity involved, a debate exacerbated by the *modus operandi* of the 1975 expedition.

An entirely different funding system applied in 1974, when Scott joined the International Alpine Camp 'Pamir', at the foot of the Soviet Union's Pik Lenin (7134m). This camp involved 200 climbers from twelve countries, supposedly in the name of détente but actually as a showpiece for Soviet propaganda. It went badly wrong: thanks to a sequence of earthquakes and bad weather, fifteen people died in four incidents. The massiveness of Soviet government was pitched against Western individuality and personal self-expression. A competitive element was encouraged, the variation on a theme which ran through Scott's thinking from his earliest climbing days to sport climbing as an Olympic event.

The invitation to the Soviet Union had been engineered by Dennis Gray, who was by now General Secretary of the BMC. Scott, Lee, Braithwaite and Nunn had been intending to return to Baffin, accompanied by Clive Rowland and Gordon 'Speedy' Smith, but their curiosity about Soviet Russian climbing got the better of them.

Somehow, Speedy acquired everyone's rail tickets from Nottingham to Moscow. Tussles with authority began with the border guards in the Eastern bloc. In Moscow, at the tendentiously named Hotel Sputnik, the climbers were welcomed by Vitaly Abalakov (1906–86), the father of Soviet mountaineering, who had made the first ascent of Pik Lenin in 1934. His boastfulness about his strength and fitness did not go down well. A troubled stay in Moscow generated some trivial offences against authority: the stroppy British (there were separate Scottish and English teams) were showing their contempt for heavy-handed Soviet authoritarianism.

From Moscow, the party flew in an old Ilyushin to Osh, in Kyrgyzstan. A smaller aircraft was then used to reach Daraut Kurgan. Several bumpy hours in a lorry brought them to base camp in the Achik Tash valley on the north side of Pik Lenin at about 3660m. Further clashes with authority began when the Soviet 'Master of Sport' Yevgeniy (Eugene) Gippenreiter (1927–97) asked a resentful English team to send their leader to the opening flag-raising ceremony. The English team declining to nominate a leader, a member of the Scottish team raised the Union Flag for them. Later, this flag was replaced by a pair of red knickers (this 'meet' was, for some, an athletic celebration in more ways than one), to the Russians' annoyance, although the serious purpose was to mock the totalitarian Russian state expressed through the meet's regimented organisation.³ Further irritation was caused by the English wanting to send a different leader each time to leaders' conferences.

English idiosyncrasy further expressed itself through wanting to try a new route on Lenin's south-east face. To reach this area, they had to cross the 5800m Krylenko Pass. A difficult climb followed: 1500m of steep crust gave way to deep powder snow. Among the Americans following a similar route was Molly Higgins: her intense relationship with Doug started here. They descended the Saukdara Glacier with the Americans, who had similar route ambitions. Scott fell into a crevasse; when hauled out by Clive Rowland, he remarked, 'It's very pretty down there, lots of icicles and crystals.'⁴ Little was subsequently achieved; Nunn and Smith fell ill, necessitating a return over the Krylenko to base camp. The northern slope had avalanched. An American camp had been buried; a search revealed food and equipment but no bodies. Another American team had been avalanched on Peak Nineteenth Party Congress (6852m); Gary Ullin had been killed.

After a recovery at the well-supplied base camp, a request to move to Lenin's south side using vehicles was refused. A return was made to the Krylenko Pass so that a new route could be tried by the north-east ridge (Scott criticised the Russians for their lack of willingness to try new routes). With three Scottish climbers, each person led in rotation over rock steps and very deep snow. A well-fed night helped them through further deep snow to join the classic *Lipkin Route* high on the mountain above Camp III. They reached the end of this long route on the summit at 3 p.m. Lee and Braithwaite were photographed in humorous poses.

High on the descent they met a team of Russian women, ambitiously intent on the first all-female ascent and traverse of Pik Lenin. The weather was changing. Several people took ill on the way down the *Lipkin Route*. Most teams otherwise seemed to be progressing well. Next day, Scott and the others reached base camp. They were elated at reaching a high summit but unimpressed by the lack of technical challenge.

At base camp, Scott learnt that the avalanche which killed Ullin and five Estonians whom they had seen a few days earlier had been set off by an earthquake, a not infrequent hazard in that area.[5] A young Swiss woman had also died of hypothermia in the storm which had hit the English party while descending. The day after, reports came in that the Russian women's team was in trouble near the summit. Scott, Lee, Braithwaite, Rowland and the American Jeff Lowe, with four French climbers, formed a rescue party but could get no higher than 1500m below the stranded women, whose radio calls increased in desperation and pathos until their final call. Drinking deeply with Masters of Sport Kostya and Boris at Camp III that night, the men 'walked together on paths normally closed to strangers'. All eight women perished.

The closing ceremony was affected by Scott's anger: infuriated that a helicopter was unavailable to transport the rescue party some way up the mountain yet could fly in visiting dignitaries, Scott got drunk and tried to overturn a Russian police car, a pointless but understandable action which did his reputation no good. On the final morning, the English, Americans and Ullin's parents attended a moving memorial ceremony – after another small earthquake.

Scott, glad to get away, left Russia with an abhorrence of the bureaucratic regimentation of Soviet life. He analysed Soviet Russian climbing as constructively collective but inflexibly over-ambitious, considering their poor equipment and lack of high-altitude experience. Subsequently, a row broke out between the French and the Russians concerning the rescue mission, for which Scott provided a dispute-resolving statement.

∽

Permission had come through during the Changabang expedition for the Everest south-west face 1975 expedition. Bonington set about raising the vast sum needed. In December 1974, the whole team headed for the Alps, for a mass climb of the *Couturier Couloir* (D3, 900m) on the Aiguille Verte (4122m), to promote cohesion and to test clothing and equipment. Scott and Braithwaite headed off on Christmas Eve to climb the *Rébuffat Route* (TD+ 6a) on the Aiguille du Midi (3842m). A hurricane overtook them. Eventually, they reached the Aiguille du Midi *téléphérique* cabin door: Scott attempted to whack it open with his ice-axe until Braithwaite pointed out that it could be unbolted. They spent Christmas there, virtually without food, sleeping under the operatives' coats until the *téléphérique* arrived on Boxing Day. The rest of the team, celebrating in Chamonix, were suitably amused.

Before the team left for Everest, Scott furthered an ambition which had been fermenting since 1967, to visit the major peaks of the Karakoram, notably The Ogre.[6] He had enquired about permission in 1969. When permission became possible from the Pakistani government, Scott, Rob Wood, Ronnie Richards, Clive Rowland, Tony Watts and Bob Wilson made something of a mad dash in July to attempt Sosbun Brakk (6413m), lying on the west side of the Biafo Glacier but from where The Ogre can be plainly seen, as a kind of reconnaissance. They were constrained by time, as Scott had to leave for Everest in August.

An unusual journey followed, by flying Afghan Air to Kabul. The 'Shoestring Expedition' then took two taxis over the Khyber Pass to Peshawar followed by a bus to Rawalpindi. The party stayed with Colonel 'Buster' Goodwin, a retired Imperial Army officer with a passion for cheese. Bad weather meant a long delay before a flight to Skardu materialised. Cutting down on porters proved a bad decision: carrying extra weight meant most members were tired out by the time they reached Askole. Porters also attempted to steal previously cached gear – the theft was discovered and the ringleader was rewarded by Scott with a punch on the nose. Unusually deep snow prevented them reaching their objective. Using Rowland's previous local knowledge, however, they crossed the Biafo to the Baintha Lukpar Glacier, then followed the Uzun Brakk Glacier to an ideal base camp site. From some minor peaks they obtained an excellent close-up view of The Ogre. The prospect of climbing its 1000m granite pillar excited Scott greatly; he and Rowland pencilled in an attempt on The Ogre for 1977. Scott returned home for a few weeks with Jan and the family before leaving for Everest.

The south-west face suggestion was Scott's, although Bonington needed very little persuasion to move from his original intention of the normal route. The expedition was very well equipped thanks to munificent sponsorship by Barclays Bank, arranged almost effortlessly by Bonington.

This strong party left the UK on 29 July. On the walk-in Bonington decided to divide the large party, quite innocently, into 'A' and 'B' teams, the 'B' team naturally feeling slighted from then on.

In an interview with the BBC, Scott raised the leadership question: 'It's a very strong hierarchy set-up here and he [Bonington] is very much the leader. However much he might say he's the co-ordinator, he is the leader. It's just something within my nature and I suspect within Mick and one or two of the rest of us, that the shop-floor mentality develops. However hard you try to suppress it, it comes through.'

He grumblingly developed his comments: 'I wasn't always in complete sympathy with the leadership, but as soon as we had a role to play, it was fine . . . we worked as one and were fully behind Chris's decisions.'[7]

The walk-in otherwise remained largely enjoyable until at Kunde Scott persuaded Pertemba to hire a deaf and dumb boy, Mingma, whom he had first met in 1972 and had seen him maltreated by his parents. Reaching Gorak Shep, Braithwaite and Scott went to camp on nearby Kala Pattar, a trekking hillock which helps acclimatisation. Mingma helped with a carry to the camp, then made his way to base camp with a load for Scott. When Scott and Braithwaite arrived there next day, the boy had disappeared. While a search party was being organised, Bonington angrily blamed Scott for the boy's disappearance. A resentful Scott, despite the peacemaking efforts of expedition doctor Jim Duff, decided to leave the expedition. Soon, the boy's body was located in a stream: it was, apparently, an accident, a simple trip leading to drowning. For Bonington, this was an acutely painful reminder of the loss of his own son, Conrad, in a similar drowning accident in 1966, at a friend's house in Scotland. He showed great understanding in this terrible situation, expressing sympathy and withdrawing his accusation against Scott; the row blew over, although it took Scott some days to persuade himself to continue. In a letter to Jan from base camp, Scott reported that the Sherpas considered the death to be 'no worse than a traffic accident' and quoted the Buddhist precept that Mingma had, as a good person who had tried hard, gone on to a better life. He concludes by saying that he will be happier when he starts climbing through the Icefall next day.

Base camp was established on 22 August. A track up the mortally uncertain Icefall was overseen by the highly experienced Icefall Sirdar Phurkipa. Camp II was soon established in the Western Cwm, many abyssal crevasses being crossed thanks to Hamish MacInnes's technical creativity in constructing suitable ladders. Here, in conditions of extended lethargy brought on by the extreme heat in the Cwm, the big questions began to be asked, notably about the prospect of cutting through the crux Rock Band on the left. Fixed ropes were very quickly put in place up long, very steep snow-slopes by Scott, Fyffe, Richards and Burke to Camp III. The weather held. Estcourt and Braithwaite pushed on to establish Camp IV; Haston, Boardman, Boysen and MacInnes reached Camp V, which was then stocked by Bonington and Richards. Meanwhile, supplies were being ferried up to Camp II to turn it into a well-stocked advance base. All was progressing well thanks to the brilliance of the Sherpa sirdars Pertemba and Ang Phurba, although a sense remained that it would not take very much, should the weather change, for the chain of camps to be broken: climbers were scattered along a nine-kilometre and near-3000m route. Bonington and his computer put in overtime.[8]

Still, the Rock Band was reached on 19 September. The next day, Tut Braithwaite and Nick Estcourt put up one of the greatest breakthrough climbs in mountaineering history. They climbed the Rock Band's left gully, encountering difficult mixed pitches within a rock cleft 30m deep, before ascending an awkward, loose ramp to take them out above the Rock Band, thus solving the problem which had defeated five previous expeditions; the way to the summit was open. Thompson, Bonington, Burke, Ang Phurba and Pertemba then carried to 8230m in support, leaving Scott and Haston in their green box to try for the summit. After fixing ropes for 500 metres, helped by 'that great natural climber, Ang Phurba', they were ready for the summit bid, going far beyond the end of the fixed ropes on the following day.

On 24 September, having dined on corned beef, mash and an orange drink, and with two deadmen, four pegs and a hammer, Scott and Haston, weighted down by oxygen apparatus, were seen by a BBC cameraman picking their way resolutely up the ramped snowfield to the gully leading to the South Summit. An avalanche passed them; Haston's face mask froze several times; the snow was powdery and occasionally chest-deep; the wind was fierce; but they were seen to reach the South Summit just after 3 p.m. A groggy discussion about continuing ensued while they drank hot water. They continued, pretty much mechanically, Scott having to change film in his camera 'with difficulty' while Haston climbed the nerve-racking loose snow on the Hillary Step. Keeping the red rags on the Chinese tripod in sight, they reached the summit at 6 p.m. They were rewarded with an incomparable view and a fabulous sunset. It was not a place to linger: their headtorches gave out when abseiling the Hillary Step. Further descent was madness, in the dark. They decided to sleep higher than anyone had ever slept before. But, as Scott, remarked, 'We knew we would survive; it was the quality of survival which mattered.'

Reaching the summit might seem like the defining moment of the expedition, and in one way so it was. The night on the South Summit, however, when linked to Scott's survival on The Ogre and his astounding ascent of Kangchenjunga in 1979, marks the hub of Scott's whirling career.

10

The Hub, 1975–79

'I get grumpy when I can't climb.'

– Doug Scott

On the South Summit of Everest, Scott and Haston survived because of their extraordinary physical strength and mental resilience. The bivouac was a pioneering piece of physiological exploration because they did not know if they could survive a night without bottled oxygen at that altitude. They hacked out a shallow cave from the icy snow then sat on their rucksacks and rope for nine hours. Their minds wandered as the time slowly passed:

> Dougal had a long and involved conversation about the relative merits of various sleeping bags with Dave Clark, our equipment officer, who was in Base Camp at the time . . . I thought he [Haston] was losing the plot and must have cerebral oedema.
>
> Before long, however, I too found myself drifting in and out of a conversation with my feet, which had become two separate conscious entities sharing our cave. I told the right foot that the left foot was just not warming up. The left foot was clearly resentful, telling me I never used it. I asked the left foot what it meant by that: 'Well, when you kick a rugby ball you always kick with your right foot.' It slowly dawned on me that I should pay the left foot more attention and when I took off my boot and sock, I found my left foot was seriously cold and turning wooden with frost . . . Dougal kindly opened up the front of his down suit to let me put my bare toes under his armpit. Then, to keep warm and not nod off to sleep, I continued to enlarge the cave.[1]

Scott later realised the significance of that bivouac: 'One night at 28,700 [feet] had broadened the range of what and how I would climb in the future. I knew from then on I would never again burden myself with oxygen bottles.'[2]

As Scott descended, he met Tut Braithwaite at Camp 4. Tut congratulated him. The trenchant reply came, 'This is only the beginning.' Scott acknowledged his success, however, would have been impossible without the support of Bonington's massive, highly organised and generously sponsored expedition.[3]

Scott also experienced the 'third man' phenomenon of being accompanied by a benign other presence. While accepting that such perceptions might well be attributable to hypoxia, Scott also claims, with extraordinary vagueness, that 'morphic fields' or 'the universal consciousness' (perhaps a misunderstood Jungian concept) might be the cause. Scott adds that he returned home, 'far more aware, stronger and with an inner peace that lasted quite some time before it dissipated'.[4]

This famous bivouac should be linked, as a survival epic, with the bad night out on Bidean nam Bian and the descent in 1977 of The Ogre (7285m), then considered the world's most difficult mountain. The story is recounted in detail in Scott's fourth book, *The Ogre*.

Three previous expeditions had attempted The Ogre; all had failed. The plan was for Scott and Braithwaite to try the South Pillar, while Bonington, invited not just for his egregious abilities but perhaps as a kind of 'thank you' for the 1975 Everest expedition, with Rowland, Estcourt and Anthoine, would tackle the south-west flank. There was no leader: Scott maintained it was too strong a team to require one.

The expedition received an official send-off from Nottingham Council House. (The previous evening, after a lively party in Raleigh Street, Jim MacDonald, a friend of Rowland who had volunteered to share the driving, ended up in hospital after a wall-bracket gave way.) The gear was transported to Pakistan by transit van. In Turkey, bureaucratic delays lost the party a few days. They then drove through Iran and Afghanistan, over the Khyber Pass to Peshawar and on to Skardu by plane after another delay. The walk-in was enlivened by Bonington and Rowland's close encounter with a bear. A Balti porter, Taki, carried a thirty-kilogram box for the twenty-kilometre march from Askole to base camp. Here, he produced from his ragged clothing thirty-one eggs, all of them intact! Scott later commended the eight Baltis who carried him, severely debilitated, down the glacier from base camp to Askole with as much gentle care as Taki had put into his egg-carrying.

The party reached base camp on 10 June and set off at once to make an advance base (4875m). On the South Pillar, Braithwaite was badly injured by a falling rock. While he was recovering, Scott climbed a nearby peak with Jackie Anthoine who, with Stephanie Rowland, had joined the team at base camp; the women were police-escorted out some days later because of their lack of a correct trekking permit. Braithwaite remained confined to base camp, a period of great frustration. Bonington was impressed by Scott's patience in the face of the disruption to the schedule caused by Braithwaite's injury. Scott wanted 'to get his body to the summit': he described it, in an interview with Leo Dickinson, as his 'John Wayne' moment.

The others, meanwhile, had been fixing ropes up an icy rib to the West Col. Bonington and Estcourt then made a bold bid for the summit via the previous Japanese route, but failed at the base of the 250m summit cone, although they succeeded in reaching the west summit. (Bonington's haste led to an uncomfortable exchange with Rowland, who had assumed from earlier discussions that they would be climbing as a team.) Scott became frustrated at having to jumar up others' fixed ropes. The ascent of the 300m Red Pillar brought them to a snow-cave at 7000m; the fine views helped.

Anthoine and Rowland led the way to another snow-cave on the ridge between the west and main summits. They remained behind next day, 13 July, as Anthoine was shooting ciné film for the Mick Burke Award. Bonington and Scott started first, with Scott leading up the final cone where some difficult climbing required a thirteen-metre pendulum swing when a crack gave out. An overhanging corner led to the summit gully.

They reached the top at dusk. Scott was moving off the summit when he stepped on a sheet of water-ice, slipped and swung in a pendulum across the cliff-face. He could only stop himself by using his feet as buffers against a rock wall: he broke both ankles. With Bonington, he took stock of their dicey situation: 'Chris had hacked out most of a long ledge in the snow down to the ice. I made the mistake of stepping on to it, only to collapse in agony. I then went down on my knees and helped Chris enlarge the ledge . . . We spent a very cold night . . . After my night out with Dougal below the summit of Everest this was the coldest bivouac I had ever experienced.'[5]

Most remarkable, however, was Scott's self-awareness at this critical moment: 'I never doubted I would get off this mountain, not with people like Chris, Mo and Clive to help, but exactly how it would work out I had no idea. I knew I was now in a very difficult position so it may seem a bit odd that I experienced feelings of exhilaration at all the uncertainty I had created.'[6]

*Descent of The Ogre, 1977. Doug abseiling the West Ridge above the
300m Pillar. Photo by and courtesy of Sir Chris Bonington.*

The descent, in a severe storm, was nightmarish: 'In the storm, I hadn't
noticed one end of the double rope was shorter than the other, so, as I
came off two ropes onto one, I shot off down, out of control. I instinct-
ively threw an arm over a short length of rope and stopped . . . Cold, and
getting colder, there was no alternative but to carry on with the descent.'[7]

Bonington abseiled off the end of one of the double ropes; he broke two
ribs and damaged his hand, his pain compounded later by a ferocious cough
and pneumonia. This excruciating pain and extreme cold when moving,
and long, sodden, marrow-chilling nights – the tent at Camp III lay under a
metre of snow – continued for four hellish days, without food. They reached
the glacier above advance base; there, Scott was sent ahead on his knees, to
test for crevasses since, being the most damaged, he was the most expend-
able! Mo Anthoine opined that Scott wasn't worth saving anyway.[8] Such
black humour had become one of several devices for maintaining morale.

On the night of the eighth day and after seven kilometres of ice, snow
and moraine, partly protected by his companions' cut-up overtrousers and
karrimats wrapped round his knees – 'bloody and swollen like melons' –
Scott crawled into base camp. Braithwaite and Estcourt had left, having

given the others up for dead. Anthoine set off in pursuit, to organise a rescue. After seven days, Estcourt returned with a dozen porters from Askole. Anthoine and Braithwaite went off to organise helicopter transport from Askole to the hospital in Skardu. Scott was carried down the Biafo then to Askole on a stretcher of juniper wood poles, climbing rope and karrimats. He was deeply moved by the Baltis' care and teamsmanship. The ordeal was not over: the rescue helicopter crashed a hundred metres short of the Skardu landing-ground. Astoundingly, Scott's injuries were not aggravated, although Bonington's rescue, to his puzzlement then anger, was consequently delayed by a week. Three days after crashing into Skardu, Scott was being repaired in Nottingham General hospital.

∞

Scott's ability to survive in extreme conditions resurfaced four years later on the world's third-highest mountain, Kangchenjunga (8586m). Arguably Scott's finest climb, he found a magnificent route up Kangchenjunga's vast, 3000m, terraced north-west face and north ridge, its openness avoiding the claustrophobia he felt on Everest's south-west face. The route tests every kind of mountain terrain. Even the base camp at Pang Pema is situated above the confluence of five glaciers. Kangchenjunga had been in Scott's mind since 1955, when he read about Joe Brown on the first ascent climbing a difficult rock barrier immediately below the summit. Scott's final book, *Kangchenjunga*, describes the climb in detail, although very much from his own point of view.[9]

Victor Saunders gives the historical perspective: 'This was to be the ultimate lightweight Alpine-style expedition. It marked the start of the new age of Himalayan climbing. The first age had been the first ascents of the 8000m peaks by the most logical and easiest route. The second age was the ascent by the more difficult and challenging faces, epitomised by the 1975 Everest route. These had been climbed with so-called siege tactics: kilometres of fixed rope, semi-permanent high camps, bottled oxygen and usually with Sherpa support. Doug's ascent of Kangchenjunga heralded the end of all that, relegating most of these techniques to the world of guided ascents.'[10]

Joe Tasker, Peter Boardman and Georges Bettembourg constituted the small team committed to the ascent without supplementary oxygen.[11] Sherpa support was minimal: Ang Phurba was sirdar, with Nima Tensing. Kami the cook and a cook's boy completed the support team with Mohan, the liaison officer. The walk-in began well: after flying to near Dharan

in eastern Nepal, the foursome with forty-eight porters trekked enjoyably along a high ridge above the Arun and Tamur rivers. While Scott on
the one hand enjoyed the 'energies flowing, as though on a ley line', his
reading of Gurdjieff in Ouspensky's *In Search of the Miraculous* encouraged negative thoughts about his emotional need to impress. For balance,
he read Buddhist scripture in a Penguin translation along the way.

Competitive needling was relentless. Bettembourg playfully knocked
Boardman off a boulder, the resulting cracked foot-bone nearly destroying
Boardman's chances of even reaching the mountain. Bettembourg was
racked by guilt. Scathing *sotto voce* comments from Boardman followed;
a discussion about Harrer's *Seven Years in Tibet* ended with Boardman's
jibe 'Don't "come on" me, Dad': Scott realised he had been pontificating
in guru style and vowed to stop. Some of his beliefs were decidedly odd:
he maintained that daily masturbation would hinder their ascent whereas
eating sperm would help by enhancing protein intake. He also claimed
that 'new moons bring strength'. Tasker's rationalist assessment was acidic:
'One has to be careful of Doug as with an awkward child. Doug prefers
followers to equals.'[12] Leo Dickinson has also drawn attention to Scott's
'Pied Piper' characteristic. Boardman thought Scott had 'a knack of self-
parody, which is why he tends to walk alone'.[13] Bettembourg criticised the
team for a lack of humour. Scott played too much Bob Dylan. Boardman
and Tasker were acting as a rather grumpy pair of Boswells to Scott's awkward Dr Johnson.

Further aggro was avoided by tripping on magic mushrooms, a regular
feature of Scott's walk-ins. From the ridge, they followed the well-
populated valley of the Tamur to Ghunsa.[14] Progress was slow because
Boardman had to be carried in a wicker basket. For part of the way they
were accompanied by an attractive Sherpani and her daughter, nicknamed
'Smile'. One evening, Scott observed them from his tent: 'I could see the
Sherpani and her four children huddling against the rain . . . She fed her
children and put them to bed, all . . . without any fuss. Everything she
did, she did with such grace and economy of effort. I marvelled at that . . .
surrounded by tapes, tape deck, books and camera equipment. It struck
me just how much of my time I spent doing things badly, whereas these
people . . .'[15]

At Ghunsa they rested, to acclimatise, re-organise the porters and give
Boardman's foot further time to heal. They then continued up the valley
to reach base camp on 4 April at Pang Pema, a grassy ledge lying at 5025m
on the flanks of Drohmo (6881m) and opposite The Twins. Its situation

is stupendous. The north face of Kangchenjunga looked like the most heavily defended (the military metaphors recur in Tasker's diary) any of them had seen.

The plan was to ascend the Kangchenjunga Glacier to a headwall leading to the North Col, between The Twins and the main summit. (This wall was estimated by Tasker at Alpine grade TD, but 'somehow more serious'.) The north ridge would then be followed over rock steps to a snow-ramp just below the summit. The ramp would be traversed to the pinnacles on the west ridge to meet the 1955 route, from where a short, breathless clamber leads to the summit. To evaluate the plan, Scott cast a number of divinations from the *I Ching*.

On their first attempt, matters began badly when hauling equipment up the headwall. Either Scott (says Tasker) or Bettembourg (says Scott) dislodged rocks which just missed Ang Phurba, unnerved Nima Tensing and injured Boardman's hand. They reached the north col (where the Sikkim side proved windless); Scott, Boardman and Bettembourg then carried supplies as far up the north ridge as possible, to the Great Terrace at about 7925m. (Tasker had become ill and had had to descend from the col.) The wind got up; they descended to a ledge but soon found themselves in great danger. On a night which confirmed the correctness of Scott's epithet, 'The Great Survivor', the wind reached an extreme hurricane by 2.30 a.m. The tent – with the climbers fully dressed inside and expecting the worst – was blown a metre along its ledge towards the 2000m drop to the Zemu Glacier. Trying to hold the framework hoops to prevent the fabric tearing was futile. Scott leapt out into the worst wind he had ever experienced: rocks moved and chips of ice flew into his face. He tried to anchor the tent with his ice-axe; the action was hopeless: the orange outer flew off into the night. The others then tumbled out of the shredding inner tent, Bettembourg having to cut through the fabric with his Swiss penknife. All then let go of the inner, which careered off into the blackness.

On their ledge they clung to each other for several hours until it was light. Then, it was time to descend: 'I thought that this time I had gone a step too far. For the second time in my life, I thought I was going to die.'[16]

That bivouac fulfilled the prophecy which Scott claimed was made to his mother by a fortune-teller. It played its part in creating the somewhat tongue-in-cheek myth of Scott as a man of destiny (see chapter two).

They retreated to base camp. The second attempt began on 9 May. Two days later, they had reached a previously built snow-cave at 7525m. After a rest-day, they reached the base of the summit cone at just short of 8000m where the two pairs made separate snow-holes. A tense shouting match in the morning – because Boardman and Bettembourg had left Scott and Tasker behind the previous evening – passed quickly. Owing to the violent weather they descended to the snow-cave at 7525m. A general perception of more than four people present was felt. A dispute broke out about their reading: Tasker's choice of Robert Graves's strange *The White Goddess* was opposed by Scott. Scott was criticised by Boardman and Tasker for bringing Castaneda with him. Scott rather petulantly resented this attack and vociferously (as far as the altitude would allow) said so. Grumbles at each other relating to pace, rests and ice-climbing technique continued, with Scott bearing the brunt of the criticism: Bettembourg chastised him for his 'imperious' behaviour and his habit of grabbing the best place in a tent. Such niggles accompanied the climbers to the summit and back.

Bettembourg decided he was too tired to continue and descended. A change in the weather decided the others for the summit. A trail-breaking slog followed, then a climb of previously fixed ropes through a rock band at 8225m, after which they made a long traverse in which all took turns in leading to reach the pinnacles only 90m below the summit. Scott, wearing only conventional double-layer leather boots, warmed his feet on Tasker's body, a bizarre but necessary diversion at that altitude. From the pinnacles, complicated ground led round the rocks which Brown had climbed, to a rock only a few metres below the summit. Here they halted, at 4.45 p.m. on 14 May, respectfully avoiding the very top. Scott grandly observed, 'We have pushed the patience of the gods to the limit.' Scott could not contain his enthusiasm for photos, for himself and for sponsors. This delayed them; they descended to the snow-cave in semi-darkness. Scott tripped on a small cliff and fell 3m; the others had observed that he was not particularly confident on steep ice. Scott blamed this on blunt crampons.

The descent largely consisted of a stagger through deep snow from one brew to the next. They did, however, throw sacks full of equipment down the headwall from the north col. At base camp, Scott immediately started thinking about home in an agitated, worried way.

✧

During this central period of Scott's climbing life, he of course went on other expeditions, notably to K2 *West Ridge* in 1978, two attempts on Nuptse, the second in 1979 reaching the summit, and a brilliantly successful ascent of Kusum Kangguru in 1979.

Scott's experience of expeditions beyond the UK and Alps now comprised an interesting mixture: apart from the four apprentice expeditions in the 1960s, he had participated in three siege expeditions; four rather laddish trips with friends and fellow NCC members to Baffin Island; the regimented and unwieldy 1974 international Pamirs gathering in Soviet Russia; the compact but highly successful 1974 ascent of Changabang's (6864m) granite spire.[17] Scott's experience otherwise related to ropes of two or three people on extended, highly technical rock face climbs, mainly in the US, such as the *Salathé Wall*. These experiences offered little consistency in terms of summit success, ethical character or personal satisfaction.

Scott draws on these experiences, however, to reach those ethical conclusions which governed his future climbing. In the siege-style expedition, Scott compares participation to being an employee in a large organisation, concerned about his position, his promotion and concern for praise from management. The implied criticism is that sieges create unnecessary tensions and rivalries, unless there is a very strong and skilful leader, because success depends not so much on the individual's assessment of his capabilities as on the leader's.

The 1975 Everest success has been described as 'the apotheosis of the big, military-style expeditions', at least as far as the UK was concerned.[18] The Japanese, Russians and Chinese, for example, continued to use such tactics when 'assaulting' the very highest peaks – military metaphors were common in describing such ventures. Siege-style expeditions had been popular as the way to climb the world's higher peaks since the French breakthrough in reaching a summit higher than 8000m on Annapurna in 1950, although such expeditions' history goes back to such massive excursions as the Duke of the Abruzzi's attempt on K2 in 1909. Scott, however, criticised siege expeditions for their ecologically destructive nature: massive quantities of firewood are used; the ground is polluted by unwanted fires, spillages, rubbish etc.; trails become open gashes on the hillside; wildlife is destroyed or disturbed; locals are corrupted by money and gifts they had not previously sought or needed; the equanimity of village life is disturbed by tricks, deceits and negotiating rows in order to make more money. This approach has been likened to trench warfare: 'Long periods of lazy inactivity led with an inevitable sense of increasing urgency towards a short, frantic, dangerous engagement on the front line, the mountain wall . . . As with the soldier . . . the same brooding, electrifying tension is in the air, the same inevitable advance towards the appointed hour for going over the top . . .'[19]

On an Alpine-style expedition, where a small number of participants is self-sufficient, the climbers are, by contrast, existentially more 'authentic': the summiteers are simply those capable of reaching the top on the day.

The main disadvantage of Alpine-style climbs is that on the highest peaks, oxygen cannot be used because the tanks are too heavy; indeed, punitively heavy loads must sometimes be carried by climbers, to the detriment of good physical readiness for a summit push. A relatively long period of acclimatisation on lower mountains consequently becomes necessary, the effect of which is to lengthen the duration and expense of the expedition and, in restrictive countries such as China, to create tiresome extra administrative problems.

Another disadvantage is that small expeditions have less bargaining power – with consequently less say over movement and timing – than very large teams. The Lake District guide Nick Kekus recounts such difficulties during the return from Scott's 1987 Everest *North-East Ridge* expedition: 'We had an epic journey back to Kathmandu as the roads were cut following a terrible storm. We had to ferry loads across landslides and negotiate with local transport. One Nepali guy was trying to rip us off with transport costs and Doug was having none of it. Firm negotiations were getting nowhere. Finally, Doug pulled out his trump card, telling the guy it would be bad karma for him if he stayed unfair on the price. It seemed to work and a better deal was agreed.'[20]

Scott's natural regard for individuals, his predilection for informality, his emotional warmth and his reluctance to be in thrall to sponsors made him not just prefer Alpine-style but advocate it as the ethical way to climb. He became one of its leading proponents, for example on his spectacularly successful Shishapangma expedition in 1982. This arrangement made democratic decision-making easier; and it was ecologically less damaging to the mountain, the trekking access routes and the integrity of the local people.

Subsequent experience would challenge some of these views: when an argument broke out on a later K2 expedition and the vote went against Scott, he stormed out of the tent. Nonetheless, for the next twenty years, all of Scott's thirty-four remaining expeditions to high peaks were completed Alpine-style (though sometimes modified to capsule style – the application of big wall climbing techniques to an Alpine-style ascent); some required financial support from trekkers paying to accompany his expeditions as far as base camp.

The Everest bivouac had demonstrated Scott's ability to survive without supplementary oxygen on the highest place on the planet; The Ogre horror had proved Scott's capacity for dealing with sustained extreme pain in very severe weather on a technically difficult descent, while the Kangchenjunga escape confirmed Scott's ability to survive through pretty much anything that mountains and their weather could throw at him. This pivotal four-year period, therefore, crystallised Scott's philosophy of expedition ethics and gave him the confidence which came from experience-defined awareness of his prodigious mental and physical abilities. This ethical belief and self-perception formed the basis for the next twenty years of high climbs scarcely equalled in mountaineering history.

Growth of a Mountaineer (II): 1970–85

'Ambition feeds on itself, it can never be satisfied, you can
only let go of it.'

– Doug Scott to Jeff Lowe

By 1971, Doug was on the cusp of international fame. Global recognition
arrived following the Everest ascent in 1975. With it came media attention:
intrusive but also useful. His loyalties were tested as his relationship developed with the outstanding American climber Molly Higgins. His ethical
principles became more sophisticated with experience. His spiritual quest
extended itself: he sought out gurus, while becoming one himself. Then,
in 1985, he first met Sharu Prabhu, his second wife. The marriage, in
1993, began happily enough with romance, passion, mountaineering and
travel. They started a family in the mid-1990s and worked together on the
founding of CAT until 2002. Their marriage, however, became turbulent
in the very early 2000s as Doug's infidelities became known. Estrangement
led to divorce in 2003.

Doug's outward appearance was changing. Following his Bill Gates
phase, he acquired his John Lennon look (possibly instigated by Jan). John
Cleare describes meeting him in 1972: 'I rushed down to Nottingham
. . . to shoot Doug [with a camera] on the Black Rocks at Cromford. He
was in his "Beatles" phase: round granny-glasses, "Pancho" moustache and
long hair.'[1]

Sixteen years later, in 1984, Maggie Burgess tells us: 'I was curious about
his hippy look. I liked the John Lennon look, the accent, the diffidence,
the humour. A gentleman. Admirable and objective, with first interest in
Buddhism, especially the life of Milarepa in Nepal.'[2]

This look derived from fashion while denoting an anti-establishment
radical. He smoked weed and listened to the 'right' music to complete
the persona. His body, however, had suffered. The compressing of the
ankle bones and appalling wear and tear on his knees during the descent

of The Ogre led to spreading arthritis and consequent operations in the early 2000s. Less well known is his horse-riding accident shortly before departure for Everest in 1987: while riding near Hesket, Doug was thrown and landed on grass and tarmac. Three ribs were broken. On at least two other occasions he was burnt by exploding gas canisters while cooking in tents. He experienced mild frostbite on Shivling, although without lasting damage, thanks to his unusual ability to function efficiently at high altitude.

Doug also enjoyed quite a powerful sex drive. At Christmas 1974, Jan caught Doug in bed with another woman. This stormy encounter did not help a marriage which, while publicly successful, was privately, after twelve years, decidedly rocky.

Doug's relationship with Molly Higgins is important because it came close to ending Doug and Jan's marriage and thus changing the course of their and their children's lives. She was also Doug's most important female rock-climbing partner.[3]

In the Pamirs, Molly had at first befriended Clive Rowland. Doug soon got to know her also. He admired her self-possession and her being the first American woman to climb Pik Lenin. She visited Rowland in Sheffield after the Russian meet, in early autumn 1974, and stayed overnight at Doug's home in Nottingham. Doug, Clive and Molly went climbing in Derbyshire, then visited the Lake District, where they climbed Pillar Rock and where Doug and Molly's attraction developed. They began a sporadic correspondence. Doug used the address of Neil Highfield, a former teacher and co-trainer of the Nottingham Moderns Rugby Club. He was frustrated at not being with Molly in the big open spaces in the US: 'I only get worse being here in the city, with all the problems zinging down the nerve fibres.'[4]

He refers to their time in a Lakeland pub, where 'the back of your hand got me going'. He tells her he is 'a born Romantic' and quotes from Hermann Hesse's 1941 poem, 'Stages', as 'appropriate to us', adding, 'my respect and tenderness you have in plenty'.[5] Doug describes life with Jan as very difficult.

His letters to Molly refer tendentiously on several occasions to Shipton. He describes his feelings when away in remote mountains: 'I cannot go on easily in the mountains beyond a certain time without the need for sympathetic female companionship.' To resolve this, he suggests having one life at home and one life with her, a compartmentalisation that Molly would not accept. He asks Molly to consider setting up a 'chance' meeting at Sosbun Brakk (where he was heading for a recce on The Ogre).

In March 1975, as preparations for Everest south-west face gather momentum, Doug tells Molly that Jan is showing 'strong signs of unease'. He sends his American lecture tour itinerary, signs himself off with 'loving you with all my heart' and arranges a phone call, with Molly pretending to be a tour promoter. The call was unfortunately accepted by the Scotts' nanny, Janet. Molly tells Doug that she misses him but not some of his 'more unpredictable and bluely [sic] moods'. She sees them as Dostoievskian lovers and tells him, 'If you love me, climb with me.' In a letter to a friend, Molly tells her that after Doug and she parted the previous autumn, she had the same dream as when her father died. Doug has become her father figure, as well as a publicly perceived father-guru.

As their meeting approaches, Doug's relationship with Jan reaches an 'all time low'. He writes that he is sitting by Lake Windermere (perhaps less of a solecism when writing to an American) trying to 'get out of a hell of a mess'; his mind has been in turmoil since Christmas. He admits, 'She knows a bit about you.' And yet he won't leave Michael and Martha, which is why he wants a 'home and away' relationship.

In spring 1975, they met in Colorado, at Eldorado Springs, near Eldorado Canyon, site of some of the finest rock-climbing in the US. (Doug was on a lecture tour.) Doug wanted Molly to remain in Colorado while he visited Yosemite, his next attempt to compartmentalise the relationship. Molly, however, travelled to Yosemite anyway. She recalls, 'Our first climb in Yosemite was *Midterm*, a 5.10 splitter fist crack: polished granite, my first true Yosemite crack. Afterwards, he said to me, "These short climbs are OK, but the real climbing is scaling these enormous shimmering walls." He launched me: *Washington Column* with Barb Eastman that spring; north-east face of Half Dome the next year, 1976; *The Nose* of El Capitan in 1977: we were the first team of women to ascend it. Doug comes back to life for me, such a very fine man, such a huge spirit. But as I read I am overwhelmed with sorrow that he is gone.'

Molly and Doug spent time at Camp 4 and put up a few climbs, despite Doug's worried insistence that they climb independently; Molly, however, did spend most of her climbing time with her partner, Barb Eastman.

By May 1975, Doug is writing to Molly on British Biafo Expedition notepaper during his attempt on Sosbun Brakk. He writes somewhat self-pityingly about 'two miserable phone calls from home', but also longingly, repeating that he loves her. He reminds her of the time they spent making love outdoors near El Portal in the Merced Valley until he was suddenly interrupted by a warm, wet tongue moving up his spine: a horse was expressing its curiosity, turning passion into laughter![6] Grudgingly, he concedes that Jan can't be blamed (!), as she is looking after two children, a dog and a cat and teaching children with special needs. He repeats that he cannot leave his family.

In 1976, when Doug returned to the US, principally to go on a lecture tour, he and Molly also visited Estes Park, where they spent several nights in the basement of Steve Komito's house. In 1975, however, Molly had met another highly distinguished American climber, Larry Bruce (they now live in Montana), the real love of her life: Doug and his compartmentalisations were relegated.

Before departing for The Ogre, in March 1977, Doug tells Molly that he finds her letters very uplifting, although in referring to 'your bloke' he now accepts that Molly's affections have become focused elsewhere. He describes how he occupies his time: an hour and a half playing rugby every Saturday and sometimes on Wednesdays; Saturday evenings, 'boozing and singing and shouting the odds'. More seriously, he is writing a 'monumental history of Everest': he works from 8.30 p.m. to midnight then, as circumstances allow, to 4.30 a.m. – the only quiet time when 'the phone's not ringing and people are calling in on me'. In 1970s idiom, he says he is 'OK for bread at the moment'. He describes life with Jan, who is teaching a class of thirty-seven nine-year-olds: 'She puts out affection but I can't return it so easily'. Jan is still 'very touchy' where other women are concerned. In fact, their relationship has altered since Everest: Jan is now fiercely possessive. He is happiest when 'out on the grit when the sun shines', but he still yearns to go climbing with Molly. He concludes, alarmingly, 'I've got scary thoughts running down the crazy corridor of my mind.'

After his success on Kangchenjunga in 1979, Doug writes again to Molly with a description of the climb. He recommends that she go to that 'very beautiful' corner of Nepal. He proudly refers to Rosie's birth and how precocious she is, like Martha. He describes Michael as fifteen and 6'2" (1.88m) and asks Molly if she will take him on a climb or two.

Another letter to Molly goes from the camp on K2's Savoia Glacier in 1980. It is baking hot. They are looking at the west ridge. The depth of the snow reminds him of the terrible winter of 1947, when he couldn't go to school because the snow came over the top of his wellies. He tells Molly about his recent trip to Australia and New Zealand and refers to the yogi whom he spent two days with in Christchurch. As he often does, he asks Molly, in a rather plaintive, childlike way, for a letter.

Doug and Jan with Rosie, 1978. (Scott family collection)

Doug and Molly did not meet again until 1982, when Doug was visiting Mike Covington in Aspen. For that occasion, Molly provides an elegiac commentary:

He was very respectful of Larry, liked him immensely; we behaved ourselves from that moment on. We did a couple of hikes above the treeline, one cold and windy day. He showed me how to use some trousers as a

Plate 1. 1962: the sandstone walls of Aiguilles de Sisse, near the Tibesti Mountains, Chad.
Photo © Doug Scott Collection

Plate 2. 1962: the Tibesti Mountains, Chad. Note the size of the expedition lorry for scale.
Photo © Doug Scott Collection

Plate 3. 1966: overview of the base camp area and climbing amphitheatre, with Reşko Tepe (left of centre, 4136m). Čilo Daği, Turkish Kurdestan.
Photo © Doug Scott Collection

Plate 4. 1966: typical rock in the Čilo Daği, Turkish Kurdestan.
Photo © Doug Scott Collection

Plate 5. 1967: approaching the Hindu Kush peaks in Afghanistan along the Panjshir Valley.
Photo © Doug Scott Collection

Plate 6. 1967: Tony Watts on Berast Sharan (5540m), Hindu Kush. The twin peaks of Kuh-i-Morusq (6436m) in the background.
Photo © Doug Scott Collection

Plate 7. 1966: Cafer Kule, Čilo Daği, Turkish Kurdestan. First ascent of this 213m tower by Doug Scott and Brian Palmer.
Photo © Doug Scott Collection

Plate 8. 1971: Doug Scott, Guy Lee and Dennis Hennek on *The Nose*, Strone Ulladale, high above Harris, Western Isles, Scotland.
Photo © Doug Scott Collection

Plate 9. 1970: Jeff Upton on the Troll Wall, Romsdal, Norway.
Photo © Doug Scott Collection

Plate 10. 1970: Peter Habeler at about 850m on the Salathé Wall, Yosemite. The first European ascent of what at the time was one of the hardest known climbs in the world.
Photo © Doug Scott Collection

Plate 11. 1971: Baffin Island, Canada: approach to the peaks by boat-sleds (and later on foot) up the Pangnirtung Fjord.
Photo © Doug Scott Collection

Plate 12. 1971: Mount Asgard (2015m), Baffin Island, Canada. The focus of several climbs by Scott and others (see Plate 13) in the early 1970s.
Photo © Doug Scott Collection

Plate 13. 1971: the Baffin Island climbers. From L to R: Steve Smith, Ray Gillies, Dennis Hennek, Guy Lee, Phil Koch, Doug Scott, Rob Wood.
Photo © Doug Scott Collection

Plate 14. (Above) 1972, spring: camp at c.7000m on Everest's south-west face. Lhotse (8516m) in the background. The Herrligkoffer expedition. Scott's first time on Everest. Photo © Doug Scott Collection

Plate 15. (Right) 1975, September 24: Doug Scott on the summit of Everest after the first ascent of the south-west face. Photo by Dougal Haston. Photo © Doug Scott Collection

Plate 16. 1976: Denali (Mt McKinley, 6190m), the highest mountain in North America. Scott and Haston made a new route on this intensely cold mountain and were involved in an extended rescue during the descent.
Photo © Doug Scott Collection

Plate 17. 1977: Scott on the summit of The Ogre at dusk. Perhaps the hardest mountain in the world to climb at the time. Shortly after leaving the summit, Scott broke both legs in a pendulum fall. He, Bonington, Clive Rowland and Mo Anthoine then endured one of the greatest 'epic' descents in mountaineering history.
Photo © Sir Chris Bonington Collection

Plate 18. 1978: high on Mount Waddington (4019m), British Columbia, Canada. Only Scott and Rob Wood completed the climb.
Photo © Doug Scott Collection

Plate 19. 1979: Kangchenjunga (8586m). Boardman and Tasker on the snow and rock ramp between the north and west ridges, about 300m below the summit, heading for the pinnacles on the west ridge. Photo © Doug Scott Collection

Plate 20. 1979: Kangchenjunga. First ascent of the world's third-highest mountain without supplementary oxygen and largely in 'Alpine' style. Peter Boardman and Joe Tasker at the pinnacles on the west ridge, about 90m below the summit. Photo © Doug Scott Collection

Plate 21. 1979: Nuptse north ridge. Looking down to the Western Cwm.
Photo © Doug Scott Collection

Plate 22. 1980: Doug and Martha Scott at about 6000m on Makalu south-east ridge.
Photo © Doug Scott Collection

Plate 23. 1980: Steep ground above the Makalu Col.
Photo © Doug Scott Collection

Plate 24. 1980: Mervyn English approaching the summit of Tūtuko (2723m), the highest peak in the Darran Range, south-west New Zealand.
Photo © Dr James Duff

Plate 25. 1981: Shivling (6543m) from base camp at Tapovan. The ascent route was by the left-hand skyline.
Photo © Doug Scott Collection

Plate 26. 1981: Rick White on the East Pillar of Shivling.
Photo © Doug Scott Collection

Plate 27. 1983: Doug
on the Lobsang Spire
above the Baltoro
Glacier, Karakoram.
Photo © Greg Child

Plate 28. 1986:
Mount Colonel
Foster, Vancouver
Island, Canada.
Ascent was by the
long prominent gully
in light and shade,
right of centre.
Photo © Doug Scott
Collection

Plate 29. 1986: High
on Grand Central
Gully (first ascent),
Mount Colonel
Foster.
Photo © Doug Scott
Collection

Plate 30. 1988: Jitchu Drake (c.6800m), Bhutan (first ascent). Victor Saunders and Sharu Prabhu (later Scott) on the summit, looking north-east along the China–Bhutan border.
Photo © Doug Scott Collection

Plate 31. 1992: summit ridge, Chimtarga (5489m), the highest peak in the Fann Mountains, Tajikistan.
Photo © Doug Scott Collection

Plate 32. 1992: Iceland: the 'Organ Pipes' at Fallastakkanöf. Scott is the lower figure.
Photo © Doug Scott Collection

Plate 33. 1994: The climb (new route) to Doug's final peak of the Seven Summits, the Carstensz Pyramid (4884m), New Guinea.
Photo © Doug Scott Collection

Plate 34. 1998, spring. Doug accompanying Arran, aged three, to Drohmo base camp just north of Kangchenjunga.
Photo © Doug Scott Collection

Plate 35. 1998, autumn. Doug on the foresummit of Drohmo (c.6850m). In the background is Kangchenjunga, showing the upper part of the north ridge route which Doug climbed with Boardman and Tasker in 1979.
Photo © Roger Mear

Plate 36. 1999: A rare view of Takpa Shiri (6885m), one of the remotest peaks of that height anywhere. On the border of Arunachal Pradesh, north-east India, and Tibet (China). Possibly the most physically arduous expedition Doug ever undertook. Photo © Doug Scott Collection

Plate 37. 2000: on the summit ridge of Targo Ri (6566m), on the Tibetan Plateau, north-west of Shigatse. Looking south. Photo © Doug Scott Collection

Plate 38. 2015: a Nepali gompa (temple) at Melamchi, north-east of Kathmandu, shattered after the earthquake.
Photo © Doug Scott Collection

Plate 39. 2018: CAN-built hostel for the elderly in Kyanjin, in the Langtang, north of Kathmandu near the border with Tibet (China).
Photo © Doug Scott Collection

Plate 40. 2018: the opening of the new school for deaf children at Bahrabise, between Kathmandu and the border town of Kodari. The previous school had been destroyed in the 2015 earthquake. Trish, Doug and the Nepal manager of CAN, Murari Gautam.
Photo © Doug Scott Collection

Plate 41. Chris Bonington and Doug protesting against the encroachment of windfarms in the Northern Lakes.
Photo © Mike and Sally Bohling

Plate 42. Doug tending his organic vegetable garden at Stewart Hill Cottage. Carrock Fell (661m) behind.
Photo © Doug Scott Collection

scarf. That had never occurred to me, to use clothing in that way. I loved it and have never forgotten it. On one of the hikes, we sat on a log and talked a long time. He missed Dougal tremendously, talked of missing him so much and thinking of him so hard and mourning so completely that the landscape before him was transformed with bright bursts of light and color. I could tell Doug was in a different 'space', mentally and emotionally and he wanted to share that with me. I respected him for that and appreciated it too. I think he had 'teachers' who were guiding him; he was traveling a philosophical path that meant a lot to him.

Doug invited Larry and Molly to join his expedition to Makalu in 1984. In September, Larry and Molly met Doug and Jan (now aware of their history) at their home in Cumbria before joining the expedition. It was the last time Doug and Molly met, although their correspondence continued intermittently. Molly does add, however, 'I deeply wish I had stayed in closer touch with Doug. He deserved it.'

✍

Doug and Jan's marriage did indeed change after Everest. On their first trip together to the US in 1970, Jan had caused controversy by speaking out in favour of student demos. The *Guardian Journal* of 29 May 1970 proclaimed 'Trainee Teacher favours US demos' and refers to Jan's visit to the radical University of California at Berkeley and to schools in Los Angeles. (Jan had obtained a scholarship to study American teaching methods.) The article carries an attractive portrait photo of Jan, describing her as having 'long blonde hair and maxi skirts', while stressing her sympathy for the 'social phenomenon' of the hippies. At this point, Doug's and Jan's outlooks must have been approximately similar, although Jan is said to have become slightly resentful of the press attention Doug received; she offered to give comments to the press but, following the prejudices of the day, her opinion was rarely sought.

Much of their subsequent time was unhappy, as Gina Madgett, an old friend of Jan, relates:

She certainly didn't like it if she knew [that Doug was being unfaithful] – but people were more guarded about such things in those days. She did have a fling or two herself while in college training, but nothing serious. Despite being aware of some of what was going on I don't think she wanted to put her marriage or family at risk. This didn't stop some spectacular rows especially in Nottingham – more than once I arrived at Raleigh Street to find Jan red faced and in tears, Michael gleefully saying 'she's thrown all Dad's clothes into the back yard' while Doug remained grim-faced! She had the sense not to throw out his photography or writing stuff, though. Despite her competence and patience as a teacher, Jan was less self-confident than she appeared, and was often undermined by Doug. I always thought this led to stress which may have made her more susceptible to the cancer later.[7]

Life at Raleigh Street, however, was always lively. Apart from the parties and frequent visits by friends and climbers, those requiring help from a day-care centre across the road often dropped in, to be listened to by Jan and to leave more confident in facing their problems.

Jan's life was made harder by Doug's conversion to vegetarianism, which began before his trip to the US in 1970. Doug expressed his fear to a friend before his departure that vegetarianism would be preferable to eating hormone-filled American chicken as he was afraid of growing breasts! He remained interested in the 'purity' of his food, to the bemusement of Kathmandu waiters. More seriously, he had seen a neighbour of his parents find relief from arthritic pain through adopting a vegetarian diet (for which there is a reasonable scientific claim). Doug suffered from arthritis from the 1990s onwards, but it is impossible now to tell if his vegetarian diet alleviated what would have been greater suffering. Doug's vegetarianism was also motivated by his growing interest in Buddhism, with its prohibition on killing sentient beings. Vegetarianism brought complications at home, however, as Gina Madgett tells us: 'Jan had to change into an inventive cook, on a small wood burning Rayburn with Campingaz stove to supplement, no matter how many were eating. And one daughter wouldn't eat fruit and veg!'

Doug maintained his commitment to vegetarianism from 1970 to about 2005, when he met Trish. Steve Razzetti tells us that Doug consistently practised vegetarianism on the 1987 K2 expedition, for example.[8] He 'went to great lengths' to transport fresh vegetables up to base camp, although because of a disorganised supply chain, most of them were eaten en route.

Lapses were only very occasional. Doug's 1975 Everest diary records him admitting to enjoying a plate of yak stew and onions. His first request to Christine Gee on arrival in Australia in 1980 was for a plate of fish and chips, permitted up to twice weekly, followed by a climb on cliffs near Sydney Harbour. His conclusion from experience came in a 1984 *New York*

Herald Tribune interview: 'You adapt to altitude faster. Meat seems to take the liquids out of the body.' (In the same interview, he confessed he had given up smoking only in 1983.)

After Everest, Jan could take public pride in her errant husband and at least enjoy reflected fame. She handled the press while Doug was away. In 1977, for example, she reproved a *Daily Express* commentator, James Murray, for writing that the Chinese tripod on Everest's summit 'mocked the efforts' of Scott and Haston. Quite the contrary, Jan asserts, as she has 'spent a lot of time with climbers all over the world' and 'doesn't know one who would agree with James Murray's belief'.

More formal advantages of fame appeared: on 28 July 1977, Mr and Mrs Scott were invited to dine with the Queen and the Duke of Edinburgh during their Silver Jubilee visit to Nottingham. Doug, however, told the *Nottingham Post* that he 'just wants to keep the same lifestyle'.

Public honours followed: Doug's first entry in *Who's Who* appeared in 1976. He was granted the Freedom of Nottingham on 17 March 1976. He and Jan attended a grand ceremony at the Council House with Lord Mayor Ivy Matthews and the Right Reverend Edward Ellis, Bishop of Nottingham. In his seconding speech, Councillor Bill Bradbury (a boyhood friend of Doug) mentions Doug's brothers Brian and Garry, although he adds, 'If you saw the three brothers together, it is doubtful if you would recognise them as such.' He also thinks he compliments Jan in saying that she 'enabled her husband to fulfil himself: it cannot be easy to stop at home and follow press reports'.

With such an honour came obligations: later that year, Doug gave a talk, free of charge, in aid of Camphill Villages for the Mentally Handicapped; not long after, accompanied by Martha, he opened an exhibition in aid of the Nottingham Multiple Sclerosis Society. These occasions marked the first of hundreds of voluntary fundraising events boosted by Doug's presence. Further spin-offs included Jan setting up a Nepal pen-pal exchange: the *Nottingham Post* pictures Jan with her pupils from Scotholme Primary School making notes at the Goose Fair. For Doug, his Freeman privilege was to put up some routes on Castle Rock in Nottingham before it was closed to the public. Another commitment, showing how far he had come since the sponsorship-begging letters of the early 1960s, saw him become patron of a Derbyshire schools Pyrenees expedition.

Martha and Rosie agree that Doug and Jan were good parents. They ended up at base camps high in the Himalayas. Rosie, on the way to K2 aged only seven, used a polo pony. She enjoyed the use of ponies for the walk-out because of bad weather. Indeed, Doug supported Rosie's passion for horsemanship by attending many of the events she competed in. In February 1979, Michael was sent on an Outward Bound course and received a highly laudatory report. Doug also taught his children to swim. He always brought them a sack of toys at Christmas and is recorded by his wider family assiduously bringing back presents from his many trips abroad.

Not all trips ran smoothly, however. On the walk-in to Nuptse in 1978, Doug and Jan were shown the largest plate-glass window in Khumjung. Later, Doug was foolish enough to opine that 'some of the magic has gone out of our marriage'. Jan threw a handy climbing-boot at him, reducing the window to non-largest status.

An offshoot of this colourful family life, Doug's driving, had not improved. John Calden, when visiting Nottingham with his fellow Estes Park bootmaker, Steve Komito, recalls, 'Of course, we were running a little late to catch our train back to London. Screeching around bends, being thrown back and forth in the car getting to the station as our train is pulling out . . .'[9]

Sometimes, however, Doug was the victim: in a letter probably written in April 1975, Doug describes to Jan an interesting hitch-hiking experience between Fresno and Ventura, California, during his lecture tour. He laconically summarises it:

9.30–1030: drunken fat woman 23 years flopping all over the car – climbed out unscathed. 12.00–12.15: 50 year old like Bugs Bunny asks me if I want to make $10. I say yes. Says he and his wife can't have children so would I give him some of my sperms in a paper cup. Said we could go down a quiet road to produce them. Told him no! 3.00–3.15 Fat Mexican student with radio warning of speed cops. 4.00–7.35 getting desperate, still 180 miles from Chouinard lecture. Stunning woman picks me up – gets higher on marijuana. Going part way but also after trying to get my sperm! Takes me to Ventura after I told her 500 people were waiting to hear me. I don't think she really believed it until she got there. She apologised for getting fresh – said she had just got divorced.

Unlike Doug's driving habits, his photographic abilities did develop. He wrote the 'Still Photography' appendix for Bonington's *Everest: The Hard Way*. He describes the Olympus cameras issued to all the climbers as part of the deal and how they performed, including several comments on lenses. (True to form, Doug used his own Pentax for the approach march.) He assesses the kinds of film issued. Doug complains that the expedition copyright rules mean that he cannot use his photographs (and thus generate income) for two years. More philosophically, he worries that his heightened perceptions of sunset from Everest's summit may have been altered by his photos affecting those memories. He concludes by praising Wendy Bonington for her scrupulous handling of the expedition's photos. Those unnamed persons who handled the photographic material more indelicately are sharply criticised for forgetting the immense trouble required to obtain them.

Networking with other photographers was part of photography, also. For example, Doug met David Oswin at Higham Hall, near Bassenthwaite, while David was on a course where Doug was a guest speaker, leading to a friendship with David and his wife Ann. David's travel company was able to get Doug to Iceland on several occasions and once even to Greenland. When the occasion arose, Doug was also able to benefit from the skills and experience of three outstanding photographers: John Cleare, Bob Holmes and Steve Razzetti.

∽

Doug's intellectual life showed real growth during this period. He developed and argued for a set of ethical principles relating to climbing and the environment.

In the winter 1976–77 issue of *Peak Park News*, Doug gave an interview after a photography lecture to students at Trent Polytechnic in which he criticised national parks. While conceding that something on an island the size of Britain had to be done, he railed against excessive new buildings and regulations, believing that freedoms were being eroded. Doug cited the stranded students on Mount McKinley to illustrate the way in which national parks give people a false sense of security and thus lead to more accidents. He stressed his wish for mountain areas to remain wildernesses, reviling 'information centres' and 'ranger briefing centres' which 'spoil the environment'.

In 1977, Doug became involved in a Peak District National Park controversy concerning the use of the Eric Byne Memorial Campsite at Moorside Farm a few kilometres east of Baslow. He prepared a history of the campsite's use from the 1930s, including by the NCC from 1961. He drew attention to problems of visitor access, water supply and use of local pathways. When the Severn Trent Water Authority closed the campsite in 1974 (because of clean water problems), a 'storm of letters' from irate climbers was directed at the Peak Park Planning Board. Complaints were made about lack of progress in establishing a permanent campsite. In 1976, a campsite was opened by Mrs Byne, a testimony to Doug's, Dennis Gray's and others' assiduousness in resolving this matter. Sadly, vandalism soon increased markedly, mainly from organised groups. Climbers largely ceased to use the site. Doug complained to the planning board once more. The campsite is now properly established, while emphasising its simplicity and peacefulness. Doug had learnt to research well, handle bureaucracies and accommodate local sensitivities.

Late in an interview about this campsite, Doug turns to the question of leading schoolchildren in mountains. Fresh in his and many others' memory is the Lochan Buidhe disaster in November 1971, in which five children and their instructor died in a blizzard on the Cairngorm plateau. The ensuing debate about schoolchildren and mountain safety was fierce. Doug links the existence of high-up bothies (mountain huts) to offering inexperienced parties a false sense of security and concurs with Fred Harper, former warden of Glenmore Lodge, that the bothies should be removed. The debate between educationists, led by Jack Longland, and climbers, represented by the BMC, became bitter and unproductive. Doug joined the criticism of certification as a substitute for experience, describing it melodramatically as a 'license [sic] to kill'. He proposed instead a 'sampler' visit after which schoolchildren and leaders could return for a more serious expedition, an impractical suggestion given the constraints most schools work under.

In 1978, Doug faced one of the biggest ethical challenges of his life. He was offered the International Award for Valour in Sport, for his descent of The Ogre. The organisers called it 'the Sporting VC'. The trophy had been initiated in 1974 by Warwick Charlton (1918–2002), a journalist and public relations worker. Previous awards had been won by Nikki Lauda and Eddy Merckx. Chris Brasher wrote about the matter after Doug had called him, in some distress, having refused the award. Doug had refused because he considered The Ogre descent to be an act of survival. He also refused because he went to the mountains to get away from a competitive, money-orientated society. Chris Bonington was misleadingly told that £25,000 (about £125,000 at today's values) went with it. Knowing that mountaineering was perennially short of funds, he tried to persuade Doug to accept the money for the whole Ogre team, with the intention of giving the money to the MEF on the twenty-fifth anniversary of the first ascent. However, giving the award to a team was against the rules. When the judging panel made their decision, it seems that they were unaware of Bonington's letter confirming that it was a team award. The Victoria Sporting Club (essentially a PR body behind the award) were gaining publicity at relatively little expense to themselves. It is hardly surprising that Doug was displeased: he withdrew very suddenly just before a TV interview in Birmingham preceding the presentation at the Guildhall in London.

Unfortunately, it turned out that little cash was on offer: the misunderstanding had occurred because £25,000 was the melt-down value of the winner's Golden Wreath. The mainstream press all criticised Doug for refusing the award because there was no cash attached to it. This opinion travestied Doug's ethical position, that climbers do not accept rewards for something they enjoy. The villain of the piece appears to have been one of the judges, Don Morley, who misled Bonington.

The affair blew up. Bonington published a summary of what happened in *Climber and Rambler* magazine within a letter from Walt Unsworth. It concluded with Doug saying that if he had accepted the award, it would have encouraged young people (he had already noted that a CSE in climbing was possible, something he strongly disapproved of) to take up climbing for the wrong reasons, i.e. to gain certificates and make money. In the same column, Bonington also published his letter to Don Morley, explaining why only a team acceptance was appropriate.

Doug went on to explain his position to the chairman of the judging panel, Sir Stanley Rous. He insisted that climbing is for enjoyment, to leave behind the competitive stresses of city life. He declared he had turned professional, while keeping 'the amateur ideal', a paradoxical position which focuses once more on his character's conflicting opposites. He told Sir Stanley that he believed the Victoria Sporting Club had acted inappropriately, effectively by hinting at the financial gains Doug might make from the award, with the implication that the award was a self-serving publicity device. Even the Minister of Sport, Denis Howell, received a letter from Doug. His reply commended Doug for his actions and expressed the appreciation of all concerned for the message from Doug to Kathy Miller, the actual winner.

The event had not died down two years later. Sir John Hunt, apropos an editorial in *Indian Mountaineer*, wrote to its editor to support Doug's decision. As Hunt rather brilliantly put it, '[Such an award] invites a spirit of competition . . . which may vitiate the purity of the deed. This spirit is aided and abetted by commercial exploitation and through . . . the press and broadcasting and its attendant "bally-hoo".'¹⁰

Thus began Doug's increasingly uncomfortable worries about the changing relationship between sport and money. Moreover, this event did nothing to lessen Doug's wariness of the media. In 1980, Christine Gee had arranged for an interview on Australia's biggest daytime programme, *The Mike Walsh Show*. Having just had a 'ruckus' with Jan, Doug arrived at the studio looking very downcast. During the interview, he offered no more than one word answers to the upbeat interviewer's questions. The interview was wound up in minutes; Gee and Doug beat an embarrassed, hasty retreat.¹¹ Doug disliked talking about himself in public and he detested inaccurate journalists of whom, starting with the misreporting of the Turkish earthquake in 1966, there were many. In his characteristically 'hot and cold' fashion, however, Doug remained happy to exploit the press if he thought they might benefit any expedition or charitable cause.

Doug's ethical interests extended to women in mountaineering. In his article in the *International Herald Tribune* in March 1985, Doug confessed to having lost too many male friends on expeditions. As the trend in Himalayan expeditions is to bring along 'family and friends' (he claimed), women should come along, as they provide a restraining and balancing effect on blind male ambition. He retained doubts, however, about women and men climbing together above base camp, a belief which history, despite some fatalities, has not borne out.

Apart from writing his first book, Doug's other principal intellectual concern was his lectures. These had two motivations: to help him earn a living and to inspire others.

The 'earning a living' part was hard work. In 1980, a lecture tour typical of those he undertook in the UK began in Glasgow on 1 December, proceeded via Aberdeen, Huddersfield, Cambridge and Birmingham, finishing on 20 December in London. Lectures across the US were even more demanding. Sometimes, a lecture circuit would occur purely in Scotland, depending on Doug's climbing plans. Some lectures came from invitations, for example at Rugby School, where Doug's talk on the 1975 Everest experience was described as 'very popular with a first-rate collection of slides' and 'from breathtaking and dramatic to truly sensitive, as Doug Scott recounted the death of one of his team-mates'. He lectured to 800 people at the RGS in 1979, a long way from his first nervous lecture at the Alpine Club in 1967. Certainly, no two lectures on the same subject were quite the same in content or presentation. Accompanying each lecture was the sale of signed photographs, books and posters, a substantial part of his annual income.

Beyond the utilitarian came the inspirational aspect. Christine Gee recalls an Ogre lecture in 1980 as being, 'mesmerising . . . and drew gasps of amazement from the audience. We even ran to two shows a night . . . his message was to inspire people to go into the hills and not to get caught in the grip of materialism, to live more simply . . .'

In the US, John Calden recalls, 'He was a great photographer and storyteller. I remember him describing a storm on Everest . . . He really commanded the stage. You felt an instant friendship.'[12]

With so much time taken up elsewhere, relatively little time was left for reading. Doug, however, became an outstanding researcher: the historical sections of many of his climbing articles, as well as sections of *The Ogre* and *Kangchenjunga*, contain fascinating accounts of previous expeditions to the area in question. Otherwise, most of his reading appears to have been carried out in tents on expedition. On Baffin Island in 1972, for example, apart from the inevitable Hesse novels, he read the suitably lengthy *War and Peace*, *The Hobbit* and Charles Reich's *The Greening of America*. It was probably during this period that Doug began to read the ancient Northern Indian religious texts, the *Upanishads*, also. His literary tastes, therefore, were divided between the escapist worlds of fantasy and mysticism (he retained an unhealthy fixation on the mystical significance of the number seven) and manuals with a practical or polemical content.

Doug's major written contribution to climbing literature during this period was the publication of *Big Wall Climbing* in 1974, a work in the tradition of Geoffrey Winthrop Young's *Mountain Craft* (1920), and a manual on aid climbing by Doug's old mentor, Geoff Sutton. *Big Wall Climbing* contains a historical survey of Europe, Yosemite and 'remote areas', followed by a description of specific big wall techniques. It concludes with advice about expedition planning. Photographs, diagrams and pictorial maps are copious and informative. In the *Alpine Journal*, reviewer Mike Ward stresses the quality and extent of Doug's research. He concludes that the work is for the 'committed mountaineer rather than the mountain lover'.

A review by Galen Rowell welcomes a book by a well-travelled, high-level participant. He criticises Scott, however, for hiding precise information behind imprecise phrasing. But he does acknowledge the truth, often amusingly expressed, of what Doug is trying to say, and Rowell praises Doug's way of blending history with environmental concerns. The usual problems of what actually constitutes a big wall are mentioned: Rowell draws attention to some American omissions, particularly winter routes. Finally, Rowell admires Doug's sense of trust in other climbers and how that enhances the integrity of the sport and the climber's personal liberty.

Big Wall Climbing was influential. For example, Victor Saunders read it when he had just begun to climb. He saw it as 'half story, half manual'. It introduced the world of 'pitons, *étriers* and vertiginous space. I was entranced and went to see Doug lecture.'[13]

This period also saw Doug's spiritual quest develop. In 1980, Doug may have visited Swami Muktananda while in Australia. Regrettably, little documentary or testimonial evidence survives of his 'intensive two days' with Mahant Swami Maharaj in Christchurch, New Zealand. As ever, it was a search for a father-figure, without Doug quite realising that for many climbers he had now become a father-figure himself.

What came across for many people about Doug, apart from his inflexibility on climbing ethics, was his naturalness and accessibility. He never 'made you feel he was famous and special', as Christine Gee put it. He was, rather, 'unfailingly kind and candid' and 'patient and respectful' towards other people's children. Ted Grey describes him as 'so easy to get on with . . . slightly shy in a way but with ability not only as a climber but in describing his experiences in a way that conveyed so well the psychological aspects of climbing, the real hard grind, the fears and relief when all went well. And of course through his photography he could share the pain, the difficulties and the scenery.'[14]

His capacity for sharing pain occurred after Dougal Haston's sudden death in January 1977. Doug and Jan did what they could to help Dougal's distraught girlfriend, Ariane Giobellina: 'I stayed with them in Nottingham, on many occasions during the five years after the accident. And sometimes for months, including travelling with the family. They were very patient with me. I was in shock; they listened and had a lot of time for me.'[15]

Doug wrote an eloquent, heartfelt obituary in *Alpine Journal* with Bonington and the late Jimmy Marshall. He reminisces about their early days together in the Dolomites and strongly dismisses the idea that Dougal's killing of a young climber in a drink-drive incident (resulting in a sixty-day jail sentence) altered his vibrant personality or affected his dominance of Scottish climbing. He saw the loss as that of a 'special young brother'. He was, 'lithesome in stature, powerpacked in flaming, unquenchable will'. Dougal's crime might have robbed Doug of an Everest ascent knighthood, but it is unlikely that Doug cared. Dougal's untimely death certainly led to speculation about what this magnificent partnership might have achieved. At any rate, it came early in the time when Doug was compiling one of the greatest lists of first ascents, new routes and explorations of hitherto unclimbed peaks in mountaineering history.

12

Classics Master, 1978–2000

'A man designed to fell mountains.'

– Georges Bettembourg

Three spokes extended from the hub of Scott's climbing life from the late 1970s onwards. He tried adventurous new routes on well-known mountains, as described in this chapter. He also explored lesser-known mountains and ranges. The third spoke was different: he began an involvement in humanitarian causes. Helping the dispossessed led to the formation of CAN in 1989. Scott's management of the charity lasted for almost as long as his climbing career; he was an extraordinary humanitarian as well as a great climber.

North-west Scotland, Alps, Yosemite, Himalayas and K2

In early February 1979, Scott and Dr Jim Duff visited Kintail, in north-west Scotland, where they climbed the iced-up Falls of Glomach, lying in a muddy-sided trench about 133m high, above Glen Elchaig. Conditions being good, Scott and Duff then headed for Skye, where they climbed *The Smear* (VI, 6) on Sgurr a'Mhadaidh. Duff recalls the Falls being the more 'impressive and fun' route.[1]

Having formerly eschewed Ben Nevis (1344m), in favour of the Cairngorms, Scott made his mark there in 1982. With the late Jim Fullalove, nicknamed 'Dan Boon', he climbed *Orion Face* (V 5), *Green Gully* (IV, 3) and *The Curtain* (IV, 5).

In February 1986, Scott returned to the north-west, this time with Colin Downer, having been invited by 'Ginger' Cain, who lived in the picturesque village of Plockton. On 28 February, Scott and Downer made the first winter ascent of *Waterpipe Gully* (VS, 4b) on Sgurr an Fheadain, in the Cuillin; Mick Fowler and Victor Saunders arrived next day with the same intention and were reportedly 'gutted'. That evening, Scott and

Downer drove to the far north, to one of the remotest Munros, Seana Braigh (927m), this long journey mitigated by joints and relentless playing of Bob Dylan. On its long gneiss cliffs, they climbed *Captain Patience* (E3, 5c, 280m), a route recommended by Al Rouse and named ironically for Downer.

On 1 March, their adventure continued in Applecross. They had intended to climb Beinn Bhan (896m) from Coire na Feola, backed by one of the finest sandstone cliffs in the UK. They found the wrong coire, however, and had to bivouac. Next day, they penetrated Coire na Feola and climbed *In Excess* (250m, V), on thin but good ice for four long pitches.

Scott also occasionally visited the Alps. In 1980, with Adrian Burgess, he climbed the *North-East (Tournier) Spur* (V, 4+, 5c) of Les Droites (4000m). Burgess had taken a long time for a ligament to heal and was confined to a *Bar National* routine.[2] In March 1980, Scott was invited to take part in a French TV documentary based at Chamonix; he contacted Burgess to try the climb, with Scott using new plastic boots to give better ankle support when using crampons. From the Grands Montets, they crossed the glacier to the Argentière hut. Three long sections began at dawn. Scott insisted on going on until dark, when they bivouacked. Burgess caught Scott writing to Jan – she wanted to know what being in such a position was like, so Scott was writing it down before he forgot.

On the second day, front-pointing was needed; the rope dragged; pack-hauling was tiresome. An aggressive few moves up a steep crack brought them to the summit, with its stupendous views of Mont Blanc and the Grandes Jorasses. On the descent, they stopped at the Couvercle hut for sleep and rehydration. The descent continued next day down the Leschaux Glacier to the Mer de Glace. Scott's ankles were punishing him. At one point, Burgess cut steps for Scott while he faced in, yet he never complained. In Burgess's words, 'He was bloody stoic as hell.' And for Burgess, Scott was a guru.[3]

In 1982, Scott tried the *North Face* (at least TD) of Monte Gruetta (3686m), with Al Rouse and Roger Baxter-Jones. They approached on skis, at which Scott and MacIntyre were both 'absolutely bad', in Christine Baxter-Jones's assessment (she had accompanied them with a friend, Catherine, as Sherpanis). They all stayed in a hut on the first night. Little else is known about this long and demanding climb, although all returned 'very happy' despite not having reached the summit.

A more unusual visit to the Alps took place in 1986, when Scott took part in a high-altitude hypoxia response test for a study by the prominent

Swiss-Austrian Professor Dr Oswald Oelz and Dr Marianne Regard of the University Hospital, Zürich.[4] Twelve of the world's leading mountaineers assembled in Kitzbühel. They climbed under controlled conditions in the Ötztal, mostly in gullies and on frozen waterfalls: the Rudolfs Hut gully is mentioned, as was a variation on *The Glass Madonna*, with a new, much-admired partner, Thierry 'Turbo' Renault. A 'hard mixed line' was completed with the Austrian climber Andy Orgler.

The study focused on 'the mechanisms for oxygen uptake'. Heart measurements were taken; all cases were found to be 'normal', probably because heart dilation is rapidly reversible at sea level. After controlled tests in two laboratories, it was found that the climbers' oxygen intake capacity was less than that of élite long-distance runners. One major conclusion showed that successful high-altitude climbers are distinguished by their ability to oxidise fat in the muscles. While successful high-altitude climbers not using supplementary oxygen operate within normal physiological limits, their success appears to depend on 'an obsessive need to be first and best'. Neurological examination of all twelve climbers showed them to have a higher IQ than the control group, although short-term memory tended to be defective. The study noted that the British pre-war Everesters who had gone to high altitude without supplementary oxygen had all subsequently carried out successful careers.

Yosemite, meanwhile, was revisited by Scott, who maintained that climbing on 'warm rock' was his favourite activity. In 1982, he tackled the relatively remote Basket Dome with Greg Child. Both men enjoyed 'looking at the natural world and how it was shaped and designed'.[5] They climbed the south-east spur, beginning with 'a jumble of dihedrals' followed for two pitches by 'a giant corner' known as Strait Jacket, then by slabs and cracks. Two bolts were placed to protect the crux, a steep slab at 5.10. For Scott, it was an ideal break during yet another lecture tour. They agreed that 'moving forward, never backward, carrying everything in a single push, was a real philosophy and the motivating essence of the way we climbed and lived back then'.

This phase of Scott's life, however, was mainly focused on the highest peaks. After Kangchenjunga, Scott felt that climbing Everest Alpine-style might be possible. Following acclimatisation on lesser peaks from a base camp, he attempted Nuptse (7861m) in 1978 then successfully climbed it in 1979, along with Kusum Kangguru (6367m).

In September 1978, Scott, Tasker and Michael Covington, with only minimal Sherpa support as far as base camp, attempted the north face of

Nuptse. The walk-in from Lamasangu was an astonishing 300 kilometres. The party reached Everest base camp on 23 September, an excellent daily average of about fifteen kilometres. Covington experienced liver trouble, necessitating descent to Pheriche; though still unwell, he rejoined the other two on 26 September. Scott and Tasker were going well: they had established Camp II in the Western Cwm by 28 September. Progress was aided by a nearby French expedition: Scott rewarded them with two bottles of whisky, 'for the use of your ladders'. Heavy snowfall – three metres of snow fell on Camp I – halted progress. Still, ferrying continued using French and German tracks, so that Tasker and Scott were ready to tackle the north ridge on 10 October. The snowfall had been excessive, however: they took five and a half hours to climb 150m. The expedition was called off at 6860m.

Scott returned the following year. Kusum Kangguru ('Three Snow-White Gods', 6367m) base camp lies on the Kyashar Glacier, a three-day walk from Lukla. On 16 September, Scott, Covington and Bettembourg attempted the 1000m north buttress which, over three days, Scott and Bettembourg succeeded in climbing over mixed ground to the north summit (which they failed to reach by 6m owing to danger from snow-laden cornices). Covington fell ill on the ascent and could not continue. Ropes were fixed on some sections above Camp II 'in order to get a good start in the morning'. Scott claimed this route as a first ascent, although the main summit was not reached until 1981. He criticised previous Japanese ropes fixed to drilled anchors.

Scott remained intent on climbing Nuptse's north buttress, which he did with Brian Hall, Georges Bettembourg and Al Rouse. Nuptse, says Hall, was completed in pure Alpine-style, insofar as they set off from the bottom and climbed the route in a single push. But when you analyse most Alpine-style ascents, they are not 'pure', Hall asserts. On this occasion, ropes fixed by a German party were used in the Icefall. Whatever label is attached, one can call it a lightweight ascent, compared to the armies clambering up its high neighbour across the Western Cwm.

The German expedition's fixed ropes were used thanks to permission from their sirdar, Pertemba: this was the second time this most remarkable Sherpa had met Scott on Everest. Scott and Bettembourg, fresh from Kusum Kangguru and Kangchenjunga, climbed straight through to Everest Camp II, near the base of the north buttress, which Bettembourg likened to a stegosaurus's spine. A rather frightening day followed while the pair traversed to the Lho La to view Nuptse and Everest's west shoulder.

Rouse and Hall (coming from a British Kantega expedition) then arrived for acclimatising, while the Scott family descended to Namche Bazar to celebrate Mike Covington's marriage to a Sherpani.

For the ascent, a recce day looked at the best way past the lower area's *séracs*. A climb to an ice-cave at 7150m followed. There, the climbers stopped for acclimatisation and rest. On the following day, they reached a second bivvy at 7620m. The summit was reached next day, steep ice and freezing winds making progress exhausting. The same day, they descended to the ice-cave, then, the day after, followed a rib of 'trembling sugar' to Camp II in the Cwm. Unfortunately, all other teams had left: the Icefall had collapsed into chaos, a considerable problem for a small team. The resulting chasms and *séracs* took a very tense nine hours to descend.

Hall describes such expeditions, in true self-contradictory Scott fashion, as 'organised chaos'. Everyone had different objectives. Scott wanted democratic decisions from a disparate group; Bettembourg, on the other hand, was impetuous. Eventually, a generally accepted strategy was agreed: 'It was an eccentric expedition: Doug with his family at Base Camp; the "Californian hippy" Covington marrying a Sherpani; a crazy Frenchman . . . Doug experimented with life and part of that was organising these Himalayan camps with international climbers, multiple peaks and friends and family. Somehow, Doug serenely rose above all the mayhem.'[6]

Scott had brought Jan, Martha (aged six) and Rosie (aged one) to base camp with him. Martha's experience was recorded in her diary, with drawings: 'It took us about a week to get there [base camp]. We camped in tents because the houses were really poor. One was just a cave. Anngphurber [Ang Phurba] was used to it and slept in them. At Everest Base Camp there were millions of boulders . . . There were lots of icicles . . . sometimes I used to take an ice-axe and play on the little ice-mountains. Daddy went off on his expedition to Nuptse. He didn't go up Everest because it was very cold.'

Towards the end of the expedition, Martha resumes her story: 'I was looking through [Ariane's] camera which brought things nearer. I saw my Daddy who was 3 miles away. I rushed down with [Ariane] for about a mile to wait for Dad. It was in a glacier which killed many people . . . The first thing I did when we got back to Base Camp was to tell sailor [Saela Sherpa?] to make two cups of tea and some rice and red beans and no proper meat as my Dad is Vegetarian [sic]. But he can eat goat meat so Sailor got that ready. Well, he had to do that on small stoves. The Sherrpa [sic] word for water is "Parni" [sic].'

This party had permission to climb Everest, but all were exhausted. Hall had two frostbitten fingers. The winter jet stream winds were descending on Everest, making an Alpine ascent impossible.

༫

After Everest, K2 was the next logical destination. In 1978, 1980, 1983 and 1987, Scott attempted K2 by different routes, but he never reached the summit. The 1978 expedition to K2's enormous 3500m *West Ridge* was led by Bonington. Seven climbers made up the party: Scott, Boardman, Tasker, Estcourt and Braithwaite, with Jim Duff returning as expedition doctor and Tony Riley as film-maker. A great deal of fixed rope was planned – nearer siege style than anything else. With Bonington's usual flair, he managed to acquire the manufacturers of Durex as sponsor.

The expedition arrived in Pakistan as the Soviets were invading Afghanistan. The walk-in via the Baltoro was uneventful until Paiju, where a row between the Skardu porters and Safiq, the liaison officer, spilled over into violence. Further porter trouble relating to food and equipment followed before base camp was established on the Savoia Glacier on 2 June. Scott could hardly contain himself from getting started on the route. Bonington remained more circumspect. The route via the Savoia Saddle was 'too technical at that altitude'. They turned to a ridge which reached the *West Ridge* higher up.

Camp I was soon established at 6000m. An easy-angled basin was crossed and Camp II was established at 6400m. Differences between Bonington's more studied style and Scott's wish for spontaneity, however, were becoming apparent. The force of Scott's personality meant his 'democratic' decisions usually ended up being what he himself forced through. As an outward sign of their differences, Scott stopped sleeping in Bonington's tent, ostensibly because of Bonington's snoring (for which there was consistent evidence!).

While talking to Duff (who had arrived with the porters), Bonington was photographing a large avalanche descending the icefall between them and K2. He suddenly realised that it was falling across their route. Shortly after, Scott came on the radio to say that Estcourt had been killed and, had the 5mm handrail rope not snapped, he would have died also; he was deeply upset. Everyone retreated to base camp. Boardman, Bonington and Riley, after a combative mess tent discussion, wanted to continue. Scott, Tasker and Duff wanted to stop, invoking the difficulties of telling wives, girlfriends and families. (Braithwaite had already left.) The expedition was called off. Scott and Bonington went ahead to Skardu to break the awful news. Without the pressures inherent in a long climb, Scott and Bonington got on very well.

Three weeks before the accident, Estcourt had a premonitory dream-vision, which he disclosed to Duff, of Scott poking around Estcourt's body among ice-boulders. When the expedition was called off, Scott searched where he thought Nick's body might be, to make sure it wasn't exposed to raptors.

In an interview for *Mountain*, 51, 1976, Messner had suggested that K2 could be completed Alpine-style. This belief perhaps gave impetus to Scott's return in 1980, to K2's *West Ridge*. Scott's small team comprised Boardman, Tasker and Dick Renshaw who, with Tasker, had made the first British winter ascent of the Eiger north face. Renshaw and Scott found compatibility in vegetarianism, to which Renshaw (virtually vegan) was strongly committed. The tactical idea was 'capsule style', where about 300 metres of rope were used to haul supplies up to successive camps. Disputes with porters about stockings and some persistent snowstorms were the highlights of the walk-in. The expedition reached 7000m before hitting high winds then running out of time as the technical difficulties mounted. Scott proposed an Alpine-style ascent of the remaining 1600m, but the others disagreed (Renshaw was anxious about frostbite after a bad experience on Dunagiri). Scott had to return home, just in time to lead an expedition to Makalu. The others tried a switch to the *Abruzzi Spur* route, resulting in a near-fatal three-night epic in a storm just below 6000m.

Three years later, in 1983, Scott returned to K2, but as part of an extended expedition to the Lobsang Spire and Broad Peak. The plan was that these two ascents would put the team, comprising Scott, Don Whillans, Roger Baxter-Jones, Greg Child, Andy Parkin, Al Rouse, Jean Afanassieff, Dr Peter Thexton and Gohar Shah, an experienced climber-porter from Hunza, high on K2. Michèle Stamos accompanied Jean Afanassieff and Beth Acres accompanied Peter Thexton. The eventual aim was to climb K2's South Rib. 'The whole thing,' Andy Parkin recalls, 'was pretty free-wheeling.' Roger Baxter-Jones opined that you knew you were leaving only when the plane left the ground. Food including fresh eggs and vege-tables for a remarkable four months was brought into the base camps. Greg Child interestingly points out what a seminal expedition this turned out to be: it led to the Scott, Afanassieff and Sustad epic on Makalu; for Rouse, it led to his death on K2 in 1986; for Whillans, it was an embittered swansong; Roger Baxter-Jones died guiding on the Triolet in 1985; Andy

Parkin suffered a terrible accident on the Matterhorn, which created a new life for him; for Child, he found many new routes on Karakoram granite in subsequent years; for Peter Thexton, Broad Peak was his final climb.[7]

The walk-in began on 12 May from Dasso; they arrived at Urdukas on 20 May. Porterage to there had run smoothly, bar one short strike: Scott was generally liked and respected by the porters as a man's man with a sense of fairness. Rock towers near Urdukas were used as preparation. Scott, with seven others, ascended the Mustagh Glacier for 300m from Lobsang meadow, a high pasture containing old buildings past which Younghusband had descended after crossing the Old Mustagh Pass in 1877. From the Pass (5422m), they climbed Karphogang (5931m) and one other previously unclimbed spire. An attempt by Rouse and Parkin on the west ridge of the Lobsang Spire failed near the top.

On 5 June, half of the expedition moved up to K2 base camp, leaving behind Scott, Child and Thexton to tackle the 600m Lobsang Spire by its *South Pillar*, which involved highly technical climbing graded 5.9 and A4. It took four days, then two for the descent. A minor pinnacle led to a col at the foot of the Spire. The night was spent in porta-ledges. An amphitheatre was exited via hairline cracks. Jumaring was sensational, with Thexton at one point hanging free for about fifty metres. The second night was spent in a snow-cave. The controversial section near the top required bolting. Child describes the event:

> We used Yosemite 'big wall' climbing techniques . . . The 'bolts near the top' was a 60 foot rivet and skyhook and bathook pitch which I led. In lectures, Doug reduced my efforts there to something akin to flagrant murdering of the impossible – though he and Pete were joyful when sitting on Lobsang's summit on a perfect Karakoram day.
>
> When we arrived . . . below the final plinth . . . we saw it was a shield of granite with razor edges. Doug announced he could forego the summit. I said I had a little pouch of drilling gear . . . Pete was non-committal. Scott's response was, 'Dougal used to say that ethics are like erections . . . they go up and down.' The final pitch – not a bolt ladder – consisted of tiny holes, [three-eighths] of an inch deep, each alternating with a little metal rivet tapped into it, or a removable hook perched on the edge of the hole. It was all drilled by a hand-held drill that works out a hole by hammer blows – not an electric drill. At the end, I placed two [one-inch-long] bolts and the lads jumared up to the top. It was a sublime time.[8]

On Broad Peak, Scott roped up with newcomer Steve Sustad, an out-standing young American climber. They climbed Scott's third 8000m peak by the *Original Route* without anything untoward occurring. Rouse and Parkin had set out on 22 June, to be joined at a 7500m bivouac by Baxter-Jones and Afanassieff. They reached the summit together on 25 June. While descending on 26 June, at 6000m, they passed Thexton and Child on their way up. Further down, they met Scott, Sustad, Whillans and Gohar Shah. Whillans and Shah had climbed more slowly, reaching just short of 7000m two days later. Scott and Sustad pressed on, to reach 7620m. They reached the summit on 27 June.

On their way down, they met Child and Thexton ascending very slowly: they were exhausted and turned back an hour from the summit. With terrible difficulty, and finishing in the dark, they struggled down to Whillans and Shah's tent. At dawn on 28 June, Thexton died, almost cer-tainly of pulmonary oedema. The others eventually succeeded in reaching base camp.

Most expedition members then went home. Such a large group had naturally fragmented: Scott and Rouse were 'oil and water', according to Child; the 'Chamonix group' tended to stick together; Whillans tended to be his own man, and so on. (Scott maintained that any expedition team greater than four would inevitably create factions.)

Afanassieff, Baxter-Jones, Parkin and Scott headed for K2, intending to try the unclimbed *South-South-East Spur* to the Abruzzi Ridge Shoulder at about 7600m. On a difficult route they established bivouacs at 6700m and 7200m. On 23 July, they reached a mere 120m short of the Shoulder. A contented night followed when Scott solicitously produced a ready-made joint. His attempt to persuade Parkin to absorb some arnica to relieve stress, despite Parkin's claim that he wasn't feeling stressed, was strenu-ously rejected. Next day, Parkin had ascended a further 30m when Scott caught up with him: Afanassieff felt ill, with pain in the kidneys, eye-sight problems and numbness in the arms and legs. The two-day descent to base camp was so successfully rapid that Scott quickly had everyone bouldering on the glacier.[9] The expedition on that route was, however, over. Three years later, Tomo Česen claimed to have completed this route, which bears his name. Scott said he could not understand why that was the case.

In 1987, Scott returned to K2 for the final time, with a large international party: Child, Tim Macartney-Snape, Steve Swenson, Phil Ershler and Scott's son Michael. Steve Razzetti headed a trekking group of ten from

Karakoram Experience. Carolyn Gunn joined as chief cook; a Hollywood film crew also participated; two liaison officers were needed. The expedition felt like a NCC outing for some of the world's finest climbers.

Tim Macartney-Snape reports that much was organised at the last minute, with even a generator for the film crew's cameras being forgotten. (The porters carried car batteries in from Skardu instead!) The walk-in was quite luxurious since everyone had their own tents, despite it inhibiting team cohesion. As Macartney-Snape points out, however, Scott had deeper experience than most to draw on.[10]

Steve Swenson, who had not previously met Scott, recalled that Scott was leader in managing the necessary bureaucracy and porters, while route choices and the like were collective decisions. What Swenson perhaps most liked about the expedition was the freedom bestowed by climbing Alpine-style, something which greatly influenced his future ventures.

The expedition was unusual in having Michael Scott as a member. In Swenson's and Child's recollections, father and son got on well. Their later estrangement came as a surprise.[11]

By 1 July, everyone had reached base camp. Phil Ershler recalls that on passing the Biafo Glacier outlet, down which Scott had been carried after The Ogre descent, Scott said he had been more worried about falling off his stretcher than on crawling down the mountainside!

On arrival at base camp, some members immediately trekked along the upper reaches of the Godwin-Austen Glacier.[12] They ferried during snowstorms to an advance base below the east face. On 8 July, a party skied up to Windy Gap (6111m). On 9 July, an unsuccessful attempt reached 900m up Peak 6812. On 17 July, a party got as far as about 6500m up Skyang Kangri (7545m) and assessed the east face of K2 as too dangerous. The attempt was abandoned. A move to Broad Peak base camp led to an attempt on it which reached only 7000m. At the end of the month, most of the party walked out to Skardu. (Ershler, Child and Swenson remained to tackle the Polish *South Pillar* route on K2, abandoning it at 7000m after heavy snow.) Thus ended Scott's four attempts on K2. In 1986, in *Mountain*, 109, when asked what his next great Himalayan challenge was, Scott quipped, 'West Face of K2, solo, in winter, without shoes.'

∽

Scott's experience of Makalu (8481m) and Chamlang, its 7319m neighbour, was not dissimilar to K2. He attempted challenging new routes on Makalu in 1980 and 1984 (*South-East Ridge*) and in 1988 (*West Face and* traverse). Again, he failed to reach the summit although he came very close indeed on a climb which he only just survived.

The 1980 attempt took place in autumn, with Georges Bettembourg and Roger Baxter-Jones, along with the late Dougal Haston's girlfriend, Ariane Giobellina. The walk-in from Tumlingtar airstrip in eastern Nepal was long and arduous. Ariane recalls incessant rain, with many leeches.[13] An advance base was established at the Chago-Barun confluence by 28 September. Climbing lesser summits for acclimatisation followed, including Kangchungtse (7678m) and some lesser peaks (Peak 6170, Peak 6250, Peak 6350 and a southern Chago peak of 6600m).

Giobellina had to descend from Kangchungtse owing to a severe throat infection. Bettembourg and Scott accompanied her part way down, then pushed up to a camp at 6700m, to reach the Makalu La (7400m) the next day. Kangchungtse summit was reached via a gully and along delicate cornices for about 800m on the following day, 5 October. The descent from 6700m was mostly on skis, although Scott opined that the skis were more trouble than they were worth.

Having acclimatised, the plan for Makalu focused on a traverse up the *South-East Ridge* then down the original 1954 *French Route*. The attempt, starting on 14 October, was beset by bad weather. The first camp was set up at 6000m. The party then crossed Peak 6260 and Peak 6825 to reach a col at 6800m. Next day, a slow climb reached 7400m. On 17 October, they arrived at 'a huge black gendarme'; the winds were too high to continue; they dropped into Makalu's eastern cwm to camp below Point 8010. On 18 October, they climbed in very high winds to 8100m. After two further days of very high winds, retreat was decided, as winter conditions were now prevailing. It took three days for a partial retracing of the upward route; an awkward descent of a heavily crevassed glacier was also needed. While awaiting the porters' return, Baxter-Jones made a solo attempt on the very difficult west face.

Scott returned undaunted in 1984, in one of the strangest assortments of participants in any attempt on an 8000m peak. He nonchalantly declared that it was 'more like four expeditions running together'. Again, it resembled a high-octane international club outing. Twelve climbers came: Scott, Jean Afanassieff, Larry Bruce and Molly Higgins, Colin 'Choe' Brookes and Brian Hall, Richard Chaplin, Jim Fullalove, Ariane Giobellina, Terry Mooney, Michael Scott and Stephen Sustad. Three Sherpas came in support: Ang Phurba, Saela Tamang and Pasang. Accompanying the climbers were family members and friends: Jan, Martha and Rosie Scott; Michelle and Jeanne Afanassieff; Clive and Sue Davies; Arthur and Rita Lees and Nick Loening. These latter were to go as far as base camp at 4900m; a guru seeking a cave retreat and an Australian herbalist strung along. Brian Hall found this phase an odd experience: 'Arthur Lees had cerebral palsy; along with his wife, they found the walk-in extremely trying, which had an effect on all of us. Molly Higgins was constantly worried about the insanitary conditions. Afanassieff's daughter Jeanne was not well, resulting in her crying and being upset throughout the trip. Dan Boon (Fullalove) was taking a lot of drugs, resulting in eccentric behaviour. Terry Mooney consumed enough *chang* and *rakshi* for the rest of the expedition put together; Jan was continually telling me we were doing things wrongly and that Doug would do it this way or that way . . .'[14]

At base camp, reached on 16 September, the party's underlying tensions were revealed: the vegetarians were at (mostly humorous) odds with the carnivores; the alcohol consumers fragmented from the drug-takers; the family groups did not mix much.

Chamlang (7319m), Baruntse (7162m) and Yaupa (6422m) had been booked by stretching the regulations. Various parties climbed some of these outliers, for example, Scott, Bruce, Higgins, Fullalove and Afanassieff made the first ascent of the south-east summit of Yaupa (6300m) by its icy east ridge. Difficulties never exceeded Scottish grade II; most of the climbers remained unroped. This climb was followed by an ascent of Baruntse by the non-technical south-east ridge, largely to give the Sherpas some introductory experience. Illnesses and other complications had set in, however. Michael Scott had stomach problems; Ariane caught hepatitis; she descended with Nick Fullalove; Hall contracted laryngitis, so he retired with his climbing partner Choe; Richard Chaplin experienced immobilising headaches above Camp IV; Pasang experienced climbing difficulties so descended with Chaplin. The 'survivors': Scott, Afanassieff, Mooney, Sustad, Saela Tamang and Ang Phurba completed the climb; Molly Higgins and Larry Bruce also climbed to Point 6730, a southern outlier of Baruntse. They reached its summit on 4 May.

A camp was stocked for the attempt on Chamlang. Scott had been on Chamlang before, in 1981, his only climb with Messner, when they had reached Point 7010 on the summit ridge. (Messner was said to be unenthusiastic about snow-holing, which he had not used before, after a 2.30 a.m. spindrift visitation.) The climb was made in two parties, the first preceding the second by a day. They ascended the east ridge (Scottish grade II or III) to a high bivouac. On 16 May, Scott's party reached the

East Summit (7235m), then the Central Summit (7180m) an hour later. The descent, thanks to Scott's poor memory of his 1981 route, led them into difficulties on 600m of very steep rock above the Chamlang Glacier. It took a day of abseils, climbs down loose rock and across green ice before Camp I was reached by nightfall.

There, they heard about Hall and Brookes's descent from the East Summit. Scott called it 'an epic retreat'. For Hall, it was rather more complicated than that: 'Terry was in great pain and snow-blind. The two Sherpas were literally shaking with fear. Terry suggested they go to the summit, by which time he might have recovered sufficiently. Just off the summit, Sustad knocked off a dinner-plate-sized piece of ice while trying to get his ice-axe to purchase. Hall was hit and concussed. Choe and Sustad "did wonders" lowering Terry, me and the two Sherpas down the mountain over three days.'[15]

At base camp the injured recovered. Hall decided to leave, however, because of his head injury. Clive and Sue Davies, Larry Bruce and Molly Higgins left to return to work. Sustad, Afanassieff (who had spent the recovery period climbing and filming) and Scott were ready for their attempt on Makalu itself. Had their intended traverse succeeded, it would have been one of the boldest climbs in mountaineering history. Instead, it became another survival epic.

After traversing Point 6285, the three arrived at Makalu's south col. The ridge climb was not particularly difficult; they reached a feature known as the Mushroom for their last comfortable night. The route became progressively steeper, on soft 'uninspiring' snow. Scott and Sustad led 150m of steep rock and gullies on the edge of the eastern cwm. Here, they descended 300m onto the cwm floor to avoid the fierce crosswinds on the ridge. They broke trail to reach the cwm's headwall at about 100m below their high point bivouac in 1980. Morale was high.

The snow proved horrible, however: a whole day gained only 200m. Carving a platform took over an hour. A fuel cartridge failed to work, leaving only one. During the night, the tent shifted, necessitating urgent new security anchors. The next day repeated the previous one: only 200m gained. Suddenly, they discovered the body of Karel Schubert, the first Czech climber to summit an 8000m peak but who died on the descent. Shortly after, they reached the summit ridge.

After discussion, they skirted a large rock tower on soft snow. They bivouacked only 100m below the summit. Afanassieff was complaining about a ringing noise in his head. All three felt drained. Scott had a very sore throat, something the others had endured since base camp. He was unable to drink hot liquid.

Next day, Scott's forty-third birthday, Sustad led off but was soon floundering in deep snow. Afanassieff argued for descent. Scott argued for the summit then descending via the *French Route*. Afanassieff, however, started descending, obliging the others to follow. They progressed rapidly to their fourth bivouac site. The gas was finished, leaving only frozen snow to quench their fierce thirst. After a cube of cheese for breakfast, they began to wade through the snow to a shoulder. Scott spotted Afanassieff sleeping in a foetal position, unroped. He had to be screamed at to move, repeated later. While reascending to reach the shoulder, their only thought was to lie down and 'sleep into eternity'. Scott drew on his extraordinary reserves of strength to break two-thirds of the trail; Sustad could not manage more than twenty metres at any time. He did, however, lead round rocks to put the party out of avalanche danger. Their strength recovered as the abseils continued. Tins of frozen fish were found at the Mushroom: morale rocketed. They continued down old fixed ropes to the south col. A little beyond it, they camped for their eighth night. Next day, they dodged *séracs* to reach base camp; just above it, Martha met them. They had to stop every few metres for a rest.

Four years elapsed before Scott's third and final attempt on Makalu. This expedition again resembled an international club meet: Al Hinkes, Rick Allen, Andy Parkin, Mark Miller, Sean Smith, Simon Yates and Scott from the UK; Sharu Prabhu, Scott's new girlfriend, later his second wife, and Praful Mistry from India; Greg Child (Australia/USA) and Terry Mooney from Ireland. The climbers were supported by sixteen trekkers, including wives and girlfriends, led by Andy Norris. The climbers suffered through a thirteen-day walk-in from Hile, at the roadhead, then up the Arun Valley, while the trekkers flew to Tumlingtar, the landing described by Yates as 'aqua-planing', where they met unusually heavy monsoon conditions. On the second night, everyone experienced an earthquake. Many porters deserted in heavy rain on the Shipton Col; a lot of food went missing. All had assembled at base camp by 29 August. An advance base at 5500m was established a few days later.

Eight of the trekkers climbed Point 6170 but on their return to base camp discovered that one of their cooks, the popular Bomb Bhadur, had died of pulmonary oedema. Yates contracted hepatitis, eliciting Scott's laconic comment, 'You don't look after yourself very well, kid.'[16] A relatively speedy walk-out then took place, with the trekkers (some of whom later complained) back in Kathmandu by 12 September. The climbers spent four days acclimatising on various 6000m peaks in the area as well as visiting the Makalu Col.

The plan was to tackle the west face, but it was 'totally out of condition'. Hinkes and Allen followed Baxter-Jones's route from 1980. On 30 September, they moved across to camp with a Spanish team on the original route at 7780m. Hinkes and Allen pressed on to 8100m. Allen was avalanched shortly after and fell at least 150 metres; his head was badly lacerated. With assistance from Spanish and Polish climbers, Allen was brought down to the Makalu La, then to the 7000m camp next day, where Scott and Child reached him, helping him to descend to advance base on 3 October. On 5 October, all reached base camp, where Allen received thirty stitches. Along with a frostbitten Spanish climber, Allen was evacuated by helicopter on 7 October, to conclude his and Alison's honeymoon! The expedition was called off.

Multiple attempts on other 8000m peaks, however, remained.

Himalayas, Norway, New England, Scotland and Spain

'It's a sad day for democracy when you have to vote on it.'

– Doug Scott

The remaining 8000m peak which interested Scott was Nanga Parbat (8126m), in particular its Mazeno Ridge, a thirteen-kilometre serrated spine with eight subsidiary peaks above 6800m leading to the Mazeno Gap (6940m), from where a 1200m ascent leads to Nanga Parbat's summit. In one of the great ascents in mountaineering history, Sandy Allan and Rick Allen completed the ridge and summit in 2012.[17] Scott made three attempts on the Mazeno Ridge, each dogged by bad luck, injury, illness and unfamiliarity with a new area.

He first visited Nanga Parbat in 1985, following a moderately successful expedition to Hunza which had nonetheless left the party weakened by illness. On 12 August, after a 'harrowing' tractor and jeep ride, the party, consisting of Scott, his son Michael, twelve-year-old Martha, Alastair Reid, David Marshall and Pakistan's most prominent mountaineer, Nazir Sabir, established base camp on the west side of Rupal Peak (5642m).[18] After three bivouacs and some Scottish Grade III ice-climbing, they reached a point about 250m below the summit. Scott and Martha, who was experiencing bad stomach pains, returned; the others summited.

The party moved round to tackle the south-west ridge. Scott, Reid and Sabir climbed 'appalling' loose rock to camp at 6400m. Despite a hurricane-force storm next day, they reached 7400m. They bivouacked about 150m lower. Reid felt ill, possibly with incipient oedema, so they all descended to base camp next day. With a panache which none of them was feeling, they hired horses and 'galloped' out to the Karakoram Highway roadhead.[19]

Scott's first serious attempt on the Mazeno Ridge took place in August 1992. Once again, quite a large international team assembled: Scott, Al Hinkes, Sean Smith, Sergei Efimov, Valeri Perchine, Nga Temba and Ang Phurba. Not only had Russians joined the team after the break-up of the Soviet Union, but the Sherpas were coming into their own as full-scale climbers. Base camp was situated near the hamlet of Latobo, at only 3500m, thus requiring more intermediate camps.

The team acclimatised on nearby 5000m and 6000m peaks, the most notable being Point 5971m, also known as Lilley Peak. The *Schell Route* was reconnoitred up to 6900m, to facilitate descent. Scott, Efimov and Pershin then placed a food cache at 7300m above the Mazeno Gap. Rockfall almost killed Hinkes when 'settee-sized' blocks just missed him. Next day, rockfall did seriously injure Perchine, who was swept down for 30m and had to be carried down to base camp with broken ribs, a crushed pelvis and skin lacerations. Smith was also hit and sustained bruised rib and chest injuries, as well as a crushed toe and shattered helmet.

Hinkes and Smith decided to go home. The others walked up to a 4800m camp on the Mazeno Glacier. Next day, they set out with twenty-five-kilogram rucksacks for eight days on the ridge, then the summit of Nanga Parbat, with a descent by the *Schell Route*. They camped first, after a very strenuous steep climb, at 5850m. On 26 August, they continued over the Ridge's pinnacles to camp at 6400m. On 27 August, they reached the first of the Mazeno summits at 6880m. Next day, they climbed to a point at 6970m, where progress was halted. Ang Phurba was demoralised after his rockfall injury and was not keen to continue. The team could not be split; they retreated. The expedition recognised the dangerous state of the mountain and called off any further attempt. They burned forty-five bags of rubbish (much of it not theirs), then left for the roadhead with their eighteen loads on donkeys.

The following year, 1993, Scott returned with one of the very brightest stars, Wojciech Kurtyka. They were accompanied by Richard Cowper, a *Financial Times* journalist who was also an excellent climber; he would

concentrate on the acclimatisation peaks. By 30 July, they had established a high camp near the Mazeno Pass at 4900m. Cowper and Scott
made probably the first ascent of the Mazeno Spire (around 5600m), a
scramble followed by 200m of VS climbing. Cowper stopped about six
metres below the top. To continue acclimatising, all three climbed what
they named Mazeno West Peak (5700m), probably another first ascent.
On the descent, a huge avalanche swept down from the peak's upper
basin. Cowper was well behind Scott and Kurtyka, so managed to avoid
it. Cowper describes Kurtyka as 'a man with the looks, sensitivity and
athleticism of a young Rudolf Nureyev'. Kurtyka afterwards recounted
the event: '. . . at the narrowest part of the gully, I heard a muffled noise.
Avalanche! I looked up and saw a long crack appear across the slope above
and then the snow began to slide. Doug was about 25m above me, running
towards some rocks. The snow was catching him up . . . Immediately, I
made three or four jumps out of the gully onto some rocks. It was just a
few seconds before the first rush of snow hurtled past.'[20]

Scott's ice-axe support failed to hold and he was carried down, bouncing
over rock and ice cliffs for some 360m. As usual, he felt no fear, only curiosity as to how the situation would evolve. He extricated himself at the
bottom, only to find that the tendons on his right ankle had been severely
wrenched, an unhappy discovery: this ankle had been pinned since The
Ogre. It took several hours of crawling over moraines – The Ogre descent
parallels are obvious – to reach base camp, three kilometres away.

The trio spent three days at base camp, but the ankle would not heal
properly. Scott headed on horseback for the roadhead then took a jeep to
Astor hospital. X-rays confirmed that he would be out of action for the
rest of the year. At the time of the accident, Scott was fifty-three.

The final attempt on the Mazeno Ridge took place in July and August
1995, by which time Scott's injuries appeared to have at least temporarily
healed. Kurtyka returned, as did Sandy Allan and Rick Allen. They were
joined by Australian climber Andrew Lock, who went on to be the eighteenth person to ascend all the 8000m peaks. Steven Thomas joined them
on the approach. This time, everyone on the walk-in used bicycles: the
sponsors were Doug's old neighbours: Raleigh. They cycled for 152 kilometres across the Deosai plains to base camp. The 1992 acclimatisation
routes were followed, to no avail: Scott fell ill – probably heat exhaustion
and the effects of an earlier operation; he walked out on 6 August. Sandy
Allan departed shortly after. The others stayed on, to reach the crest of the
Mazeno Ridge. In poor conditions, they reached the Ridge's third peak

but lack of supplies and bad weather forced a retreat. Scott's extraordinary powers were waning. He had some important climbs still to accomplish, but he gave up major expeditions five years later.

∾

During this 1978–2000 period, it was inevitable that Scott would wish to return to Everest to attempt it by a new route. In 1987, he tried the *North-East Ridge*, on which Boardman and Tasker had died in 1982.

The expedition was sponsored by Altos Computers and also supported by the MEF. Once again, it enjoyed quite a large international membership: Scott, Michael Scott, Rick Allen, Sandy Allan, Nick Kekus from the UK; Sharu Prabhu, from India, took part in one of her earliest climbs with Scott; Robert Schauer from Austria; Steve Sustad was an American working and living in the UK; Eva Jansson, from Sweden, was base camp manager. Mangal Sing (Nima) Tamang and Sila Tamang joined the expedition as cooks. They had been with Scott on all his expeditions to Nepal since 1979. The permit came from Rick Allen. Through his climbing partner Sandy Allan, they invited Scott, who 'accepted with alacrity'.

Several previous expeditions had failed, using both Alpine and siege tactics. The *North-East Ridge* is seven kilometres long and very exposed to wind and bad weather. It involves a range of climbing surfaces.

Acclimatisation was spent in the Langtang, north of Kathmandu. The most notable ascent was Naya Kanga (5846m). The party then travelled via the Friendship Highway to Shekar Dzong, arriving at Everest base camp on 4 September. With the help of yaks, advance base at 6400m was established on 14 September. Because of high winds, the lowest camp on the ridge, on Bill's Buttress at 7090m, became a large snowhole. Ropes were fixed to that point. In late September, progress was halted by very deep, avalanche-prone snow. Michael, who was ill, left with Eva Jansson. By 3 October, nonetheless, progress had been made to the first buttress. Sharu became ill after eating a sharp, salt-edged plum stone which left her throwing up stomach blood, although she gamely carried gas cylinders to 7500m. (Scott had brought the *umeboshi* plums, as he believed that dried fruit was an aid to acclimatisation. He had never been a fan of Diamox.)

Meanwhile, Rick Allen forged on to the top of a second rock-step to make a snow-cave at 7900m. Frostbite or frostnip, however, was spreading through the team. On the first summit push on 14 October, Scott and Allen reached 8100m in very high winds. A further attempt on 15 October failed to make the previous day's height. Everyone retired to base camp where, on 19 October, the first of the winter storms blew in: the expedition was over.

Its conclusion was marred dreadfully by the death of Nima Tamang in an avalanche, the only time on the expedition, according to Nick Kekus, that Scott became angry. (When friends were lost in accidents, Scott often reacted angrily rather than sadly.) Sharu describes the incident: 'Tamang's body was found after two days with some digging help from a nearby American team but also by using the new Avalanche Rescue Equipment that Robert Schauer had brought with him from Austria. Robert simply went over the area with his beeper. He poked with a long stick exactly where it had beeped and felt Tamang's body. We all started digging; the body was soon found. Doug was very impressed with that piece of avalanche rescue equipment; he tried to buy it off Robert, but Robert had to take it back to the manufacturers.'[21]

Tamang was cremated at Rongbuk gompa on 24 October. Scott travelled all the way to Khumbu to talk to Tamang's family before re-joining the expedition on the border at Nyalam. As Scott wrote in a subsequent article for *The Guardian*, 'By caring for each other, we are relieved of the burden of our own self-importance.'[22]

The way home was disrupted by transport problems occasioned by heavy snow. Sandy Allan skied out via Lhasa.

By the time he stopped going on large expeditions in 2000, Scott had attempted seven of the fourteen 8000m peaks and succeeded on four of them (and all but climbed a fifth, Makalu). Fortunately, he had the imagination not to try all fourteen as a list. While more interested in climbing in adventurous areas, Scott nonetheless continued to put up new routes on lesser but still more familiar mountains. These occupied a substantial amount of his time and energies from the late 1980s onwards.

Scott returned to Norway in 1988. He visited Sissel and Tomas Carlström at their home in Hemsedal, a mountain area and ski resort in southern Norway, together with Stein P. Aasheim and his wife at that time, Ragnhild Amundsen. They made a first ascent of a frozen waterfall in Herad, some way down in the valley from Hemsedal. Aasheim recalls that in the late 1980s, Scott gave a lecture and they did one short (two rope-lengths) climb together in Romsdal.

Although Romsdal lies towards Norway's southern end, Scott travelled to northern Norway to climb with 'local hero' Sjur Nesheim on at least two occasions. In March 1998, Scott (on his own) was invited by the local club to talk about his life and climbs. Scott and Nesheim then visited the

Lyngen Alps, lying east of Tromsø at about 400 kilometres north of the Arctic Circle. The made a first ascent (route 24.2 in the *Lyngen Alps* guidebook; 700m, IV) on the Urdtinden south face, which is quickly accessible from the road. This long, mixed route includes a waterfall pitch. Despite the pain he must have been suffering, Scott never complained and seemed to Nesheim to be in good shape, completing the climb 'in good time'. He and Nesheim also put up the first ascent of the *Scott-Nesheim route* (III-4) on Munin, a mixed 200m pillar next to Vågstind, on the Kvaløya, an archipelago lying between Tromsø and the Arctic Ocean. As Nesheim records, Scott was interested in 'many cultures and ways of thinking', very much in keeping with the way his mind was developing.

After the Caucasus expedition in 1994, Mark Bowen and Scott met quite often during the 1990s (and thereafter), especially as Scott continued to lecture regularly in the US. They often went climbing together in New Hampshire:

> Aside from the *Black Dike* (WI4-5M3), a mixed climb, and *Chia Direct* (WI4+), pure ice, Doug climbed *Recompense* (5.9), one of the best lines on Cathedral Ledge, and *Across the Universe* (5.10a PGI3) on Mount Willard. Doug, Sharu and I also did some climbing at Lake Willoughby, the most impressive ice and mixed climbing area in New England. I remember him leading a long, vertical ice pillar wearing a pair of my old plastic boots, which didn't fit him very well. Very impressive, what with his beat-up old ankles from the Ogre. Sharu didn't have a chance on the thing, being a rank beginner, so he and I literally hauled her up to the belay hand over hand. Doug made six or seven visits to New England on his lecture tours, and we managed to go climbing on all but the last two, when his ankles were so bad he could barely walk.[23]

During the 1990s, Scott was equally active in the UK. He took a new interest in Scottish sea-stacks, beginning with the Old Man of Hoy (137m), known to 15 million BBC viewers from its first ascent in July 1967. Probably in 1994, with Jim Duff and his girlfriend, Scott and Prabhu arrived late and topped out at 10 p.m. on midsummer's day, still in daylight.

Lacking snow in Glencoe in February, probably 1995, Duff and his girlfriend, with Scott and Prabhu, headed for Scotland's north-west coast, where they tackled Am Buachaille (easiest grade: VS 4c), requiring a short but often choppy swim to reach its base. Duff recalls that they swam out to the stacks in windproofs, with their clothing in their rucksacks. This was a major coup for both of them and was typical of Doug's imperturbable confidence. After that feat, they continued to the furthest north-west, to the Old Man of Stoer (70m, VS 5a as the *Original Route*) on the beautiful sweep of Sandwood Bay.[24] This sandstone stack is accessed either by a short swim or a Tyrolean traverse.

In 1997, Scott, despite being somewhat arthritic and having to use two telescopic poles for support, joined Sandy Allan, Richard McHardy and Tut Braithwaite in Spain's Picos de Europa, a region he had previously visited as far back as 1964. The group flew to Madrid then drove to a mountain village house owned by Tut's friend, Adrian Garlic. Egg on toast tapas at the bar on arrival went down well. Scott, says McHardy, was well-prepared, with plastic bivvy sheets. From Garlic's house, they walked up to a mountain hut.

Only one 'big' route was achieved: *Murciana* (ED inf/A1, 530m) on the West Face of El Naranjo de Bulnes (2519m). On the climb, McHardy and Braithwaite led off, into cold mist. The rock was clean limestone with good belays. Allan and Scott missed the way at a divide and so suffered an unplanned bivvy (which Scott had brought clothes for). From the cliff-face, they could hear McHardy and Braithwaite toasting them in wine. A plan to haul up a bottle of wine went unrealised. They probably completed Route 124, *Almirante* (ED/A3, 530m). This close-knit foursome then drove back to Madrid, with the Rolling Stones and Bob Dylan courtesy of Allan's cassettes; what Scott called 'real music'.

Most of the climbs above were completed on mountains familiar to climbers of Scott's class. What was happening in parallel, after 1979, was twenty years of exploration.

13

Explorations, 1980–2005

'You'll never find enlightenment on a full stomach.'

– Doug Scott

While trying new routes on frequented mountains, Scott also explored peaks and areas unfamiliar to most climbers. He was also in a position to complete his version of the Seven Summits – the highest mountains on each of the continents.

New Zealand and Himalayas

Scott first ventured into the Southern Hemisphere in 1980. From Nepal, Scott, Jan and Martha flew to Auckland, where Jan and Martha were to stay in Peter Hillary's beach house. Jan wrote to Michael that they had visited Lake Taupo for a climbing meet. A Maori lady asked Doug for his autograph which, Jan says, 'at first freaked him out!' She told Michael that she had earned her break after a very hectic time. Michael was asked to mow the lawn at home as 'Doug won't have time to do it as he rushes in and out to K2'. Jan continued to feel homesick, however, for her 'ramshackle old house, ramshackle old family and friends'.

Martha recalls the black, magnetic beach sand visible from their house overlooking Hobson Bay. The Scotts set about exploring North Island; at Lake Taupo, Scott only just avoided falling into a pool of hot volcanic mud. From North Island, Scott, Dr Jim Duff, Mervyn English and Ariane Giobellina flew to Milford Sound on the south-west corner of South Island, to climb in the Darran Mountains.

The Darrans appear to have been named after the Y Darren Widdon crags in Glamorgan, a belief supported by Welsh names for other local features. The Darrans' highest point, Mount Tūtoko (2723m), named after a Maori chief, resembles a compressed version of The Ogre. The range mostly comprises sandstone, granite, gneiss and diorite. Access is hard work. In a mountain profile in *Alpinist,* June 2014, Paul Hersey comments, 'For more than 100 years, small bands of climbers have struggled through rain-soaked forests to reach the great ice and rock lines of the Darran Mountains in New Zealand. And yet, even today, many of the vast walls remain largely unknown.' The first guidebook was produced only in 1990.

Duff was present to make a film about recent deaths on Mount Cook (now Aoraki). Filming involved transport by helicopter. By chance, the party ran into one of the helicopter pilots in the Milford pub. He flew them into Bivouac Boulder, thereby avoiding a day's 'bush bash'. On the approach to Tūtoko, an exposed *brèche* had to be traversed. This turned out to be a leap too far for Ariane. She and Scott turned back; Duff and English continued to the summit. On the return journey, Duff fell while trying to leap across a stream he should have waded and broke his knee cap. Scott carried his rucksack for him to Milford, which they reached at midnight. As Ariane says, 'The walk-out seemed to last ages and ages, with heavy packs. We arrived back in civilisation in the dark – and hungry!'[1] Scott returned via Christchurch, for his intensive course with a swami, before heading to Pakistan for an attempt on K2.

Scott's first big expedition of 1981 settled on Shivling, 'the Matterhorn of the Himalaya'. Shivling, for obvious reasons 'the lingam of the god Shiva', is a strikingly steep, technically difficult granite twin peak situated just south of Gaumukh (the 'Cow's Mouth'), at the snout of the Gangotri Glacier; this source of the Ganges (starting as the River Bhagirathi) is a very important Hindu pilgrimage site.[2] Above Gaumukh lies Tapovan (4500m), a moraine meadow where base camp is usually sited. While not remarkably high at 6543m, Shivling offers a formidable climbing challenge from all sides except the west face, by which it was first climbed in 1974. As a place of great spiritual resonance with a tough, unclimbed route, it was an ideal peak for Scott after his success on Kangchenjunga.

For his team, Scott chose his friend Don Whillans, the self-indulgent genius whose quips – real and invented – still do the rounds in climbers' pubs. Given his lack of mobility, Whillans was included for his lively banter and immense experience (and as consolation for not being picked for Everest 1975). Georges Bettembourg persuaded Scott to choose Stephen Sustad, who climbed with Scott on several subsequent expeditions (see chapter twelve).

Scott had first met the outstanding Australian climber Rick White in Yosemite in 1973, where they climbed *The Nose* of El Capitan. In the mid-1970s, the forceful White had put up some awe-inspiring rock-climbs with

Australian wunderkind Greg Child. Child had first met Scott at a pub near Sheffield in 1979. He was immediately impressed by Scott and Jan, an apparently glamorous couple. That encounter led to him 'helping' Scott the following year with a Scottish lecture tour combined with ice-climbing on the sandstone terraces of Torridon, in the North-West Highlands.[3] As Child gratefully remarks, 'Scott was willing, unlike most mountaineers, to open doors to younger climbers in whom he saw promise.'[4]

Also joining the team was a Scott climbing partner from the Lake District, Colin Downer, chosen for his mastery of high-quality European and British climbing routes. The eighth member was New Zealand climber Mervyn English, returning after a disastrous attempt on Ama Dablam west face during which a partner had died and he had been badly injured.

The expedition started from Delhi. For the neophytes, it almost over-whelmed them: 'Lining the roads, rambling shanty towns of mud brick, cow dung and tin sweltered beside plush air-conditioned hotels. Families of beggars sifted through garbage within sight of Rolls-Royces.'[5]

At the Indian Mountaineering Foundation (IMF) for their obligatory briefing, Scott learnt that the cost of permission was giving a seminar on modern climbing techniques and advising eight Indian-led climbing teams.

Reaching the road-end at Gaumukh began with an eighteen-hour overcrowded bus journey to Uttarkashi. They moved from dusty plains to misty, forested hills above the roaring Bhagarinathi River; pilgrim buses competed with each other, thieving monkeys, elephants engaged in log-ging, importunate hooch sellers and noisy market traders. At Uttarkashi (Whillans called it 'Uttar Chaos'), the expedition was joined by its Indian co-leaders, Colonel Balwant Sandhu and Ratan Singh, respectively the Principal and Chief Instructor of the Nehru Institute of Mountaineering.

After another terrifying bus ride along the unstable road to Gaumukh, they reached the temple-town of Gangotri. Scott was spotted enjoying Bob Dylan while sitting next to a near-naked saddhu. Sleep was denied by fleas, chanting and the blare of horns from nearby temples.

At Gangotri, forty-five porters were hired for the two-day trek to Gaumukh then Tapovan. This short walk-in was sensually rich: the scents and colours of the plants and trees; the colours of the birds and butterflies; the textures of the granite; the turbulence of the muddy, white water; the broiling heat of the May sun – all in sight of the gleaming snows. Impervious to these glories, Whillans encountered an ash-covered saddhu, who extended his hand for alms. Whillans shook it and asked, 'Are you on some sort of sponsored walk?' The saddhu left, bemused. Whillans's humour, however, disguised his pain. Unseen by him while resting at Bhojbasa, Scott observed his friend hobbling by: Whillans was too proud to admit that his painful knees were already restricting his progress.

After reaching Gaumukh, the climbers made their way to the Bhagirathi, issuing from the glacier's snout. Scott briefly tried a pilgrim's cleansing bathe. An easy day's walk next day, 17 May, brought the 1,220-kilogram *bandobast* to Tapovan. Twenty young Indian climbers arrived two days later. 'Seminar' week helped the Indians to gain first-class instruction while cragging and bouldering near Tapovan; the Westerners acclimatised progressively on the Meru, Chaturangi and Gangotri Glaciers. The badly equipped Indians were dissuaded from attempting over-ambitious climbs.

Following several forays above 5500m during this training period, from 18 to 29 May, the real climb could now begin. Acclimatisation rates decided that Scott, Bettembourg, Child and White were to tackle the unvisited East Pillar ridge, a long climb resembling a warped power-saw blade. The 1300m climb alternated corniced arêtes with walls, finishing on a headwall then the summit cone. The descent was planned for the west face, partly because of its relative straightforwardness and because the other party might leave guiding tracks.

As it was anticipated the climb would take nine days, all the equipment and food bags would have to be hauled up manually – proof that Alpine-style does not necessarily mean lightweight. Six loads of twenty-three kilograms each were needed. Hauling mechanisms were not included.

On Scott's fortieth birthday, 29 May, an advance base was established at the foot of the ridge. Heavy snow began to fall almost immediately, in whirlwinds. Retreat was sounded; two hours of boulder-hopping and bum-slides covered the ground back to base camp. Life there was enlivened by complaints about Whillans's laziness. Whillans roused the camp at midnight with a cry that his fiftieth birthday had arrived. In fact, it was only his forty-eighth, but the occasion demanded whisky in any case. To pass the time at base camp, the party visited local lakes and hermits in caves, several of whom were refugees from Chinese Tibet.

On 3 June, the party returned, carrying ten days' food. Scott and Bettembourg led along a coxcomb ridge while Child and White laboriously hauled up the awkward sacks. For two days, the climbers chopped and kicked their way over pinnacles, cornices and sharp crests to a bivouac hanging over the abyss. They slept in their climbing harnesses attached to a piton.

On the second night, Child and White mistakenly believed their gas cartridge to be empty; changing it sent a fireball through their tent, leading to screams and burnt eyebrows.

'What the hell is going on?' shouted Scott.

'The tent! The tent!' Child yelled back.

'Is it insured?' was Scott's deflating response.

On the fourth day, they reached the top of the rock dome: it had taken them the whole day to climb only two pitches. Time to tackle the Golden Pillar, a sheet of granite sharpening into a phallic tower. Child led the way: 'I sling the rack of gear over my shoulder, wedge my hip inside the wide crack and shimmy up it. After 10m, the crack becomes smooth-faced, bulging and choked with ice. I chop hand-holds into the ice with my Alpine hammer's pick and wedge my boots across the slick crack. There is no protection. After 15m, the crack narrows enough to cam a friend into it. Georges leads another pitch, after which we rappel back down to our tents.'[6]

The weather worsened. Scott and Bettembourg found a ledge for the tents, but it was midnight before the site had been cleared and the merciless bags hauled up. Their bivouac sat below a rock spire resembling an anticipatory crocodile. A whole day of freezing climbing yielded only another 150m of ascent. Even an evening meal of sardines, mashed potatoes and soup failed to restore circulation properly. Scott asked with fatherly kindness, 'Think you can make it home, kid?'

The climb up the tower ground on. White had to swing in a pendulum of twelve metres to reach a place where the ice-axes would bite. Scott burrowed through a tunnel of overhanging snow. Once the tents were up, tepid water was gulped down as soon as the snow melted. From Scott's and Bettembourg's tent oaths emanated when someone knocked over a pot of boiling water, soaking the sleeping bags.

Day nine dawned: movements were clumsy from tiredness; irritation showed at their slow progress. Only a day's food remained. To speed up, Bettembourg did some re-packing and sent one of the haulbags trundling down the south face, hoping that those at base camp would not think it was a climber.

Scott led, smashing his way past cornices while straddling the ridge. For the next bivouac, Scott and Bettembourg established themselves relatively securely under an overhang. Scott was asked why he managed to get the better spot; the laconic answer came: 'You've already wrecked your tent, so a good site won't make any difference.'

Greg Child on Shivling East Pillar, 1981. (Doug Scott collection)

After two more pitches the views began to open out. On the tenth night a storm broke, forcing spindrift into the tents. A rest-day was called. Food was down to cereal with sugarless tea. Scott asserted that they must move on tomorrow: crossing the summit was now necessary for survival. They turned to Scott's paperback of Castaneda's *Teachings of Don Juan*. The teachings tritely declared, 'Find a path with heart and follow it to the end.'

Now on their eleventh day, the food had all but given out. The final 150m of cornices, towers and ice runnels had to be negotiated to reach the headwall below the summit. Putting a boot through the cornices revealed the glacier over a kilometre below. The headwall, fortunately, looked manageable. Scott and Child climbed the first 100m using ice-screws and pitons. By darkness, with insufficient room for two tents, all four climbers clambered into one two-man tent. The last of the food was some cereal and a packet of mushroom soup.

Next day was cold and windy. Complaints about lack of food were met with Scott's pithy dictum 'You'll never find enlightenment on a full stomach.' Bettembourg and White led the way, with Scott and Child hauling up the leaden packs. By mid-afternoon, the headwall had been climbed. At only 125m from the summit, Scott, disturbingly, declared he could hear voices. All four picked up sounds coming from the dip between the summits. Scott spotted four figures: the other party. They shouted a description of the way down, a heartening moment.

The foursome arrived by 5 p.m. at a ledge just short of the summit. They were too tired to go on. The gas for melting snow gave out. In a screaming wind, everything superfluous was buried in a crevasse. On their thirteenth day, at 7 a.m., they reached the summit. Bizarrely, Scott and Bettembourg danced a jig. But the monsoon storm clouds were massing: it was time to descend after only ten minutes on top. Scott advised caution because of weakness from lack of sleep, liquid and food.

Scott's warning was timely. The first 200 metres to the col between Shivling's summits went well. Tracks left by the other party, and fixed ropes from a previous Japanese expedition, helped. A steep ice-wall followed, leading to a wide bowl. The Scott and Bettembourg rope reached the bowl first. White, on blunted crampon points, slipped. His ice-axe failed to hold him. He slid rapidly past Child, who was thrown into the air. Both climbers tumbled for almost 250m. Bettembourg and Scott watched in helpless horror. They hurried towards what they expected to be two corpses, but the snow had cushioned the fall. Everyone continued, bruised and shaken.

Near the bottom, Whillans appeared. The climbers fantasised about what food he had brought. Scott reached Whillans first and told their tale while awaiting the others.

'Well done, lads. You made it back,' was Whillans's dry welcome. He then departed for the Meru Glacier and base camp.

'Did he bring anything to eat?' Child asked.

'Yes, but he got hungry while he was waiting and ate it all himself,' came the appalling reply.

Back at base camp, however, the feasting began. Not all the stories had happy endings. Two of the young Indian climbers had died on Bhagirathi II.

Scott had one of the last words: 'It's simpler up there, isn't it?'

Greg Child had the other: 'Shivling was like El Cap for me, but with hell and Antarctica added. Doug turned me to Alpinism and for this he must be held accountable!'

∽

Shortly before leaving for Shivling, in March 1981, Scott received permission from the Chinese to climb Shishapangma (8027m, 'The Crest above the Grassy Plain', or, from an Indian perspective, Gosainthān, 'The Home of God'). Although the Chinese had first climbed the mountain from the north, in 1963, Scott aimed to make an Alpine-style ascent of the unclimbed 3000m south-west face, overlooking Nepal.

Scott teamed up with Alex MacIntyre, the ambitious *enfant terrible* of the high-altitude climbing scene, Roger Baxter-Jones and Tut Braithwaite. They were joined by Nick Prescott and Elaine Brook for the acclimatisation period. Prescott was an enthusiast, but without previous Himalayan experience. Brook hoped to make cultural connections with local Tibetans while Prescott supported the main team on the south-west face. This rather tetchy expedition of petty quarrels was also one of the most smoothly successful Alpine-style ascents of an 8000m peak in history.

The expedition arrived in Lhasa via Beijing and Chengdu on 9 April. A frustrating, expensive administrative delay at Nyalam almost stopped the expedition altogether. By 3 May, however, they had established an advance base below the subsidiary peak of Nyanang Ri (7071m). Braithwaite and Prescott remained out of action for most of the acclimatisation period. An attempt on Nyanang Ri reached 6000m. The party then broke up, Braithwaite to return to avoid more serious illness, Brook to work among the Tibetans. The break-up was really caused by underlying tensions between Scott and MacIntyre. Scott was relaxed about the two inexperienced people getting their fair share of the experience (being fully paid-up), whereas MacIntyre regarded them as a restriction on the main climbers' progress. Tensions were intensified by shortness of time thanks to the earlier administrative delays.

Castle Camp was established five kilometres from advance base, at 6000m. From 17–19 May, Pungpa Ri (7445m), a shoulder-outlier of Shishapangma, was successfully climbed by Scott, MacIntyre and Baxter-Jones. On 25 May, these three and Prescott set out for the base of the south-west face, about three and a half kilometres away. A straightforward mixed climb of about 300m brought them to a bivouac site in a small basin. From there, Prescott, more or less at MacIntyre's insistence, descended to Castle Camp. A route dispute followed, with Scott following a rock rib while Baxter-Jones and MacIntyre climbed a steep snow and ice slope. They all met at a bivouac site in a 'pea-pod' couloir at just on 7000m. On 28 May, they climbed the couloir to reach the summit ridge, then arrived at the summit at 2 p.m. Scott and MacIntyre headed for the slightly lower west summit, about 300 metres away, but stopped short because of dangerous cornices. Remarkably, they descended with relative ease and were safely back in Castle Camp on 29 May.

The return to the UK began with a banquet provided by the Chinese Mountaineering Association in Beijing, where the vegetarian dishes met with Scott's enthusiastic approval. Certificates of summit success were issued. Back at their hotel, they decided to visit a disco for foreigners. In a moment of abandon, Scott whirled MacIntyre round – then let go of him. MacIntyre was enraged; the month's tensions erupted: the pair brawled, insulted and threatened each other. Outside, MacIntyre punched Scott, breaking his glasses. Separate taxis were taken back to the hotel. The evening ended in a lachrymose reconciliation and a rough morning. The gist of MacIntyre's insults was that Scott was 'past it', a hopelessly inaccurate assessment given his performance on Shishapangma, where they had summited on the day before Scott's forty-first birthday. The insults were perhaps a projection of MacIntyre's own febrile self-concern. Such speculation became irrelevant, however: MacIntyre, one of his generation's most brilliant mountaineers, was killed a few months later by a falling stone on Annapurna.[7] Greg Childs adds, 'Doug only spoke highly of Alex. Doug was in my kitchen in Seattle when Jan phoned me to tell Doug of Alex's death. He was very upset, but Doug held much inside. It was clear he was much affected.'

The route on Shishapangma confirmed Scott's reputation as one of the leading advocates of Alpine-style ascents. His enormous strength and talents were now amply confirmed by this first visit by any mountaineering party to Shishapangma's southern faces, culminating in nearly 3000m of direct ascent.

Pakistan, India, Jordan, Bhutan, Australia and the Karakoram

June 1985 saw Scott in a new area: Hunza, Pakistan. His assertion that 'people only get killed in the mountains for two reasons: excess of ambition or lack of luck' was about to be tested to the maximum. An over-ambitious expedition was compromised by porter trouble and illness. Scott, his son Michael, Greg Child, Steve Sustad, Sean Smith, Mark Miller, Alastair Reid, Snævarr Guðmundsson and Helgi Benediktsson headed for northern Pakistan. Clive and Sue Davies, old friends, joined the expedition as trekkers. The main intentions were to climb rock pinnacles in Hunza, to attempt the north face of Rakaposhi (7788m) then Nanga Parbat from the south. They failed on all of these, but they succeeded in climbing Diran (7273m) and some minor summits.

In their bus through the Karakoram Highway furnace, several expedition members lay on the roof for coolness. Below Rakaposhi, a tyre blew. A few minutes later, another bang, as a second tyre went. The bus started to tilt above the long drop into the Indus. The driver's Walkman, and his brain clouded by weed, had isolated him from near disaster. Replacement tyres had to be fetched from Gilgit, delaying arrival in Hunza by several long, hot hours.

They were joined on arrival by Pakistan's most famous climber, Nazir Sabir, as liaison officer. The group divided: Michael Scott, Reid and Guðmundsson took themselves to the Passu Glacier. The others, minus Benediktsson, lying ill in Islamabad, climbed to a camp three hours above Karimabad at 2400m, next to the Ultar Glacier. Next day, they reached a high col below Bubli Motin (Ladyfinger Peak, 6000m) from where Scott and Sustad climbed a minor summit. Everyone, however, felt ill and lethargic. In the valley, the temperature had reached 47 degrees. The Passu team returned, also feeling the heat. Base camp was then shifted to below the north-east ridge of Rakaposhi. Here, trouble blew up with the porters, who threatened the Europeans with sticks. According to Sabir:

> Our verbal agreement with the porters was that we would pay for two camps but as we walked up to the next camp, we heard they were expecting [the] same payment as for other teams . . . Our four hours

of negotiations went without any result. Suddenly our seventy-eight porters left our base camp, chanting slogans but after an hour we saw them heading back towards us again. The procession by now had grown larger, turning mob-like, with the slogans getting a lot louder . . . Some of our members were taking pictures of this drama from atop nearby huge boulders. That annoyed the porters; some of them grabbed the cameras, yelling, with some even threatening to burn our camp . . . Doug finally agreed to pay three days' wages.[8]

Sabir complained to the authorities about the porters, which led to some of them being arrested, jailed and flogged. Scott pardoned the culprits, however, and Terry Mooney QC, who had just arrived, successfully pleaded for their release.

Meanwhile, Sabir flew to Islamabad to get permits to climb Diran. He takes up the account of one of the most perilous periods on any Scott expedition:

As I reached [base camp] with the climbing permit, I learnt Doug and his team had left for Diran two days earlier, taking advantage of the good weather and taking it for granted that I would manage the permit. They planned to reach the summit in two days. The only member at [base camp] was Sean Smith, who was not well. Doug, as usual, didn't have any communication equipment between him and the [base camp]. I decided to follow them up the mountain. Early next morning I left with our kitchen crew, Mohamad Nabi of Hussaini in Hunza, to help me carry some supplies to the foot of the mountain, hoping to catch up in two days.

There was news of a huge brown bear hanging around Minapin Glacier since 1978. It was reported to have developed a taste for Western food. I was told the same bear approached the advance camp when Doug and his team were there but his team had some huge guys like Michael Scott and Mark Miller, who chased him away. It also visited the Austrian base camp; their [liaison officer] opened fire into the air for safety after perceiving it near his tent. The bear was infuriated on hearing the gun shots and destroyed several tents before it went away. At the advance camp where Doug and his team were confronted by this visitor, I was anticipating his visit too and left every food item outside the tent, a stove ready to go just outside the tent and ice axes under my pillow, just in case.

I spoke to Nabi but he told me he had killed several [bears] in the Astore valley when he was working in Gilgit Scouts. I tried to sleep while listening to my favorite country songs of Olivia Newton-John but it just didn't help. My sixth sense told me I heard the bear approach our tent and then tear apart our tinned fish cans. I didn't make any moves and just kept quiet, hoping he would go away. Interestingly he carried away all the food in three shifts and started eating in a relaxed atmosphere. I woke Nabi up and slowly dared to open the tent door. I lit the stove but the bear didn't seem to even bother. His eyes shone against my head torch and I saw him staring at me before disappearing behind the hill as if he was saying 'good bye and thanks for a rich meal.' Nabi and I managed to stumble back to base camp with empty stomachs as our special guest made sure of not leaving anything.

Doug and his team returned to [base camp] next day after reaching the summit of Diran . . . Some years later I heard this famous bear was killed by someone from Minapin while it was feeding on their domestic animals.

On top of all this, injuries and illness were taking their toll, and Mooney, Child, Guðmundsson and Sustad all left. From Minapin base camp, Mark Miller made a fine solo climb of Point 5677 (now marked on maps as Sumayar Peak). The expedition was rejoined by Benediktsson. Together, they moved up to a camp at 4000m. From there, a two-day push took them to Diran's summit by the *Original Route* and down to a bivouac 600m below it. From there, Benediktsson reached the summit with an Austrian climber the following day. Sabir and Smith reached Diran's summit plateau shortly after.

For Sabir, Scott remained 'my brother mentor'. In the typical 'club' fashion of Scott's later expeditions, Jan, Martha and Rosie arrived at base camp with other spouses and friends. Unfortunately, an Austrian climber had died on the descent from Rakaposhi, leaving the party with little stomach for continuing on the mountain's east side. A plan for the south flank failed owing to bad weather and exorbitant porter rates. It was therefore decided to move to Nanga Parbat, which they reached on 12 August.

∽

On the other side of the sub-Continent lies Darjeeling, now used by the IMF for regular international conferences on tourism and related topics.

In 1985 Scott, with other big names such as Messner and Bonington, attended. Here, he met his second wife, Sharu Prabhu.

Sharu (familiar for Sharavati) Prabhu had been invited on the strength of her sporting and climbing record, having been on a major Indian Everest expedition. An immediate attraction was felt by both, although at this stage the relationship remained purely friendly.

Prabhu visited Europe in spring 1986, for a Women Alpinists' gathering at Chamonix. She went on to climb with Scott in Wales and the Lake District. She recalls that Scott's marital problems were obvious. He returned to India in autumn 1986, to a conference in Manali. At the end of his talk, he asked if anyone would like to climb with him. Two climbers answered: Helen Urquhart (*née* Padday) and Andy Jess, just returned from a Scottish Youth Expedition to nearby peaks. Their reply led to a hitherto unrecorded attempt on Ali Ratni Tibba (5492m), a giant spire at the head of the Malana Glacier, south-east of Manali.

This expedition, which lasted about a week, started from Bhuntar, on the main road south of Manali. Scott, Prabhu, Padday and Jess trekked up the Parbati valley then zig-zagged over a col leading to the Malana valley. They camped somewhere near the col, where it rained for most of the day. Their toilet rolls got wet and had to be dried on a rock when the sun came out.

Next day, they carried on east-north-east up the Malana valley to camp on the lip of the Malana Glacier, originating below the Ali Ratni Tibba west face. A brief icefall recce was carried out. Helen recalls that a snow wolf came sniffing around their tents after dark. Doug asked them quietly to set off a flash from Andy's camera to scare it away. On the following day, Doug, Jess and Padday threaded their way through the glacier icefall into a high cwm at around 4125m; it took about four hours. Padday and Scott carried on to reach an outlying top south or south-west of Ali Ratni Tibba, somewhere between 4950m and 5100m; further progress was thwarted by excessive loose snow; it was time to return to glacier lip camp.

In the morning, the porters returned; they struck camp and walked for several hours down the Malana valley to just short of Malana village. At some point a waist-deep river-crossing had to be managed. Their most probable exit followed a trail north-west over the Chandra Khani Pass (3660m) to come out at Naggar, on the main road back to Manali. Padday's assessment of Scott was: 'Great to climb with and very interesting and inspiring. Well organised and had so much experience.'[9]

After the conference and expedition, Scott and Prabhu headed to the Western Ghats, the long range stretching down the Indian west coast.

They tried some rock-climbing in Maharashtra, where a 200m corner crack and chimney climb, over two days, on the fortress cliff at Harihar was named *Scottish Kada* in Scott's honour. The climb had been arranged by Harish Kapadia. They then took a bus to Bengaluru, where they put up several climbs, notably *Scott's Crack* in Savandurga and *Ramagiri Betta* in Ramanagaram (where *A Passage to India* was filmed); they bivvied in local temples. They were accompanied by the renowned Indian climber K.V. Mohan. Scott and Prabhu visited further sites near Pune, Mumbai and Nashik, where Scott put up several new lines, mostly hard two pitch routes of 'flared off-width cracks and chimneys, on generally loose rock'. It was a wild, romantic trip.

Scott and Prabhu next met in 1987, this time in Jordan, at the behest of the Jordan Ministry of Tourism. Scott had been intending to visit Jordan, with Jasmin Tours, having met its managing director, James Smith, at the Manali conference. The ministry wrote to Scott on 31 January 1987 to offer him every support, including his air ticket, should Scott wish to extend his visit to Wadi Rum, in order to open Jordan up as a new adventure tourism venue. Scott was accompanied by the Chamoniard climber Bernard Domenech and by Martha, the first time she had met her father's new girlfriend.

They arrived on 5 April. Two complimentary nights' accommodation in Amman and Aqaba followed, the same repeated at the end of the tour. At Aqaba, their swim was enlivened by suddenly coming across a masturbating Arab. The climbing at Wadi Rum had been arranged for Scott through his friend Tony Howard, author of the local guidebook.[10] Scott, Prabhu, Martha and Domenech put up one new route before Domenech was obliged to leave. Martha then climbed a new route: *Martha's Steps* (D+). Scott and Prabhu climbed the long *Gulab Tower*. They had one very cold, unplanned bivouac, a desert echo of Everest's South Summit. They completed *Skyline Buttress*, consisting mainly of chimneys and stepped ledges, and three or four other routes. A helicopter took them to the top of the Rum for interviews. Martha was presented with a fine ornamental knife.

∽

Away from adventure tourism, one hot Kathmandu day in 1984, Steve Berry, the affable managing director of Mountain Kingdoms, expressed a wish to Elizabeth Hawley, the chronicler of Himalayan summiting expeditions, that he would like to attempt the Bhutanese peak of Gangkhar

Puensum (7570m), the highest unclimbed summit in the world. Hawley put Berry in touch with Colonel Penjor Ongdi, who promised the permit, which arrived two months later. Berry readily concedes that he invited Scott, his boyhood hero, for the sake of sponsorship. They met in March 1985. Scott's first action of rolling a joint was no doubt for persona projection. Berry, however, hoping for clarity, was somewhat put out.

Money was still insufficient when Scott introduced Berry to the inimitable Maggie Payne, later Burgess. Maggie organised a support trek, where the trekkers paid a premium for being part of the expedition as far as base camp. Owing to administrative problems, however, the permit was cancelled. In 1986, Scott and Payne used their influence with Sir Robert Wade Geary, British High Commissioner in Delhi, to persuade the Bhutanese to reinstate the permit. They succeeded.

At this point, however, practical and philosophical differences began to surface. Scott insisted on 'doing things his way': Jean Afanassieff was to come along as film-maker. Berry had already committed to a different film-maker; he turned for advice to Al Rouse, whose comment was, 'If you let Doug have his own way, fine – he would look after everyone in a paternal sort of way, but if you started to take any decisions yourself, Doug would go out of his way to reverse them.' On the matters of climbing style and filming responsibility, neither Berry nor Scott would back down. Scott withdrew, leaving some bitterness in his wake. Later, Berry and Scott did make up: Berry recognised Doug's immense contribution to Nepalese wellbeing through CAN; Scott fundraised for Berry, giving public lectures in Bristol and a talk in Berry's village to raise funds for the tennis club. Steve concludes, 'We all loved Doug. He undoubtedly was a force of nature, a great bear of a man with serious eyes and impossible ideals. May his soul be free to wander unhindered.'

Discussions with Berry had fired Scott's imagination, however. He had been interested in Bhutan since the mid-1960s, after seeing Augusto Gansser's photos published in *Mountain World*. Bhutan was also a Buddhist country, in a relatively 'pure' way, unlike the compromises reached in Nepal and the terrible destruction wreaked by Mao in Tibet. At the Darjeeling Tourism conference in 1985, Scott had met Nedup Dorje of the Bhutanese Tourism Corporation, who interested Scott in his government's policy of 'controlled development': King Jigme Wangchuk IV had opened up their mountains in 1983. With Mike Westmacott and Maggie Payne, they visited Sikkim after the Conference. There, they discussed the idea of a support trek as a way of paying for an expedition.

Maggie, through her ambassadorial connections, was instrumental in 1987 in gaining permission for Scott to attempt Jitchu Drake ('The Angry Bird, or Swallow'). Its uncertain height appears to be around 6800m. The expedition would be sponsored by *The Guardian,* who sent David Rose along as a climbing reporter. This north-easterly neighbour of the elegant Chomo Lhari lies in little-visited territory, which thus interested Scott. Only four previous attempts were recorded: a Japanese women's and an Austrian men's expedition in 1983, the latter reaching the south summit; a 1984 Japanese siege which fixed 3000m of ropes to the south summit, and the Italians who met with disaster in 1984 on the south-east ridge. In 1988, Scott's expedition, the only one on Jitchu Drake, made the first ascent (the north summit being a few metres higher than the south summit).

Scott arrived two and a half weeks before the main party, having flown in, unusually, from Bagdogra, in West Bengal. He was to lead a trek for the first time. The members were all from the RGS, aged from twenty-four to seventy-eight. From the border with India at Phuntsoling, the group proceeded through the Dooars, or 'Gates', low-lying passes providing access to Bhutan from India, then through teak and pine forests to Paro. Scott enjoyed the trekking, which concentrated on the Phobjikha Valley (home of rare black-necked cranes) in Central Bhutan. These treks helped Scott with his fitness: he admitted he was feeling rather run-down after a particularly demanding tour of seventy lectures, designed to pay off debts, part of which were induced by his separation from Jan.

As the RGS trekkers were leaving at the beginning of May, the mountain-eering team of Victor Saunders, Lindsay Griffin, Sharu Prabhu and David Rose met Scott. Maggie Payne and her three support trekkers joined them in Bhutan's pleasant capital, Thimphu. They drove to the roadhead, past the start of the trek up to Taktshang (the Tiger's Nest gompa), one of Bhutan's most spectacular sights. Despite heavy rain, the trek to base camp through conifer and juniper forest proceeded well; from there, they hoped to explore the west side of the mountain. An acclimatisation programme began, during which the party looked at all but the mountain's north side. At this point, Saunders severely strained a tendon after landing awkwardly when jumping off a boulder. He was put on a horse, to which he declared an allergy.

'Antihistamine, old bean?' asked Lindsay.

'It's the fur dust that gets me.'

'We'll cover you up and throw buckets of water over you while you ride!' said Doug, with a gleeful glint. The horse shied frequently in reaction to Saunders's antihistamine doses.

From an attractive base camp at a high lake, the climbers looked at the ridge separating the two east-face glaciers. Snow conditions, however, dictated that the attempt should be from the south. After a recce by Griffin and one of the trekkers, Neil Lindsay, Camp I was established on 23 May at 5500m above an icefall.

The party was not in great shape: Saunders was hobbling; Griffin had a bad shoulder; Prabhu had stomach problems. On 26 May, the weather cleared and morale lifted; they set off up to the base of the south face. Saunders and Scott, next day, broke trail to the bergschrund. During the usual afternoon storm, they fixed a one-pitch climbing rope for an early start the next day, which required a 750m ice-climb. Gear was whittled down to the minimum. Around 1 a.m., they discussed the line to reach the south-east ridge. By the eighth pitch of the day, they found themselves in a violent storm; somehow, though, Scott felt confident they should carry on. His instinct was right: they reached the south-east ridge two pitches later. Scott hacked out a bivvy site for himself and Sharu on the flat part of the ridge. Saunders, Griffin and Rose slept in a nearby snow tunnel discovered by Griffin.

On 30 May, the party moved up to a camp on a shoulder not far from the south summit. Griffin felt unable to continue and Rose remained to look after him. Saunders, Scott and Prabhu left at 2.30 a.m. Dawn colours were enhanced by extreme cold. They were helped by old Japanese fixed ropes which, as Scott wryly remarked, 'would have been churlish not to use'. Saunders led up to the south summit. By midday, they had traversed the corniced intervening ridge and stood on the summit. As on Kangchenjunga, they stopped a metre below the very top out of respect for local religious sensibilities. The astounding view extended from Kangchenjunga to Arunachal Pradesh, 300 kilometres away.

Two days of careful downclimbing and strenuous abseils brought them back to base camp. Here, an altercation blew up between Scott and Saunders, mainly to do with Scott and Saunders's conflicting views about publicity for the expedition, although underlying tensions also contributed. Griffin believed these tensions might have developed from Scott's obvious drive to get Prabhu to the summit. (Prabhu, however, believes that the main motive was a sudden weather window opportunity which needed to be capitalised on.)

Saunders, nonetheless, declared how impressed he was with Scott's resistance to altitude: he was strolling around on the high ground with not a hint of breathlessness, while Saunders 'wheezed asthmatically behind'. Griffin asserted that Scott 'climbed strongly throughout': he too was impressed by Scott's strength, but – as did David Rose – he found the Scott–Prabhu combination hard to take on such a small expedition. Griffin and Saunders both found Scott's style, of careful acclimatisation followed by a committed, relentless climb, something requiring exceptional strength, not to their taste.

With their use of the old Japanese ropes, this could not strictly be called an Alpine-style expedition, yet it was no siege either. Nor was it capsule style. In the end, it was just a group of mostly very experienced and strong climbers, reaching a summit using their skills and equipment as their experience deemed best.

∾

The globetrotting continued. During the 1980s, but perhaps most notably in 1986 and 1989, Scott visited Australia, principally on lecture tours, but also to climb, to visit friends and to visit a guru, Sri Aurobundo.

In 1989, while on a lecture tour organised by the dynamic Christine Gee (the first one had been in 1980), Scott, Prabhu and Rick White climbed 'crags and canyons' around Alice Springs. He visited the Blue Mountains, for example, on The Three Sisters when it was allowed; Mount Boyce and Mount Piddington (Wirindi) in the Explorer Range; and climbed on Mount Arapiles in West Victoria, probably the best rock climbing in Australia. Christine Gee observes, 'Really, Doug would climb anything . . . He often climbed with Chris Baxter, the founder editor of Australia's *Rock and Wild* magazine. Out of Brisbane, he would go climbing with his great friend Rick White at for example Kangaroo Point, at sea cliffs around Sydney, or even bouldering up at Lindfield Rocks with Dr Jim Duff.'

On Mount Arapiles, a 140m rock wall in western Victoria, Scott put up several climbs with Dennis Kemp (originally from Wales but living in Australia, author of a climbing handbook). Scott climbed on Frog Buttress, on Mount French, in Queensland, a system of cracks first discovered by Rick White and Chris Meadows in 1968. In 1989, with Simon Yates, Prabhu and Rowland Tyson, he climbed on the fantastic granite sea cliffs at West Cape Howe on Australia's south-western extremity: their routes were all first ascents. Yates gives a detailed description of one climb in his lively, autobiographical *Flame of Adventure*. The climb had it all: cracks, ledges, overhangs, with a great sea-swell below. As Yates says, 'These cliffs were a huge adventure playground, yet they had hardly been climbed on.' At the top, they shook hands and returned to their car in a golden sunset;

one of those perfect days. Scott and Prabhu then went off to explore King's Canyon, south-west of Alice Springs.

Another lecture circuit in July 2005 led to Scott and Tim Macartney-Snape touring eastern Australia. In between lectures Scott and Macartney-Snape climbed when they could and stayed with friends whenever possible.

They climbed in three places. First, at one of Macartney-Snape's local crags, Mount Alexander above Mittagong, then at Mount York in the Blue Mountains and at Morialta in the Adelaide Hills. All offer fairly small crags rising above steeply wooded hills. At Morialta, on top of a climb they both had a feeling they were being watched. They were: by a koala.

Visiting Australia also offered a good chance of climbing on Australia's 'best kept secret', Tasmania, with Dr Jim Duff. They climbed there twice; in 1986, on the Organ Pipes above Hobart, on *Fiddle Sticks*. Sailing the coast, Duff had spotted a sea cliff and as a 'present' he took Scott there by road to put up a new route. Previously the crag was unclimbed.

These Australian venues are thousands of kilometres apart; the urge to travel and to explore, despite worsening health, remained as strong as ever. This decade of exploration ended on a frustrating note, however, on the Rimo range, just east of the Siachen Glacier war zone in the East Karakoram.

The malfunction possibilities were obvious from the outset: an Anglo-Indian expedition, and to a war zone; an expedition joining civilians and military. Scott invited Nick Kekus and Stephen Sustad; with his usual foresight, he had been planning the expedition since 1986. He also invited old friends Rob and Laurie Wood and the outstanding Austrian climber Robert Schauer. Prabhu, with whom Scott was infatuated at the time, completed the team. The Indian team, which lacked the experience and cohesion of the Westerners, was led by Sonam Palzor of the Indo-Tibetan Border Police, with Tsewang Smanla, Kanyaiha Lal and Mohan Singh. The team was augmented by liaison officers and a doctor.

On 27 May, this group assembled at the IMF headquarters in Delhi. They were told that the original application for Apsarasas (7245m) was no longer valid. On 29 May, most of the team flew to Leh while Scott and Palzor remained in Delhi to negotiate with the IMF. The Leh team spent a long three weeks there, on tourist trips to the magnificent nearby gompas and on acclimatisation walks, including an unpermitted ascent of Stok Kangri (6153m). Eventually, permission for Rimo III (7233m), particularly its spectacular south-west face, was obtained.

On 17 June, the party left Leh by the military road for Panamik, an outpost below the Siachen Glacier's snout. Schauer, however, had run out of time; he departed. Porters were hard to hire because they earned more by assisting the military. Students were found in Leh (an attempt to hire local Nepalis foundered on poor India-Nepal relations); they returned from base camp at 4300m between the North and South Terong Glaciers on 24 June. The delays and uncertainties adversely affected morale. Loads had been ferried up by twenty local porters from Panamik to base camp but the climbers had to carry very large loads themselves. However, by 28 June, an advance base had been established at 4800m on the North Terong Glacier. Here, Rob Wood developed chest pains, an immediate cause for concern; he too had to leave the expedition.

Camp I was established at 5400m on the west ridge of Rimo II, as an alternative approach to the south-west buttress was being constantly swept by powder snow. (Rimo II became an acclimatisation ascent before tackling Rimo III.) The Westerners and the Indians then chose alternative routes, agreeing to meet at a notch below where the west and north ridges merge. Scott climbed with Laurie Wood and Prabhu; Sustad and Kekus soon overtook them. They all camped 600m up on a level area above a *sérac* wall. Scott led every pitch while Wood and Prabhu jumared up with loads. More interesting climbing followed next day; the Indian climbers were spotted shouting excitedly but unclearly near the notch rendezvous. As they got higher, however, the Indians were identified on a col near their tent. On reaching the notch, burnt juniper, signs of a prayer ceremony, were spotted, adding to the mystery. Meanwhile, Scott, Wood and Prabhu had stopped 400m lower down.

The weather continued fine: Sustad and Kekus climbed on for ten pitches to reach the fore-summit. At 2 p.m., they found difficulty circum-venting a large black tower of very loose shale surrounded by deep powder. Other monster blocks had to be passed before they reached the summit of Rimo II (7373m) at 3.30 p.m. On the way up, they noticed the Indians heading up the south-west flank of Rimo IV.

The descent was completed over two days: a series of abseils to the notch, by dark, then two more days to reach advance base. Scott, Wood and Prabhu turned back at the notch, as Wood and Prabhu felt unable to continue on steep, hard ice covered in powder. Scott, Sustad and Kekus decided on an attempt on Rimo III by the south-west buttress. Suddenly, however, the expedition was called off on 15 July by Palzor. It was a hasty, annoying decision.

In a 1990 *Alpine Journal* article, an angry, frustrated Scott analysed twelve circumstances which prevented the expedition achieving its aims and made positive recommendations for avoiding future problems he had identified.

Despite this setback, and the fact that he was now approaching fifty, Scott still had a decade of outstanding explorations ahead of him before concluding his big expeditions in Tibet in 2000.

Iceland, Canada, Pakistan, Greenland, Nepal, Antarctica, Argentina, Tajikistan, Russia, Chile

Altogether, Scott made six visits to Iceland. These changed that country's mountaineering history. The inspiration for Scott's enthusiasm for Iceland originated with Ted Grey. In 1964, he was assistant leader on a Derbyshire Schools Expedition to Iceland. One member was David Baker, a promising young expeditioner. Baker met Scott on a course at White Hall. This meeting initiated a long period of support by Scott for Derbyshire school expeditions.

Scott's first expedition to Iceland, in October 1984, was sponsored by David Oswin. Jan was present, also. Snævarr Guðmunsson and Scott began on the Stardalur crags, about ten kilometres east of Reykjavik, making a new 5.6 climb known as *Scott's Leið (Route)*. Next day, after Scott's lecture, they travelled to the steep outlet glacier, Gígjökull, towards the extreme south of Iceland. It lies on the volcano which caused flight havoc in 2010. With other Icelandic Alpine Club members, they carried out some ice-bouldering.

Scott's appetite was stimulated. He returned in May 1985, this time concentrating on the Hrútfjallstindar, at the southern extremity of the Vatnajökull; the party, consisting of Helgi Benediktsson, Jón Geirsson and Þorsteinn Guðjónsson, also visited the Svínafellsjökull.[11] Geirsson recounts what happened:

A classic hour to get through the crevasses and the hard work was behind us. When Doug saw the huge frozen waterfall on the south side of Hrútsfjalltindar, we set off. That night, we slept in a snow cave at the foot of the slope. Doug was first up – he said he was a morning person. The rest of us shook our heads, amazed at Doug's eagerness and Helgi's energy in carrying his skis with him. Doug waited for us at the foot of the waterfall.

'Shall I solo it?' asked Doug.

'Really?' I hacked a bollard out and Doug hammered in a piton. We climbed the waterfall, simultaneously, in two pitches, Helgi and Doug on one rope, the rest of us on another . . . Above the waterfall, the climb changed to long snow slopes, risky traverses and ice-ridges until we reached the vertical iced-up rock wall at the top of the face. We had no helmets; Doug had a baseball cap despite the final pitches being serious: grade 6. I increased my speed. Doug tugged on the rope: 'Too much oxygen; enjoy the view, youth. You take the photos.'

We ran into cauliflower ice. Water dripped down Doug's neck. He swore and shouted at me to watch the rope. Doug then brought the lads up one at a time. We waded through slush to the South Peak. On the summit, whisky.

On the descent we got into mist. Even Helgi admitted his skis were not very helpful. Back at camp, Doug shared his beers with us.

They then travelled north-east up the coast to make the first ascent of Rustanöf, in Vestrahorn. Scott's verdict: 'If it had rained, this would have been the worst climb in the world.' The igneous rock was brittle and dangerous: while abseiling, Scott's long hair got caught in the descender. Dangling freely, he removed the hair, which was starting to rip off his head skin.

At nearby Fallastakkanöf, Doug spotted a rock face: the Organ Pipes (basaltic columns). The columns were smooth, divided by narrow vertical cracks. Snævarr tied himself onto Doug's rope. Snævarr takes up the story: 'The first pitch was very difficult, a 25m crack. The next pitch no better, sustained and overhanging, topping over a small roof. After that, we climbed an exposed traverse to the belay ledge; things then became easier. Snaevarr was peppered with pebble buckshot as Doug cleared the route. I shook Doug's hand at the top. Six hours of excitement were over. I saw Doug lift a pair of Wellington boots out of his "big wall" bag. The name "Pete Thexton" was written on the bag. Mountains take as well as give.' Not only the climbing was exciting. Benediktsson 'looked pale' after experiencing Scott driving at 70mph in second.

In 1991, Scott returned with climbing partners from the UK: Sharu Prabhu, Guy Lee, Colin Downer and Jim Fotheringham. Unfortunately, Scott's knees were troubling him; he was not able to climb any long routes. After some disagreements over vehicle choice, they left Reykjavik. The group first headed to Skaftafell on the fringe of the Vatnajökull. Helgi Benediktsson and some friends joined them here. They made a ski mountaineering ascent of Hvannadalshnjúkur (2110m) and climbed a few local peaks. From there, with Helgi driving, they headed to Lake Jökulsárlón, at the south-east corner of the Vatnajökull, where *A View to Kill* had been filmed. Scott wanted to meet some of Helgi's friends camped at the head of a nearby glacier. The way to the camp led up the trackless glacier. In their two-wheel drive rented minibus, streams, boulders and ice had to be negotiated for between five and eight kilometres, destroying the sump plug and cam belt. The rental people were waiting when they eventually reached Reykjavik after some costly repairs. Scott denied all knowledge of going off-road. Each member of the party had to fork out about £100 for the damage, 'too much' in the general opinion. No one missed the irony of sitting stormbound in the vehicle once it had been repaired.

They then moved via Gullfoss and Reykjavik in a full blizzard to new territory on the west coast, near the Snæfellsjökull, where they managed to ski and climb. While in that area, they made a ski ascent of the dormant volcanic chain of Helgrindur (873–988m). At the nearby Lóndrangar viewpoint, Benediktsson and Scott climbed a 60m seastack. While the van was being repaired at Ólafsvik, Scott visited a storm-bound fishing-fleet and acquired a huge cod. He cooked it in the hostel where they were staying. The cod stank the place out: the warden was unimpressed and made the cooking continue outside. Scott did, however, feed all the hostel guests. On the way back to Reykjavik they stopped near Borgarnes and did some ice-climbing.

Scott next returned at Easter, 1992. With Guðmundsson and Benediktsson, he travelled once again to Skaftafell. It was one of the coldest winters for decades. First, they attempted a ski approach to the rock spires of Tindaborg on the west flank of the Öræfajökull, but a fierce snowstorm forced a hasty retreat. Next day, they revisited Fallastakkanöf. Guðmundsson and Scott completed a new three-pitch route (5c, 6a, 5b), although the final pitch coincided with the 1984 Organ Pipes. As sunset approached, Guðmundsson thought about suggesting they descend. Scott, meanwhile, after a long pause, made an 'amazing' lead in below zero temperatures (lower inside the cracks), fisting his way through holes in the snow adhering to the rock up the final five metres. Next day, while reminiscing about the climb, Guðmundsson confessed to his wish to go down. Scott then confessed to the same thought but did not want to bring it up as it might make him seem a quitter.

In 2001, Scott returned once more, this time with Sharu (now Scott), David Oswin, Jim Fotheringham and Chris(py) Bacon. Scott and Sharu were taken for a day's climb to Skarðsheiði (highest point, 1054m), about forty kilometres north of Reykjavik. The aim was to climb the north-west face of the Skessuhorn, legendary birthplace of an old troll-woman. The climbs of about 250m generally comprise about twenty layers of 10m–20m vertical basaltic steps. Scott and Sharu roped together; Guðmundsson roped with Björn Ólafsson (later the first Icelander to climb Everest). Although visibility was partly hindered by rock, Scott and Sharu were seen to be stuck on pitch two; later, they downclimbed. Scott was perceived to be 'not happy' about this decision, although he did not express it publicly.

The final outing to Iceland was a family holiday: in September 2004, Scott, Arran and Euan arrived during Scott's post-divorce period. His lecture was entitled 'Sacred Summits': Guðmundsson noted how Scott's focus had shifted from climbing towards spirituality. With Helgi Benediktsson, the boys and Scott travelled to Landmannalaugar, in south Iceland, where they hiked to the top of Grænihnjúkur, a two-hour walk up a zig-zag track. Scott's knees troubled him greatly; he used walking-poles. He did have time, however, as the boys recall, to throw a stick into a geyser.

Back at the hut at Landmannalaugar, a discussion which became rather too dismissive on Guðmundsson's part arose on the nature of religion and of Scott's 'out of body' experiences. (Scott was, however, used to such challenges.) Scott and the boys subsequently stayed at Guðmundsson's house for two nights. On the first morning, Scott was interviewed by a young reporter who wanted to discuss different kinds of extreme sports. Scott was surprised to hear of such an attitude. 'If you want to make a success in sport, you must only focus on one,' was Scott's opinion. He seemed, says Guðmundsson, to realise that youthful attitudes and his had diverged.

Heading much further west to Canada in January 1985, Scott, with Greg Child, took up Rob Wood's challenge of a visit to Mount Colonel Foster (2135m), on Vancouver Island, mainly for the largely unexplored ice-climbing on its 1000m east face. Wood boasted that the ice-climbing was better than 'the whole of Scotland put together . . . bigger and better than the Rockies . . . possibly the best in the world'.

Mount Foster, named after Major-General William Foster, an administrator and keen mountaineer, was only identified in 1912. It was first climbed in 1968. The first winter ascent of the east face was by Bajan and Nicol in 1979. Scott, Child and Wood chose a parallel couloir and made its first winter ascent.

Wood met Greg Child, from Seattle, and Scott at Campbell River. Some of the staff at nearby Strathcona Lodge 'volunteered' to carry packs for them. They wound their way through the Elk River canyon, to emerge on a geomantically – according to Scott – favourable campsite. They were bequeathed supplies of marinated smoked salmon. Next day, they reached a great amphitheatre, with the face on one side. They walked across Lake Landslide, heading for the Grand Central Couloir (Alpine Grade VI). The snow in the couloir and its subsidiary gullies was mostly *névé*.

The first day's climbing led up 350m to a bergschrund, which offered protection from snow sliding from above. The second day's climb, in cloudier weather, followed a steepening ice-chimney. Wood describes their progress as 'superb pitches of classic ice-climbing, with front points and ice-axes biting in perfectly'. Steepening ground, however, led to the packs having to be hauled up behind them. The weather began to close in. Wood had to overcome an intimidating green-blue ice bulge. He succeeded; his fear diminished, replaced by pride at having skilfully completed his pitch. A delicate, exposed traverse over steep slabs followed. Beyond it, Scott found a bivvy spot and got a brew on.

A good night's sleep was followed by a sunny day. Child led up a vertical sliver of ice. This led to exit cracks and then the summit ridge. By 10 a.m. they had reached the summit. All experienced an unusual degree of euphoria and wellbeing. Scott expatiated on listening to 'the voice within': he believed survival was not dependent on external events but letting the external environment become part of you, and letting it adjust your will accordingly.

A series of long and dangerous rappels followed down the west face, then a tiring contour round the mountain's south side to reach Landslide Lake. Scott just avoided rockfall slicing through his rope. On the way out they revelled in the silence, broken only by the occasional clink of glass containing Whiskey Jacks.

༄

Scott began the final decade of his exploratory life with an attempt on the north ridge of Latok I (7145m), next to The Ogre. On 12 June 1990, Scott, Sandy Allan, Simon Yates and Rick Allen had established a base camp at 5100m on the Sim La. The first objective was the nearby Biacherahi Peak (5900m), one of several towers, but they were halted by masses of unstable snow on the summit ridge. They turned their attention to the Biacherahi Dome (5750m) and succeeded there. Treacherous snow conditions made for an awkward descent.

The party had been joined by a missionary called Cindy, Rick's wife Alison, *Financial Times* journalist and climber Richard Cowper and Allan's sister Eunice. (Prabhu was not present because of difficulties in getting a visa for Pakistan.) On 15 June, with Allan and Yates, these three headed for Hanipispur South (6047m), just north of base camp. Again, deep, unstable snow halted progress. Scott and Allan, after an exploration of the Choktoi Glacier, attempted a clean, rocky ridge on Latok III (6949m). A recce to look for a descent route led to a gear cache and naming the ridge *Indian Face Arête*. Back at base camp, Yates and Allen's decision to explore the long Nobande Sobande Glacier and to attempt Bobisighir (6411m) resulted in withdrawal thanks to dangerous snow conditions.

One month into the expedition, the party was joined by Robert Schauer, the film-maker and climber, who arrived by army wagon from Iran. Filming was carried out at the foot of Latok I.

On 18 June, Scott and Allan reached their previous high point on the arête. The rock started to turn to powder as Allan then Scott tried to place pitons. After a very uncomfortable bivvy partly covered in spindrift, Scott made a strong 5c lead next day. More technical climbing followed, ending with another cheerless bivvy (cold tea and Snickers bars). They then reached the summit; from the final steps to it, they abseiled to base camp with great difficulty. There, nobody could agree on a common goal; the expedition was called off.

Richard Cowper recorded the arrival of the three women (Alison, Eunice and Cindy) at base camp; Alison and Cindy departed on a trek to K2. Scott, Allan and Eunice departed by jeep for Hushe, followed a few days later by Allen. They stayed in this area for ten days and became well acquainted with the locals. Schauer and Yates remained at Latok base camp for a fortnight and climbed Ulu. Yates and Schauer used the army wagon to reach the Hushe area, where they explored the Charakusa valley. Certainly, the isolation and frustrations resulting from thwarted ascents (and disappointment for the sponsors, Inspectorate-OIS) put a strain on relationships. The debate about whether mixed expeditions are beneficial resurfaced. Scott was generally in favour, although his approval tended to coincide with self-interest. Cowper, while sceptical, did join the women on their Baltoro trek.

In August 1990, a poorly documented expedition, under the auspices of David Oswin's trekking company, took place in southern Greenland. The aim was to 'go off the beaten track and enjoy peace and quiet in one of the world's last wilderness areas'. The principal areas to visit were the Narsaq Peninsula (mainly trekking) and the Tasermiut Fjord (mainly climbing). Accommodation was mostly in tents. The fee was £1,800 (nudging £4,000 at today's prices). The duration, London to London, was seventeen days. No other records appear to exist of Scott's only foray into Greenland.

Rather better fortune came in 1991, with an expedition to Tripura Hiunchuli IV (Hanging Glacier Peak, 6563m) in the Kanjiroba Himal of Nepal. At the time, this area was relatively unvisited. After flying on 30 September to Bangula, west of Pokhara, this mixed group (Scott, Nigel Porter, Prabhu and John Cullen) undertook a long walk-in via Beni, the Kagmara La and the East Jaghdula Khola, to reach base camp on 25 October.

Advance base was established at 5200m below the intended rocky ascent route. On 27 October, the attempt on Hiunchuli IV from the west was called off. Next day, Scott, Prabhu, and Porter succeeded on the South Buttress, despite 500m of loose rock (which Cullen decided not to tackle) before gaining good ice and snow. The descent required an unplanned bivouac. On the way out, they walked to Jumla for a flight to Kathmandu on 4 November.

∽

Scott's exploratory mind was turning to South America. Completing the Seven Summits was evidently an ambition. Two of the seven were accomplished in late 1991 and early 1992: Mount Vinson (Antarctica) and Aconcagua (Argentina). Vinson, though not particularly high at 4892m, is subject to some of the most extreme weather on the planet. Being very isolated, lying about 1,200 kilometres from the South Pole, it is expensive to reach. Scott solved the expense problem by guiding a group of six climbers.

This trip was a challenge of endurance, logistics, navigational skills and instincts. It also succeeded through teamsmanship. The whole party, comprising Scott, Prabhu and Roger Mear (of *In the Footsteps of Scott* fame) as climbers, and Chris Brown, André Hedger, Sundeep Dhillon, Frank Musgrave, Ian Newell and Mike Parsons as supporting climbers, left London in November, in time for the Antarctic's optimum December good weather window. Scott's dogged persistence worked wonders at Heathrow check-in, where he managed to get their airline to carry twice the normal weight allowance without extra charge.

They reached Punta Arenas, the conventional departure point for Antarctica, without mishap. Here, they were obliged to wait for a suitable weather window for their next flight in an old DC-7, which had its return fuel bolted to the floor in large tanks. Food had to be procured

in Punta Arenas. Mear and Parsons organised this on the basis of food
bags per person per day. When laid out, some items were missing. Scott
had been given a shopping list, which he promptly lost. Nor were Scott
and Prabhu to be seen at departure time. An hour later, they turned up
carrying cabbages, smoked salmon and much else supposedly unsuitable
for polar travel where economy of weight is vital. Scott's response was, 'I
must admit I'm a bit of a big bag man.'

An eight-hour flight brought the party (and others, including an
American élite climber, Sue Giller, who considered the 'real treat' was to
'rub shoulders with climber extraordinaire, Doug Scott') to Patriot Hills
air base at eighty degrees south, from where a ski-equipped Twin Otter
flew to near the base camp on the Branscomb Glacier. En route, they had
to land without navigational instruments in thick cloud, before continuing after a three-hour wait. The weather turned very sunny, however: two
men stripped to the waist and were given a row by Mear: sunburn would
require an expensive airlift out.

The climb up the Branscomb Glacier took four days. A steep section led to the col between Vinson and Shinn followed by a scramble
along the summit ridge to the top, which they reached on 7 December.
Unfortunately, views were obscured by thick cloud. On the descent, Mear
took a bearing in the whiteout. Scott didn't bother; the parties separated.
Mear's party walked for two miles down the glacier on rigorous compass
bearings. Part way down, Scott's team appeared briefly through mist.
Mear's party eventually reached their camp. As a brew appeared, so did
Scott and his team. 'How,' asks Mear, 'is it possible for someone to follow
their intuition in whiteout conditions, with no tracks to follow, for more
than an hour and find a few tents in the snow?' Nothing was said; the
difference in navigation techniques was never mentioned.

The return flight to Punta Arenas was hair-raising, with thick cloud
forcing the plane to fly so low that the passengers could identify seals
on ice-floes. Like the aftermath of the Shishapangma success, Scott got
involved in a scuffle with a well-known American climber during the
celebrations.

Scott and Prabhu left the others at Punta Arenas and travelled across
Argentina to Aconcagua (6961m), reaching it by February 1992. Aconcagua
hardly counts as exploration; it is included as an extension of the adven-
ture on Vinson and the even wilder foray into Patagonia thereafter. Scott,
Prabhu, Sandy Allan, Tut Braithwaite and Paul Moores then visited
Patagonia. They attempted the *Chouinard Route* on FitzRoy (3405m), one

of the wildest places on Earth. They got high on the route but were turned back by storm and excessive snowfall. Scott mentioned to a climber whom he met at Aconcagua base camp, Robert Mads Anderson, that there was 'too much snow in Patagonia'.

Anderson recalls that Scott and Prabhu approached the mountain via the Vacas Valley before heading up the *Polish Glacier Route* on Aconcagua from the Plaza Argentina (4206m). He also recalls how 'British' Scott was: while everyone else at the base camp was rushing around worrying about weather, gear and teammates, Scott remained remarkably calm. He invited Anderson for tea. This ascent did not make a strong impression on Scott, as he does not record it in any of the usual ways. He had now completed five of the Seven Summits.

∽

Despite increasing problems with his legs, Scott remained busy: in June 1992, he headed for the obscure Fann mountains in Tajikistan, thus becoming one of the first non-Russians to climb there since its independence in 1991. His destination was this range's highest peak, Chimtarga (5489m). Rick and Alison Allen joined him, along with Sharu Prabhu. Their Russian hosts were those redoubtable experts Sergei Efimov and Valeri Pershin (or Perchine), one of Russia's greatest rock-climbers. On generally good roads, they reached base camp just north of the beautiful Alaudin Lake. For acclimatising, all of them bar Alison climbed Zamok (5070m) from a camp at 4020m. Their route followed the Zamok Glacier to a couloir, followed by a long traverse to the north, to reach the southeast ridge of Zamok. From there, five hours of scrambling brought them to the summit.

On 24 June, everyone moved up to a camp at 4000m above Mutne Lake. Scott, Prabhu and Efimov roped together, while Allen roped with Pershin. Difficult, snow-covered rocks led to a bivouac at 5000m. The next day required many hard, time-consuming pitches; they stopped 50m below the summit. On 27 June, they roamed over several summits, including the highest one, before dropping to a pass via the north ridge followed by an awkward abseil through deep snow into a gorge. After returning to base camp, Allen reclimbed Zamok with Alison. On 30 June, they left for Samarkand, arriving in London two days later. Scott comments that he enjoyed the local markets and the communal approach favoured by the Russians, of everyone staying in one tent, with a pressure cooker; he was sufficiently impressed to try this system later that year on Nanga Parbat.

The sixth of the Seven Summits was not long in coming. In June and July of 1994, Scott, Braithwaite, Stephen Sustad, Mark Bowen, an American physicist whom Scott had got to know during one of his lecture tours, Malcolm 'Pike' Cundy, his friend Ken Tilford and Richard Cowper were organised by one of Joe Tasker's brothers, John, to travel to Elbrus. (Tasker had visited Russia several times previously and knew how to work the system.)

The party flew to St Petersburg. Thanks to excellent contacts with the local police, John Tasker obtained visas and rail tickets (insisting that they would understand Russia better through rail travel) with great efficiency. Tasker's then girlfriend, Irina Smirnova, a professor of linguistics, came along as interpreter. The train journey to Mineralnye Vodi was marked by the party's laddish indifference to the regulations imposed by Olga, the redoubtable carriage stewardess. (Tasker declared he was exhausted by the end of the trip.) From there, buses brought them to Terskol, in the valley to the south of Elbrus (5642m). The normal ascent route is a straightforward one, with only minor altitude problems. The party climbed Elbrus, from a base at the famous Priut-11, a cable-car ride and short walk above Terskol.[12] Stephen Sustad colourfully recalls, 'We ran up and down the hill (which is not remotely technical) and then played around on some smaller peaks. The country was on the verge of unravelling. The local mafia extracted "protection" of $1 each for every day we were there. Threatened to "disappear" our guide, Leonid Zamiatnin, if we didn't pay.'[13]

Bowen recalls Doug unsuccessfully trying to drink the thugs under the table to avoid paying the extortion 'fees'. A distracting brawl occurred between the thugs and some Russian paras, with uncertain results. From Terskol they ascended to the German Bivouac in the Shkhelda Valley; Bowen and Sustad attempted Peak Shchurovsky but were beaten back by melting ice and rockfall. Scott and Braithwaite decided to try Ushba (4710m), the Caucasus's most striking peak, which Braithwaite had been on before. An avalanche on the Ushba Icefall, however, looked ominous. Extensive crevasses and deep snow also threatened progress. Scott declared to Braithwaite, 'I'm not too happy with this,' a very unusual utterance.[14] Had they pursued their intended route, they might well have been killed. Once again, Scott's intuition had avoided disaster. The expedition concluded on a 'rock and snow lump' called Railway Workers' Peak. The party returned to Mineralnye Vodi from where they flew to St Petersburg and so to London.

Scott returned to South America, in December 1994, on one of his most unusual expeditions, on board the Southampton-built yacht *Pelagic*. This powerful craft was captained by the renowned American sailor James 'Skip' Novak. First mate was Hamish Laird; other crew were Laird's brother Alex and sisters Joanna and Emma Ellis. Francis McDermott came along as a sailor-climber, as did Julian Freeman-Attwood, who had invited Scott.

This complicated voyage began interestingly in Punta Arenas, Chile. A certain ritual is followed: at 5 p.m., a steam-bath is taken at the Baños Touristos (a run-down establishment run by a gay, blind local). Pisco sours are then absorbed at Sotito's Bar, followed by dinner there. Maria Theresa's is then visited, around midnight. When the party arrived there, they were accosted by girls with heavy lipstick and fishnet stockings. Scott absorbed the scene, then declared to Freeman-Attwood, 'This isn't a nightclub, lad. It's a bloody knocking-shop!'

The *Pelagic* left Punta Arenas on 2 December, for the straits of Magellan and the southern end of the Cordillera Darwin range. In remarkably good weather (Scott, fuelled by 'warm Cabernet', was allowed to stand watch and take the wheel) and after passing Tierra del Fuego, they reached Agostini Fjord.

The first object was to climb in the Cordon Navarro, on the fjord's south side. Supplies were fetched ashore using an Avon dinghy. Scott was the leader on land; he climbed the only technical rock pitch leading to 'Mount Pelagic's' summit ridge. Freeman-Attwood and Scott hacked their way through almost impenetrable thorn bushes and dwarf beech in a quest for an advance campsite. (Back on the *Pelagic*, a nearby glacier calved off a piece 30m high and 250 metres wide.) On 4 December, despite heavy rain, more loads were humped up to advance base. Despite a leaky tent, all the climbers attempted a nearby 2000m peak via a Grade V ridge. Rain halted them high up. Next day, they attempted to dry out between showers, although their gear was scattered by a confident Fuegan silver fox. On 7 December, they retraced their steps to the summit, which they reached at about 1 p.m. Scott estimated the overall grade at TD inf. (Some debate ensued about this being a first ascent.) Scott and Freeman-Attwood climbed a neighbouring 'minor frosty concretion' which they named Mount Poltroon,[15] referring to one of Captain Haddock's curses in the *Tintin* series. Scott was impressed by his view of so many unclimbed peaks; sadly, the weather permitted few more for the rest of the month.

Two days later, still in heavy rain, the party explored a nearby island, where sights of skuas and shags appear to have been the high point.

On 11 December, they moved slightly north to Enchantment Bay. The weather prevented much happening, however, so they motored up to

Hyatt Fjord, passing a vast cruise ship on the way. They approached the
Serrano Fjord and could make out high mountains through the mist. On
returning to Agostini Fjord, they met two French climbers, Dr Emmanuel
Cauchy and Nicolas Tingasson, whom they invited to dinner.

Plans were devised to attempt Monte Sarmiento (2246m), according to
Darwin, 'the most sublime spectacle in Tierra del Fuego', but the weather
continued to prevent purposeful activity. A decision was made to help
Novak plot safe havens around the Tierra del Fuego fjords. They headed for
the impressive Beagle Channel, still in poor weather. Some 500m buttresses
on the Tres Picos (1546m) were admired as the best rock they had seen on
the trip. After proceeding by sail for about 160 kilometres, they switched
to motoring to penetrate the Seno Ventisquero, a narrow, deep-water fjord
with many huge icebergs. From there, they proceeded to the Garibaldi
Fjord off the main Beagle Channel. As the impenetrable bush prevented
landing, they turned their attention to the Fiordo Chueco, which Scott
declared was the most impressive of all. At the fjord's north-west end, rich
in animal and bird life, they set up a camp about 500m above sea level. The
terrain, said Scott, combined Rannoch Moor bogs with Malaysian jungle.

They had set their sights on a 2100m peak. On 20 December, Scott,
Freeman-Attwood and Alex Laird reconnoitred a couloir to reach about
800m. Next day, they moved a camp up to a ridge at about 1200m. Rain
– as bad as any monsoon, Scott declared – fell for eighteen hours, turning
to heavy snow; retreat was sounded on 24 December. Back on the glacier,
Freeman-Attwood thought he heard a helicopter, but it turned out to be
Scott practising his Buddhist 'Om' mantra. They returned to the *Pelagic*,
which sailed across the Beagle Channel and on to the remote Kanasaka
estancia (ranch), where they enjoyed Christmas Dinner with the rancher,
Eugenio Martinez, his wife Estelle and their three children. They left the
estancia for Puerto Williams. There, by a happy chance, they bumped into
John Ridgway, who had just arrived on *English Rose IV*.

Skip Novak mentions that Scott had no maritime experience at all – a real
landlubber, as Freeman-Attwood put it. Even in the dock in Punta Arenas
he felt queasy! However, he did enjoy the novelty of the experience. On the
way to the Agostini Fjord, Scott's principal contribution consisted of boiling
potatoes in the galley. (A photo of Scott on watch with shading hand across
his eyebrows is clearly self-satirical.) His attitude when leader on land, however, appeared to be 'every man for himself': there was no safety briefing.

On 27 December, Scott's expedition ended when he flew from Ushuaia,
where the party dispersed, over the Darwin Mountains and so to Punta

Arenas. He described the view of the Darwins as 'unsettling', knowing that so many peaks to climb remained in that area: his appetite for new exploration remained strong.

The final peak of the Seven Summits was attempted the following year, 1995. Scott claims that box-ticking the Seven Summits was a 'disreputable concept' which had not occurred to him until he discussed an ascent of Carstensz, New Guinea, with a group of climbers from Mapala University Climbing Club (Jakarta) whom he met at the base of Aconcagua. For someone of Scott's experience, this claim stetches credibility: the first completion had occurred eight years before the Aconcagua discussion, amid hefty publicity.

The Carstensz Pyramid is surrounded by glaciation despite lying close to the equator and requires getting through extensive jungle to reach it. The party consisted of Scott, Sharu, Tom Callaghan, Mark Bowen, David Macrae and Chris Brown.

After Scott had lectured in Jakarta and following bureaucratic delays, they flew in early May to the village of Ilaga. Scott was immediately fascinated by the Dani's dress and customs; he enthused about their vegetable growing. Fifty-three porters carried their equipment through fields then dense, swampy jungle – another new medium for Scott after his sea-voyage to Patagonia – and provided moving solo and chorus music in the evenings. They reached base camp after crossing the Mbla-Mbla Pass (3800m) in the rain, on 9 May.

On 12 May, they stood at the base of the coarse limestone north wall by 6 a.m. The ascent was made by a variation left of a prominent gully, with a further left variation above a big scree basin at grade 5.6/5.7. (Bowen's estimate, however, is 5.9+.) They reached the summit at 11 a.m., after some brief but helpful sack-hauling on an enjoyable Alpine route. Scott was applauded on top for reaching his Seventh Summit. Other routes followed: one new route was named *Middenspits,* to the east of the Pyramid. They reached a cairn only 30m short of the summit on a climb (5.7/5.8) left of the *Original Route* before heavy rain forced a withdrawal. Finally, they visited the local copper mine, one of the largest in the world, and stood aghast at the environmental damage.

After returning to the UK, Scott received stories from Bowen of the Indonesian government's maltreatment of the Dani, something he had witnessed (a villager kicked in the face by a government administrator) at Ilaga. He likened the Indonesian government's maltreatment of the Dani to that of the Chinese in Tibet. Scott's ethical sensibilities, deriving from his empathy with indigenous peoples were now, with experience, developing into beliefs which would cause controversy in retirement.

Himalaya, India, Tibet, Switzerland

> 'Many climbers like mountains and they come to climb
> peaks and go home. But Doug Scott is a different person.'
>
> – Pertemba Sherpa

After his Seven Summits, Scott returned to the Buddhist areas of the Himalaya. In 1996, Scott fixed his sights on the beautiful triangle of Chombu (6362m) in northern Sikkim. A large body of talent assembled to tackle this remote peak. Scott was joined by Lindsay Griffin, Julian Freeman-Attwood, Mark Bowen, Skip Novak and Phil Bartlett. An old friend, Balwant Sandhu, came along as liaison officer. Two support trekkers, Paul Crowther and Mike Clarke, joined the expedition; Sherpa support was provided by Pasang Namgyal, Tenzing Norbu, Sungay and Nawang Zongda.

Although Scott was an experienced organiser, 'Doug's democracy' worked well as long as Scott got his way. On this expedition, however, he had considerably mellowed: members often did their own thing; it was a harmonious adventure. The decision was for a post-monsoon expedition, the first Western expedition to penetrate this area since the 1950s. In his *Himalayan Journal* report, Scott provides a lengthy account of their bureaucratic difficulties in Delhi, mainly because of tensions between the IMF and the Indian military.

From Delhi, they travelled by rail to New Jalpaiguri. Thanks to Freeman-Attwood's connection to the American climber Ed Webster, they were met by Princess Hope Leezum Namgyal; she provided extensive assistance with transport as far as Sikkim's capital, Gangtok. Here, after additional payments and paperwork, they took on their Sikkimese liaison officer, Lalit Basnet. On 27 September, the party set out up the Tista River valley. They passed the Inner Line and spent the night in a dak bungalow, where Scott particularly enjoyed the hot springs. Much disquiet was expressed at the environmental damage wreaked by Indian Army roadbuilding, particularly in destroying ancient forests and consequently altered drainage systems.

Base camp was set up by 1 October, close to the Tibetan border, at the head of the Lachung valley. Fox, marmot and bharal (Himalayan blue sheep) were observed. The valley to the south of Gurugongmar was explored. A recce was carried out to the Sebu Cho (lake); Bowen and Balwant found the route to the plateau between Chombu and Chombu East. Griffin and Bartlett climbed Gurung (5691m) and examined the col between Chombu and Chombu East. Meanwhile, Scott, Novak and Freeman-Attwood crossed the Sebu La (5352m), to view Chombu's north face and Kangchenjunga's east face.

The weather remained consistently unstable; now acclimatised, they set out on 14 October to climb Chombu East from an advance base on the south-west flank. They traversed awkward moraine then ascended a glacier until a very steep ice slope led them to a ridge at 5000m. As they followed the summit ridge, a storm broke. False tops were overcome, followed by a section *à cheval* then an awkward gap before the summit. Return was by the same, sometimes technically tricky, route.

Interest remained focused on the main Chombu peak, however. An icefall was outflanked to put in a starting camp near the Sebu Chu. After the usual moraine and loose rock, the snow conditions presented such danger that the attempt was abandoned.

They turned their attention to their second permitted peak, Gurudongmar (6715m). To its north lies the lake of the same name, the source of the Tista and at 5414m, one of the highest lakes in the world. An advance base was established on the south side, but three days of bad weather were enough to call the expedition off. Scott had to hurry home to be with Sharu at the impending birth of Euan, their second son (Arran is the elder). Novak, Sandhu and Freeman-Attwood remained to explore the northern versant of this attractive group of mountains. (Bowen had left the expedition slightly early, with the trekkers, as he could see that conditions were unsuited to further climbing and wanted to include some local travel before returning to the US.) Generally, however, this was an enjoyable expedition, if frustrated in its aims by poor weather.

Major expeditions were becoming less frequent: CAN was occupying much of Scott's time. And his legs needed medical attention. Nevertheless, in April 1998, Scott travelled with Lindsay Griffin, Skip Novak and Julian Freeman-Attwood to attempt Drohmo (6881m). Permission had also been granted for Jongsong peak (7462m), in the Janak area. Remarkably, Sharu, with three-year-old Arran and 15-month-old Euan, came along to base camp (even reaching Pang Pema, 5451m): a chance encounter with a *Daily Telegraph* reporter led to an article on their return. The other support trekkers were Freeman-Attwood's wife-to-be, Emmy Rothschild, Eleanor

Caputo and Terry Mooney QC. Sheru Zangbu accompanied as *sirdar*, with Norbu Zangbu and Nawang Karsang.

Julian's girlfriend became quite ill not long after reaching base camp (4650m). She and Julian left, along with Skip's girlfriend. The usual acclimatisation and recce period followed on such lower peaks as The Wave (6050m), climbed by Griffin and the Sherpas. Scott, Novak and Griffin established Rock Camp on Drohmo at 5180m; on an initial reconnaissance of the south face, the three climbed to around 6000m on the central rib; Scott was set on reaching a point where they could obtain a fine view of Kangchenjunga. 'The sight of it,' Griffin observed, 'clearly meant a lot to him.' They then descended, leaving some ropes in place.

Scott then insisted on trying for the summit. Although Griffin had a stomach bug, he, Scott and Novak did start. The weather turned; with Griffin still unwell, they descended. Griffin offered to try again but on 2 May Scott was ready to leave. Griffin was left with the impression that Scott was seeking partners of the stature of Boardman, Tasker, Baxter-Jones or MacIntyre which the current luminaries could not equal. Scott's concerns might also have been related to his own declining performance.

The unclimbed South Rib remained a challenge for Scott. He returned in September 1998 with Roger Mear to complete the route and attempt Teng Kongma (6215m), another outlier of Kangchenjunga, north of the Pang Pema base camp. Twenty-three loads were portered in; the Westerners were joined by 'old friends', Shera Zangbu, Nawang Kasang and Janak Tamang.

Mear admitted that until he was asked by Scott to join the expedition, he had never heard of Drohmo. The organisation was entirely Scott's: he obtained an MEF grant and assembled the food, equipment and other paraphernalia. CAT organised the portering and trekking. Mear paid £4,000 as his share. For him, it was like a package holiday, if more Saga than '18–30'.

Base camp was covered in yak pats; it was a pleasure to leave it. Acclimatisation and recces began immediately with a scramble to Point 6019 on the Teng Kongma ridge north-east of Lhonak. A 'rock camp' was then established at 5200m, just off the central glacier moraine between Lhonak and Pang Pema, after which they attempted the north-east ridge of Teng Kongma. They ascended its east glacier to reach the base of the north-east ridge. Continuing on two ropes, with Scott and Mear on one and the Sherpas on the other, after three hours and a six-metre ice-step, they reached the rock summit at 1 p.m. They then re-traced their steps to the rock camp.

A recuperative break forced by rain and snow lasted until 2 October. On 1 October, however, Scott visited a Nottingham expedition based at Pang Pema, a pleasing coincidence. On 3 October, a camp was set up at the head of the glacier leading to Drohmo's very steep South Rib. The climb began on 5 October. Mear and Scott, with very heavy rucksacks, had planned a four-day trip. About 300m up the route, a dispute arose about the route. Though quickly resolved, Mear thought it took some courage to disagree with Scott; the altercation was never subsequently mentioned. Pitches over red granite and up snow gullies followed until they reached a site for their tent at 6207m above a cauliflower ice-tower. In fine weather, Mear led over steep ice the next day. Sound belays were hard to find. From the tent, that night, protected in an ice grotto, they viewed sunset over Everest and moonrise over Kangchenjunga. Next day, hoping for the summit, they left the tent and much else behind. Mushy snow was unhelpful, but they reached the top of the South Rib by 2.30 p.m. They continued along the lengthy ridge for half an hour, to a subsidiary top at 6855m. The main summit was at least a kilometre away and 26m higher. At this point, they wisely turned round, to return to their bivouac, then next day reached the glacier after a strength-sapping twenty-five abseils.

The North side of Kangchenjunga from high on Drohmo, 1998.
Most of the 1979 ascent route up the glacier then the North Ridge is visible.
(Doug Scott collection)

Back at base camp, another coincidence occurred: Aberdonian neighbours of his old climbing schoolfriend, Geoff Stroud, turned up. (They
were attempting a repeat ascent of a neighbouring peak, first climbed by
Kellas in 1898.) Scott offered them freshly cooked chips, for which they
offered a half bottle of whisky. Scott turned this offer down in favour of
three Mars Bars.

Scott remained uneasy that they had fixed ropes for part of the climb:
his ethical commitments and sense of purity remained strong. (He could,
however, have reminded himself that he was fifty-seven.) He also, however,
felt that he had not done his fair share on the climb as regards leading: few
climbers of that age would have responded that way.

∽

After the mountain and the sea (Patagonia, 1994), Scott's next elemental
change led to the jungle, to Arunachal Pradesh, India, with Greg Child
from September to November 1999.[16] Scott's Ogre injuries were returning
to haunt him, but in a way which he refused properly to recognise.
Such stubbornness compromised the trip and strained its protagonists'
relationship.

Child and Scott were accompanied once more by Balwant Sandhu,
and by Akhil Sapru and four Darjeeling Sherpas: Pasang Futar, Phurba,
Thukpa Tshering and Dorji. It was the first civilian expedition permitted
to enter the Khurung River valley and its surrounding mountains since
Partition, a measure of Scott's powerful influence over the Indian authorities. The aim was to explore the mountains around Takpa Shiri (6885m),
an extremely remote holy peak on the Arunachal Pradesh-Tibet border.

The expedition left Delhi by train for Guwahati on 18 September. The
eighteen-day walk-in, in constant rain through difficult jungle, proved
very arduous. Blood poisoning and leg injuries affected Scott; typhoid
and malaria were also prevalent. On 21 September, they took a bus full of
equipment and provisions to Itanagar. From there, jeeps brought them to
Ziro. Promised helicopter support was unhelpful: they were ordered off
the helicopter minutes before departure thanks to the military suddenly
refusing to transport foreigners. Child was ready to leave the expedition at
this point, until Scott persuaded him not to.

Scott and Child travelled in jeeps for two days through the incessant
rain to the valley head at Kloriang. From there, they walked to Sarli to
meet Sandhu and Sapru. A government official advised against antago-
nising the machete-bearing locals and warned of venomous snakes. Porters

were hard to come by: government subsidies meant they did not need to find extra work. They were still two weeks away from base camp.

On the trek to base camp they stayed in long-houses and crossed rock steps using ladders: it was not possible to walk more than fifteen steps without slipping on greasy, vegetation-entangled boulders. By 12 October, all the porters had disappeared. Next day they crossed the Khurung on a rickety bridge of creepers, to enter the rhododendron and conifer zone. Pasang had malaria; Child had blood poisoning. On 15 October, they reached open pasture, a decent site for a base camp. Unfortunately, Scott had slipped the previous day and torn a knee ligament. Child was angry because Scott had not previously mentioned his arthritis. (He also found Sandhu's condescending manner towards him, that of 'a colonial pantry-boy', irksome.) Thukpa had now caught a malarial fever also.

The two men talked during the walk-in of their respective marital problems. When combined with the cyclonic monsoon, malaria and fever, mud and raging rivers, it made, as Child sardonically suggested, for 'good *Heart of Darkness* stuff'.

From 16 to 28 October, they tried to recce the mountains. Balwant, while trying to find more porters, caught typhoid. Sapru had run out of time. Then Scott dislocated a big toe while crossing a stream. Child decided he had had enough and left. Part of their failure to achieve anything, Child asserts, was Scott's 'blowing out' his knee, which was already near to collapse from arthritis, implying that Scott should not have attempted this expedition in the first place. Scott and Sandhu (who had kept a journal of his condition, described by Child as the 'diary of a madman') were evacuated by helicopter on 24 October. (Sapru walked out with all the gear, which took two weeks.) They were flown to Din Jan Military Hospital near Dibrugarh, further up the Brahmaputra from Itanagar. After treatment, and a safari through an elephant sanctuary, Scott reached home on 8 November.

He said afterwards he had experienced a degree of despondency and helplessness not felt on any previous expedition. Despite the warnings, Scott spoke highly of the local people, the Atapani, the Nishi and the Bungaroo, all of them extraordinarily skilled at hunting and moving effortlessly through dense jungle. They had not met white people before. Child agreed: despite its grimness, the expedition left a stronger impression on him, thanks to the local peoples, than 'other expeditions which had real success'. Scott particularly commended their honesty – not a piece of gear went astray. Scott's 2001 article for the *Alpine Journal* encapsulates his relationship with indigenous peoples: 'A belief in the importance of truth, a hardness of moral and physical fibre, courage before impossible living conditions, the love of adventure and exploration, a fresh, candid simple attitude to life's problems are among the other qualities that the [Nishi] people have to give the world.'

Despite the demands made on him by CAN, the collapse of his second marriage and increasing problems with his legs, knees and ankles, Scott rallied his forces. He was invited by Julian Freeman-Attwood to Targo Ri (circa 6550m) on the Tibetan Plateau, a route to which Freeman-Attwood had found after a chance meeting with an Italian anthropologist the previous year in Lhasa. Scott then invited Richard Cowper. They headed in October 2000 to this very remote range about 300 kilometres north of the Lhasa–Kailas highway, between the Shuru Tso (lake) and the Dangra Tso. The party enjoyed a brief acclimatisation trek above Bahrabise, in Nepal, at the end of September before heading to Lhasa.

Their secondary aim was to visit the Sezhik Bön gompa to the north of the peak, from where Sven Hedin had been turned back in 1907. They travelled by truck from the highway and set up their base camp at 4930m to the south of the peak on 3 October. With the help of local yak-herders, mostly women, an advance base was established at 5280m and a high camp at 5760m. The locals then descended. The three Westerners climbed the mountain's south ridge to reach a point on the final snowdome just 3m below the summit, to respect its strong local religious significance. The climbing was never more than Difficult. Scott thanked Freeman-Attwood for doing most of the trail-breaking. The locals confirmed that no one had climbed in the Targo Ri area before.

When at the lamasery, they asked the rinpoché (abbot) if he minded them climbing his mountain: 'I do not mind,' came the cryptic reply, 'but I cannot speak for the gods.'

∽

Targo Ri concluded the two principal strands of Scott's climbing life from 1978 onwards: attempts on new routes up familiar mountains and expeditions to unexplored mountains or unfamiliar areas. Humanitarian work occurred elsewhere, however, and in 1990 and 1991, Scott and Sharu participated in the UN's Climb for the World scheme.

In March 1989, the legendary Edwin Drummond was floundering at the base of the Eiger. He imagined himself climbing it to promote Amnesty International's prisoners of conscience. Drummond's friend,

Mike Hollingworth, a long-standing broadcaster, suggested the UN's next International Day of Peace, on 18 September 1990, could be celebrated by climbers from every nation scaling the Eiger by every route in the name of the unjustly imprisoned and the disabled. On top, they would fly the UN flag and, by lantern-light, the message from UN Secretary-General Javier Perez de Cuellar would be read out and transmitted globally by satellite. Expressing concern about the state of the environment was a secondary aim. The project was financed by Anthony Fretwell Downing, a Sheffield IT company director.

Drummond received strong responses from all 159 UN countries. Eventually, it was decided that one man and one woman from each continent would make the climbs on the Eiger, with a blind mountaineer and guide tackling the *West Flank*. In addition, a climb for people could be made in every country. The hope was that by the year 2000, 2,000 people would stand on 2,000 summits throughout the world.

In the UK, the main political leaders (Thatcher, Kinnock, Ashdown and Owen) acted as patrons, while Lord Hunt became climbing patron. Bonington was appointed ambassador-at-large, although his involvement was not great. Sharu Prabhu volunteered, as did Scott, who agreed to accompany a blind climber up the *West Flank*. John Cleare was invited as official photographer. (He also bivvied on the Eiger summit and helped with letting off the fireworks.) Cleare and Drummond carried out publicity activities such as putting banners on top of Ilam Rock and Cnicht.

For the ascent of the Eiger on 12 to 26 September 1990, Alpinists from about twenty countries turned up, including some important climbers such as Scott and Catherine Destivelle. The Swiss provided a bunkhouse at Kleine Scheidegg free, as well as free passes on the Jungfraujoch railway and the occasional helicopter trip. On the summit, fireworks were let off, then most people descended by the *Normal Route*.

At the Mitteleggi Hut, however, a characteristically Scott-esque incident occurred. John Cleare takes up the story:

We had just settled down for the night, Sharu and Doug in the centre of the lower *Tratzenlager* [layer of mattresses on the floor]. I'd already dozed off when the door crashed open and two Germans stomped in. They started shouting when they discovered the *Tratzenlager* was chock-a-block and the blankets were all taken. Then they saw not only a Kenyan but an Indian also! They became belligerent and started to pull Sharu out of bed.

They'd hardly got the blanket off her when Doug was awake, on the floor and throwing punches. He knocked one of the Germans down. And by now several others of us were awake, up and in support. Doug threw the two Germans out into the night, which they spent in the lean-to woodshed; we saw them slink away at first light. Doug was a big fellow; he had no time for fools. He was not a man to cross. But he could be generous and utterly charming. Undoubtedly, he was a Hard Man – tough as old boots.

So much for world peace!

The Eiger climbs had been filmed by a BBC crew from *Blue Peter*, the event presented by Diane-Louise Jordan. This was not Scott's first encounter with *Blue Peter*, however. Back in February 1984, with the assistance of Julie Tullis in charge of sound and Kurt Diemberger working the cameras, Scott took *Blue Peter* presenter Peter Duncan climbing in the Lake District. Described by Julie Tullis as 'the only disastrous film that Kurt and I have made', the film shows a late start on a very wet, snowy day. Diemberger was wearing only an Icelandic sweater as an outer layer. By the time they reached the climb, the iced-up waterfall of a tributary of Combe Gill on Raven Crag in Borrowdale, the rain had washed away much of the lower part. (The climb is a grade III of 100m over two pitches.) An inelegant scramble followed up snow-covered boulders. The cameras were successively drowned out of use. The microphone ceased to function: no great loss as Scott did little more than mumble. (The film does show the meticulous care he applied to safety, however.) Back at the studio, Duncan interviewed Tullis, who put a brave face on the washout. The last question to Tullis was, 'What do you intend to do next?' Heading for K2, was the poignant reply. Here, Tullis lost her life on the descent; Diemberger barely escaped with his.

∽

Since the late 1950s, Scott had been punishing his super-strong body on long climbs in thirty-seven countries. Even he recognised by the early 2000s that major expeditions were over for him. Since 1990, he had in any case devoted more and more time to CAT and CAN, as the number of CAN schools, health posts and Sherpa shelters increased. CAN was a brilliantly productive and beneficial way of spending his post-expedition years.

14

Growth of a Mountaineer (III), 1985–2003

'Whatever Doug Scott's political views may have been, or
are now, his level of energy and efficiency as president of the
Alpine Club is very impressive. His sheer drive and crispness
at a lecture/symposium event were awesome.'

– Simon4, contributor to the UKClimbing chat forum

Doug and Sharu had two boys, Arran and Euan, to add to his family with
Jan. Doug took an increasing part in international environmental events
and discussions about mountaineering, while continuing to earn his living
from lectures. He published two books and was working on at least five
others, as well as writing for major mountaineering journals. His spiritual
quest received its deepest test through a close relationship with 'NE', a
Buddhist adept at the Samye Ling lamasery in the Scottish Borders.[1] Much
of his time was taken up with CAT and CAN. Somehow, in the early
2000s, he had to contend with a form of homelessness, mental anguish
and physical decline that was only reversed on meeting Trish in 2005.

Sharu Prabhu came from a well-to-do family in Mumbai. After university and a time in industry, she joined the historic 1984 Indian expedition
to Everest on which Bachendri Pal became the first Indian woman to reach
the summit. In 1985, after the loss of the man she loved in a mountaineering accident, she met Doug, for the first time, in Darjeeling. She was
'awestruck by his personality'. In Maria Coffey's *Where the Mountain Casts
Its Shadow*, psychiatrist Sam Naifeh suggests that the intensity of a close
relationship being suddenly cut off, the bereaved person seeks it out again.

Sharu was always an 'outdoorsy' person and 'loved freedom'. For Doug,
Sharu represented Indian charm, something he was ready to embrace.
Doug introduced Sharu to rock-climbing and mountaineering in the
Alpine style. They climbed, among many other places, in the Western
Ghats, Wadi Rum and the Alps. In the UK, they climbed, for example, the
Old Man of Hoy and the *Pincushion* (E2 6a) at Tremadog. They reached

the summit of Bhutan's Jitchu Drake in 1988, although the expedition's tensions resulted in modified tactics which prevented *The Guardian* reporter, David Rose, attaining the summit. Doug, however, could not readily see the problems within the group dynamic.

With Doug developing his relationship with Sharu, he and Jan separated definitively early in 1987, with Jan retaining the marital home. Their divorce was declared absolute on 6 April 1989.

Doug, Arran (foreground) and Euan at the wedding of Garry's daughter Jennifer in 2017. (Scott family collection)

In 1987, Doug and Sharu consulted Lyn Birkbeck, a well-known Keswick astrologer. While the detail of their charts remains confidential, Birkbeck did link Doug's wish to (re-)climb Everest to his 'interior topography of similar proportions'. In Sharu's case, he suggested that her profession or reputation would soon change radically, although he stressed that being alone might make close relationships 'impossible'. How seriously Doug and Sharu took these readings is uncertain, although Sharu did consult Birkbeck again when her marriage was falling apart.

Doug did express doubts to Sandy Allan, with whom he climbed regularly in the early 1990s, about the wisdom of marrying someone eighteen years younger.[2] Nonetheless, the marriage went ahead. The couple lived at Bewcastle, north of Brampton. From there, they moved to Winton, near Kirkby Stephen. After that, they made a more durable home in an attractive hamlet near Carlisle

These few happy early years – when they were mischievously referred to as 'John and Yoko' – were followed by increasing difficulties, some of them cultural. Sharu had to adjust to life among a group of high-powered climbers, some of whom had 'come up the hard way'. Doug was, initially, possessive; Sharu became over-protective. Seeing Doug's attractiveness to other women, and even his relaxed friendliness towards his professional female acquaintances, she insisted on keeping them distant. Christine Gee was warned by Doug not even to send 'thank you' notes during a lecture tour in Australia; Doug, with a rueful shrug, described his marriage as 'pure possession'. Maggie Burgess, another of Doug's female friends, was deeply hurt by this embargo and did not see Doug for a long time. Doug's compliance with such wishes was probably motivated by a wish to keep the marriage going.

Sharu's life changed with the arrival of Arran in 1995 and Euan in 1996, although exotic travel remained possible: the children, even when very young, did reach base camp on occasions, for example on Aconcagua and Drohmo.

Among Doug's friends and climbing partners, opinion about the marriage remained divided. In 1994, for example, their visit to Bob Holmes in California passed off well. Others found Sharu an engaging hostess while detecting an underlying tension. On one occasion, Sharu attended a New Year's Eve party without Doug or any explanation as to his absence. On another occasion, Guy Lee and other friends were invited by Doug to a New Year's Eve party at Chapel House. When they arrived, the house was very quiet: they eventually found Doug and Sharu watching TV. After entertaining themselves for an hour or so, everyone left.

After a few years of marriage, Doug began his affair with 'NE'. Sharu had previously intercepted a letter from another girlfriend; the consequence was separation, in 2001.

The following four years became Doug's 'nomad' period, when he depended on others for accommodation. With friends, he overstayed his welcome: he was untidy and kept erratic hours. He slept on the Oswins' sofa, as well as at Colin Downer's house at Blea Farm, under Saddleback, and at Tom Morrell's house, near Penrith – Doug, it seems, did not sufficiently recognise the Morells' situation, in that life had to revolve around Pam Morell's long-term care needs: Tom had to ask Doug to leave.

Doug then moved to a bungalow he bought near Samye Ling at Eskdalemuir: Craighaugh. Sherpas worked in the garden. Dr Jim Duff helped out, as did Colin Downer and Jim Fotheringham. Doug, however, continued to live in a kind of scruffy expedition style. He was 'looking terrible' at this time, although Jim Fotheringham says the change after he met Trish was 'staggering'.[3]

To escape, and for income, lecture tours took place to Australia, the US and Iceland, among others. This rootless existence, and anxiety about the fate of his children, accompanied a physical decline.[4] Dez Hadlum describes Doug around 2001: 'When I met him . . . I was shocked about his appearance. He still had a powerful torso, but he seemed to have shrunk. He was bent over, slightly bow-legged and walked with a strange gait. I literally winced at each step he took.'[5]

Others testify to hair loss, loss of weight and boils on the neck (suggesting a poor diet). Physical decline was only one part: on a drive from Glenmore Lodge to Edinburgh, and despite his customary calls to 'Drive faster!', his fellow passengers remember his depression and incessant anxiety about his situation, a state of mind echoed by others.[6] In 2004, he was rushed to Dumfries hospital with acute appendicitis. Here, he was visited on 9 April by Lucie and Steve Goodwin, who observed that this event probably marked Doug's lowest point.[7]

Certainly, his driving had not improved! Richard Cowper recounts how Guy Lee had mentioned that the Grey Mare's Tail waterfall, near Moffat, was frozen and ready for climbing. He, Sharu and Doug drove there, with Doug using his knees for steering while concentrating too much on the surroundings. Consequently, Doug's old Volvo left the road and tumbled into a riverbed. After a couple of minutes, Sharu and Doug were able to crawl out of their windows, but it took longer to extricate Cowper, unbelted, in the back seat. Astonishingly, none was seriously injured.[8]

A different sort of driving hazard is described by Tim Macartney-Snape: 'I visited Doug and Sharu in Cumbria in 1999. A Sherpa, Lhakpa, was staying with them. Lhakpa had smuggled into England some *tongba*, a favourite drink from the eastern Himalaya. We sampled quite a lot one evening, after climbing. When it came to deciding what to eat for dinner, the cupboards were a bit bare, so Doug suggested we drive to the Duke's Inn at Armathwaite, some distance away, as it had a good menu. Doug insisted that he was OK to drive. Despite my own state of *tongba*-induced happiness, I was rather nervous. Worse when we drove back after a great night in the pub. Doug's driving was terrifying!'

Doug and Sharu's divorce was vigorously contested. Sharu gave up her management of CAT; Jan lost ownership of Doug and Jan's joint property.

Gina Madgett takes up the unhappy remainder of Jan's story:

When Doug moved, life became difficult for Jan financially. I believe her parents decided to give up their home and move into the annexe [originally Doug's workroom] to help out.

Jan was first diagnosed with cancer around this time, but she appeared to make a reasonable recovery. She continued teaching her special needs classes, was involved in village and school life, was herself artistic, and still welcomed many climbers and friends who needed a bed for the night. After the return of the cancer and chemo treatment, Jan felt she needed to be nearer her daughters – Michael was in New Zealand by then – so she rented a flat in Bournemouth where Martha was doctoring . . .

Money became a bit tight, and her sister Tena let her stay in their holiday cottage in Veryan, between Falmouth and St Austell in Cornwall. She was very ill and weak by then – brain cancer as well as breast, and though I often drove down for a weekend she was likely to say the black dog had got her and I'd better keep out of the way until evening. The Doug-Sharu divorce was a cruel cross for her to bear when she was so dreadfully ill, knowing by now she didn't have much time left.

It was while she was in Bournemouth and Veryan that Doug used to call in to see her – probably regretting some of his past conduct – and they became close again. In fact, one day talking affectionately of their past he suggested they get together again. Jan merely looked him in the face and said, 'I've moved on Doug.' He laughed, but it stung. I truly believe that he absolutely meant it [at Jan's memorial service, when he gave the eulogy] when he said Jan was his best friend.[9]

At that service, Doug testified to Jan's capacity for hard work, her dislike of bureaucracy and fondness for Bob Dylan. He recalled her 'big, welcoming smile' and her pride in her children. Finally, he said how much they were fatefully bound to each other and how love existed between them until the end.

The remaining bone of contention during the divorce period was the whereabouts of Doug's RGS Patron's Gold Medal, one of his most precious possessions, and his CBE insignium. These disappeared at some point during the separation and divorce. Enquiries and a search in England have led nowhere.

Doug's and Sharu's divorce was declared absolute on 12 August 2003. Originally, Sharu had been awarded custody of Arran and Euan, but this was contested. After a protracted toing and froing between solicitors, Doug was awarded custody of the children (as being best placed to provide for their accommodation and education, he no longer being an absent father); Sharu was awarded 'reasonable access'. The final order was made in February 2008. As Doug somewhat disingenuously put it to Trish on their wedding day, 8 December 2007, 'I have a big wedding present for you.'

∽

Meanwhile, climbing went on, mainly cragging and winter climbs. One day, for example, Doug, Colin Downer and Guy Lee were heading up to Tarn Crag, to make a winter ascent of Chock Gully, when they met a man heading downhill to alert the mountain rescue. A girl in his party of six had broken her ankle. It was suggested that they had enough people in their team to effect a self-rescue. On reaching the casualty, Doug suggested she attempt to crawl down, Ogre-epic fashion. She found this too difficult; her friends just looked on. Guy Lee organised a carry down with a makeshift stretcher, using their kit. Doug and Colin continued on to the climb, which turned into a real epic, with Doug narrowly avoiding being swept off the last pitch by an avalanche. The improvised rescue got the girl down to the road and off to hospital.

As international lectures continued, so did the associated climbs – and the impression they left. Mark Bowen says, 'My wife and I used to give the annual slide show for the beginners' rock-climbing program run by the Boston Chapter of the Appalachian Mountain Club. I always used to show a slide of Doug with his fists raised in triumph and a look of glee as he stood at the top of a climb at the Quincy Quarries, a small urban rock-climbing area south of Boston. I used to say something like, "This man climbed Mount Everest, but he still gets a charge out of climbing the little outcroppings around here that you'll be climbing in a couple of weeks.'"

Doug, never very proficient, still occasionally skied. In 2001, he and Dez Hadlum headed for the Rocky Mountain National Park on a 'Colorado bluebird' day. Dez picks up the story:

I offered to break trail through 6 to 8 inches of fresh powder snow. We reached a high alpine lake with only a few snowdrifts to contend with. The descent was good, across untracked powder. We skied into the next valley and up to two high lakes. The descent was trickier, more wooded and a bit steeper. Near the bottom, Doug missed a turn; he had to make a quick decision: hit the rock face on the left or go down the snow bank on the right. He chose the latter. He ended up shoulder height in a tree well full of fresh snow.

While he was thrashing around, two people approached. One asked, 'Are you Doug Scott?' Doug asked how they knew this. One had seen his Everest lecture in Baltimore the previous week! The conversation ended with Doug's remark, 'You know I climb better than I ski.'

Half an hour later we arrived at the trail head. My knees were hurting, so I know Doug's must have been killing him. Despite this, he was enjoying the outdoors, overcoming pain and showing the Scott determination to see things through.

When not preparing lectures, Doug was writing hard. During the 1990s and thereafter, he published two books and was working on five others. *A History of Everest*, which had been gestating since the late 1970s, never, fortunately, appeared: its history has been comprehensively covered. A regrettably unfinished work, however, was Doug's anthology of mountain poetry, ranging from Wordsworth and Geoffrey Winthrop Young to Buddhist meditational poems.

In the late 1990s, Doug began work on the second volume of his autobiography, *Up and About*, although the first volume did not appear until 2015. *Up and About* is a useful reference work, although many dates are wrong and some of the stories present Doug rather tendentiously. Its length is excessive, with trivia and banal discursive comments on global affairs. Around 2007, Doug collected a set of tales of 'inspiring mountain rescues', something which would have made for interesting, personal reminiscence. Perhaps longest in gestation was Doug's history of the

Himalaya, a comprehensive piece of research covering everything between Chitral and Namche Barwa. When Doug asked me to edit his final book, *Kangchenjunga*, the typescript he submitted, including this history, ran to a hefty 173,000 words, something the publisher was keen to reduce. Sadly, Doug's final illness overtook him and *Kangchenjunga* was published posthumously.

In 1992, Doug published *Himalayan Climber*, an account of his major climbs. Something of a coffee-table book in format, it nonetheless contains descriptions, sometimes very brief, of twenty-seven of Doug's major climbs in the Greater Ranges, enhanced by superlative photos. The *Himalayan Journal* reviewer, Jim Fotheringham, noted the revelatory photos of local people and the captions' creation of a 'kaleidoscope of mountaineering'. While detecting some occasional departures from ethical principles, Fotheringham praises Doug's admirable aesthetics. The book, he says, follows the British tradition of initiative, adventure and eccentricity in mountaineering: it tries to capture Doug's complexity and his attempts to make sense of mountaineering and life. John Porter's review in *Mountain Craft* echoes the admiration for the photos but finds the arrangement of the text occasionally repetitive and rather perplexing, with an editorial oversimplification which undercuts the magnitude of the experiences portrayed.

Of course, a promotional lecture tour from 24 February to 29 March 1992 accompanied the publication of *Himalayan Climber*. Only seven of these thirty-three days were free, with never fewer than six consecutive nights of lectures. (At that time, Doug was also carrying out fundraising lectures for CAN.) These lectures generated human interest beyond their content.

David Baker, who had first met Doug at White Hall, recalls, 'When I last saw him in Oban he was giving a talk to raise funds for CAN. I didn't particularly want to impose myself on him after so long as there were lots of others wanting his attention. He spotted me when I was bidding for a signed photo in the post-talk auction. We chatted and reminisced. About a week later I got a framed signed photo in the post from him and I sent him a donation for CAN. He didn't need to do that, but the photo has pride of place in my lounge.'[10]

Doug's final major writing contribution of the 1990s was his chapter on climbing the Carstensz Pyramid, in Steve Bell's *Seven Summits*. Of course, Doug continued to contribute to journals and magazines and was invited to write the forewords for several books.

∾

Aside from writing, Doug's time was taken up increasingly with environmental and ethical matters. The International Climbing and Mountaineering Federation (UIAA) had been making ethical declarations since Kathmandu in 1982. The first Tyrol Declaration came in 2002. It aimed to define human values in terms of mountain sports.

The most notable discussion concerning mountain wilderness began at the Alpine Club's 1984 'Environment and Lightweight Expeditions' symposium, followed by the Theses of Biella in 1987. Concerned about the inroads into mountain wilderness areas, and sponsored by the Sella Foundation, various distinguished mountaineers, notably Scott, Bonington, Messner and Chouinard, met in Biella, between Milan and Aosta, in 1987. Their declaration, the Theses of Biella, declared that man was no more than a visitor, or perhaps a guardian, to places unaffected by civilisation. Opposition, for example, was led against heli-skiing; they opposed the proposal to place a ladder on the Hillary Step (an action made irrelevant by the 2015 earthquake); a European controversy about bolting began which rumbled on for the next thirty or so years.

Doug strongly criticised several European national climbing institutions for actually encouraging bolting. He supported Mick Fowler's dictum to 'shun the bolt completely'. At the time of the 2002 Tyrol Declaration, Doug formed a friendship with the German rock-climber Alexander Huber. Together, they campaigned against bolting and retrobolting, sanctioned and indeed encouraged by several European national mountain bodies.[11] As Huber states, 'I discussed these things mainly with the DAV, the German Alpine Club. Of course, the DAV with more than a million members is more concentrated in giving a service to the big majority. To a certain extent I understand their service, but on the other side there is no other body than the DAV for preserving the Alpine heritage. And this Alpine heritage is not just the mountain huts but every mountain with routes from each era. All these routes need to be preserved as Alpine heritage.' I asked Huber if his, and by implication, Doug's, main objection to bolts was aesthetic or about taking the risk out of outdoor climbing, or both? Huber answered, 'It is definitely the risk because the risk demands the competence and skills of an Alpinist. That's what Alpinism is all about!'

In 2009 a UIAA mountaineering ethics declaration was issued. Another, concerning indoor climbing walls, followed in 2012. One on the preservation of natural rock came in 2013, followed by a statement on climate change in 2015. Doug became the UK's representative on the UIAA's management committee from 2008 to 2012.

A large part of Doug's Valedictory Address as President of the Alpine Club, in 2001, was devoted to preservation of the environment.[12] He covered the questions of litter, removal of camps, removal of bodies (a topical concern following the re-discovery of Mallory's body in 1999; he created a new Alpine Club policy in relation to the possible discovery of Irving's body), bolting, retro-bolting of Classic Alpine routes and the local human environment, particularly the wellbeing of porters. He dates many modern concerns from 1986, when the Nepali government lifted most climbing restrictions there. He recommended 'education', to see a tin can as 'litter'. A distinction was drawn between leaving oxygen bottles on the mountain, where they cause aesthetic offence but little environmental damage, and the deforestation along access trails to provide many expeditions with firewood.

Doug became President of the Alpine Club during the most difficult period of his life. While a distinction in itself, this presidency at the millennium (1999–2001) provided the occasion for revaluation and renewal. By common consent, Doug was a very successful, innovative president, despite his flagrant disregard for protocol. I recall a meeting in 2002, where elder members would vociferously interrupt Doug with their corrections to the procedures for the meeting.

Early in his presidency, Doug offered a critical paper on the club's activities. He stressed the importance of getting more young people to join and of making the club more internationally accessible.

Doug drove the club towards increased membership, improved recording of and promulgating of information, protection of the Alpine heritage (new thoughts on which came from Mike Esten) and how to make better use of the club's assets, various environmental projects and prizes for wider-context achievements, such as research literature and science – but not for 'great climbs'. He suggested a new edition – in his typically paradoxical way of bringing tradition up to date – of *Peaks, Passes and Glaciers* (a kind of Alpine Club adventurous excursions anthology). The club's *Handbook* was updated and the club's policies, particularly on topical debates were clearly set out. A new *Club Rulebook* was produced, although some members quickly pointed out the irony of Doug Scott promoting rules! He tasked a sub-committee with improving the *Newsletter*.

William Newsom was asked to produce a much-admired paper on the club's future management structure, which led to better use of time at committee meetings, improved operation for sub-committees and the establishing of a marketing committee. Doug commissioned the setting up of a video library, although that was soon overtaken by technological improvements. He invited more foreign climbers to lectures and social events. He initiated special Alpine Club discount deals with manufacturers and retailers. He hired people to set up a website, to make the club more publicly interesting. It supplied information which would generate fewer tiresome, expensive bureaucratic delays abroad. Another innovation was to move the annual dinner from London to the provinces. The first such dinner took place at Shap, not very far from Doug's house! (Altruism playing self-interest: another Scott paradox for those who are collecting them.)

There were other, more peculiar presidential duties. In 2002, Royal Mail corresponded with Doug about the design for 2003 stamps to commemorate Everest's first ascent fiftieth anniversary. Rather more unusual was having to respond to Norman Dyhrenfurth's request to the Duke of Edinburgh to be considered for a knighthood! Protocol required support from the appropriate sporting body, but the committee felt that because so few outstanding British climbers received knighthoods, it would be inappropriate to support an application from a non-British person. The request was therefore rejected. Dyhrenfurth accepted it in good part.

Overall, Doug instituted generally beneficial, constructive initiatives. His vision, his perception of likely trends in the mountaineering world and his drive kept the club moving in a cohesive, purposeful way.

In his little spare time, Doug continued to read Gurdjieff for what he considered his spiritual benefit. His interest, however, had been turning more strongly to comparative religions (mainly Islam) and to Buddhism in particular. Stewart Hill Cottage contains several dozen books on Buddhism: historical, theological and cultural. His particular interest centred on Milarepa, the Tibetan spiritual teacher who committed murder while young before turning to religious dedication and mastery. Milarepa is associated with Tantric and Kagyu (oral tradition) Buddhism, aspects which Doug was able to learn about from 'NE' at Samye Ling.

Christine Gee points out the metaphorical connection between Doug's interest in physical exploration and the unknown spiritual territory of Buddhism. Doug came to realise that the intricacies of Buddhist theology, which require a lifetime to master, were too much for the time he had available and that he was too uncritical to follow the Buddhist path on his own. What he needed was a teacher, a guru, and this he found in 'NE', the adept at Samye Ling.

Their affair appears to have lasted about three years, from about 2000 to 2003, thereafter fading. It was terminated by 'NE', who said she was going into a long retreat; Doug was shocked and upset. Nonetheless, their connection was sufficiently interdependent and passionate for them to seek the guidance of a rinpoché, a senior incarnate lama, on their course of action.[13]

Kagyu Samye Ling was founded in 1967, the first Tibetan centre in the West following China's illegal invasion of Tibet in 1959. It lies about three kilometres north of Eskdalemuir, some thirty kilometres north of Carlisle. The Scott connection appears to have arisen through businessman Harry Milward and his wife Gwen, who 'had a conversation' with Doug about Gurdjieff 'sometime in the '70s or '80s'. Further interest was raised by the Dalai Lama's visit in 1984. A plan was formed in 1998 to build a stupa (shrine). Doug, with Bonington, Fotheringham, David Oswin, Hamish MacInnes and others, helped from 1998 onwards to fund and to build it. Doug lent posters as well as giving fundraising lectures at the Rheged Centre outside Penrith. He ran a fundraising trek in 2000. 'NE' was reluctant to become involved but was overruled by Lama Yeshe, the abbot. Each trekker paid CAT for the trek while also raising sponsorship to cover donations to the stupa building programme, to include a prayer-wheel house, statues and landscaping of a peace garden. Sixty trekkers contributed. They followed a sacred pilgrimage route in Nepal researched by a nun. 'NE' met Doug in Kathmandu, where they were received (and probably counselled) by Akong Rinpoché, the abbot at that time. They received teachings, lit butter lamps and prayed for world peace. Doug led one group of thirty while Jim Fotheringham led the other.

At that time, Samye Ling had attracted a lot of angry, alienated young people. Some were disruptive and problematic. Therapeutic walks and climbs in the Galloway hills and coastal cliffs were organised by Jim Fotheringham at the rinpoché's request. He recruited Doug, helped by Andy Fanshawe and Nick Kekus.

Craighaugh remained as a bridge to the Lake District. Samye Ling became a place of refuge, construction and learning. Even after marrying Trish in 2007, Doug returned once a year.

Doug's teacher at Samye Ling, 'NE', had studied with the Karmapa Lama (third-highest lama in the Buddhist hierarchy). While refusing to judge others' spirituality, Doug, says 'NE', was sincerely interested but attributed his deeper insights to his climbing. She adds that Doug was a great communicator but that his interests were eclectic, comprehending many subjects. Doug did not attend important teachings although he participated in occasional early morning meditations. He always attended the annual open day. Doug, 'NE' concludes, was generous, kind, quite self-aware and self-critical. But she criticised his mountaineering as 'non-Buddhist': Buddhism sets the highest value on the preservation of sentient life. High-level mountaineering continually risks death.

The impressive stupa was consecrated on 3 August 2000, an auspicious date for Samye Ling and its founder. Doug, 'NE' and Jim Fotheringham each sponsored a layer. Indeed, they went to considerable trouble to find red hemlock for decorating the interior. With his departure from Eskdalemuir, when Doug and Trish moved to Stewart Hill Cottage in 2006, this tumultuous, rather isolated period of Doug's life came to an end. Much public controversy, fortunately balanced by private happiness, lay in store for his remaining fourteen years.

15

CAN and CAT

'I think he was literally a god for Nepal . . . It seems likely
he will be reborn as a Serag, a mischievous spirit who
consumes the potent essences of food and wealth.'

— CAN Health Supervisor Alija Shahi

Scott gave thirty remarkably energetic years of his life to found and
develop Community Action Nepal (CAN) and its supporting company,
Community Action Treks (CAT). CAN was formed for the benefit of
those 'specialists' and their families who worked for Western expeditions
and for Nepalis living in remote communities who wanted to establish
or extend their village schools and health posts. No other mountaineer
– indeed, no other individual – has come close to improving Nepal's infra-
structure in this way. CAN has supported and established (at the time
of writing) eighteen schools, eighteen health posts and health centres,
three porter shelters, one Sherpa heritage house (including an elderly
persons' complex with warm accommodation and a community/prayer
room), eleven livelihood programmes and ten water supply projects – a
prodigious achievement. CAT and CAN thus comprised, for Scott, an
astonishing second career, begun almost twenty years after he became a
professional mountaineer in 1972.

Origins, ethos and structure

CAN's origins are complex. At base lies Scott's deep affection for indigenous
peoples, going back to his life with them during his first four expeditions
beyond Europe in the 1960s; he often commented enthusiastically on
these people's hospitability and friendliness, and on the simplicity of their
lifestyle with its lack of material possessions. Such an enthusiasm can be
seen in *Kangchenjunga*, where the principal ethnic groups of Nepal are
described in affectionate detail. In return for freely given hospitality, Scott

wanted to pass on Western building know-how while preserving vernacular appearance, the benefits of Western medicine and hygiene and, after the 2015 earthquake, Western knowledge of geoscience and architecture.

Another personal stimulus derived from Scott's belief in being fatefully connected with Sir Edmund Hillary. Since the 1960s, Hillary had dedicated his life to the wellbeing of the Solu Khumbu Sherpas through his Himalayan Trust. Hillary and Scott had met at the Alpine Club, the RGS and in Nepal itself during the 1970s, although they never climbed together. They also met in Darjeeling in West Bengal on 15 May 1985, at a seminar on mountaineering: both would have been fully aware of the other's activity. Thanks also to his early reading on leadership, and his later mountaineering literature consumption generally, Scott knew of Hillary's extraordinary achievements in Solu Khumbu and of the reverence in which he was held. Hillary, however, largely confined his humanitarian activities to the Solu Khumbu area; Scott's schools, health posts and shelters stretched across at least four Nepali provinces, from north-west of Pokhara across North Gorkha, Langtang and Bahrabise to Khumjung in the Solu Khumbu then a long way east as far as the Bajramai secondary school at Bodhe in Dhankuta.

That the Sherpas were badly paid and badly looked after by Westerners rankled with Scott. He had first observed the Sherpas' poor pay and working conditions on the Herrligkoffer expedition to Everest in 1972, where some porters went barefoot while carrying heavy loads over rocky ground up to base camp above 5000m. Lt Col J.O.M. 'Jimmy' Roberts (1916–97), the 'father of trekking' in Nepal, had consistently tried to ensure fair pay and conditions for porters. In the case of the high-altitude Sherpas, Scott and Roberts had discussed as early as 1973 making them full members of a proposed Everest team by seeking their advice as well as sharing tents, equipment and food, a 'democratic' way of avoiding the 'officers and other ranks' mentality which had bedevilled British-Sherpa relations since 1921.[1]

Scott's discussions with Roberts connected to another influential force: ex-pat Mike Cheney (1928–88), who worked with Jimmy Roberts in the first Nepali trekking agency, Mountain Travel, founded in 1964. Cheney, as Sherpa liaison officer, first met Scott on Bonington's 1975 Everest South-West Face expedition. He campaigned consistently for better working conditions and pay for the Sherpas, including setting up a Trekking Workers Welfare Fund. As Scott said in his diary when describing the founding of CAT:

All of us who went to Nepal used the services of Mike Cheney and his Specialist Cooperative. We were impressed by the total altruism of the man and the effectiveness of his trekking agency. He ploughed back all the profits into the Cooperative for the benefit of the staff and porters and provided a friendly and sound service for British climbers and trekkers visiting Nepal.

Mike died in 1988. We had to use other agents who were not always as caring of their employees. In 1989 whilst walking up to Kangchenjunga with various friends, I made a decision that would eventually associate me more intimately with the local hill people of High Asia. Sitting around the kitchen fire our Sherpas and porters were bemoaning the fact that the trekking industry in Nepal seemed to offer little security or return for all the hard work they put in. If only they could set up their own co-operative then they would have a guaranteed and regular income and a chance to determine their own futures and that of their children.

Cheney died prematurely, aged only fifty-nine. Scott took up his mantle, and the Specialist Trekking Cooperative (STC) came into being. It fulfilled a banking role also, helping Sherpas paid in cash while on trek to keep their money safe; Ang Tsering, a UIAA member and past-president of the Asia Mountaineering Federation, took a leading hand in creating deposit banks for the Sherpas' benefit.

Another contributory founding idea occurred after a Sherpa, Nima Tamang, died in an avalanche on the 1987 Everest expedition. The sponsoring company, Altos, provided £3,000 for Tamang's widow and children, an act of decency which inspired Scott to think further about how Sherpas could be better looked after. In fact, Scott established Specialist Trekking Expeditions as a cash-support organisation for the STC, much in the way that CAT was established to help fund CAN.

A more immediate stimulus to the founding of CAN occurred in 1990. On his way out from the Latok peaks, near Askole, a heavily laden porter tripped, fell and disappeared into the Braldu. In Askole, the porter's family had to be found to pay them their insurance money and to wait for the police to issue a death certificate. Scott saw that the village was experiencing over 50 per cent child mortality because of water polluted by excrement emanating from the local irrigation system. Scott became 'angry that in this day and age there was such unnecessary suffering.'[2] Ever practical, and in recognition of help from the people of Askole after his terrible epic on The Ogre in 1977, Scott decided to act: he contacted the Aga Khan Rural Support Programme in Skardu; from a nearby freshwater stream, a feeder pipe was installed, which supplied seventeen standpipes throughout the village. The project cost $10,000, half of which was paid for by Jed Williams of the American Alpine Club. Scott concludes, 'This was the project that gave me the confidence to react positively to requests in Nepal to put in schools, health posts and porter shelters as well as pipes for clean water. So indirectly from that drama on The Ogre, and the ensuing publicity, we were able to set up Community Action Nepal.'[3]

The word 'request' is important in marking CAN's ethical basis: the request for assistance had to come from the Nepalis themselves. Such a positive ethical outlook began as a reaction to the Nepal government's corruption, its lack of democratic structures and Kathmandu-based insularity where power and wealth were concentrated. Scott was never afraid to speak truth to power. As trustee and fundraiser Phil Powell remarks, not just secular power, either: 'He would criticise schoolteachers who drank or absconded . . . At a meeting in Kutumsang he told local men to do less drinking and help the women (who did the bulk of the hard physical work) more. He remonstrated with the esteemed Thrangu Rinpoché about young children migrating from North Gorkha to Kathmandu or India and advocated they remain in their village for their primary education. When we visited Tulku Kama Minjur Rinpoché at Serang Monastery, Doug expressed his alarm at the amount of plastic waste the monks and nuns were dumping down the hill.'[4]

Scott was an advocate of self-sufficiency and sustainability. Help, furthermore, was given only where it was most needed. CAN projects exist in remote places: Ghunsa, in the southern extremity of Khumjung is an eleven-hour (at least) jeep drive from Kathmandu. In North Gorkha, health workers have a six- or seven-day walk from the roadhead to reach their health posts. Scott was insistent that help was not for those places at the end of a road from Kathmandu, where city values and practices could compromise local ethics and lifestyle.

The operating principle was *shramadhan*, or community self-help through voluntary labour. This would normally take the form of local materials and labour being used – normally about 30 per cent of the total – to construct community buildings: if villagers were significantly responsible for these improvements, they would look after the buildings responsibly. No project could begin until a local committee, ideally with a gender and ethnic mix in its composition, was formed with a chairman sympathetic to CAN's ethos. Every building project was unique: a 'one size fits all' approach was to be avoided. Local construction professionals were encouraged to maintain an overview of each project. The commitment was to vernacular architecture and building practices, although this principle underwent some modification after the 2015 earthquake and changes to government re-building legislation. Principles governing construction dimensions and materials, quality assurance and so on were established. Reinforced concrete, for example, was avoided unless absolutely necessary – decisions were made according to the size, situation and nature of the land available. Unlike other charities which he had seen vying with each other to 'help' locals, who thereby became dependent on them, Scott strongly opposed the principle of donor dependency.

Scott, of course, had been a builder for several months with his brother Garry, and enjoyed a lifelong interest in construction – particularly where it involved one of his favourite materials, wood. He was naturally drawn to help for local communities which reflected such an interest. He used his skills: numerous stories describe Scott expertly assessing constructions, for example the roofing plank at Melamchigaun in Helambu, or physically assisting with stone-breaking or wood-cutting.

After *shramadhan*, the next most important principle required sustainability through using local people's skills and initiatives, such as producing garments from looms, raising goats, growing mushrooms (for a fast turnover), making honey and, dearest to Scott's own heart, growing organic kitchen vegetables.

As far as schools were concerned, specific ethical aims were established: educating children in the locality, not in Kathmandu or India, was stressed, to give children a pride in their community. Every school had a library, many of them dedicated to Scott's friend Roger Fox, who left a legacy for library provision. Reliable information was mandatory to sustain democracy. Once a school was successfully up and running, it was handed over to the government. Nepali government cuts in 2019–20 forced a redistribution of CAN resources in favour of North Gorkha. CAN schools elsewhere have consequently enjoyed mixed fortunes: the Bahrabise School for the Deaf continues its excellent work while the school at Ghunsa, which has 230 pupils, is now urgently in need of support teaching staff (as well as funds for the health-post workers to buy medicines in Kathmandu).

Health posts have their own ethical basis, in the belief that local knowledge becomes local effectiveness. Primary health care is supplied where none previously existed, although still initiated by local request. Western medicine provides the model. Scott, however, was enthusiastic about traditional Tibetan medicine practitioners working alongside CAN health staff. Preventative care is offered. Guidance comes from Dr Rob Lorge's formulary for health-post medicines and his handbook of primary health care, later expanded by Dr Gerda Pohl. The psychological effects of natural disasters are also treated. Queries from the field can now be discussed with Kathmandu specialists thanks to better connectivity. *In situ*, minor operations, such as for cataracts, are performed. Simple research projects are followed. The health programme is tied to health education, particularly relating to mothers' groups and schools, enhanced by a once-yearly visit to Kathmandu for retraining and updating of medical knowledge.

∞

Scott describes the financial ethos and practices underpinning CAN thus: 'We work very closely with the local village committees at all stages of our operations through our CAN office in Kathmandu. CAN directs all monies received in the UK out to Nepal where it is low profile and grass roots in its approach. Administration costs are kept to the minimum – our staff do not travel around in 4×4 jeeps or run up huge entertainment bills in hotels and restaurants.'[5]

The bulk of CAN fundraising occurs in the UK. Scott travelled on endless lecture tours across the UK, redoubling his efforts after the 2015 earthquake. These lectures, which were given as far apart as Ullapool, the Isle of Mull, Pateley Bridge, Hull, Holyhead, Builth Wells, London, Exeter and St Austell (a small proportion of the total) generated ancillary sales from books, Nepali crafts, photographs and posters. One fundraising venture is the highly profitable biennial open day at Stewart Hill Cottage in Cumbria, Doug and Trish's home, with its fine gardens, ponds, interesting plants and Scott memorabilia.[6] Fundraising events also generated income thanks to UK supporters, such as Paul Hodges' marathons from the Moel Siabod Café. Scott's dictum was 'cash is king'. His long-suffering but amenable accountant, Neil Edgar, begged to differ. He first got to know Scott in 1994. Despite his 'trepidation at meeting someone famous', Edgar found Scott easy to get on with – most of the time. It was always possible, he recalls, to have a chat with Scott about family or sporting matters.

Around 2002, Edgar tells us, at the time of Scott's divorce from Sharu, the STC evolved into CAT to maintain trekking income. When Jeff Frew was running CAT, he managed to get 500–600 trekkers interested each year, providing CAN with £35,000 profit per annum. These trekkers, in turn, often spread the word – there were very few bad experiences – since the treks, for example to Helambu and Langtang, often visited impressive CAN projects which would be discussed then supported from the UK. Successful word-of-mouth promotion avoided the need for expensive advertising.

CAT also contributed to providing Sherpas with a fair wage and fair treatment. It never quite achieved the success of the STC, however. Scott's attitude to money, Edgar says, did not change greatly over the years. He always complained when his tax bill was too high, but his aim was not so much for profit as to provide an income to support his family. Record-keeping was never Scott's strong point: quarterly VAT returns began with a pile of loose records evolving into a concertina file for each month – Scott citing this as an example of progress – after much gentle nagging from this dedicated accountant. Scott, however, remained sceptical about the value of record-keeping. Trying to get him to record mileage to lectures or the sales of posters and memorabilia proved very difficult: carefully focused sessions between Edgar and Scott remained necessary to keep the tax man happy. Scott was 'never really worried about the minutiae of figures and how they'd been arrived at'. Deadlines were only kept because Edgar had the sense to chase Scott to meet them well in advance of when they occurred.

Conversations between Scott and Edgar occasionally became difficult, usually concerning legal constraints. Detailed records of expenditure did not interest Scott greatly, as long as he knew the monies had been spent in a way he considered satisfactory. When Edgar tried to explain legal requirements, however, Scott would listen; sometimes, though, he became quite angry about the niceties of company law. Even after a bad phone call, Edgar recalls, he knew that a good conversation could quickly be resumed. In sum, the relationship between company and charity law led to frustration, but Scott was 'ultimately kept under control and within the law'. Scott's drive, assisted by trustees, staff and volunteers, Edgar concludes, created CAN's achievements. His legacy in so doing should remain 'as great as his mountaineering exploits'. Other trusts and foundations, such as the Juniper Trust (patron: Sir Chris Bonington), run by the tireless writer-poet Angela Locke, also provided funds. Locke recalls a

Nepali guide telling her that CAN was a model of best practice, 'not one where the 4x4s drive round Kathmandu and never help the hill people', thus worthy of funding.

As a friend of David Durkan remarked about Scott, 'The world's most enthusiastic fund-raiser! You meet him, you shake hands, he talks CAN and you automatically contribute. I bought one of his £10 posters and paid £200! Just because it was Doug.'[7] Many volunteers, some mountaineers, others simply people happy to give their time, money or labour for a good cause also contributed enormously, such as Linda Orritt's inimitable sales of books and cakes. In addition to UK volunteers, CAN managed to attract the support of organisations such as Porters Progress UK, the International Porter Protection Group, Promise Nepal and bigger institutions such as CAFOD and the Big Lottery Fund, as well as those working under CAN's umbrella, such as the Ulleri Library Project run by James Dauman. These volunteers and organisations run to several hundreds. Discovering the spectacular extent of fundraising support via the CAN website, www.canepal.org.uk, is an uplifting experience.

While Scott was the powerful driving force behind CAT and CAN, these companies were run since 1998 by an administrative team in Nepal, led by Murari Gautam at the time of writing. In 1993, CAN offices were established in central Kathmandu for a Nepali manager with a secretarial and administrative support team, supplemented by health and education staff in the field. CAT was run by Westerners whom Scott knew personally. In the UK, Scott's ideas and policies were supplemented by trustees, both Western and Nepali, chosen largely in Scott's own image. Infrequent disagreements would occasionally generate a walk-out by Scott, who was found at the end of one such meeting chopping wood with considerable force. Sporadic problems occurred with Scott's management style. They illustrate the ever-present contradiction in Scott's psyche: that of a beneficent humanitarian prevailing in a manner which often infuriated those around him.

The formation of STC in 1989–90, was followed by CAN's first request for assistance, from Tej Tamang at Ghunsa in 1994. It began a history which embraced highly turbulent years for Nepal, encompassing the ten-year Maoist uprising, Prince Dipendra's massacre of the Royal Family in 2001 and the 2015 earthquake.

CAT's history does not entirely correspond to CAN's pattern. As Scott and Sharu tackled their acrimonious divorce, finalised in 2003, Sharu, who had been in partnership with Scott since 1990, wanted to take on the STC, but came to a business arrangement with Doug about the future ownership of CAT. Up to about 2006, radical office restructuring became necessary; about the same time, the occasional piece of financial malpractice surfaced, a breach of trust which led to lowered staff morale. The period 2008–12 proved turbulent despite relative stability in the country at large. The CEO, Martin West, presided over a loss of £90,000 by 2011, much of it caused by rapidly rising prices. At that point, Scott reacquired CAT; his director's loan, thanks to cooperative work with Bhai Tamang, was reimbursed by 2013. Over the period 2010–12, the breach with Ian Wall, an experienced trekking leader and an old friend of Scott, widened until a definitive confrontation with Wall in 2012. Trekking numbers did improve, though not to earlier levels: by 2018, CAT clients amounted to sixty-six trekkers. Then COVID struck. Trekkers are now returning to Nepal, as I witnessed there in September 2022, although numbers have not yet attained pre-COVID levels.

The following sections are not a history of CAT and CAN. They should be seen as a description of Scott's founding of these companies, then how he handled and developed them through the personal, political and natural upheavals which beset him and this country to which he was so attached.

The God-Father

Scott continues to be revered in Nepal. CAN staff have described him with awe – 'He is like a god to me' – because of Scott's ability to create something quickly out of, apparently, nothing. CAN health posts have saved countless Nepali lives through reducing disease; horrifying infant mortality rates have been reduced by building properly staffed and equipped birthing rooms. CAN schools assist the escape from poverty. CAN hostels and shelters protect from the harsh environment. The title image of fatherliness is a strong one. As Phil Powell says, 'Doug was "very hands on" with CAN and knew the projects in meticulous detail. He was generous: for example, when Doug met some honey hunters he promised he would give them some of his mountaineering ropes. He always delivered on his commitments. When he went to the new CAN Kyanjin Hostel for the elderly he took warm Berghaus fleeces for everyone. He wanted us to build "small palaces for the elderly poor". He would always listen to staff concerns about pay and conditions.'[8]

It helped in CAN's development that Scott was also so knowledgeable about building methods, materials and construction, and enjoyed building as an activity. Purna Gautam, headmaster of the school at Melamchigaun, recalls a moment in 2000 when 'my school building was being constructed. Masons had built a wall three feet high without interlocking the stones. Scott then asked them to demolish the wall and taught them the right way. After six months, when Scott visited the school once again, he witnessed a hole in the ceiling of the building and replaced the wooden plank himself while encouraging the carpenter to work efficiently.'

Such knowledge extended to vehicle mechanics, going back to Scott's experiences with motorbikes and lorries as a young man: Scott would help in getting jeeps out of mud or repairing them when they broke down.

Scott always advocated self-development, self-sufficiency and self-help while opposing donor dependency. He wanted to support grass roots community development. Despite all his participation, however, Scott would describe Murari and his team in Kathmandu as the bedrock of the organisation. Certainly true, but CAN's long-standing secretary, Ruth Moore, was vital in keeping a semblance of routine going at the CAN office while also helping to steer Doug through the choppy waters of his disintegrating relationship with Sharu and his sometimes fraught relationship with both trustees and administrative staff in Kathmandu.

Scott's effectiveness was indubitable. He would win over people by talking about their family, what they most cherished in their lives. He would encourage people to look forward. He was generous and thoughtful: whenever he visited Nepal, he always remembered to bring presents. He was also cast in the heroic mould: passionate and defiant in the face of strangulating bureaucracy and armed Maoists, yet at the same time a pragmatist, if sometimes too trustful. He built excellent partnerships with other organisations. But if we accept the argument that Scott's dynamism derived from the energetic clash of opposites in his character, we have to look also at the less happy consequences for others of living and working with this driven soul.

༄

Curiously, although Scott had set up the beginnings of a co-operative and trekking agency with Jimmy Roberts and Mike Cheney, it was two friends of Scott who provided the catalyst for these developing into CAT.

In March and April 1989, Nigel Porter joined Scott and Sharu and his friend Terry Mooney QC for a trek to Scott's 1979 base camp at the foot of Kangchenjunga, starting from the airstrip at Suketar, near Taplejung in Eastern Nepal. The trek was organised by fellow Cumbrian David Oswin, a trekking specialist. By all accounts, despite some unseasonal snow, this was a much-enjoyed trek, as Porter's detailed account makes clear. For example, at Hellok, the party was surrounded by a group of Nepali schoolgirls. Sharu asked them if they were Sherpas, to which they replied, 'Chhetri.' 'Warriors, eh?' replied Scott, who knew the Chhetri to be a warrior caste.

Further along, Porter went down with 'yeti's revenge', allowing Scott with perhaps too great alacrity to try out his homeopathic medicines on him (orthodox medicines being successfully applied later). Scott's medical skills were further exercised two days later when he gave Ang Phurba 'eye-drops and pills' for snow-blindness. On the following evening, too much 'Mustang coffee' (*rakshi* and melted yak-butter) led first to over-exuberant renditions of 'Wild Rover' and 'The Leaving of Liverpool' before Scott dissolved the evening in laughter by falling backwards into the metal kitchen equipment stacked next to the cooking tent.[9]

Such events are all part and parcel of a memorable trek. While no explicit discussion of conditions for Sherpas is recorded in Porter's otherwise detailed account, the sight of a Sherpa porter attached to a Russian expedition being brought down in a body-bag must have provoked some comment. On another occasion, Porter helped a local porter over difficult ground by carrying some badly attached kitchen equipment for him. Nearer Pang Pema base camp, a porter badly gashed his head when hit on steep ground by falling ice blocks. The expedition doctor patched him up, but Scott came across him an hour later still carrying his full load supported by his head-strap! Scott immediately re-distributed his load among the other porters. Such incidents would have provoked thinking about Sherpa working conditions.

We know that this very harmonious trek constituted the germ of CAT treks thereafter, as Jeff Frew, whom Scott had first met in Coire an t-Sneachdha in the Cairngorms in 1984, was again invited in 1989 to lead a CAT reconnaissance trek with a view to establishing a sustainable tourist model. (On this trek, a stray dog turned up. It was nicknamed 'Dog Scott' as Scott had wandered onto the wrong ridge with some Sherpas and only joined the trekkers several days late. Such conduct was unsurprising: Dr Rob Lorge, CAN doctor and trustee of long standing, maintained that he never saw Scott wear a watch.)

Another early trek, in 1994, saw Terry Mooney centre stage once more, this time with Ghunsa resident Tej Bahadur Temang as cook. Tej's strong sense of civic responsibility led him to ask Mooney if STC might consider fixing the roof of his village school at Ghunsa, in Khumjung. In December, Mooney visited Ghunsa, completed a survey and spent £200 buying enough land for a school and play area. In January 1995, Sharu visited Ghunsa to find the villagers had already started to level the ground. Sharu contacted the Department of Education in Kathmandu and the school project formally began. At the same time, Scott launched an appeal for funds. Thanks to STC profits of £3,000, the Bill Reaper Memorial Fund contribution of £2,000, the Irish Himalayan Trust's £1,000 and various other donations, £9,000 was raised over the following eighteen months. In April 1996, a group from Plymouth College, who had themselves raised £1,000, established a health post using materials from the old school. In February 1998, the Ghunsa school was officially opened. A school at nearby Lapcha was also officially started.

These two treks act as the paradigmatic foundations for CAT and CAN. All future developments generally followed the patterns established by them. Thanks to Scott's drive and enthusiasm, his experience and background knowledge and his ability to get on well with the indigenous peoples, CAN had established its own momentum. Then the complicated political history of Nepal intervened.

✍

The Maoist insurgency, which began on 13 February 1996, set the Communist Party of Nepal (Maoist Centre) against the country's government. The Maoists' purpose was to overthrow the Nepalese monarchy and establish a people's republic. The end came with the signing of the Comprehensive Peace Accord on 21 November 2006. During the insurgency, massacres, executions without trial and kidnappings were widespread: over 17,000 people died. Several hundred thousand people were obliged to move their homes throughout rural Nepal.

Despite these difficult conditions, CAN continued to expand its work. In 1997, after discussing the matter with Oldham solicitor Allan Hargreaves, Scott decided to put the STC on an official footing. On 9 December, the STC Charitable Trust was registered in the UK and as an NGO (non-governmental organisation) in Nepal. Terry Mooney was one of the trustees; Chris Bonington became patron.

Innovatory excitement coupled with the generosity of the donations made for immediate expansion. In March and December of 1997, information was gathered on the feasibility of starting a schools' project in

Langtang, the mountainous area bordering Tibet north of Kathmandu. In 1998, a busy year, Scott visited Langtang to discuss the rebuilding of Mundu School with the villagers, as well as the restoration of the 500-year-old Langtang gompa. In mid-October, Scott, Pip Hopkinson (one of the original trustees) and Captain Tek (an ex-Army officer who had been appointed to run STC in January 1996 alongside STC office manager Gyaldzen), found their way to the upper reaches of the Dudh Kosi (the 'Milk River', which drains the Everest area) to remote Walung. There, they left glass and tools, the starting materials for a health post, clean water supply and gompa renovation project.

Still in this extraordinary year, Scott began to consider Melamchi school for support. Purna Gautam, its headmaster, comments:

In 1998, I got an opportunity to share my dream of establishing my school, Melamchi Ghyang Primary School, established in 1985, as one of the best schools in Sindhupalchowk. I sought support for building our own school and enhancing the quality of education with the help of British trekkers who were active in Helambu through CAT. In 1999, I got to meet Doug Scott in person. In 2000, CAN provided support to build an eight-room school building and provide a salary for two school teachers.

The school that started with only nineteen students grew to have ninety-five students by the end of 2002. With this increase, rooms began to get occupied and congested. Gradually, we began to build more rooms and upgrade to the lower secondary from the primary level. In 2005, we upgraded to full secondary level school. In the same year, Melamchi Ghyang Secondary School was the first English medium school in the district to achieve 100 percent first division results in the School Leaving Certificate examination conducted by the National Examination Board.

Scott and his team also trekked in 1998 in Helambu, along the Gosainkund Circuit near the Tibetan border, and in December 2000 established a health post at Kutumsang, a village situated on the border of the Sindhupalchowk and Nuwakot districts, in answer to a request for help from Sonam Dorje Sherpa. (When Scott turned up on a return trek, he was greeted with cries of 'He's here!') Pasang Wangchu Hyolmo, Sonam Dorje's nephew, came down from Helambu to Kathmandu to tell me the story. His uncle had shown land available to Scott. The village council promised *shramadhan*. CAN would supply the non-local materials, which the villagers would then carry from the roadhead. So far, general happiness. But Sonam left for the US in 2000, unable further to accept a compromised existence under the Maoists (he had owned a hotel but the insurgency and other events had wrecked the tourism industry). Nonetheless, the health post was established; Scott took part in lifting the timber required. The health post began to provide, free of charge, more than 177 different medicines. A birthing centre came into operation: it contributed strongly to minimising infant and maternal mortality rates.

The millennial year also proved to be busy. Thanks to a chance encounter on a plane, Scott met Dr Rob Lorge, who was asked if he might be interested in working in Nepal. Lorge's tentatively affirmative replies led both men a fortnight later to a fundraising event at Shap where Scott publicly declared that Lorge would be spending six months in Nepal! Lorge remains a hugely influential figure in the development of CAN's practices and ethos.

CAN, geographically continuing to spread its wings, established a well-equipped school in Bode village, near Dhankuta in the eastern province of Kosi, with responsibility for providing teachers' salaries as well. Similarly, health posts and schools were established in the remote Ghyamrang and Rohigau villages in Kaski district, north-east of Pokhara. Salary and allowances were provided for teachers and nurses. Not without difficulty, however: field nurse Kalpana Khadkha, one of CAN's longest-serving employees, relates how the Army at Pokhara instructed Scott not to proceed to a Maoist-held area. Scott, however, insisted on going on alone: 'If I make mistakes, they can kill me. The others needn't go.' A courageous declaration which led to successful action.

One of the most conspicuous CAN successes during this period involved Hira, a boy with a cough who appeared at the Ghunsa health post. The cough was diagnosed by Lorge as a congenital heart condition. Lorge called Scott via satellite phone to see if fundraising for his treatment were possible. Hira was transferred to Kathmandu to be seen by a private cardiologist, who confirmed the diagnosis. Lorge emailed the results to a cardiology colleague at the Royal Brompton Hospital in London, where a surgeon offered to operate free of charge. After Lorge contacted Chain of Hope, a charity founded by Sir Magdi Yacoub, CAN funded the travel for Hira and his father while Chain of Hope covered the operation's costs. The corrective surgery was successful. Hira's recuperation in hospital was also funded: other charities helped until he was well enough to return to Ghunsa to lead a healthy life. In December 2003, Scott met Hira: 'Hira rushed with outstretched arms and both parents were overcome with emotion.'[10]

Because the projects were expanding, and because personality clashes, such as Gyaldzen's inability to work with Captain Tek, were leading to managerial ineffectiveness, it was decided also in 1998 to re-structure the management in Kathmandu. Jiban Kharki was appointed project manager. At this time, Scott got to know an auditor, Murari Gautam, who began by providing a legal framework for Scott's plans. By 2002, he was doing part-time work for CAN and CAT. Scott was in Nepal every year: they discussed money flow from the UK to Nepal and how it could best be distributed.

Two other CAN managers were appointed. While designed to share the increasing administrative burden, these managers tended to develop differing views as to how the charity should be run. Scott was inundated with conflicting emails as the managers became increasingly competitive. To relieve the stress, Jiban was let go in 2006, although the 'three managers' structure survived until 2008, when Murari, who shared Scott's ethos, fired the two remaining managers and became operations director in Nepal, a post he continues to occupy with great effectiveness and professionalism.

The insurgency, however, was spreading like an infection across Nepal. The health-post nurses were frightened. Scott knew they faced extortion demands. With only one nurse in each health post, they naturally felt isolated; at least two nurses per health post were introduced where possible. The Army harassed the nurses also, because they believed them to be treating the Maoists sympathetically. In fact, Scott decided on the policy of agreeing to treat all combatants, as long as they were non-uniformed and unarmed. The nurses would also work in civilian clothes.

Very difficult moments continued to occur, such as a bloody shoot-out at Phaplu, not far from Ghunsa, when Scott, Trish and Dr Lorge were nearby. As Scott recounts, the District Commissioner told them that the Maoists were aware of their presence and needed medical care and medicines: they were therefore at risk of kidnap. Because of this, they found themselves stuck in Khandbari with a sub-machine gun-toting soldier posted outside their hotel room to deter kidnappers! It was here that Dr Lorge decided to use his time to write a formulary listing the medicines appropriate for CAN health posts, later updated by Dr Gerda Pohl. The day after they flew out, the airstrip control tower was blown up. Scott, in characteristically laconic fashion remarked that, 'a kidnap would be good publicity for CAN'.

Powell comments, 'Doug had remonstrated with a local Maoist Commander about having to pay a "contribution" and it was then I believe that Doug explained what drove CAN's philosophy and how we were more communist than the insurgents! The Maoist Commander I believe was shot dead the next day in a battle in a village where our team were hiding out.'

However, matters improved. The nurses became safer by foregoing their uniforms. The Maoists recognised that CAN's projects were community-driven, thus allowing them to look at the projects sympathetically. Even-handedness in treatment of casualties also helped.

Overall, CAN maintained a relatively good relationship with the Maoists. They knew CAN was an independent NGO. Despite the pressures, staff turnover was not too high. Scott often said CAN's support was vital during the insurrection as the government had diverted all its spending power into the war effort.

Of course, the insurgency marked a bad time for CAT; revenue virtually collapsed. The STC was stopped in 1999 and became CAT and CAN. CAT, as the STC, had operated as a partnership between Scott and Sharu, from 1990 to 2001. After Scott came to a business arrangement with Sharu about CAT's future ownership in 2002, he invited friends to become shareholders in what became Community Action Treks Limited. Many CAT supporters had fortunately become long-term supporters of CAN. From 2002 to 2007, income dropped because of the uncertainties of organising safe trekking during the insurgency and adverse publicity following Dipendra's massacre of the Royal Family in 2001. A global financial crisis was in the offing, with the particularly detrimental effect of a sharp rise in long-haul flight prices. Even getting cash into Nepal proved problematic. On at least one occasion, Scott and Lorge carried $10,000 in cash through Nepali Customs (where Scott was well-known) in a rucksack. On other occasions, substantial quantities of banknotes were imported under hats.

Despite the experienced Martin West taking over the directorship of CAT in 2008, he wound it up in 2011 with losses of £90,000. Overall, therefore, the insurgency marked a remarkable period of project expansion, administrative difficulties and changes, personal and political uncertainties and the loss of income in Nepal.

༄

Having ridden the Maoist storm, Scott was in a position to expand CAN after the Peace Accord had been signed. Expansion, however, brought its own difficulties: increased human involvement meant increased managerial problems.

New buildings were supplemented by extensions to existing construction. With the justifiable pride of the successful headmaster, Purna Gautam of Melamchigaun, says, 'In the following years, 2007, 2008 and 2009, our school was able to achieve high distinction marks in the Secondary Education Examinations . . . Numbers of students began to grow. Students from various districts began to enrol in the school even from Kathmandu and other cities. In 2008, thanks to the support of CAN and the West Yorkshire Scouts, a new hostel building was constructed for the students, with more in the following years. By then, Melamchi Ghyang School had established itself as one of the model schools despite being located in one of the remotest Himalayan villages of Nepal. Without the support from CAN, it would have never been possible.'

Expansion depended on fundraising. In the UK, earnings came mainly from Scott's lecture tours.[11] These raised over £100,000 per annum. Sarah Powell comments that Scott was a very good speaker; he planned carefully; no two lectures were the same. He was also meticulous about thanking people. Although not at first warming to Scott because of his taciturnity – he was at times notoriously monosyllabic – Sarah organised a successful musical evening in Oxford at the Jacqueline du Pré Music Building. Success there led to the first big Oxford lecture, at the Said Business School, in 2007. Ticket sales for the first two lectures met expectations: word had got out that Scott had caused chaos by rearranging tables in contravention of fire regulations, resulting in an ultimatum from the building administrators. Later that evening, he drove up the disabled persons' access ramp to collect his equipment. Scott did not like the Said building: it was 'only good for climbing'. He had flu but stayed up with others at the Powells until 2 a.m., yet at 7 a.m. was directing porridge preparation for all who stayed overnight. The Powells managed to acquire the august Sheldonian theatre free: perhaps ten lectures took place in Oxford, altogether. Sometimes, the stresses of relentless travel, handshaking, hastily grabbed meals told: Scott could become shirty, for example when being rather brusque with the staff of a museum in north Oxford. Still, his Oxford experiences summarise much about him: phenomenal stamina, brilliant lecturing, the capacity to infuriate through bloody-mindedness, his charm and approachability.

Other UK fundraising events supplemented these lectures. First Everest then wider mountaineering lectures were organised by Robin Ashcroft.

He had first met Scott when masterminding the National Mountaineering Exhibition, *Everest: the Top of the World*, for the Everest First Ascent fiftieth anniversary in 2003 at the Rheged Centre outside Penrith. A comment by Scott that the South Summit bivvy replica was inauthentic because it lacked pee stains in the 'snow' led to several years' cooperation on lectures about Scott's 1975 ascent and other fundraising initiatives. (Everest '75 reunions were also used as fundraising ventures, for example the thirtieth anniversary event at the Blencathra Centre in 2005.) Ashcroft was invited to work for CAN on fundraising and publicity, which he did until standing down in 2018 to go into politics.

Other lecturers chipped in: Professor Hildegard Diemberger, a Tibetan expert and daughter of Scott's climbing and photographer friend, Kurt, lectured at Rheged. In 2008, Steve Sustad lectured on his own remarkable mountaineering exploits; Doug's 'Crawl Down The Ogre' lectures began.

Ancillary events such as the Day of the Dog, a kind of annual dog-walking festival, were staged at various prestigious venues, such as the impressive Lowther Castle, near Penrith, with its splendid gardens. At events such as the Kendal Mountain Film Festival, there would be sales of books, signed posters, ethnic Nepali crafts and cakes. After one such sale, Scott and his assistant had left when the assistant suddenly realised they had forgotten the cashbox. On mentioning this, Scott replied, 'Don't worry. Someone who needs it will get it.'

In Nepal, fundraising treks continued. A memorable trek in 2008 took a large party, requiring thirty porters, to the restored gompa at Walung on the route from Tumlingtar airstrip to Makalu. The CAN health post at Walung had been restored. At the opening ceremony, the exuberance of the dancing led to the collapse of the floor. Scott had brought his bike along on this trek, carried (on this and other treks) by the irrepressibly fit and charming Mangale Tamang. On another occasion, in 2007, Scott's old friends Barney (expedition doctor and occasional peacemaker on the Bonington Everest 1972 expedition) and Rachel Rosedale, participated in a trek organised by Ian Wall and were impressed by the quality of the equipment. Many of Trish's friends also enjoyed CAT treks, for example to the remote former kingdom of Mustang. Generally, CAT treks were led by guides from Kathmandu, although Scott, with his reputation for appearing suddenly out of nowhere – though not always by design – accompanied as many of the treks as his knees would allow him.

Treks were administered from the Kathmandu office. Despite Scott's and the Kathmandu staff's best efforts in the UK and Nepal, making a profit became increasingly problematic and, as we have seen CAT was wound up in 2011. Directorship of the new version of CAT, sustained by a loan from Scott, was handed in 2012 to the experienced Bhai B. Tamang, who had been running his own trekking company for eighteen years. Tamang's Army connections were found very useful when the British Army (including Prince Harry) made its preparations in Nepal for its engagement in Afghanistan. Fortunately, Tamang found it 'very easy' to work with Scott, who impressed him by giving his shoes away when he saw poor people.

To help develop CAT in particular, Ian Wall, an experienced Plas y Brenin instructor who had known Scott in Cumbria since 2000, became a CAN trustee in 2003. He was employed in Nepal from 2005 to oversee CAN and CAT operations in Nepal and some years later took up permanent residence there. CAT's financial problems, however, led to down-sizing, with half of Wall's salary being cut in 2010. (Such a drastic change led to Wall being invited to take part-time employment elsewhere; the manner of Wall's side-step became a major matter of contention when the final split occurred.) During the difficult post-insurgency period (2006–12), Wall became increasingly obliged to point out to Scott that Nepali laws and procedures governing employment, human rights and equal opportunities relating to trekking companies, thanks to a radical change of government, had changed. Policy could no longer be dictated by non-Nepalis, a situation Scott found hard to adjust to, sensing a fraying of his authority and frustration at not being able to manage CAN and CAT as he had done hitherto. Their relationship consequently deteriorated as the UK-Nepal misunderstandings grew.

Scott and Lorge therefore travelled to Nepal in February 2012, 'to sort this mess out'. After acrimonious discussion, Wall was summarily sacked on 26 February, with effect from the end of that month. The split was temporarily damaging to CAN and CAT's reputation.[12] Scott and Wall never spoke again. Wall recounts, 'I last saw Doug in 2018, in Kathmandu, while sitting in a hotel. Doug walked towards me but I had my back towards him. The person I was talking to told me of Doug's approach. At the last minute, Doug, I assume, recognised me and then took a circular route round the garden, although Trish did acknowledge my presence later with a small wave.'[13]

Failures of perception and communication bedevilled this relationship from the outset. Wall (as did others) found it difficult to accommodate Scott's driven, sometimes infuriating management methods: 'Doug Scott's way is the best way', especially where such an approach conflicted with the new anti-foreigner laws. Yet it was such a relentlessly focused approach by Scott which made CAN such an outstanding success, not just as one of the best-run charities in Nepal, but as an organisation of such sustained benefit to so many Nepali lives.

Resolving disputes was another preoccupation. A quarrel in 2011 at Melamchigaun between a CAN health co-ordinator, Rajani, and twenty nurses, and on the other side, a village leader and president of the CAN management committee, Purna Gautam, was resolved through Scott's understanding of Buddhism. Gautam had been attempting to sack Rajani by not renewing her contract, perhaps owing to professional jealousy. Scott reminded Gautam, a Buddhist, of the Buddhist precept of being kind to others in thought, action and speech, while admitting to his own failings in such matters! He reminded Gautam of the wheel of life, with the pig, cockerel and snake, the representation of ignorance, passion and malice, at every gompa's entrance, their effect being to destroy others' reputations. Scott went on to talk about the wheel's six segments representing the realms of the gods, the demi-gods, humanity, then the animals, the ghost realm and finally the fiery hell realm reserved for those consumed by a hatred for others. In the light of these comments, Scott asked Gautam to reconsider his attitude to Rajani and the nurses, as no one is without fault.

Scott went on to support Rajani, as loyal (always first on the Scott list), hard-working and effective. He praised the nurses for their hard work and their remarkable courage in not leaving their posts during the insurgency. Gautam, in turn, was praised for his astounding achievements in creating a flagship school which is admired by all in the locality and beyond. Finally, Scott told Gautam not to spoil this well-earned reputation through attaching himself to negative thoughts and emotions, or 'your ability to help others' will be diminished. He promised to return in October (the letter was written in April) with Trish and Dr Rob to see how matters have progressed.

This unusual version of dispute resolution draws attention to the conflict or paradox within Scott's psyche: the compulsion to behave with egotistical forcefulness in order to help others. Scott had to repress his ego because he was treated as royalty wherever he went.

After the earthquake

The earthquake of magnitude 7.8 on the Richter scale which struck north-west of Kathmandu on 25 April 2015 principally affected Gorkha,

Sindhupalchowk, Nuwakot, Solu Khumbu, the Langtang and Kathmandu. For Scott and everyone at CAN, the shock was correspondingly high: millions of pounds' worth of fundraising and twenty-five years of hard work were wiped out in twenty minutes. Scott, however, met this challenge, which would have broken others' spirits, with renewed vigour. He re-trebled his fundraising efforts, assessed the damage very briskly and produced an action plan which CAN could coalesce around and follow.

Within five months of the earthquake, £1 million had been raised; reconnaissance visits had taken place; meetings had decided on a plan of action: a newsletter (promoting single-mindedness of purpose) was sent to all interested parties to describe the damage and what it would cost to restore the projects affected. Because large sums of money were now involved, a longstanding CAN trustee in England, David Absalom, was appointed to oversee the quarterly funding requests in conjunction with Nepal operations director Murari Gautam. Phil Powell was appointed as a professional fundraiser. The highly knowledgeable Keshab Adhikari guided new engineering and construction overseers. Sanjeev Singh became programme officer. Glyn Utting, an exceptionally talented structural engineer on loan from WYG, an international engineering consulting group, added his considerable expertise, derived in part from MoD work in Afghanistan. (Glyn is now chair of the CAN trustees.) WYG's gift of personnel after the earthquake was a central reason for CAN's success in dealing with the crisis.

The 2015–19 period was occupied in approving projects and making field inspections, so it was a period of extensive, sometimes hazardous travel: in 2017, a helicopter containing Scott, Trish, Phil Powell, Rob Lorge and others, while heading back to Kathmandu, lost a door in mid-flight; two sets of luggage tumbled earthwards, one of which, Trish's, was lost forever. On another occasion, a local CAN nurse sat in the front of a helicopter in order to help navigate through the clouds to visit a CAN school project. Unfortunately, the helicopter got lost and was obliged to land on a mountainside. Scott disappeared for some bouldering, his characteristic excuse being, 'Maybe climbing will bring the answer to us.' Once the correct location had been established, upon re-entering the helicopter, Scott turned to the nurse and dryly suggested, 'Maybe you'd be better sitting in the back.'

Visits in July and November of 2015 to the Bahrabise School for Deaf Children by Scott and Trish, with headmistress Maina Karki, Bhoj Raj Shrestha (school chairman and founder), Murari Gautam and others, assessed specific damage. A rebuilding plan had to be submitted for government approval. The visitors noted that the fifty-one pupils had got over their trauma of being inexplicably suddenly flung around their classrooms and were again working purposefully, albeit in temporary accommodation. Artistic creativity was fostered by Scott's sometime climbing partner, Andy Parkin, who paid this school several extended visits as a kind of artist-in-residence. Children's paintings, inspired by Andy, could still be seen in the wreckage. Andy visited the school on several further occasions to encourage the children and, through sales of their paintings, earn themselves some pocket-money, an extension of CAN's sustainability policy. When first built, this school was termed 'a palace for the poor'; now, the wreckage would be removed and a better structure would replace it. This was not just idealism: new buildings, with anti-earthquake foundations and other features compliant with new government anti-earthquake legislation, would be constructed.

The successful Melamchigaun school's headmaster had his own tale to tell:

> On the fourth day after the earthquake, seven porters visited my tent, where my family and I were living . . . One of the porters, Pasang Tamang, told me that Mr Doug Scott wanted to talk to me. It was around 4 p.m. After a missed call, Scott was on the phone again in no time. I then told him about the situation and he said, 'Don't worry, we will rise again.' His words filled me with hope.
>
> After the earthquake, CAN was the first organization to distribute relief materials, within three days [from the phone call]. Within one month, my school was able to resume classes, building Temporary Learning Centres with support from CAN. Within three years, reconstruction of my schools and health posts was completed. Likewise, a Cash for Work programme was launched in Melamchi Ghyang to reconstruct an eighteen-room hostel, science lab and health post building which provided a huge relief and job opportunities for the disaster ravaged community.[14]

Health posts were appraised in similar fashion. At Kutumsang, in the Langtang, materials for a new post were quickly ordered; plans were drawn up by Keshab and the materials assembled where road access might make transport of the materials feasible. Such material included insulation foam to make the nurses' temporary accommodation more tolerable; they were also supplied with head-torches and down jackets. A plan was drawn up for the kitchen garden to become productive and to be protected from grazing buffalo. Finally, an improved access road was funded. The approximate cost was £37,000.

Several other kinds of building were being repaired, such as gompas, boarding hostels for schoolchildren and the elderly and even a Sherpa heritage house. Also needing reconstruction were the porter shelters, most of them situated on the high ground in the Everest area. At Machermo, for example, the shelter was redesigned to fit a change in demand. At least thirty-two other constructions across Nepal were affected and treated similarly in what was named the Build Back Better campaign. In spring 2017, Scott visited Langtang, to come across a harrowing sight: the village of Langtang had been obliterated. Temba Lama, CAN Nepal's management committee treasurer, lost twenty-two family members in the catastrophe, in which more than 400 lives were lost: the vast, fanning landslide which had engulfed the village recalled the Aberfan disaster. Many charities, several from the US, had stepped in to help. CAN joined in.

Naturally, matters did not always proceed smoothly. In Langtang, the wipe-out had divided the community, although Scott used the earthquake as a way of unifying the inhabitants. In Kutumsang, a conflict arose between the landgiver, Prem, and the contractor. Scott and the grants officer from CAFOD were present. 'Prem, sit down and shut up,' was Scott's contribution. The CAFOD officer was shocked. (On an earlier occasion in Langtang, Scott discovered that a village headman had been appropriating funds destined for the village. At an investigative meeting, Scott made his feelings very emphatically known to the malefactor.) Such disputes illustrate the kind of challenge to be overcome when reconstructing several dozen CAN projects across several Nepali provinces.

∽

As a result of the continuing work and negotiations with the Nepali government, a new policy was announced: to bring all building work up to a 'good' standard by 1 January 2020. Such an aim helped to focus fundraising. From 2015 to 2019, site visits continued, to encourage, to solve problems, to prevent delays, to cut through the red tape as tangled as the electric cables festooning the streets of Kathmandu.

Such a change of direction had been foreseen by Murari. In 2020, following the direction of the Nepali government's Social Welfare Council, which monitors domestic and international NGOs, CAN handed over all its projects to local government and decided to launch programmes and projects only in the Chum Nubri region of North Gorkha. Such a withdrawal was carried out 'with some reluctance'. The council had recommended that CAN launch its project only in certain local districts, for ease of monitoring as well as better conservation of resources. In the following years, CAN reconstructed eleven health posts in this region, provided free health services and health education and launched income-generating programmes and training in all seven wards of the Chum Nubri rural municipality. CAN continues to concentrate much of its resources in North Gorkha.

By Scott's own admission, the speedy, widespread reconstruction programme necessitated an ethical compromise: the principle of *shramadhan* was relaxed in view of the extreme hardship being suffered.[15] When CAN withdrew from effectively all areas except North Gorkha, it had succeeded, thanks to an astounding collective effort, in handing over by 2019 eleven schools and five health posts to the Nepali government.

One aspect of the CAN ethos which continued to thrive was sustainability. Income-generation and organic food production were priorities. Projects were supported until they became self-managed or handed over to the Nepali government. Health posts worked in partnership with local health committees, for example at Ghyamrang (near Pokhara) or Gola (near Walung).

Income-generating initiatives were designed to supplement CAN funding. Support for local tourism and homestays was encouraged. A hundred lemon, orange and apple plants were grown in health posts' organic kitchen gardens. Beehives, as well as cash crops of cardamom, ginger, potatoes and apples were introduced. Apple, walnut and apricot trees were distributed in North Gorkha. Mushroom cultivation at Bahrabise raised £600 in local markets. Campsites for tourists were planned. Other projects included fish farms, market gardens, reforestation and manufacture of craft goods. Expert agricultural and horticultural knowledge – some of it from the wonderful Chelsea Physic Garden – was brought in to help. A horticultural centre at Phaplu tried diversification of crops, to improve productivity. Joined-up thinking was applied: water supplies and composting methods were improved to encourage better crop yields.

Scott saw such cottage industries as an antidote to the threats to the mountain communities posed by the big agro-tech companies and the lack of income opportunities driving younger people into the cities. The consequent Build Back Better project following the 2015 earthquake based itself on the introduction of an organic Livelihood and Agriculture programme which has grown into one of CAN's most successful endeavours today.

Dr Claire Souch and her husband, Dr Till Pellny, first met Scott in 2016. She is now CAN secretary and oversees the Livelihood and Agriculture programme: it has helped over 2,000 villagers to grow their own vegetables in order to improve nutrition and food resilience, much needed during the COVID pandemic. Training and equipment have been provided and 237 poly-tunnels built. A network of over 200 organic kitchen gardens, which continues to expand into new villages, has been established. Specialist Junior Technical Assistants (JTAs) and agricultural helpers based at CAN's health posts run the programmes in the communities, working closely with the nurses on the health programmes.

Iron-deficiency anaemia is particularly prevalent in Nepal, affecting the health of women and children especially. Flour in Nepal is fortified with minerals such as iron during the milling process. However, in the mountains, the villagers mill the grain they harvest themselves, thus missing out on the fortification process. Through the professional connections of Dr Pellny with the Nepal Agricultural Research Council, CAN has introduced new varieties of bio-fortified wheat with enhanced zinc and iron levels to local farmers; these can be milled locally into flour to produce healthier bread.

CAN's Livelihood and Agriculture programme also creates sustainable income sources for communities through growing high-value crops, such as saffron, apples or walnuts, which can be sold to tourists or traded in markets. All the revenue is put into local community funds.

The programme continues, but not without its problems: landslides, heavy snowfall and wild animals (particularly monkeys and bears) combine to challenge CAN's work. Nonetheless, in 2021, 280,000 kilograms of vegetables were grown across CAN's sites, raising the Nepali equivalent of £27,000.

Sustainability stretched to traditional female skills, also: CAN provided income-generating training to mothers' groups in Ghyamrang and supported them in producing fibres from plants (hemp and nettles) to make clothes and sending them to market in the UK. Hundreds of women thus gained employment opportunities, earned a living and learned to be economically stable and independent. What is best about these projects, though, is their positivity in the face of terrible destruction: they offer hope, the kind of moral sustainability which so many villagers, with their properties in ruins, need.

A broader sustainability question involved the environment. Scott had been fascinated by trees from his earliest years. Many CAN projects began reforestation projects. Scott supported Nepali government successes in establishing national parks (to avoid deforestation) and saving the rare Nepalese rhino from poachers.

Unsurprisingly, Scott's other main environmental concern focused on high-altitude tourism. Many have mentioned Scott being vocal about the ruination of Everest, particularly in his 2018 speech advocating a change in government policy. This, he suggested, would require people who wanted to climb Everest to first climb a 7000m peak to spread the economic benefits of mountaineering across Nepal. The policy did change but the government went for a lower altitude threshold. He described people who went up fixed ropes as 'high altitude tourists', and mountaineers who kept doing the same thing as 'lacking imagination'.

As a result of these ideas and efforts, CAN in 2018 became the winner of the UIAA Mountain Protection Award. Nepali government practice scarcely reciprocated; money from international sources has disappeared. Victims are still sleeping under tents, tarpaulins and salvaged wreckage.

While this reconstruction process was developing, thanks to the tireless efforts of the CAN staff in Nepal, extraordinarily vigorous fundraising continued in the UK. CAN acquired 5,000 donors and 100 UK volunteers. It was a gigantic task: pre-2015, CAN operating costs amounted to about £215,000 each year. In 2016, £1.5 million was needed, dropping to £700,000 in 2017–18. The aim thereafter was to generate annual income of £500,000.

Fundraising methods were highly diverse. Obvious social media outlets were used. International organisations such as CAFOD and Switzerland's Caritas contributed substantially. Other activities included cake stalls, sponsored activities – such as one little boy giving up his chocolate allowance for the year – lunches, barbeques, art exhibitions (including Scott's own wildly successful High Exposure exhibition in Mayfair) and concerts. An annual film night was established at the RGS. A 'Mountain Film on Tour' was organised by Ben Ayers. Keith Partridge and Brian Hall made a film about Bonington, screened at the RGS in 2018. Some unusual lectures were set up; for example, the National Trust for Scotland's Scottish tour of lectures focused on Himalayan plants.

Some assistance was also provided through direct application of skills: British Expertise International, for example, helped with building projects. One of the most remarkable stories was that of the Oxford college porter, Peter Hack, who bought a Scott print every year for several years (by saving his £2 coins) then donated the money to CAN during COVID lockdown.

Meanwhile, Scott's relentless lecture tours, organised for ten years by the tireless Denise Prior, continued. In 2017, he gave twenty-three Ogre lectures in the sixty-four days between 3 October and 6 December. Scott's sale of his photographs in limited editions at the D-Contemporary gallery in Mayfair raised several thousand pounds.[16] Scott's exceptional auctioneering skills succeeded in charming even large groups of people into parting with more money than they had intended to. Another method was to appeal to a mass audience: Scott appeared on Border TV and ITV for interviews. In the last few exhausting months of his life, this indomitable humanitarian was still exerting himself with superhuman strength. As Victor Saunders states about the Everest Stair Challenge, 'Doug is raising funds for reconstruction, climbing indoors with Sir Chris Bonington. Over the weekend, they plan to raise thousands of pounds for the earthquake relief effort. They are at an indoor centre in Keswick, climbing the equivalent height of Everest, pitch by pitch. You have to raise your hat to this pair of wonderful old men revisiting their past.'

Funding and assistance grew through connections to schools and universities. A relationship with the London School of Medicine at Imperial College was established from 2016: second-year students visited CAN projects. They returned in 2019, headed by neuropathology specialist Professor Steve Gentleman, and helped to finance the Kutumsang health post using funds earned in rag week. Long-term contact has also been established with Egglescliffe School and Sixth Form college in Stockton-on-Tees, started by a Scott-Tut Braithwaite lecture, resulting in Ghunsa becoming a partnership school with Egglescliffe.

By 2018, Scott was able to report in CAN's *Three Years After* brochure that £3 million had been raised. And in the CAN newsletter of September 2018, it was reported that fourteen health posts, seven schools, three porter rescue shelters – one of them, at Gorak Shep, is the highest inhabited building in the world – one community centre, one home for the elderly and two memorial gompas had been rebuilt.

In the frantic rush to acquire donors, mistakes were occasionally made: in 2019, an energy company phoned to offer a substantial donation. A preoccupied, rather stressed and tetchy Scott grabbed the phone and told them to 'bugger off', only to find out that they were offering sponsorship of £12,500 annually! (The matter was later successfully resolved.)

CAT, during these post-earthquake years, was still functioning. Bespoke trips were still being arranged. Every kind of individual was catered for, from retirees to schoolchildren. COVID, however, then struck, and the world tourist market effectively collapsed. A recent visit to Kathmandu (September 2022) does show the market reviving, however.

CAN continues to function well, despite the inevitable vacuum being created following Scott's death in December 2020. (Scott was becoming co-ordinator rather than director; he had been working on his succession in the months leading up to his death, although without reaching any firm conclusion.) Concerns about supplies during the pandemic were met by Murari Gautam, who ensured staff were double vaccinated. The unusually bad monsoon floods of 2021 stretched resources, but a porter relief fund was established, and vaccines procured by the Nepali government were successfully delivered to remote areas with the help of other charities. Two new health clinics have been set up, while the problem of future food security has been met through developing the Livelihood and Agriculture programme. Restructuring intentions have focused on streamlining job descriptions and the creation of subgroups for health, education, construction and income generation.

Some problems have to be worked through, such as trustee consensus about future policy and the composition of the trustee body to ensure it has 'new blood' coming through. A stable number of trustees has continued, in the UK and Nepal, however. Scott generally chose trustees who shared his views. Thumping the table sometimes occurred when matters did not go Scott's way; he could be impatient with those not wholly committed. As Phil Powell says, 'With CAN, Doug held everything in his head.' And, as my fellow trustee Roy Welford put it, 'Doug operated a centralised system of control and had all his hands on all the levers. As Trustees we were there to support Doug and on occasions challenge the way things were done, but Doug drove CAN.'[17]

Thanks to an excellent team in Nepal and hard-working support in the UK, CAN continues to help Nepal's poorest.

16

Non-retirement

'The honoured are the ambassadors of an art, a passion.'
– Doug Scott, as chairman of the Piolet d'Or jury, 2009

Doug's final two decades pitched domestic happiness against fractious public crusades. Doug and Trish's life at Stewart Hill Cottage, with its sociability, the tending of the vegetable garden, making building improvements to a fine property, walking the fells and taking part in extensive voluntary work gave great satisfaction to both. Honours were awarded: national, academic, environmental and mountaineering. Doug's internationalist roles brought satisfaction as well as trials: while he undoubtedly enjoyed ethical crusades, perhaps rather too many surfaced. Some management problems associated with CAN, as well as the 2015 Nepal earthquake, made for a very testing public life. These years were also punctuated by health problems, mostly concerning the state of Doug's hips, knees and ankles. Mental stress exacted by the above led to Doug's final illness and his death at the age of seventy-nine. This illness in the middle of the COVID pandemic, moreover, prevented many friends from visiting him or attending his funeral and memorial services to honour him in the way they wished to. The obituaries, however, recognised his greatness.

Trish Lang and Doug Scott first met in 1999. Trish had been brought up in Greenock, attending prep school in the village of Kilmacolm, west of Glasgow, before going to boarding school in Wales. An ambition to be a wine-taster was disregarded by her father; the compromise was domestic science college in Glasgow. The effects of a youthful car accident required five years of plastic surgery. She had (and has) an adventurous spirit: a course at the Sorbonne was insufficient to curtail her interest in Africa, from which she returned to a mercifully short and unhappy first marriage. Her second marriage, to Peter Lang, lasted for thirty happy years. Peter was CEO of a family ship-owning and steel stock holding firm. Life was divided between the world of business and that of a Scottish country laird.

Trish in 2008, the year after marrying Doug.
(Scott family collection)

Trish, along with Peter and Sir David Carter, who at that time was Regius Professor of Clinical Surgery at the University of Edinburgh (later Chief Medical Officer for Scotland) had founded their own charity, Surgery in Nepal (SIN). It, however, was in danger of being wound up around 1999. Trish was advised to speak to Doug Scott, someone she had not previously heard of. Doug's advice by phone came across as a mono-syllabic mumble. Trish and Peter then organised a CAT trek, comprising mainly wealthy Scots, in 2000. Peter fell ill with pneumonia at the last minute; they were unable to go. The money raised from the trek, however, would go to funding the health post at Kutumsang; its costs were also underwritten by SIN. Peter and Trish were invited to the Kutumsang opening in 2001, but Peter was unable to attend. He died in 2004, a much respected, well-loved person with a wide circle of friends.

Doug invited Trish to Kathmandu in February 2005 to open the Milarepa health post. Against friendly advice, owing to the political turmoil in Nepal, Trish decided to go anyway: one of the remarkable features of their happy marriage was the way two sets of friends from entirely different worlds succeeded in accommodating each other. The trip provided the kind of interest which kept their marriage adventurous. On their way up country by jeep, they came across a mined Maoist roadblock. Doug's suggestion that they should detonate the mines was not welcomed. From the other side, a local truck proved too dangerous: they walked on to Thimbu. There, they were greeted by the local Maoist commander. A potentially dangerous situation was defused by Doug, who told him, 'I've never met a Maoist before.' At Thimbu, Ang Phurba, remarkably, produced a birthday cake for Trish. Looking back over the trip, Trish realised that Doug Scott was 'quite something'.

Back in Kathmandu, however, a saturnine Doug, evidently interested in Trish, faced up to a confessional. He named three women with whom he was currently involved. Trish realised that Doug would have to sort himself out! A closer relationship developed when Doug visited Kilmacolm in April 2005, to comfort Trish after the death of an old friend. Once Doug had returned from a trip to Australia and New Zealand in September 2005, he, Arran and Euan joined Trish at her then home, Ardrannoch, near Oban, on the beautiful Argyllshire coast. They then flew to Bulgaria, where Doug was giving a talk on the environment. The media recorded Doug's 'every move' while rock-climbing near Sofia; Trish felt she was with someone of notoriety.

As part of the 'getting to know you' process, Trish had to be introduced to Joyce. Trish recounts, 'We took Joyce out to a pub for lunch. Doug went to pay the bill. Joyce turned to me and said, "Dear, I hope you know what you are taking on." I replied that I felt I was old enough to cope. Her response was, "Well, I have to tell you that he has never had a proper job and never had a proper haircut!"'

Other travels soon followed: Nepal in October saw Doug working with a French film crew with Trish acting as interpreter: Doug remained entirely resistant to learning languages, even Nepali. Christmas 2005 was spent at Ardrannoch, followed by a travel show in London, then on to Chamonix for another lecture, with media attention from the French, who called him 'the living legend'. The couple proceeded to the Gers, in the south-west, to meet Trish's relations, the de Taillac family, the senior member of whom claims descent from Porthos, one of the Three Musketeers. Doug immediately took to the area – and the family – including an enthusiastic appreciation of one of the de Taillacs' friends, a descendant of the philosopher Montesquieu. Back in the UK, Ardrannoch was sold in May 2006, as was Craighaugh around the same time. Stewart Hill Cottage, in the quiet, scenic fells of the northern Lake District was bought, their home thereafter.

In July of 2006, thanks to Maggie and Patrick Burgess, whose Sherpa Heritage House charity helped to restore Pertemba's domicile in Khumbu as well as Kathmandu's Durbar Square, Trish and Doug were invited to Clarence House by Prince Charles to extend his longstanding interest in Nepali architecture.[1] The then Prince of Wales spoke without notes and with a love and respect for Nepali architecture which his guests enjoyed and appreciated.

Doug and Trish returned to Nepal in October 2006 for the opening of the Machermo porter rescue shelter, funded in part by pictures signed by Sir Edmund Hillary of Doug's photo of Dougal Haston on the Hillary Step. At a Buddhist ceremony, also attended by Dr Jim Duff, 300 locals and dignitaries treated Doug 'like a living god', although he remained 'sanguine, unfazed and modest' throughout.

Christmas 2006 brought visits to Leysin, to see Ariane Giobellina and to set about buying a property there, realised in 2009. A trip followed to Nepal in March 2007, to Helambu, to view CAN's projects, balanced by five weeks of diggers, cement and topsoils occupying their time and effort in the garden of Stewart Hill Cottage on their return. (Regrettably, Doug's peremptory treatment of a former climbing partner who was helping extensively with the building work, Colin Downer, led to a breach which, despite a late attempt by Doug to make peace, never healed.)

On the Helambu trek, Jamie Mellor, a farming friend from Argyll, recalls its physical and emotional ups and downs. Two cooks and more than forty porters helped. Butterflies, wildflowers and magnificent views were memorable. 'Sherpa stew' (curried leftovers) was preferred to porridge. The lama's speech at the Melamchigaun school inauguration was 'interminable'. Doug was feted in every village; requests for help were incessant. The switchback route, which reached a stupa at 3771m, was both trying and exhilarating. Like similar mountaineering ventures, this trek enjoyed a 'club outing' character.[2]

Before going to Zermatt in June 2007 for the 150th anniversary of the Alpine Club, the flying Scotts managed two visits to the Salzburg Film and Music Festivals, and to give lectures. At Salzburg, they met Franz Wintersteller, the hero of the early Alpine-style climbing era. The drive to Zermatt was frantic, in true Scott style: they arrived at 11 p.m. Doug was scheduled to appear at 5.30 a.m. for an interview at 4000m on the Breithorn. Thanks to oversleeping after their journey, Doug appeared in cords, brogues, a green jacket and broad-brimmed fishing hat; he was nicknamed the 'English eccentric' by Swiss TV. He was more smartly dressed – Trish's purposeful sartorial influence was beginning to exert itself – for the unveiling of Whymper's statue. The trip finished in the Maritime Alps and Aix-en-Provence.

No sooner had the garden work been concluded than Doug and Trish set out in September 2007 for a lecture to the RGS in Hong Kong. Here, in a romantic setting, Doug proposed and was accepted. The trip continued to Australia to see Trish's son Ken and daughter-in-law Moni, and renew acquaintance with Christine Gee. They flew home via South Africa, where Doug gave lectures in Johannesburg and Pretoria, then returned to Carlisle for their wedding on 8 December. On the big day, best man Bonington was stuck in Korea, but made it back in time for pudding. The 'honeymoon' was spent lecturing and climbing in the Adirondacks and Lake Placid, in New York state.

The couple's happiness had been compromised by a four-year legal exchange with Sharu concerning parenting arrangements for Arran and Euan, culminating in an injunction to prevent the boys being taken to India. The matter was resolved on the Friday before the wedding by Doug being awarded custody: 'a big wedding present', as he described it to Trish on their wedding day. Such a decision came as a shock for Trish, becoming part-responsible at the age of sixty-three for the boys' upbringing.

In 2008, they visited the new health post at Walung in eastern Nepal. An excursion was made to the holy caves at Kambalung, in the Yaphu area. The passages lie deep underground and require some scrambling. Claustrophobic progress was completed by a violent thunder and lightning storm reverberating through the caves. Also in 2008, Doug pulled off the remarkable negotiating feat of entering Iran, for a conference of the UIAA, of which he was the British representative, without a visa or money (credit card use having been stopped by sanctions). During the conference, he was observed wagging a finger at Iran's vice-premier. Perhaps Doug and Trish's most interesting excursion, however, occurred in 2009, when they flew to Chile (a UIAA venue) to travel through the Atacama Desert, on the edge of which they climbed, with some acclimatisation difficulty, a 5800m mountain. They then flew south to stay on an *estancia* in the Torres del Paine region. A hike to a glacier confirmed Trish's view that with Doug, 'every event seems an adventure'. Wine-tasting – organised for Doug despite Trish being the wine expert – followed near Santiago. They returned via Miami and Madrid, where Doug gave yet another lecture.

∽

International travels and domestic improvements, media attention and lectures set the tone for the Scotts' married life. In many countries, for example Bulgaria and Sri Lanka, media attention at the airport and at lectures was considerable. Doug conducted endless interviews for the press and TV, all with the same diffident courtesy despite the repetitiveness of the questions. Many of his interviews are on YouTube. In fact, he appeared on TV in at least fourteen countries, as far apart (in any sense) as the US, Slovakia, Greece, Nepal and Australia.

Film had also been part of Doug's life since he was in his early twenties, with the private silent film showing the Picos de Europa trip in 1963. In fact, his filmography shows him mentioned in at least twenty-five films. Leo Dickinson's *Rock Island Climb*, about *Sidewinder* on Strone Ulladale, was screened on BBC in 1971. (A subsequent invitation to join Dickinson's 1971 Cerro Torre expedition was turned down: Scott maintained that Dickinson's team was 'too good' for him because of its high-powered solo climbers. He might also have been concerned at being a 'bit too John Waynish', as he said to Dickinson in their post-Ogre interview.) Doug's association with the BBC extended to his *Blue Peter* appearance described in chapter thirteen. He also enjoyed a long association with broadcaster Clive Tully. Shortly after Strone Ulladale came Mick Burke's film of the 1971 expedition to Baffin, *A Dangerous Alternative*. Their connection developed in the ensuing four years until Mick's death on Everest in 1975. After The Ogre, in 1977, Leo Dickinson interviewed Scott separately and with the team on their return: he was struck by the differing tone and substance of Scott's contributions, a measure of his sensitivity.[3] Several later films were made for French and Swiss television, in Europe and Nepal, including an investigation of the UFO seen over Chamlang. As technology advanced,

Scott became the subject of numerous podcasts. And during the recent past, an Italian company has been working on a film version of *Up and About*.

Vegetarianism was left behind in 2005. His appearance altered: John Lennon no more but a new resemblance to a benign version of William Hartnell, the first Doctor Who. He also dressed differently, acquiring a country gentleman style in tweeds: one neighbour mistook him for the Duke of Norfolk! He also tried his hand at fishing.

Such positive changes were, however, compromised by Doug's increasing problems with his legs: he had on occasion been using crutches from the late 1990s. Doug had reached his lowest physical and mental point in the spring of 2004. Knee problems had begun earlier. In 2003, he made his first appointment at Basingstoke Hospital to replace his left knee, followed in 2004 by the operation. In 2006, his right knee was replaced. In 2007, he found himself in hospital with neck pain (possibly brought on by stress). Failing teeth also became a problem, as Jim Fotheringham remembers: the solution was implants from Trish's dentist in Glasgow. A two-year period of relatively good health followed until 2009, when hip problems resurfaced. The hip operation was carried out in 2012; it was complicated by a wound infection. Remarkably, however, such difficulties were not sufficient to stop him climbing when he was lecturing in the US in September of that year, as Tom Hornbein relates:

> Doug spoke at Neptune's in Boulder. The memorable moment came on our backyard critter, *The Platypus*, with Douglas Snively. Doug was on crutches after the hip replacement but wanted to climb. We took a slow hour to get to the base, another hour plus to get us all up and a third hour to get Doug back to level ground with the crutches, which Snively tucked in his pack for the climb. Doug was slow and at times immobile as he figured out the next moves on this slightly sandy, at times total friction sloping slabs. At one point, Snively called down to Doug, 'I can lower you down, if you'd like.' I, number three on the rope, called back, 'Douglas, Doug does not have a reverse gear in his transmission!' Talk about stubborn persistence! I suspect this was not his last climb.[4]

In 2013, a bone fusion operation on Doug's ankles was attempted, once more at Basingstoke. Sepsis developed, this time identified by the Scotts' GP, Dr Kate Keochane. Fortunately, Martha was at hand and prevented a fatality. The sepsis recurred in India in 2018 but was treated in time. In the spring of 2020, when reading Doug's typescript for *Kangchenjunga*, I noticed some technical slips which suggested that Doug's brain was not functioning consistently. The final illness had begun.

To balance these trials, however, Doug received a series of academic, civil and mountaineering honours. Hovering above these remains the question of a knighthood. Being the first Englishman to reach Everest's summit – and by a very difficult route – combined with thirty years' dedicated service to the people of Nepal made this honour richly deserved. A process was initiated by Chris Bonington but got 'lost in the system'. A friend of the Scotts comments, 'I did write to the Honours and Appointments Secretariat at the Cabinet Office a couple of years ago about this omission. I was told that my letter of support had been added to the record and "would be taken into consideration when the nomination is next considered". I enclosed letters of support from Angela Locke, David Huxley and a statement from Chris Bonington. Alas, events overtook us and it was not to be.'[5]

Knighthoods cannot be awarded posthumously. It is iniquitous that the Honours Office did not respond as it ought to have done. Doug's achievements had previously been recognised by his CBE in 1994. His view was that it was a useful device for promoting the ways available for helping others, particularly, of course, the Sherpas and other Nepalis.

Still, Doug's work received many awards and public recognition. In 1984, he and Alex MacIntyre (posthumously) jointly won one of the first Boardman-Tasker Awards for *Shishapangma*, a fascinating multiple-perspective expedition account. In 2015, *Up and About* won India's Kekoo Naoroji prize. Doug and Trish travelled to Mumbai in 2017 to receive it. Here, he took the opportunity to climb in the surrounding hills.

Academic honours came during this period, giving considerable satisfaction to the man who had struggled with English O-Level, yet who had produced six books, dozens of articles, lectures, forewords and blogs. Nottingham University awarded him his Master of Arts in 1991. A Master of Education degree was conferred by Nottingham Trent University in 1995. Derby University made him an Honorary Doctor in 2007, while the previous year Heriot-Watt University in Edinburgh made him an Honorary Blue for his mountaineering achievements. The award which Doug appreciated most of all, however, was the RGS's Patron's Medal, one of its two highest honours, in 1999, the citation reading: *Doug Scott, CBE, for contributions to mountaineering and the knowledge of mountain regions.* Most of these honours meant little to Scott: he remained ironically detached from them, with the exception of the RGS Gold Medal and the Piolet d'Or (see below). He saw them as a source of mild humour and as devices which might be used to promote his humanitarian work.

Environmental awards were conferred also. In 1996, Visa gave him their Tourism & Community Award. The Explorers Festival in Poland designated him Explorer of the Year in 2004. Perhaps most telling of all was the Golden Eagle, the John Muir Lifetime Achievement Award, in November 2005, a recognition for all Doug had done to promote respect for wilderness, mountain environments in general and the nature of national parks (in the UK, US, elsewhere on Continental Europe and in Nepal). Associated with these came awards for CAT and CAN, for example the Responsible Tourism Award in 2008. In 2017, WYG (now the Tetra Tech Group), the company which helped to supply CAN with personnel in the post-earthquake rebuilding period, was recognised by British Expertise International for its work. In 2018, the UIAA gave CAN its award for Mountain Protection and Humanitarian Work. With little sense of its belatedness, considering how Doug had cleansed the UIAA stables in 2012, the UIAA awarded Doug honorary membership in 2020.

Doug became involved in three ways in the Piolet d'Or (Golden Ice-Axe), the annual climbing award given by the Groupe de Haute Montagne (GHM). After Walter Bonatti in 2009 and Reinhold Messner in 2010, Doug justly received the lifetime achievement award in 2011, presented by Bonatti, with whom a like-minded friendship developed. In 2009, as chairman of the jury, he oversaw the first (climbing) award to a female climber. At the award ceremony, the intention had been for Doug, then his co-jurors Jim Donini and Peter Habeler, to speak in turn. Doug, selfishly, yet with passion, spoke at such length that the other two were unable to say what they wanted.[6] His expansive energy combating such narrowness of focus constituted one of the many oppositions which coursed through Doug's life; they were the principal source of his mental energy, other than the effects of his Freudian relationship with his parents.

The third involvement with the Piolet d'Or occurred when Voytek Kurtyka, in 2010, turned down his lifetime achievement award, having already declined to be a juror: 'This is a devilish offer,' he said. 'I always had a sense of escaping to the mountains from everyday social bullshit, and now you propose to me to take part in it. I was always escaping to the mountains to find encouraging proof that I'm free from the social bonds of award and distinction and now you offer it to me . . . Don't even try to honour me.'

Doug had at that time been moved to write a substantial, pertinent piece on the matter of awards in mountaineering: London was holding the 2012 Olympic Games. He wrote about competitiveness in the BMC magazine in 2011. It is worth quoting at some length, as it represents Doug's final position on the matter of competitions and awards:

What the mountaineering fraternity do question is that there should be competition in the high mountains . . . The idea of competitive mountaineering is still far from alien in the former Soviet bloc, where mountaineering competitions were first promoted in 1948. The tragedy of the death of eight Russian women mountaineers making the first all-women traverse of Peak Lenin in 1974 brought home to many the folly of promoting high-altitude mountaineering as another Olympic event.

I heard no grumbling when eventually Chris was made a CBE – after all, he was the main spokesman for British climbing. Rumour even has it that Dougal Haston and I, as summiteers of Everest, might have expected some recognition from Her Majesty if Dougal hadn't served three months in one of HM's prisons during his misspent youth.

In 1994 I received a letter from the Ceremonial Branch of the Cabinet Office, Westminster, asking if I would accept becoming a Commander of the British Empire. I have to say I accepted without a second thought and have never regretted doing so. My parents were overjoyed.

None of us seem to have attracted any criticism for accepting such awards . . .

For myself, I've always been ambitious: to be appreciated for what I've done . . . We all like to be liked and I am no exception. At the Piolets, I was given the chance to extol the virtues of the freedom of access that we have in the Alps – by keeping out politicians, bureaucrats, insurance companies and other commercial interests. But the most important message is that the only climbing that is going to get this kind of acclaim has to be done in an original and committing style – without compromise.

In 2011, Doug and Chris Bonington were awarded honorary membership of the Alpine Club, a fitting occasion to mark fifty years of friendship. The relationship between the two was complex.

It would be unfair to both to describe the Bonington-Scott relationship as an opposition between, on the one hand, an autocratic 'top down' leader creatively acquiring funds for publicly high-profile siege expeditions, and on the other hand, a 'democratic', egalitarian proponent of unobtrusive financial and climbing-style self-sufficiency. As their climbing together shows, as well as their joining together on any number of causes, their differing personalities – Bonington as the diplomat, Scott as the 'man of the people' – were subsumed into a genuine liking for each other.

They had first met in 1961 on the summit of Mont Blanc, when Bonington and Whillans with Clough and Długosz surfaced from their groundbreaking climb on the Central Pillar of Frêney. Scott, something in awe of this sudden encounter with greatness, prepared a meal, the generosity and practicality of which Bonington never forgot. Bonington often called into the Scott home in Nottingham if he was in the neighbourhood for a lecture; they climbed together in Derbyshire.

As far back as the K2 expedition in 1978, Bonington – despite the flare-ups on Everest in 1972 and 1975 – could happily declare, 'I feel a real affection for Doug. He has a good sized ego which he doesn't really acknowledge, but he has a tremendous warmth of heart and a great climbing drive which will stand us all in good stead.'[7]

Differences on that expedition between Bonington's more studied strategic style and Scott's drive became apparent. The force of Scott's personality could not be trifled with: his 'democratic' decisions usually ended up being what he himself forced through. Bonington was a superb fundraiser and planner; Scott was brilliant at the kind of organisation which keeps red tape to a minimum. They accepted such differences in each other. On a filing card from January 1977 (thus predating The Ogre), Scott drafted comments about his relationship with Bonington, almost certainly a basis for writing his autobiography. He said, 'The one thing that keeps us together is our urge to be in and climb the mountains, despite my open criticism of him assuming strong leader roles and being commercially greedy.'[8]

Scott talked to himself about Bonington's commercial shadow: 'Am I envious of him? We are kept together as the child keeps the man and woman together through bad times and good until out of rebellion, then confusion, into a period of mutual acceptance, and see we both have our special gifts and at one level he's right, right for him, and at another my beliefs are right for me. It's just a question of him asking, "What's my problem?" but he probably doesn't see it as a problem because it's everyone he mixes withs [sic] problem, so he's no other term of reference, except at home, and that is what he knows can save him.'

Despite Doug's idiosyncratic grammar, he makes an acute point. Bonington's two marriages, to Wendy, then to Loreto, have been satisfying and secure. Doug's first two marriages flew through almost constant turbulence. Bonington always had a stable home life to fall back on, whereas Doug sought satisfaction (in climbing, companionship and sexual relations) where he could find it. Of course, things changed with Trish: her ability to provide a happy, elegant yet homely home, to maintain consistent standards of behaviour, along with her mastery of social know-how, gave Doug, for his final fifteen years, the fulfilment of a collaborative, symbiotic home life which he had never hitherto properly enjoyed.

Chris and Doug did not go on any major expeditions after K2 in 1978 (which had involved a dispute after Nick Estcourt's death). They did, however, work well together on many committees in the UK and they gave many joint lectures, as well as attend fundraising events. Bonington became patron of CAN. They lived only fifteen minutes from each other in the Northern Lakes; their friendship rightly developed in this private situation, to the extent of Chris being Scott's best man on his marriage to Trish in 2007.

Regrettably but perhaps fortunately, no other document exists to define what they thought of each other. However, the BMC rebranding crisis in 2016 (see the next chapter) put a strain on their friendship at a time, during the post-2015 earthquake period, when Doug and Trish were faced with exceptionally strong demands on their mental and physical resources.

During the dispute with the BMC, Doug sided with Bob Pettigrew and Dennis Gray, and a group of about thirty like-minded senior mountaineers. Chris and Doug were both patrons of the BMC. Doug, with his crusader's passion, continually lobbied Chris to join the 'BMC 30'; he, the diplomat, refused. Chris supported the 'work for change from within approach'; Doug preferred direct confrontation. The whole dispute between Doug and some individuals in the BMC became very personal. Because the BMC had trolls, Doug came out worse. He was accused publicly of being a racist and a colonialist which, absurd as it was, hurt him a lot. Worried for his health, Trish encouraged Doug to step back from further confrontation. Doug had expected Chris to come to his defence, but Chris, along with the other patrons, favoured the diplomatic approach. This division came as no surprise to those such as John Porter and Tut Braithwaite who could see their respective characters at a distance, although those more directly caught in the Scott whirlwind were less pleased.

Chris's extensive obituary piece for Doug in the 2021 edition of the *Alpine Journal* retold their story and concluded with praise for his happy home life.

∽

The period around 2010–12 required broad shoulders from Doug. In 2008, as vice-president of the BMC, he became the UK's representative on the UIAA. In 2010, the organisation was rocked by a crisis around the issue of potential financial irregularities. Doug became involved in much internal wrangling, and matters came to a head at a showdown at the UIAA General Assembly, which took place in Kathmandu in late September and early October of 2011.

When the Scotts arrived in Kathmandu on 23 September, an earthquake measuring 6.8 occurred, a sign of things to come. On 4 October, the meeting was 'raw'. Doug got on to the agenda a motion of reforms which clearly implied that the UIAA president Mike Mortimer and certain members of the board had failed the organisation. Doug lost his temper, but Mortimer, among others, was voted out: Doug, with backing, had won the day. Gloom and tension followed on 5 October. The Scotts ended up in the same restaurant as Mortimer and his associates, with the opposing parties sitting at opposite ends of the room.

More than a year of tension and anxiety, plus hundreds of emails, meant a wearisome, edgy time for Trish and Doug. Fortunately, they were distracted to a degree by their work on CAN, although in 2012 managerial complications involving Ian Wall also led to high emotions. If Doug and Trish then thought that a quieter life lay ahead, they were wrong: not only was the devastating 2015 Nepal earthquake about to change their lives, but a bitter, convulsive row between Doug, with his friends and associates, and the BMC was about to engulf British mountaineering in an unprecedented manner.

Another ethical challenge erupted just after the evening with the Prince of Wales. Doug and Trish were called to the BBC so that Doug could comment on the case of David Sharp, left to die on Everest only 300m below the summit while up to forty other climbers, gripped by 'summit fever' and a reluctance to have their fees wasted, walked past him. Doug wrote the paper 'No Morality-free Zone in Climbing' as a result. As Doug pungently expressed it, the problem was that clients of commercial climbing organisations absolved themselves of conventional moral responsibilities at high altitude, 'as dogs on a lead'. He advocated much more careful commercial guidelines about emergency procedures. He commended the selflessness of the Sherpas, citing Ang Phurba, who give up the summit prize to save those in desperate need. He maintained that reaching a summit was a hollow victory if climbers did not fulfil their moral obligations en route. He reminds us that those indigenously connected with the land show generosity, kindness and help to others. Our sophistication, he suggests, has distanced us from these essential qualities.

In a regrettably undated and unpublished paper (which evidence suggests might have been written in the 1990s), on a similar humanitarian theme, titled 'Expedition Medicine: an old-fashioned view', Doug began by citing Ch'i-Po (Qibo), the mythical doctor to the Chinese Yellow Emperor. Doug drew on his experience to advocate nurturing the 'life force' for sudden bursts of strong energy; he advocated conservation of energy and planning an expedition on the basis of harmonising spirit and energy, to reconcile 'inner and outer freedoms'. He rejected the importance of 'success', the wish to impress the rest of the world.

He expressed concern about the effects of the 'commercial side of expeditions'. Mountaineering should be a 'personal pilgrimage' on a path like any other. He advocated recalling our youthful spirit of curiosity as a healthy emotion. Also constructive, he argued, is to recognise a woman's spiritual qualities because that will lead to help in developing (as a man) your own. (Some comments concerning women's relative lack of ambition and greater emotional intelligence seem somewhat uncomfortably dated now.) Homesickness is designated an illness, cured only by leaving home without too many problems remaining in it. It can be escaped from through ambition, books and alcohol, but the pangs of homesickness may take up to five weeks to subside. He consoles himself with a quote from Ralph Waldo Emerson's poem 'Goodbye': 'We are but river-arks on the ocean brine.'

Doug went on to recommend a vegetarian diet as the best way of avoiding the 'terrors' of insufficient food, although he conceded that the Eskimo on Baffin and the Masai in Kenya exist on an almost entirely meat-based diet. He claimed that since adopting a vegetarian diet free from additives his pains brought about by mountaineering and rugby had lessened or disappeared. He further claimed such a diet had helped with acclimatisation. He reminded us that chewing garlic and smoking are both aids to acclimatisation. Doug considered that homeopathic remedies may work but admits to not knowing much about the subject. If all else fails regarding a climber's health, Doug suggested consulting Dr Peter Steele's

Jan with Michael, c. early 1970s, place unknown.
(Scott family collection)

handbook on expedition medicine. An Alpine-style ascent should only be done when there is unity about the route, the weather and the state of acclimatisation.

The paper's bibliography is short and contains references to the Tao and Buddhism, as well as to Castaneda, Gurdjieff and Rudolf Steiner. While the essay is fascinating in what it reveals about Doug's concerns, its conclusions do not consistently reflect Doug's own mountaineering experience.

A test closer to home occurred as Doug became estranged from his eldest son, Michael. They had climbed together on several occasions. In 2006, Doug and Trish visited Michael, his then wife Eva and their two children in New Zealand, to where Michael had emigrated. Not long after, Michael and Eva separated, and Michael's business ran into financial trouble. He was bailed out by Doug, to a limited extent. However, a difficult letter to Doug followed. While Doug wrote a diplomatic reply, communication between the two collapsed and continued, to Doug's infinite regret, until Doug's death in 2020.

17

'A Very Different Man'

> 'When I first met him, I thought he was a mixture of Albert
> Schweitzer, Crocodile Dundee and one of the Goons.'
>
> – Trish Scott

Doug had been aware of the controlling power of money, through private
sponsorship or government funding, since the Herrligkoffer expedition
in 1972. With his friends, he had witnessed the increased intervention
of money in his sport over the following forty years. With money came
competition on climbing walls or at international gatherings such as the
Olympics. While conceding that climbing wall competitiveness was una-
voidable, he always resisted any kind of commercial open-air climbing.
Not just competition, either: climbing tourism revenue could be increased
by reducing risk, through bolting: this horrified him. As the UK's representative at the UIAA, Doug led the Traditional Values Working Group
from 2011 onwards. Tradition, however, was anathema to many younger
climbers and to moneymaking bodies: Doug was in danger of becoming
an old fogey.

Indeed, Doug's conservatism in ethical matters may have led to his
defeat for the BMC presidency in 2009 (although he did become a patron
in 2016). This claim extends to Doug's attack on the BMC management
in 2015–17 being a 'sour grapes' consequence of that rejection. Doug was
not a vindictive person, however: with few exceptions, generosity of spirit
held sway throughout his life. He was, moreover, demonstrably concerned
with mountaineering ethics from an early age; he saw BMC rebranding
as an ethical and managerial problem, as his speeches and writing make
clear. He regarded the rebranding as undemocratic (a significant word in
the Scott vocabulary), motivated primarily by commercialism (the search
for funding from Sport England through increased membership and the
promotion of commercial services and activities), an ethical offence. He
regarded the BMC as departing from those traditional values which he

espoused. A particular focus for Doug, Bob Pettigrew and others was the energy and resources which the BMC were putting into competition climbing, thus diverting such resources from the mass membership.

For Doug and others, the rot in the BMC had set in during the run-up to the 2012 London Olympics. Government money went to any organisation which would represent the ideals the government wished to promote. Once money had changed hands, however, government could exert some control over any organisation it was even part-funding. The complacency of assured funding set in; jobs were allocated without proper competition; like-minded views held sway. As one BMC critic satirically put it, 'The BMC have to invent new policies to attract more government money, so that they can employ more officers, who can then generate more imaginary "issues" to attract more government money.' The membership was being distanced and denied.

Beyond such criticisms, Doug had a more personal motivation for the coming attack: he would invoke Shipton and Smythe. In his mind, he was climbing shoulder to shoulder with the ghosts of these noble mountaineers, to further their adventure ethic.

His goal was never to promote himself, or to make money from what he saw as the achievements of others, but to focus on the serious endeavour of finishing that which others had started.[1]

The other part of the historical context ran as follows: 'I think it upset Martin [Wragg], Stephen [Venables], Martin Scott and Doug that their turn on the main committee of the Alpine Club, which saw a golden period of Alpinism towards the dawn of the Club's 150th anniversary was being overshadowed by a movement which ran counter to those achievements, and which in time could undermine the Club's remit.'[2]

Doug's personal position regarding money was clear: Doug did accept fees for speaking and media interviews, but he always did so in conjunction with charitable causes, while keeping a deep sense of legacy and obligation.

In 2015, chief executive Dave Turnbull and the executive committee began a rebranding of the BMC, with the intention of renaming it Climb Britain. As John Roberts tells us, 'In general the rebrand became the lightning rod for grievances and an opportunity to air various issues from insurance to staff salaries. Many grievances were conflated; it was also seen as an opportunity to attack certain senior staff figures. Those attacking did not seem to be wholly aligned. There was probably an element of truth in some of their grievances. I think essentially they wanted some senior staff change, but they were unable to effect anything with such confused messaging and a broad brush Motion of No Confidence.'

Thirty members collaborated on the process leading up to the motion of no confidence. (Known as the 'BMC30', they comprised influential climbers who had mostly occupied senior positions in UK mountaineering.) 'Heated exchanges' occurred between this group and their opponents, who supported the necessity for continued funding and believed themselves to represent a progressive faction. One pernicious exchange involved gin and tonic being poured over Bob Pettigrew at the Plas-y-Brenin AGM; the police subsequently cautioned the offender, made her apologise and provide restitution.

At the crucial AGM in 2017 a motion of no confidence (originating from Bob Pettigrew, Doug Scott, Dennis Gray and other senior signatories, although Scott and Gray were both absent on the day) was raised, with the principal aim of restoring 'the democratic process of accountability to the grass-roots membership'. Although the Climb Britain rebranding had been dropped by September 2016, in the proposers' view this initiative should have been subject to a membership vote. (A disapproval rating of 93 per cent, divided between the 'naffness' of the rebranding term and the undemocratic manner of the change, was recorded in a consultative vote, reflected in countless pages of members' online comments.) The motion, however, was defeated – for: 359; against: 2,100; abstentions: 62 – as recorded in the AGM Minutes.[3] Doug considered removing his name from the twenty-six signatories before the final motion, a mark of the proposers' lack of cohesion.[4] In the event, he did not, as such a removal would have invalidated the motion. Doug's preparatory paper in fact concentrated on a wide range of problems which the BMC needed to deal with, such as access, climbing walls, government money and so on.

The consensus, now, appears to be that Doug, Bob Pettigrew and others had some longstanding grievances (for example, concerning insurance, *Summit* magazine, the role of competitions) which a complacent management had failed to address: their criticisms were in several respects justified (although by no means everyone in the group agreed with all of the criticisms: Doug called it a 'scattergun approach'). Opinion is divided as to how well Doug presented his case. I recall reading his Alpine Club missives with a groan, believing that with more crafting of expression and by cutting his messages' length by about two-thirds, he could have been much more persuasive. Nor did his abrasive manner win him friends or persuade his opponents: he spoke and wrote, as usual, with passion and complete conviction – including some unjustifiable *ad hominem* attacks which, however, were objectionably launched by both sides: more alienation than persuasion was achieved. Others, however, including a prominent member of the Scottish Mountaineering Club (SMC), praised (in private correspondence) the cogency of Doug's and Bob's case. Sustained, hurtful, personal attacks on climbing forums, not least the BMC's, sharpened the bitterness of the conflict. Nor could the diplomat Bonington back Doug the crusader, thus putting a strain on their relationship.

As a result of the motion of no confidence, Siddiqui resigned his presidency on 3 May 2017, citing vituperative personal attacks on him. A difficult period followed for the BMC, as Doug had foreseen. A new CEO was appointed in November 2020, and relations between Turnbull and Doug never recovered.

In 2017, Doug received a personal letter from a senior officer in the BMC suggesting he was now *persona non grata* as a BMC patron; he interpreted this as an effective sacking. For him, other than the emotional and personal detritus left by this event, that concluded his part in this matter, although he maintained a 'behind the scenes' interest in the BMC thereafter.

∽

Set against such public trials, Doug and Trish, who had evidently met at just the right time in each other's lives, continued their frenetic international travels. One place offered sanctuary. In 2006, they acquired a new house in Leysin, Switzerland. and moved in during 2009. Every year, the Scotts would enjoy three months of relative tranquillity during the winter, for ski-ing or snowshoeing. Usually, they drove over, although Doug's excitable attempts at passenger-seat driving instructions to Trish led to some of the marriage's frostier moments. Brexit and a Swiss wealth tax made the house more difficult to enjoy; it was sold in 2019.

Brexit, of course, raises the question of Doug's politics. He could not be pigeon-holed into consistent support for any one party. Doug had been brought up in an Empire-Conservative voting household in a Labour city: tensions of ideological allegiance existed from the outset. He unquestionably went through an egalitarian phase, tending towards Labour support, during the main part of his climbing career, a belief consistent with his views on democracy. Later in life, he made it explicitly clear that he opposed Brexit as well as the Hydra of Scottish Nationalism. He got on well, unsurprisingly, given their adventurous backgrounds, with Rory

Stewart, who served as MP for Penrith and The Border from 2010 to 2019. It would be tempting to conclude, in a Gilbertian fashion, that Doug's political views were those of an extremely moderate, socially democratic conservative.

Despite his injuries, operations, travel and demands of local life, Doug continued to climb. In 2002, Jim Fotheringham's son, Joseph, went missing in the Russian Pamirs. Doug immediately volunteered to accompany Jim to Russia for the search, with its unhappy outcome, a selfless act never to be forgotten.

Climbs occurred in almost every place where Doug gave a lecture or attended a conference, for example in the Algarve, or on the island of Telendos, next to Kalymnos, where a 2010 UIAA meeting was taking place. The Scotts averaged two trekking trips a year to Nepal, sometimes with the help of Doug's personal bike Sherpa, Mangale. In 2017, Doug and Trish collected the Kekoo Naoroji Prize for *Up and About* in Mumbai. A blogger connected with Harish Kapadia, known only as 'Outrigger' tells us, 'Scott visited the hills of Ratangad and Katrabai near Bhandardara. His family joined him on the outing and the idea was for his wife and children to trek to Ratangad while Scott tried some rock climbing on Katrabai. Senior Himalayan Club member, Rajesh Gadgil, recalled that Scott had no hesitation in backing off once he concluded that the proposed route was not in the best state to be climbed. Although among the greats of mountaineering, Scott had no bothersome ego or attitude about him. "He was a strong person and believed strongly in the values that mattered to him," Rajesh said. He remembered Scott telling local climbers not to bolt rock indiscriminately.'

Travel continued: a US tour in 2012 extended to Salt Lake City, followed by a visit to Tom Hornbein at Estes Park, where Doug signed 300 books. Social events among Boston's high society broke the journey home. Lectures followed in Norway and on Harris. In October, Doug and Trish were in Amsterdam on UIAA business. In April 2013, they travelled through Sri Lanka in Doug's capacity as patron of a Sri Lankan charity. Trips three or four times a year continued. After the 2015 earthquake of course, travel was focused much more on Nepal, although because Doug was on a lecture fundraising tour in Scotland in 2018, Trish had to travel with Murari Gautam to Mongolia to receive the UIAA Mountain Protection Award for CAN, a trip which included a frightening unscheduled detainment in Kyrgyzstan. Doug and Trish's last foreign trip took place in March 2020, to Jordan, to Amman, the Dead Sea and Petra, which they reached by mule (Trish also being a confident horsewoman). They arrived at a Bedouin village, an echo of Doug's expedition to the Atlas in 1962. The trip finished with a return to Wadi Rum, where Doug had climbed in 1987.

In the UK, several friends recall Doug's propensity for climbing anything, such as a rafter or beam, even in their own homes. Regular cragging featured. A fine 2001 Berghaus photo shows Bonington and Scott on top of Shepherd's Crag in Borrowdale, having thoroughly enjoyed their climb together. After they married, Trish and Doug enjoyed many walks, often with visitors, on nearby High Pike (658m) and Carrock Fell (661m). Trish was even persuaded to climb the awkward sandstone ridge of Stac Polly in the north-west Highlands in 2011.

In 2016, Tony Greenbank visited the seventy-four-year-old Scott, for a climb, and wrote in *The Guardian*, 'He points above his garden to Carrock's crags. "Up there, youth," he says, his Nottingham accent discernible. "Trough Gully! It's as good as a Scottish ice climb. I've climbed the Trough a dozen times when it's choked with ice."'

Other favourite venues lay nearby: in the Eden Valley, a place almost as idyllic as it sounds, Doug climbed near Armathwaite with Simon Yates, or in Borrowdale with Steve Goodwin. Simon's wife Jane, a teacher, readily empathised with Doug; both had a special fondness for the Eden Valley and its views. They had known each other since 1993, when she and Simon had moved to Cumbria together.[5]

Even cragging produced its controversy, however, as the problem of bolting appeared. Doug's Traditional Values Working Group produced a summarising paper, *The Preservation of Natural Rock for Climbing*, in August 2012; it was endorsed by Bonington, Kurtyka and Messner and became BMC policy. It did not, however, prevent bolting occurring on the top of a crag in Borrowdale in February 2016. Responses on the UKClimbing website were overwhelmingly in favour of the bolts being removed, an action strongly encouraged by Doug.

The environment of the Northern Fells, quite different from the Southern Fells, lying south of the Penrith–Keswick line, also occupied Doug's time. Not long after moving to Stewart Hill, Doug joined forces with Bonington in 2007 to protest about new wind farms to be sited near Blencathra. National Wind Watch stated, 'Bonington and Scott say they want to "highlight the fragility and sensitivity of the area and preserve its unique vista for future generations, and in the process keep the Northern Fells a breathing space for the nation."'

In a much more amusing way, Joe Brown's shop's fiftieth anniversary was in part celebrated by a treasure hunt called, unsurprisingly, 'Joe's

Golden Nuts'. Clues were to be found on climbs which Brown had made in earlier days. Doug, with Angela Soper and James McHaffie, chose the routes. *Eliminate 'A'* (VS 4c) on Dow Crag was the most popular climb chosen by the three.

When not climbing or travelling, the Scotts' Cumbrian surroundings offered an enjoyable local life. The Rheged Centre was the place for lectures, a gallery, a cinema, shops, workplace and a creative space for exhibitions. Sally Bohling, with her husband Michael, comments that Doug, socially, was 'self-effacing, modest, humble, totally without ego . . . a very spiritual man, with a wonderful "on the button" sense of humour.'[6]

In winter, regular Scottish reeling (country dancing) sessions, run by Robin and Melanie Davies, took place in Mungrisdale village hall. Doug was not light on his feet; he was over-enthusiastic; his partners felt his iron grip; he scratched the arm of author Angela Locke. Nonetheless, Locke admired Doug and asked him to give talks on spiritual matters locally. He was, she adds, 'huge' at dinner parties. His wildness was tempered by discipline and a degree of self-irony.[7]

Perhaps one of the most surprising developments in Doug's cultural life was his new passion for opera and ballet. Going to the opera began with *Boris Godunov* in Bratislava in 2008. He was 'enthralled' by it. A notable *Carmen* in Budapest, in May 2012, had been part of the UIAA conference trappings. Doug began to accompany Trish in the UK and soon found that he himself enjoyed it. From there, ballet took on a sustained fascination, largely because of Doug's interest in how the body worked, balletic movement in some respects, such as balance, muscular strength and stamina, being not dissimilar to rock-climbing.

More time for reading and writing came about in the writing-room chalet which Doug had built in the garden, near the Nepali flag. This room housed the books and journals he needed for writing, as well as his private papers. Here, writing continued, often through the small hours.

As many as forty lectures in a year took place when well into Doug's seventies. A 'big' lecture could bring in £20,000, a significant sum for CAN. Many lectures, however, were motivated by fundraising for local projects, for example, at the Borders Writing Festival in Peebles in 2006 on 'Moments of Being', a reference to a Virginia Woolf short story with perhaps Wordsworthian and Buddhistic echoes. He and Trish returned several times to the Arran Mountain Festival. He would sometimes begin with a favourite lecture quip, on seeing a large audience: 'Well, there can't be much on telly tonight.'[8] In December 2012, he launched the first Otley

Mini Mountain Fest with a lecture on Everest. Tied to such voluntary lectures, sponsored events took place, such as abseiling off the clock tower in Brampton.

Lectures for income and for CAN continued. They increased after the 2015 earthquake. David Nightingale, who first met Doug through a CAT trek in 2004, became a paid road manager in 2010 because 'Doug wouldn't take "no" for an answer' to suggestions that a trekker might like to support CAN. David describes a typical (insofar as there was one) Scott day:

> Doug would get up at 4 a.m., for a few hours in the writing-room. He would phone me about 7.45 a.m. to ask if I was free. Breakfast about 9 a.m., followed by CAN work in the office. For an evening lecture, we'd jump in the car about midday for a mad dash ('Drive faster!') to the lecture hall. The lecture would finish at about 10 p.m. after which we'd dash back to Cumbria, and so I'd get to bed, exhausted, around 2 a.m. Doug could keep this schedule up without seemingly needing to eat properly. He would promise that we'd stop for fish and chips, but it didn't often happen; I learnt to bring a bag of butties and bottles of water to survive these journeys.
>
> On one occasion, when Doug, Peter Habeler and Tut were driving to a lecture, Peter said he was looking forward to stopping somewhere nice, like a country pub, for lunch. Doug agreed with a blithe 'no problem', then drove to a filling-station shop where pre-packed sandwiches and crisps were thrown in Peter's direction before the full-pelt drive continued!
>
> Nor were lectures just about driving. Accommodation was makeshift: It was often about blagging a night with one of Doug's many friends across the UK. On the Edinburgh trip mentioned above, Habeler got a bed, while Doug and Tut used their sleeping bags on the floor. In the morning, my wife Lynne cooked a breakfast of porridge, eggs and bacon, while Doug did a spot of bouldering on the house's outside wall.[9]

At lectures, Doug was a very effective salesman. Several people have testified to his extraordinary persuasiveness as an auctioneer. In his obituary in the *Nepali Times*, it reported that 'Doug Scott was "the world's most enthusiastic fund raiser".'

As Robin Ashcroft relates, after some lectures, including even at the august RGS, he would organise 'Doug's Glamorous Assistants', several attractive young ladies who would present themselves, as if in a bygone television game show, to hold up items for auction, the whole executed with such irony as to refute charges of sexism. Lectures continued abroad, also, particularly in Europe and in the US, for example at the Banff Mountain Festival in 2018.

∽

When at home, two aspects of life made Doug happy. He enjoyed the company of his family. After a serious riding accident, for example, Doug helped Rosie to rebuild her life. Those of the extended family, such as Garry's son Richard and his family, also enjoyed their time with him. Richard recalls that as a small child, Uncle Douglas often used to bring gifts from Nepal for him and his older sister. He would also call in frequently during lecture tours.

Naturally, Doug's mountaineering interests rubbed off on some of the family. He taught Richard how to climb at the Black Rocks in Derbyshire, where he himself had started. They would also visit the climbing wall in Nottingham whenever Doug's busy schedule allowed. He was always generous with giving Richard posters of his expeditions. As Richard became older, Doug introduced him to such well-known travel journalists as Clive Tully. Clive recalls, 'One moment which sticks out was when I was visiting the Oswins with my wife and baby, Aislinn. We'd progressed to a few drinks after our evening meal. Doug joined us. Aislinn was fretful. My wife brought her downstairs to soothe her, but Aislinn was having none of it. "Come here, child," said Doug, as he took hold of Aislinn, cradling her against one shoulder. Within a minute she had quietened down and within the next she was fast asleep. We carried on chatting, with my daughter asleep on the great man's shoulder for a good hour. Others have spoken of Doug's extraordinary Zen, but this was it in action!'[10]

Nor did happy times have to be about mountains. Richard, Arran and Euan had 'good days out' together with Doug when they were young. A pleasant memory for Richard was a day trip to Wells-next-the-Sea in Norfolk. Of course, Doug attended Joyce's eightieth and ninetieth birthday parties, which Doug helped to turn into 'fun family events'. And he attended Richard's wedding to Laina in 2018, as did Brian and Garry. Doug and historical continuity within the family was strong and proactive.

Richard also tells us that he and his wife stayed on occasion at Stewart Hill Cottage. As with virtually every other visitor, Doug would show them his organic vegetable garden. No other activity outside his writing and

*The last photo of the three Scott brothers together. L to R: Brian, Doug, Garry.
At the wedding of Garry's son Richard to Laima, May 2018.*

lectures provided Doug with so much interest and enjoyment as the cultivation of his organic vegetables.[11] Doug jealously guarded his half-acre plot
of organic leeks, onions, potatoes, marrows, cabbages and carrots, while
also earning a reputation for showing it off to visitors at any time of the
day or night. The garden had a long ideological history, stretching back to
his father's allotment. Scott's evangelism was robust: he reacted very badly
to Trish being caught spraying her roses. His evangelism carried over into
CAN, with its sustainability health posts. In Cumbria he had entered local
competitions, with some success.

   Unlike much of his previous life, Trish recalls Doug's domestic efficiency. No sooner would she remark on a carpet requiring hoovering when
Doug would take it up and clean it at once. Doug also, 'with very good

taste', chose some of Trish's clothes for her, for example a very chic raincoat in New York. Both were deeply involved in Arran and Euan's education and upbringing, a widely agreed success story: Arran is an electrician and Euan is an e-discovery consultant. Where the two previous marriages were often confrontational or running on separate tracks, Doug's and Trish's marriage was symbiotic.

In spring 2019, however, Doug's mental co-ordination and emotional equanimity began to falter. He was diagnosed with an inoperable cerebral lymphoma. Nonetheless, with the indefatigable determination which had seen him through the critical moments of his life, he continued fundraising by climbing the stairs at Stewart Hill in the Everest Challenge 2020, his final activity for CAN. He described it as 'hellish', but it was mentioned on the BBC and the inspiration it generated was widespread.

Doug died early on 7 December 2020, with Trish and his family present. His funeral took place at Castle Sowerby church on 16 December. Attendance was limited by COVID restrictions, but ice-axes were raised. Two memorial services had to be cancelled for the same reason. Eventually, a tribute evening was held at the Kendal Mountain Festival on 8 November 2021. A full house greatly enjoyed stories and insights from Tut, Guy Lee, Andy Parkin, Victor Saunders, Chris Bonington and of course Trish, their comments added to in a movingly appreciative film from Reinhold Messner. This event was followed on 24 March 2022 at the RGS. A full house, with Tut, Leo Houlding, Chris Bonington and Rob Lorge and including Pertemba and Murari in the audience, heard a highly varied account of Doug's colourful life and ideas. The auction of several of Doug's most famous photos raised a proportionately large sum.

While all the UK's major newspapers and news outlets, such as the BBC and Sky, carried obituaries for this national figure, tributes and obituaries appeared worldwide. Most referred to Doug as 'one of the world's greatest mountaineers'. Some rightly stressed the importance of the Alpine style of his ascents. The UKClimbing website brilliantly captured that interaction of opposites which generated such energy: 'Tough guy rugby player fascinated by Buddhist mysticism; anarchic hippy with a deep sense of tradition; intensely ambitious one day, laid back the next. He was as egotistic as any climber, but was also demonstrably generous and compassionate, admired universally for his philanthropy.'

Many online forums offered more personal memories. Most stressed his gentlemanliness, his approachability, his ordinariness and his climbing ability. The *Nepali Times* averred that he was now on the list of 'great givers to Nepal'. It called him a 'giant among giants'. *Outdoors Queensland* focused on his legacy: 'Scott became a mentor to new generations inspired by the idea of lightweight climbing and the ideas he espoused.'

Bonington's summary was apt: 'His mountaineering achievements pale alongside his creation of Community Action Nepal and the schools, hostels, health clinics and Porter Rescue Shelters it has built and sustained over twenty-five years for the people of the high Himalayas. It is an outstanding charity. Well run and widely respected.'

In his eulogy for Doug at his postponed memorial service, Phil Bartlett commented, 'Many of us can remember being ready to set out for a day's climbing only to find Doug in some interminable phone call or tending his cabbages. When he did at last appear, there was no apology: this was the price we paid for the privilege of his friendship.'

Phil stressed Doug's openness to new ideas and his endless curiosity, despite his weakness for gurus. His conversation was 'first-rate'.[12]

For polymath Marcia Fotheringham, Doug had great emotional intelligence, even when he referred to her as 'a shilling rabbit' (actually a form of compliment!).[13] The *New York Times* drew attention to his humanitarian character. In the *Alpine Journal*, 2021, Stephen Venables underscored how important the manner of the climb was for Doug. He was, for Venables, 'visionary and adventurous, yet rooted in the traditions he valued'. Perhaps the CAN obituary's comment summed up the feelings of so many people across the planet: 'There will be great sadness today as we remember Doug and reflect on what we have lost. However, there will also be feelings of gratitude and thanksgiving for the impact that Doug had in the world.'

Doug's legacy, through his books, talks and lectures, inspired thousands of schoolchildren, students and other young people to take to the hills, to climb and to reflect on their experiences. The NCC lives on. He was among the earliest and most consistent proponents of Alpine-style climbing, now the established way.

David Baker, who first met Doug on a White Hall course found him inspiring in this typical way: 'Rather than have us just follow him up routes, he was keen that we learnt how to be safe and to be able to lead. I know he pushed me in my lead climbing; I will always remember my first VS lead at *Earl Sterndale* (south-east of Buxton) under his guidance.'[14]

Baker and his friends were moved to buy a truck and drive to Chitral, where they enjoyed 'a great learning experience'.

Doug's astonishing list of new routes, first ascents and exploratory climbs in at least thirty-seven countries gives the benchmark to those prepared to eschew box-ticking in favour of adventure. Doug's six visits to Iceland were particularly influential. As Snævarr Guðmunsson tells us, it was Doug's books as well as his climbs which inspired the Icelanders, while his climbs helped to establish certainty about route standards: his visits led to 'an enormous progress' for Icelandic climbers; 'the sport of climbing began developing in a broader way than ever before'.

His writing provides a permanent record of an astonishingly productive life not least through his ethical principles, of looking after our environment, of being scrupulous about what we eat, of enjoying adventure for its own sake, untainted by the values and practices of the city.

In the UK and Nepal, CAN's trustees are committed to maintaining Doug's legacy of providing security, education and a chance of improved diet and health for thousands of Nepalis. Best of all is the gift of hope for a better future in one of the world's poorest countries. CAN proves that life can be improved, and can be done so, quickly and effectively.

∽

Doug Scott was one of the greatest mountaineers in history. During his fifty years of serious climbing, he put up possibly more new routes and reached more new summits than perhaps any other climber. He set an example of good climbing style which has been fully recognised by the other 'greats', such as Messner, Kurtyka, Bonatti and Bonington. His views on the way we manage our wilderness and mountain environments were ahead of their time. A poet, an avid reader, a fanatical researcher, a gardener and a quester for philosophical truth lay within him when not climbing. Scott's unusual dynamism was the product of co-existing opposites, derived from a home which was disciplined yet free: he showed both tunnel-vision and generosity of spirit; infidelity was set against uncompromising loyalty; Romantic passion strove against cool reflectiveness; a disregard for protocol and stuffiness contended with ethical rigour. For all the irritation and fury Doug could generate, for all his exasperating belief that Doug Scott's way was the only way, in the final perception, love and affection triumphed. No British mountaineer has dedicated thirty years of his life with the unsparing energy and purposefulness he put into improving the lot of the people of Nepal. The depth and largeness of Doug Scott's humanitarianism remains unsurpassed.

Appendix

A Timeline of Doug Scott's Recorded Climbs and Expeditions

'(f)' signifies a successful first ascent or new route.
'(u)' means that the climb did not reach the summit.
The list is not exhaustive as far as
single rock-climbing routes are concerned.

1955

Easter
Derbyshire: Black Rocks, Cromford: *Fat Man's Chimney, Lone Tree Gully, Central Buttress*

Summer
Birchen Edge
Kinder Scout and Bleaklow
Beddgelert

1956

Easter
White Hall: Windgather and Castle Naze

Whitsun
Tryfan: *Milestone Buttress* (u), Little Tryfan
'Ogwen Cliffs'
Glyderau

August
Kinder Scout

1957

August
Arran: *Cir Mhor: Rosa Pinnacle South Ridge Direct*

1958

January
Sprinkling Tarn and Wasdale

Easter
Eskdale OB Centre: Scafell Pike, Skiddaw, Helvellyn (u)
Yewbarrow

July
Bernese Oberland: Blüemlisalphorn (u)
Chamonix: Mer de Glace, Aiguille du Peigne: *Boeuf Couloir* (u)

October
Great Gable area

1959

January
Scafell Pike
Ben Wyvis

Summer
Snowdonia: *Cemetery Gates*
Chamonix: Dent du Requin (u), Dent du Requin, Aiguille de l'M, Mont Blanc: *Goûter Route*
Julian Alps

December
Sty Head, Langdale, Wasdale Head

1960–65

Numerous new routes in the Derwent Valley

1960

January
Torridon: Liathach, Beinn Eighe, Beinn Dearg, Beinn Alligin
Kintail: Five Sisters
Glencoe: Bidean nam Bian

Easter
Ben Nevis
Mamores and Grey Corries

Summer
Dauphiné: Les Bans (u), Pic Coolidge, Dôme de Neige des Écrins, Barre des Écrins

December
Scafell

1961

Easter
Old Man of Coniston: Dow Crag

July
Bregaglia: Ago di Sciora, Pizzi di Gemelli: *Ferro da Stiro*, Piz Badile: *North Ridge, Cassin Route*
Chamonix: Aiguille du Moine, Pointe Albert, Aiguille du Chardonnet: *Forbes Arête*, la Nonne, l'Évêque, Aiguille Mummery, Aiguille Ravanel, Mont Blanc

October
Raven Tor: *Traverse*
High Tor: *M1, Flaky Wall*

December
Glencoe: Bidean nam Bian

1962

April
North Wales: *Cenotaph Corner*

July–September
Chamonix: Grand Capucin: *Bonatti Route*, Dent du Géant, Aiguille du Plan, Aiguille du Fou, Cornes du Chamois (f)
Ötztal Alps
Sierra Nevada: Veleta, Tajo de los Machos, Caballo, Mulhacén, Cerro de los Machos
October: Atlas Mountains: Ouanoukrim, Tizi Ouanoums: *Beetham Route*, Toubkal, Tadaft n'bou Imrhaz: *South-East Cracks* (f), Jebel Siroua

1963

Easter

Cantabrian Mountains: Tiro Alfonso XIII (probably u)

Pyrenees

High Tor: *Mecca*; Chee Dale: *The Big Plum*; Kilnsey Crag; Malham Cove; Gordale Scar

High Crag: *Cataclysm*; Wildcat Crag: *Catastrophe Grooves*

July–August

Dolomites: Cima Picolissima, Punta di Frida, Cima Piccolo: *Spigolo Gallo*, Cima Grande: *Comici Route*

1964

February

Cairngorm, Northern Corries and Lairig Ghru

Stac Pollaidh

Suilven

Summer

Gordale Scar: *Grot, Twilight*

Chamonix: Aiguille du Peigne: *North Ridge,* Aiguille de Blaitière: *West Face,* Aiguille du Midi, Mont Blanc: *Frendo Spur*, Midi-Plan Traverse

Dolomites: Sassolungo area, Sella Pass area

1965

Spring

Tibesti Mountains: Aiguilles de Sisse; Trou au Natron; Tierso Toroko: *West Ridge* (f)

1966

Thirteen successive weekends in North Wales

Anglesey: *Crowbar, Syringe*; High Tor: *Girdle*; Dinas Cromlech: *The Thing*; Clogwyn Du'r Arddu: *The Corner, The Boulder*

August–October

Čilo Dağı: 'thirteen' rock-climbs above advance base, Reşko Tepe (u), Cafer Kule (f), Sirt Tepe

1967

January

Coire an Lochain: *Savage Slit, Milky Way*

May–July

Hindu Kush: Kuh-i-Bandaka: *South Face* (f), Kuh-i-Sisgeikh: *East Face* (f)

Sakhi Valley area: 'eight summits between 5500m and 6100m' (all f)

Sharan Valley: 'a number of granite peaks around 5500m' (all f)

July

Chamonix: Aiguille du Plan: *North Face Direct*

Summer

Cumbria, Castle Rock: *Thirlmere Eliminate*

Staffordshire: The Roaches

Donegal: Mount Errigal, Slieve League

Gogarth: *The Big Overhang* (f)

October

Donegal, Sail Rock: *Roaring Forties*

1968

April
Donegal, Sail Rock

May
Gogarth: *Whip*

Summer
Bernina: Piz Palü Traverse
Chamonix: Aiguille du Petit Dru: *Bonatti Pillar*

November
'Three successive weekends in North Wales'

December
Coire an Lochain: *Chute Route*

1969

January
Ski-tour: Cairngorm, Bèn Macdhui, Lairig Ghru

Easter
Harris: Strone Ulladale: *The Scoop* (f)

Summer
Dolomites: Cima Ovest: *Rudolf-Baur Route* (f, British)

1970

February
Strone Ulladale: *The Nose* (u)

Easter
Yosemite: *Steck-Salathé Route*, Cathedral Spire: *Braille Book*, BHOS: 'five-pitch route', *Lost Arrow Spire*, Reed's Pinnacle, 'various roof climbs', Leaning Tower, El Capitan: *Salathé Wall* (f, European)

June
Norway: Adelsfjell: *South-East Cracks*, Troll Wall: *Høibakk's Chimney, Rimmon Route*

1971

Spring
Pyrenees: Tozal del Mallo: *Spanish Route*

June
Strone Ulladale: *Sidewinder* (f), *The Nose* (u)

July
Baffin Island: 'two 2000m peaks South of Mt Asgard' (both f), Freya Peak, Killabuk: *East Face* (f), Breidablik: *North Face,* Asgard North Peak (u)
Shawangunks: *Broken Sling*

September
Strone Ulladale: *The Nose* (f)

1972

April
El Capitan: *The Nose*
Estes Park: 'several routes' on the Twin Owls
Washington State: Cascades: Index crags

Spring
Everest south-west face to 8000m (Herligkoffer Expedition) (u)

June

Baffin Island: Asgard west face (u), Asgard north peak (f)

Tetons: Devil's Tower

August–September

Everest south-west face to 8300m (Bonington Expedition) (u)

1973

Summer

Baffin Island: 'a dozen unnamed peaks' in the Mount Turnweather area, Overlord Peak

1974

May–June

India: Garhwal: Changabang (f)

July–August

Russian Pamirs: Pik Lenin: *South-East Ridge*

Derbyshire and Lake District

December

Chamonix: Aiguille Verte: *Couturier Couloir*, Aiguille du Midi: *Rébuffat Route*

1975

March

Estes Park: Long's Peak: *Diamond* (u)

Colorado: Front Range: Taylor Peak

Eastern Sierra: *Keeler Needle* (u)

Yosemite: *Washington Column, Meat Grinder, Little Wing, Outer Limits, Midterm, Anathema, Plumkin*

July

Karakoram: Sosbun Brakk (u), 'Minor peaks above the Uzun Brakk Glacier'

July–September

Kala Pattar, Everest: *South-West Face* (f)

1976

April

Denali South Face: *Scott-Haston Route* (f)

May

Baffin Island: Baffin Fjord Peak, Overlord Peak: *South-west Buttress* (f)

June

Colorado: Long's Peak: *Diamond Lil* (f)

Summer

Mount Kenya north-east face: *Grey Pillar* (f), *Diamond Couloir* (f?) to Batian and Nelion, Hell's Gate: Main Wall: 'two new routes' (both f), *Olympian*

Kilimanjaro: *Breach Wall*

Month uncertain

Climbs on Nottingham Castle Rock (f?)

1977

May–July

The Ogre: *West Ridge* (f)

1978

April–May

Canada: Mount Waddington: *South-East Chimney* (f)

May–July

K2 West Ridge from Savoia Glacier (Bonington Expedition) (u)

September

Everest region: Nuptse: *North Face* (u)

1979

February

Kintail: Falls of Glomach

Cuillin: Sgurr a'Mhadaidh: *The Smear*

April–May

Kangchenjunga (f, without supplementary oxygen), *North-West Face* and *North Ridge*

September

Everest Region: Kusum Kangguru to north summit (f), Nuptse *North Buttress* (f)

1980

March

Chamonix: Les Droites: *North-East (Tournier) Spur*

June

Australia: cliffs near Sydney Harbour New Zealand: Darran Mountains: Tūtuko (u), 'two Alpine rock climbs' (both f)

July–August

K2 West Ridge (u)

September–October

Everest Region: Kangchungtse: *Original Route*, Peak 6170, Peak 6250, Peak 6350, Southern Chago Peak 6600

Makalu: *South-East Ridge* (u)

1981

May–June

Gangotri: 'several minor peaks above 5500m', Shivling *East Pillar* (f)

Nepal: Chamlang: *North Face of Point 7010* (f)

1982

Probably winter

Ben Nevis: *Orion Face, Green Gully, The Curtain*

Monte Gruetta: *North Face* (u)

April–June

Tibet-Nepal border: Nyanang Ri (u), Pungpa Ri (f), Shishapangma: *South-East Face* (f)

Summer

Yosemite: Basket Dome: *South-East Spur*

1983

April–June

Karakoram: Karphogang, 'one other spire' (both f)

Lobsang Spire, *South Pillar* (f)

Broad Peak: *Original Route*

K2: *South-South-East Spur* (u)

1984

February

Blue Peter climb, Borrowdale

September–October

Everest region: Yaupa, south-east summit (f), Baruntse, Chamlang East and Central Summits (f), Makalu: *South-East Ridge* to 8370m (u)

October

Iceland: Reykjavik: *Scott's Leið* (f); Vestrahorn: Rustanöf (f); Fallastakkanöf: *Organ Pipes* (f)

1985

January

Vancouver Island: Mount Colonel Foster: *Grand Central Couloir* (f)

May

Hrútsfjallstindar: *South Face* (f)

June

Hunza: minor summit above Karimabad; Diran

August–September

Rupal Peak (u), Nanga Parbat: Mazeno Ridge (u)

1986

February

Sgurr na Fheadain: *Waterpipe Gully* (f)

Seana Braigh: *Captain Patience* (f)

Applecross: Beinn Bhan, Coire na Feola: *In Excess* (f)

Easter

Ötztal high altitude tests, *The Glass Madonna*

Autumn

Manali Area: Ali Ratni Tibba (u), Pinnacle circa 5000m South of Ali Ratna Tibba (f)

Western Ghats: Maharashtra: Harihar: *Scottish Kada*, Savandurga: *Scott's Crack*, Ramanagram: *Ramagiri Betta*

Climbs near Pune, Mumbai and

Nashik: 'two first ascents'

Tasmania: Hobart Organ Pipes: *Fiddle Sticks*, 'new route' on coast

1987

April

Wadi Rum: *Martha's Steps* (f), *Gulab Tower* (f), *Skyline Buttress* (f), 'three or four other routes', all (f)

Probably May

Wales: Tremadog: *Pincushion*

June–August

Peak 6812 (u), K2: *East Face* (u)

August

Langtang: Naya Kanga

September

Everest: *North-East Ridge* to 8200m (u)

1988

Winter

Hemsedal and Romsdal

May–June

Jitchu Drake (f)

August–September

Makalu: *West Face* (u)

1989

March–April

Trek to Kangchenjunga base camp

Spring

Alice Springs 'crags and canyons', King's Canyon

Blue Mountains: Three Sisters

Explorer Range: Mount Boyce, Mount Piddington

West Victoria: Mount Arapiles

Brisbane: Kangaroo Point

Sydney: sea-cliffs

Queensland: Mount French: *Frog Buttress*

Western Australia: West Cape Howe

May–June

Rimo II (u)

Late 1980s/1990s

Climbs with Mark Bowen in New England

Franconia Notch: *Black Dike*

Frankenstein Ice: *Chia Direct*, Cathedral Ledge: *Recompense*, probably in late 1980s

Mount Willard: *Across the Universe*

Whitehorse Ledge: *The Last Unicorn*

1990

June–July

Karakoram: Biacherahi Peak (u), Biacherahi Dome (f), Latok III: *Indian Arête* (f winter), Latok I (u)

August

Greenland: Narsaq Peninsula, Tasermiut Fjord

September

Eiger: *West Flank*, Jungfrau

1991

Probably summer

Iceland: Skaftafell: Hvanndalshnjúkur (ski ascent)

Snæfellsjökull, Helgrindur (ski ascent)

Lóndrangar sea-stack (f)

October

Kanjiroba Himal: Hiunchuli IV (aka Hanging Glacier Peak) (u), Hiunchuli IV: *South Ridge* (f)

December (to January 1992)

Mount Vinson

1992

February

Aconcagua: *Polish Glacier Route*

Patagonia: FitzRoy: *Chouinard Route* (u)

Easter

Iceland: Skaftafell: Tindaborg rock spires (u)

Fallastakkanöf: three-pitch route (f)

June

Tajikistan: Fann Mountains: Zamok, Chimtarga (f, British)

August

Nanga Parbat area: Point 5971 (Lilley Peak) (f?); Point 6880 (Mazeno Ridge), Point 6970 (Mazeno Ridge), Mazeno Ridge (u)

1993

July–August

Mazeno Spire (f), Mazeno West Peak (f) Mazeno Ridge (u)

1994

June–July
Old Man of Hoy
Caucasus: Elbrus, Railway Workers'
Peak

December
Tierra del Fuego: Cordon Navarro:
Mount Pelagic (f), Mount Poltroon (f)
Fiordo Chueco: '2100m Peak' (u)

1995

February
Am Buachaille, Old Man of Stoer:
Original Route

May
New Guinea: Carstensz Pyramid
(several routes, all f)

July–August
Mazeno Ridge (u)

1996

September–October
Sikkim: Chombu East, Chombu(u),
Gurudongmar (u)

1997

Spring
Picos de Europa: El Naranjo de Bulnes:
Murciana

1998

March
Lyngen Alps: Urdtinden *South Face* (f)
Kvaløya: Munin: *Scott-Nesheim Route*
(f)

April
Kangchenjunga area: Drohmo (u)

September
Kangchenjunga area: Teng Kongma:
North-East Ridge (f), Drohmo (subsid-
iary summit) (f)

1999

September–November
Arunachal Pradesh: approach to Takpa
Shiri

Late 1990s

Climbs and walks in the Galloway hills
and sea-cliffs

2000

September
Nepal: Trekking peak above Bahrabise

October
Tibet: Chang Tang: Targo Ri (f)

2001

Spring
Colorado: off-piste skiing

Probably summer
Iceland, north of Reykjavik:
Skarðsheiði (f), Skessuhorn (u)

2004

September
Iceland: Landmannalaugar:
Grænihnjúkur

2005

February
Nepal: Thimbu trek for CAN

September
Near Sofia: rock-climbs

Late autumn/early winter
Blue Mountains: Katoomba, Mount York
Mittagong: Mount Alexander
Adelaide Hills: Morialta

2006
October
Nepal: Helambu trek

October
South Africa: Cederberg Mountains

2008
January
US: Adirondack Range: cragging
White Mountains: skiing and climbing, Mount Washington

April–May
Nepal: Walung and Kambalung Caves
Bratislava: cragging

September–October
Nepal trek

2009
Each winter until 2019
Leysin, Switzerland: ski-ing and climbs

September–October
Chile: Atacama Desert: 5800m peak

October
Portugal: cragging near Oporto

2010
March–April
Langtang trek

May
Greek Islands: cragging on Telendos

2011
April
Chamonix: 'some climbs'

Summer
Stac Pollaidh

October
Milarepa trek

2012
September–October
Cragging in Vermont

2013
April
Sri Lanka: Dambulla Caves

2016
February
Carrock Fell: *Trough Gully*

2017
April
Near Mumbai: cragging

2020
March
Jordan: revisiting Wadi Rum

Spring–summer
Cumbria: Everest Challenge 2020

Notes

Notes on the Text

1   For a comparison of climbing grades around the world, see http://www. alpinist.com/p/online/grades

Chapter 1

1   Moritz, C.P., *Reisen eines Deutschen in England im Jahr 1782* ('Travels in England in 1782').

2   Lob is the name given to a mischievous fairy with a dark raincloud as a body. It can be confused with Lob Lie-By-The-Fire, a strong, hairy giant which helps humans. In this case it must be the former, as Great-Grandma Sansom's intentions were clearly intimidatory.

3   This length of service is calculated on the assumption that Joyce began to work at Player's when she was fourteen before giving up her job on marriage when she was twenty.

Chapter 2

1   Brian Scott, in correspondence with the author.

2   Sutton-in-Ashfield lies just south-west of Mansfield, about twenty kilometres north of Nottingham.

3   Freddie Mills (1919–65) was the world light heavyweight boxing champion from 1948 to 1950. His style relied on two-fisted aggression, relentless pressure and the ability to take punishment to carry him through; in more cases than not these characteristics were sufficient.

4   Evidently, Prime Minister Harold Wilson had not been well briefed before the reception at Number 10 – or was incipiently suffering from the Alzheimer's which forced his resignation not long afterwards – when he asked Scott, 'Are you one of the climbers?' A kind of inverse event occurred when Scott was presented many years later to the Queen: in a comical attempt at naturalness, he observed to Her Majesty, 'You're looking well!'

5   There is uncertainty about dates, here. Scott says he entered Middleton when he was five, in 1946, which seems likely, that being the statutory starting age. But he also claims that he spent only two years at Middleton before he entered

Robert Shaw when he 'turned seven', i.e. in 1948. This school did not open
until 1950, however. So, 'two' years must be a slip for 'four'. Scott would therefore have been nine, not seven, when he entered Robert Shaw.

6   Brian went to grammar school and does say that his brother was 'very intel-
ligent', a description there is no reason to doubt. Fortunately, the brothers
remained close despite this parting of the educational ways. He also says that
it was Douglas who advised him to go into medicine, a career in which he was
conspicuously successful, finishing as Consultant Physician at Lincoln County
Hospital. Scott might secretly – his lack of academic achievement never made
that a realistic career choice – have wanted to go into medicine himself, if only
to gain the approval of grateful patients. His interest in expedition medicine,
and particularly in his frequent 'clinics' for the benefit of locals on expedition
walk-ins, is dealt with in chapter 15.

7   It is not clear if the House was named after the famous mountaineer who dis-
appeared high on Everest in 1924, or, more likely, his younger brother, Trafford
Leigh-Mallory (1892–1944), the Head of Fighter Command and eventually Air
Marshal, who was instrumental in the Allied victory in the Second World War.

8   As an English teacher for thirty-seven years, I find it surprising that someone
would read such difficult texts for English O-Level. Scott's memory may be
playing tricks on him: some of these are more likely to have been read in the
sixth form, though almost anything by Orwell survives as a standard GCSE
text.

9   The school (now a housing estate) was named after A.J. Mundella (1825–97),
a prominent and popular public figure in Nottingham who became Sheriff of
Nottingham in the 1850s.

10   Susan Holland, née Webster, in email correspondence with the author, 11
November 2021.

Chapter 3

1   In *Up and About*, Scott says the Mamores trip occurred in 1957, which, from at
least two external evidence sources, cannot possibly be right.

2   The Black Rocks are situated just above the High Peak Trail as it passes above
Cromford, giving very fine views of the sub-Alpine Derwent Valley.

3   Jack Longland (1905–93), properly Sir John Longland, was an educator, broadcaster and mountaineer. A brilliant climber who put up the first whole-height
route on Clogwyn Du'r Arddu, Longland became famous on the 1933 Everest
expedition for safely bringing eight Sherpas down in a blizzard from the highest
camp. He spent some years in the 1930s as an academic at Durham University,
working mainly for the benefit of unemployed people.

4   Geoffrey Winthrop Young (1876–1958) was technically one of the finest rock-
climbers in the UK, indeed anywhere, before the First World War. A pacifist,
he served in an ambulance brigade first on the Western Front then on the
Isonzo Front in north-east Italy, where he lost a leg at the Battle of Caparetto

(1917). During his recovery, he devised a new kind of artificial leg and returned to UK and Alpine climbing for fourteen years. He was Mallory's mentor. He was Hahn's closest friend and became a governor of Gordonstoun (sometimes Chairman of the Governors) during the 1950s and 1960s. He was president of the Alpine Club from 1941 to 1944 and effectively created the BMC. Young was a highly accomplished mountaineering poet, perhaps the finest to date. He wrote copiously on almost every aspect of mountaineering, including Outdoor Education, an integral part of the Gordonstoun syllabus along with public service.

Kurt Hahn (1886–1974) was a German educational philosopher and headmaster of Salem and Gordonstoun. He was secretary to Prince Max of Baden when the latter had to ask the Kaiser to abdicate at the end of the First World War. Prince Max and Hahn went on to found Salem, at von Baden's seat just north of Lake Constance. After the notorious Potempa Incident in 1932, when Hitler congratulated some SS troops on beating a young Polish Jew to death, Hahn courageously spoke out against Hitler. He was interned by the SS then released after eleven days, to be forced into exile in the UK. In 1934, he founded Gordonstoun, and went on to found Outward Bound in 1941 then, with Sir John Hunt, the Duke of Edinburgh's Award Scheme in 1956. He thought deeply about the moral, social and physical aspects of young people's education (in the broadest sense) but wrote no thoroughgoing work on the subject.

5   Quoted in Wilson, K., *The Games Climbers Play*, p. 528. Longland's letter was in response to a letter in *Mountain*, 51, by Rod Bulcock.

6   *Bidis* (pronounced 'bee-dees') are thin, hand-rolled cigarettes made of tobacco and wrapped in tendu or temburni leaf (*Diospyros melanoxylon*), a plant native to Asia. *Bidis* are principally manufactured in India and other South-East Asian countries. They contain four to five times the amount of nicotine found in conventional cigarettes. Adapted and edited from www.verywellmind.com

7   A royal chivalric order, chartered in 1888 and dedicated to 'prevent and relieve sickness and injury, and to act to enhance the health and well-being of people anywhere in the world'.

8   One day in 2016, Doug phoned me to ask if I would edit the historical section of *The Ogre*. After I had agreed, he characteristically asked if the task could be completed by yesterday. He then asked if I knew about the Knappach rowan. Despite my strong connection with the little Highland town where I live, I had to confess I didn't. Doug informed me that it was situated only two kilometres from my house, so I duly tramped over a few fields to reach this tree, which still produces berries and may be 400 years old. From it, there is a fine view of A'Chailleach (928m), the final Munro which Doug climbed. I reported my excursion to Doug and, the following week, I received a copy of Max Adams's *The Wisdom of Trees* (Head of Zeus, London, 2014), a work of some beauty in content and as an artefact. I consider myself duly educated.

9   A waterfall on the western edge of the Kinder Scout plateau; highly spectacular when the winds which scour this isolated spot force the water upwards.

10   Dez Hadlum, in email correspondence with the author.

11   Harold Drasdo (1930–2015) was a leading climber in the post-Second World War era, and an early member of the Bradford Lads. He also climbed with the Rock and Ice Club. He wrote guidebooks and several works on Outdoor Education.

      Joe Brown (1930–2020) was another of the UK's leading post-war rock climbers. With Don Whillans, also a member of the Rock and Ice Club, he put up many very hard new routes, particularly in North Wales and the Peak District. He broke several other barriers: that of social class, as the very working-class first ascentionist of Kangchenjunga in 1955, and as a TV broadcaster. He joined White Hall as an instructor in 1961 (so not while Scott was involved there).

      Gordon Mansell (1932–2016) was an instructor at White Hall in the 1950s and a painter until the end of his days.

12   Geoffrey Byrne-Sutton (1930–2000) was expelled from Harrow but went on to Cambridge, from where he completed some of the most serious routes in the Alps. He became warden of White Hall in November 1955 and qualified as a BMC Guide in 1956. Sutton and Harold Drasdo opened up new climbs in the Poisoned Glen, Donegal, from 1956 to 1959 (perhaps a stimulus to Scott's expeditions there a few years later).

13   McDonald, P., *The Story of White Hall Centre*, p. 287.

14   *Up and About*, p. 64.

15   Munros are Scottish Mountains over 3,000 feet (914.4m). The original list was compiled by the SMC stalwart Sir Hugh Munro in 1891. He listed 277. Thanks to re-surveying and prolonged, animated discussion about definition, the current number stands at 282. There are also 226 Munro tops (at present), these being points above 914.4m with insufficient drop on all sides for them to be considered separate Munros.

16   Scott is unclear in his route description. He does not mention the outlier of the Grey Corries, Stob Ban (977m), yet it would have been on his route. It is hard to imagine him not including it, despite referring only to the eastern extremity of the range, Stob Choire Claurigh (1177m). If including Stob Ban, Scott would have covered a further seven Munros, making seventeen for the day altogether. In *Up and About*, Scott mentions that he had climbed twelve Munros, which is unlikely to be correct as it would have meant shunning many of the best summits along the walk.

17   The *Cenotaph Corner* climb meant a lot to Scott, not just because he was emulating a difficult route by arguably the UK's most famous rock-climber of that era. In his final book, *Kangchenjunga*, Scott refers to Brown's legendary first attempt at *Cenotaph Corner* in 1948, when Brown dropped a mason's hammer which flattened his belayer. Brown, of course, had famously climbed a crag

immediately below Kangchenjunga's summit while making its first ascent with George Band in 1955. The story had first been told to Scott by someone at White Hall, most probably Gordon Mansell. The implied link connected Brown's humble beginnings and subsequent ground-breaking ascent with Scott's own spectacular progress.

18   Lyn Noble, in correspondence with the author. At the time of Scott's visits to Yugoslavia, the ruler was Marshal Tito, who pursued a policy of encouraging as much contact with the West as he dared. As an example of Tito's 'soft power' he encouraged nude bathing on the Adriatic from as early as 1960. Scott had evidently heard about this in choosing Yugoslavia as his destination.

19   Lyn Noble, in email correspondence with the author.

20   My thanks to John Cleare and various members of Peter Biven's family for the detective work in confirming that the school was Rushey Mead.

21   Peter Biven: 1935–76. John Cleare's climbing obituary of him in the *Alpine Journal* for 1977 is excellent.

22   Geoff Stroud, in correspondence with the author.

Chapter 4

1   The biblical allusion initiates the theme of Scott as having a kind of god-like presence.

2   Steve Smith, in email correspondence with the author.

3   Evans was a prolific illustrator and went on to co-found the Cicerone Press.

4   A cheater is a form of home-made aluminium nut.

5   Lyn Noble, in correspondence with the author.

6   Peter Thompson, in correspondence with the author. This was the first occasion of several in which Scott just beat other distinguished climbers to the first ascent of a difficult climb.

7   Bob Holmes, in correspondence with the author. In calling Bob 'Youth', Doug was assuming an adult role which he could justify by experience if not by age. He was twenty-two at the time; Bob was two years younger.

8   Steve Read, in correspondence with the author.

9   This quote and subsequent quotes in this chapter from Bob Wark are edited extracts from Bob's correspondence with the author.

10   Almost certainly Ryvoan Bothy, well under an hour's walk from the nearest road.

11   The source for this is a manuscript at Scott's Stewart Hill Cottage, Cumbria. There were no deaths on Ben Nevis that night. Four young men, however, were killed in a storm in December 1956 on Ben Nevis. Scott makes the correction in *Up and About*.

12   Jean's Hut was built in 1951 on Cairngorm to commemorate the life of Jean Smith. It was moved in 1964–65 to about 900m in Coire an Lochain. Owing to vandalism, it was dismantled, to widespread dismay, in 1986.

13   Peter Thompson, in correspondence with the author.

14 Dennis Gray helpfully points out that Crew in fact came from Elsecar, near Barnsley; he had grown up in a pre-fab and, when young, was a wonder at maths. He won a scholarship to Oxford but walked out at the end of his first term. He went on to set up Mountain Equipment with Peter Hutchinson and moved to Wales, where he began to study again and climb a lot with Joe Brown.

15 Brian Palmer, in correspondence with the author. The sack-hauling system anticipates the strenuousness and pain involved in employing a not dissimilar system on Shivling fourteen years later.

Chapter 5

1 One notorious episode involving British pilfering passed into legend as the Great Fish Finger Robbery; it led to the local *gendarmerie* bringing out their sniffer dogs.

2 Rather judgmental on my part: on one of my first Alpine outings, I attempted to climb the Grande Casse (3855m) from the Refuge du Col de la Vanoise (Félix Faure) via the *voie normale*, solo and without crampons.

3 It is mildly interesting that the Vallot guidebook describes this route as 'suitable for a late start'.

4 The heights and grades in this section are taken from the guidebook *Écrins Massif: Selected Climbs*, by John Brailsford, published by the Alpine Club, London, 1987.

5 Not the Col de la Selle, as wrongly stated in *Up and About*.

6 The 'flares' here are trousers, not incendiaries for attracting a helicopter's attention.

7 It is not recorded how Jan and the NCC climbers reached Chamonix: probably train in Jan's case and by hitching for most of the rest.

8 Scott's recollection is different from Lyn Noble's in that Scott maintains they descended the fixed ropes together.

9 The *Expedition Report* consistently misspells this river and its valley as 'Gentil'.

10 If 'Bonington' is the most widely misspelled person's name in mountaineering, then the 'Blaitière' is possibly the most widely misspelled mountain name.

11 Brian Palmer, in correspondence with the author.

12 'Sid' Smith, in email correspondence with the author.

13 In *Up and About*, Scott admits his avowed 'greed' extended to a drive to see his name in print.

14 Dave Wilkinson, in phone conversation with the author.

Chapter 6

1 Inexplicably, in his *Alpine Journal* 2002 review of the history and possibilities of climbing in the Atlas, Hamish M. Brown fails to mention Scott's expedition.

2 In *Up and About*, Scott claims to have caught hepatitis B, but the family's two medical experts, Martha and Brian, concur that hepatitis A is the correct diagnosis.

3   Lionel Terray (1921–65) was a major French first ascentionist in the Alps, on Makalu and Cerro FitzRoy.

4   Gaston Rébuffat (1921–85) was another major French figure, the first to climb all six great north faces of the Alps. He was a member of the French team which climbed Annapurna, the first ascent of an 8000m peak, in 1950.

5   This Turkic word for 'mountain' should more accurately be in the plural, 'Dağı', but I have left it here as Scott wrote it. The 'Čilo' pertains to the Jilu people, an Assyrian-originating tribe who left the area after the 1915 massacres.

6   The 'minor problem' has continued: I travelled through the edge of this area in 1997. Between Lake Van and Diyarbakir I counted at least 248 Turkish tanks and pieces of heavy artillery along the roadside, all of them pointing at Kurdistan.

7   Mike Webster, in email correspondence with the author.

8   *Cilo Dağ Expedition Report*, p. 18.

9   Hans Bobek (1903–90) was an Austrian geographer noted for his works on cultural and social geography and urban geography as well as on the regional geography of the Near and Middle East.

10   Henry Robin Fedden, CBE, (1908–77) was a writer, diplomat and mountaineer who went on to work for the National Trust.

11   *Cilo Dağ Expedition Report*, p. 29.

12   The Nestorians became a branch of the Eastern Christian church from about the fifth century CE.

13   *Cilo Dağ Expedition Report*, p. 32.

14   The powerful Varto earthquake of 19 August 1966 killed well over 2,000 people. The epicentre, however, to the north-west of Lake Van, was several hundred kilometres from the expedition area.

15   *Cilo Dağ Expedition Report*, Appendix VII.

16   Bob Holmes: private interview with the author, December 2021.

17   *Up and About*, p. 170.

18   *Hindu Kush Expedition Report*, p. 21.

19   Ibid, p. 28.

Chapter 7

1   Tena Walton, Jan's elder sister, in correspondence with the author.

2   On several occasions in *Up and About*, Doug mentions Jan's 'irregular periods' in a near-accusatory way, as though they were a kind of illness requiring his attention and thus a hindrance to his own life's continuity. (He did, very unkindly, once accuse Jan of 'holding him back'.) That Jan's periods might have been irregular because of stress or other causes seems not to have occurred to him. In that respect, Doug was very much a man of his time. Jan was in training to be a nurse.

3   Dennis Gray, in correspondence and conversation with the author.

4   Doug records in his diary one memorable occasion when Jan threw a frying

pan at him; it missed and sailed through a window to land on a car outside. Such inflammatory events seemed to be over very quickly, however.

5 Coffey, Maria, *Where the Mountain Casts Its Shadow*, p. 34.

6 Jan's elder sister, Tena Walton, describes her mother as a very outgoing home-maker 'who made friends wherever they moved'. Her father, she says, was much quieter and 'lived by the Queen's Regulations'.

7 Perhaps the previous year's Tibesti expedition had persuaded them that there was no turning back from mountaineering as a lifelong passion for their eldest son.

8 *Up and About*, p. 190.

9 John Cleare, in correspondence with the author.

10 Adapted from *Up and About*, pp. 92–93.

11 Geoff Stroud remains adamant that the accident was Doug's fault. Certainly, his date of June 1961 (rather than July 1966) seems to be the more likely. And there are other instances of Doug shifting moral responsibility for misdemeanours onto others when a young man.

12 The date is uncertain: the summer of 1961 or 1966. I favour the latter on this occasion because the story concerns a minivan with Doug at the wheel; he had bought his first minivan in 1965.

13 Bob Holmes, in correspondence with the author.

14 Garry Scott, in correspondence with the author.

15 Nick Kekus, in correspondence with the author.

Chapter 8

1 For the adventurous and weather-indifferent, Strone Ulladale lies about ten kilometres north-west of the Outer Hebrides' highest peak, Clisham (799m). Access is by a supposed path along Gleann Chliostair for about ten boggy kilometres from the B887, at a point about fourteen contorted kilometres west of its junction with the winding A859 from Stornoway to Tarbert.

2 Yannick Seigneur (1941–2001) was considered to be one of the most brilliant Alpine guides of his generation. He was the first Frenchman to climb three 8000m peaks.

3 Peter Gillman, in correspondence with the author.

4 At the end of his *Alpine Journal* article Scott nonetheless claims the first British ascent for 16 July 1969.

5 Leo Dickinson, in conversation with the author.

6 Normally referred to as 'The Gunks', these rocky mountains make up one of America's leading climbing areas. They are situated only 130 kilometres from New York City. The rock is solid quartz conglomerate with horizontal cracks. Climbing is characterised by airy roofs, big jugs and traverses. It offers one- to three-pitch climbs at all levels of difficulty.

7 Royal Robbins (1935–2017) was one of the greatest rock-climbers in American history. He pioneered single-push routes on El Capitan and Half Dome. He

advocated boltless climbing. While he often climbed with Yvon Chouinard, he sustained a long rivalry with Warren Harding, another great pioneer of climbing in Yosemite.

8   The crag's unusual name derives from Chuck Pratt's remark that it was a 'big hunk of shit'.

9   Adapted from *American Alpine Journal*, 1971.

10 Habeler says that this climb occurred after the *Salathé Wall* which, given the state of their hands after the *Salathé Wall* climb, seems less likely.

11 Peter Habeler, in correspondence with the author.

12 Scott and Habeler graded their route as: 6, 5.9, A3, with 37 pitches of which approximately half are free climbing.

13 Snap is a Nottinghamshire miners' word for lunch, adopted by local climbers.

14 *Up and About*, p. 246.

15 The exclamation mark in brackets is mine: Scott has picked up, in a description resembling a drug trip, on Jimi Hendrix's phrase ('Purple Haze').

16 With the exception of the 'frog anecdote', all the quotations relating to the *Salathé Wall* climb come from 'On the Profundity Trail', Scott's excellent article in *Mountain*, 15, pp. 12–17.

17 Scott calls them 'Eskimos'. This is a contentious term, generally applied to both Inuit and Yupik peoples. 'Eskimo' is by no means inappropriate for the peoples of this part of the Canadian Arctic, however.

18 The colour film was the twenty-six-minute *Dangerous Alternative*, premiered in 1971.

19 Elaine Matthews, in email correspondence with the author.

20 From *Alpine Journal*, 1973, pp. 85–88. The article is accompanied by excellently captioned, beautiful photos of these astounding mountains.

21 I have not so far been able to trace this piece of writing, although Scott describes it as a valuable insight into how others saw him.

22 See also *Mountain* magazine 37, July 1974, p. 10. Boardman's *The Shining Mountain* and Tasker's *Savage Arena* describe their 1976 ascent of the very difficult west wall of Changabang.

23 This is a bit of persona-building by Scott as by 1975 he had been to neither New Guinea nor South America. In the event, he climbed Aconcagua in 1990 and the Carstensz Pyramid in 1995.

24 The Gate of Mists seems to go by several different versions ('Gate of the Mists', etc.).

25 Rob Wood is an interesting character who, like Scott, reacted badly to city life and so climbing was a means of escape. He trained as an architect and developed the idea of an alternative global settlement of self-sufficient villages surrounded by farms. Presciently, he envisaged electric cars. On climbs in Yosemite with Mick Burke in the early 1970s, he considered that their successes were due to psychic phenomena as much as technical expertise. Wood married Laurie Manson, a person of very similar cast of mind and spirit. Their story

and beliefs are fascinatingly related in *At Home in Nature: a Life of Unknown Mountains and Deep Wilderness* (2017).

Chapter 9

1   The expedition gets only a very brief mention in the following year's *Alpine Journal*, perhaps reflecting its unhappy, unsuccessful nature and perhaps also for legal reasons.
2   Scott archive at Stewart Hill Cottage. The original is unpunctuated.
3   Guy Lee, however, assures us that Gippenreiter was the good guy among the Russians: 'He spoke good English, sympathised with our frustrations and always mediated on our behalf.'
4   Rowland, Clive, *Towards the Ogre*, McRay Press Ltd (Scarborough, 2022) p. 195. See https://towards-the-ogre.company.site/
5   In July 1990, in the worst mountaineering disaster in history, forty-three climbers were wiped out by an earthquake-triggered avalanche on the *Razdelnaya (Razdelny) Route* on Pik Lenin.
6   The Ogre, a.k.a. Baintha Brakk, is one of the few mountains in the Karakoram to have a western name which preceded the local name. K2, or Mount Godwin-Austen, is another example.
7   Bonington, Chris, *The Everest Years*, p. 42.
8   Bonington famously used a computer to work out the logistics of this expedition, at home and in the field. (It took Scott to remind us that Bonington, away from his computer, did more than his fair share of carrying and other more physical expedition duties, from dawn to dusk.) While the personal computer had not been created, at least for general use, in 1975, a friend of Bonington, Iain Macnaught-Davis, ran a computer company and lent a kind of 'board war games machine', as well as giving help from programmers and use of time on his main computer.

Chapter 10

1   *Up and About*, p. 380.
2   Ibid.
3   Next day, on their way down, Haston and Scott passed Boardman and Pertemba, who duly reached the summit in worsening weather. Near the top, they met Mick Burke, who was never seen again. An avalanche hit Camp 2 on the descent, causing a variety of minor injuries. Scott had to use his teeth on the fabric to bring air into his snow-laden tent. The expedition walked out without further incident. Scott met Jan and Michael and went trekking in Khumbu with them.
4   *Up and About*, p. 388.
5   Scott, Doug, *The Ogre*, p. 139.
6   Ibid.

7   Ibid, pp. 145–146.

8   Mo Anthoine (1939–89) was a distinguished British climber, both on rock and in the Himalaya, mainly in the 1970s and 1980s.

9   Tasker wrote an article on the climb for *Alpine Journal*, 1980. Georges Bettembourg's always interesting *The White Death* gives his account of his experience. Bettembourg died while crystal-hunting on the Aiguille Verte in 1981; Boardman and Tasker died in 1982 on the north-east pinnacles of Everest, though both left diaries.

10   Victor Saunders, in conversation with the author.

11   The previous year, 1978, Messner and Habeler had made their historic ascent of Everest without supplementary oxygen, although they were part of a larger Austrian team which did use it. Scott's expedition was the first to make an ascent of one of the 8000m peaks without supplementary oxygen from bottom to top.

12   Joe Tasker's diary, Scott archive, Stewart Hill Cottage.

13   Peter Boardman's diary, Scott archive, Stewart Hill Cottage.

14   Not to be confused with Ghunsa in Khumjung, the site of the first CAN school and health post.

15   Scott, Doug, *Kangchenjunga*, p. 238.

16   Ibid, p. 247. It is unclear which previous event Scott is referring to: he had over the years taken several falls, any one of which under only very slightly different circumstances could have proved fatal.

17   An epithet usually attributed to Whillans, but which Scott credits to Hamish MacInnes.

18   Thompson, Simon, *Unjustifiable Risk?* p. 302.

19   Scott, Doug and MacIntyre, Alex, *Shishapangma*.

20   Nick Kekus, in conversation with the author.

Chapter 11

1   John Cleare, in correspondence with the author.

2   Maggie Burgess, in conversation with the author.

3   Trish, however, went on many more treks and expeditions with Doug during their time together.

4   Letter from Doug Scott to Molly Higgins. Undated, but probably autumn 1974. Molly has kindly supplied a group of ten letters between them, and two from Molly to female friends, from 1974 to 1982.

5   Hesse's poem can be seen as a 'death is not to be feared' poem, or as an enjoining to 'gather ye rosebuds in the face of death/mortality'.

6   There are some variants to this story (regarding the animal involved).

7   Gina Madgett, in correspondence with the author.

8   Steve Razzetti (leader of the Karakoram Experience support trek), in correspondence with the author.

9   John Calden, in correspondence with the author.

10   Letter from Sir John Hunt to Mr Motwani, the editor, 20 May 1981.

11   Christine Gee, in correspondence with the author.

12   John Calden, in correspondence with the author.

13   Victor Saunders, in conversation with the author.

14   Ted Grey, in correspondence with the author. Grey was a founder member of the Young Explorers' Trust in 1972.

15   Ariane Giobellina, in correspondence with the author.

Chapter 12

1   Dr Jim Duff, in correspondence with the author.

2   Bar National (sic) is Chamonix's legendary watering-hole for climbers (and inquisitive tourists).

3   Adrian Burgess, in correspondence with the author.

4   The results are described in the *American Alpine Journal*, 1987, p. 83ff.

5   Greg Child, in correspondence with the author.

6   Brian Hall, in correspondence with the author.

7   Greg Child, in correspondence with the author.

8   Ibid.

9   Andy Parkin, in correspondence with the author.

10   Tim Macartney-Snape, in correspondence with the author.

11   Steve Swenson, in correspondence with the author.

12   The glacier is named after Henry Haversham Godwin-Austen (1834–1923), the first person to fix K2's height and position, which he did in August 1861 from a point about 1000m above Urdukas on a spur of Masherbrum. For a detailed account of his unusual life, see my biography of him: *The K2 Man (and His Molluscs)*, In Pinn (Glasgow, 2013).

13   Ariane Giobellina, in correspondence with the author.

14   Brian Hall, in correspondence with the author. *Chang* is beer brewed from millet, rice or barley. (It is now often written *chhaang* to distinguish it from a Thai commercial brand.) *Rakshi* is a millet or rice spirit.

15   Edited from Brian Hall's account of the descent, in correspondence with the author.

16   Scott frequently addressed people as 'youth' or 'kid', irrespective of their age. The habit no doubt derived from early Nottingham experiences but was preserved as part of the clubable Scott persona.

17   The account of this climb, from which both climbers only just succeeded in descending, is given in Sandy Allan's superb *In Some Lost Place*.

18   In 1989, passing through Pakistan en route to Xinjiang, I asked Nazir what it felt like as he approached K2's summit: 'It was like passing a very, very big exam.'

19   Scott was an accomplished horseman. His daughter Rosie is an expert horsewoman.

20   Quoted by Richard Cowper in correspondence with the author, from his article in the *Financial Times*, September 1993.

21   Sharu Scott, in correspondence with the author.

22 Undated, but almost certainly in November 1987.

23 Mark Bowen, in correspondence with the author. The grades cited come from the American grading system.

24 Not to be confused with the Old Man of Storr, a crumbling pinnacle resembling an elongated spearhead, on the Trotternish peninsula of Skye.

Chapter 13

1 Ariane Giobellina, in correspondence with the author.

2 This mountain should not be confused with the so-called Kishtwar Shivling (circa 5935m), in Jammu and Kashmir. Unhelpfully, it too has an East Pillar.

3 The word 'helping' is in inverted commas because assistance on Scott's lecture tours often required much more labour than was initially suggested.

4 Greg Child, in conversation with the author.

5 Ibid.

6 Ibid.

7 For further comment on this expedition, I recommend John Porter's biography of MacIntyre, *One Day as a Tiger*.

8 Nazir Sabir, in correspondence with the author.

9 Helen Urquhart, in correspondence with the author.

10 Howard, Tony, *Treks and Climbs in Wadi Rum, Jordan*.

11 *Jökull* means 'glacier' in Icelandic.

12 The Priut-11 (*priut* means 'hut' in Russian) lies at 4100m. It was completed in 1939, named after eleven Soviet scientists who had used it as a base in the 1930s and could accommodate 120 people.

13 Steve Sustad, in correspondence with the author.

14 In a slightly different version, Scott declared, 'We'll wait and see what happens,' and disappeared into his tent to meditate.

15 Scott took great pains to point out afterwards that these were names of convenience only and should not appear on any map unless endorsed by the Chilean authorities.

16 Arunachal Pradesh, mostly the former Assam, is beautifully described by Ian Baker in *The Heart of the World*, Souvenir Press (London, 2007), one of the most remarkable travel books ever written.

Chapter 14

1 'NE', not her real initials, has asked not to be identified. She has been helpful, however, in keeping me informed about Doug's life at and near Samye Ling and about his interest in Buddhism.

2 Sandy Allan, in correspondence and interview with the author.

3 Jim Fotheringham, in conversation with the author.

4 At this time, Sharu had custody of the children. Doug was worried that Sharu might take them to India.

5   Dez Hadlum, in correspondence with the author.
6   Allen Fyffe, in conversation with the author.
7   Steve Goodwin, in correspondence with the author.
8   Richard Cowper, in correspondence with the author, and corroborated by Guy Lee.
9   Gina Madgett, in correspondence with the author.
10 David Baker, in correspondence with the author.
11 Alexander Huber, in correspondence with the author.
12 See *Alpine Journal*, 2002.
13 Regrettably, because of a professional connection between 'NE' and the rinpoché, he too must remain anonymous. It was not, however, as some have suggested, the Dalai Lama.

Chapter 15

1   John Hunt diplomatically left out from *The Ascent of Everest* the incident in Kathmandu when disgruntled Sherpas expressed their dissatisfaction with inconsiderate British treatment by collectively peeing in the British ambassador's garage!
2   Scott, Doug, *The Ogre*, p. 173.
3   Ibid.
4   Phil Powell, in correspondence with the author.
5   https://www.catreks.com/
6   The 2022 open day, thanks to quite extraordinary preparatory work by Trish, raised £7,500.
7   David Durkan, in correspondence with the author. Doug had peculiarly magical persuasive powers, as I know to my cost having acquired a couple of Scott limited edition photos for far beyond the price I had been intending to pay.
8   Phil Powell, in correspondence with the author.
9   Both songs, of course, by The Dubliners; no climbing meet in the 1970s and 1980s was complete without a raucous rendition of these songs.
10 Trish Scott: diary entry in December 2003.
11 The main source of income came from donors, but that is not strictly 'earned' income.
12 Wall, however, wrote a generous piece about Scott in the 2021 *Alpine Journal*. It concluded, '. . . without Doug I would never have moved to Nepal and been able to lead the life I so enjoy today. I am forever indebted.'
13 Ian Wall, in an interview with the author.
14 Purna Gautam, in correspondence with the author.
15 'CAN's ethos', in CAN brochure *One Year After*, p. 13.
16 I know of at least one person present on that occasion who had intended to spend £200 on a limited edition photo of the Shishapangma area, but was seduced into paying £800 instead.
17 Phil Powell, in correspondence with the author.

Chapter 16

1   Maggie Burgess, in conversation with the author.
2   Jamie Mellor, in correspondence with the author.
3   Dickinson recounts that when on a climbing wall in Bristol with Scott on an E3 route, the manager instructed Scott to come down because his 'belaying was dangerous'. When told that it was the great Doug Scott, the manager remained dismissive. While it is generally agreed that Doug was a safe and careful climber, several stories suggest that Doug's belaying practices could at times be uncomfortably relaxed.
4   Tom Hornbein, in correspondence with the author.
5   Sally and Mike Bohling, in conversation with the author.
6   Stephen Venables, in conversation with the author.
7   Bonington, Chris, *The Everest Years*, p. 131.
8   An unfair criticism, in my view: Bonington had his mountaineering aims and worked for the best deals to realise them.

Chapter 17

1   Mark Higton, in correspondence with the author. The two following quotations are also edited versions of part of our correspondence.
2   John Roberts, in correspondence with the author.
3   Andy Syme, in correspondence with the author.
4   This paragraph's information is an amalgam of comments from Andy Syme, now president of the BMC, Jonathan White, Bob Pettigrew and me.
5   Simon and Jane Yates, in conversation with the author.
6   Michael and Sally Bohling, in conversation with the author.
7   Angela Locke, in conversation with the author.
8   Alice Maxwell in *Voice for Arran*, a monthly online magazine.
9   David Nightingale, in correspondence with the author.
10   Clive Tully, in correspondence with the author.
11   Richard Scott, in correspondence with the author.
12   Phil Bartlett's eulogy for Doug Scott, January 2021.
13   Marcia Fotheringham, in conversation with the author.
14   David Baker, in correspondence with the author.

Bibliography

Books and other publications by Doug Scott

Scott, D.K., *Mountaineering in Spain and Morocco: Expedition Report*, privately published (Nottingham, Autumn 1962)

Scott, D.K., *Tibesti: Expedition Report*, no publication details provided (presumed Nottingham, 1965)

Scott, D.K. (ed.), *Climbs on Derwent Valley Limestone*, Nottingham Climber's (sic) Club (Nottingham, 1965)

Scott, D.K., *The Cilo Dağ Mountains, S.E. Turkey: Expedition Report*, (Nottingham, 1966)

Scott, D.K. and Cheverst, W., *The Midlands Hindu Kush Expedition 1967: Expedition Report*, Dividend Token Press (Nottingham, 1968)

Scott, Doug, *Big Wall Climbing*, Kaye and Ward (London, 1974)

Scott, Doug and MacIntyre, Alex, *The Shishapangma Expedition*, Granada (London, 1984)

Scott, Doug, *Himalayan Climber: A Lifetime's Quest to the World's Greater Ranges*, Diadem Books (London, 1992)

Scott, Doug (ed.), *Philip's Guide to Mountains*, Philip's (London, 2005)

Scott, Doug, *Up and About: The Hard Road to Everest*, Vertebrate (Sheffield, 2015)

Scott, Doug, *The Ogre: Biography of a Mountain*, Vertebrate (Sheffield, 2017)

Scott, Doug, *Kangchenjunga, the Himalayan Giant*, Vertebrate (Sheffield, 2021)

Books to which Doug Scott contributed

Bell, Steve (ed.), *Seven Summits*, Octopus Publishing (New York, 2000), with an article on the Carstensz Pyramid by Doug Scott

Bonington, Chris, *Everest: The Hard Way*, Hodder & Stoughton (London, 1976), with an appendix on photography by Doug Scott and Ian Stuart

Bonington, Chris et al, *Changabang*, OUP (New York, 1976)

Bonington, Chris and Salkeld, Audrey, *Great Climbs: A Celebration of World Mountaineering*, Mitchell Beazley (London, 1994)

Child, Greg, *Thin Air: Encounters in the Himalayas*, Patrick Stephens Ltd (Yeovil, 1998), with a foreword by Doug Scott

Durkan, David, *Penguins on Everest*, Swami Kailash Publications (2012), with a foreword by Doug Scott

Haston, Dougal, *In High Places*, Canongate (Edinburgh, 2003), with an introduction by Doug Scott

Hornbein, Thomas F., *Everest, The West Ridge*, Third Edition, The Mountaineers (Seattle, 1989), with a preface by Doug Scott

Howard, Tony, *Troll Wall: The Untold Story of the British First Ascent*, Vertebrate (Sheffield, 2011), with a foreword by Doug Scott

Lewis-Jones, Huw, *Mountain Heroes: Portraits of Adventure,* Conway (London, 2011)

Norton, Lt-Col E.F., *The Fight for Everest 1924*, New Edition, Vertebrate (Sheffield, 2015), with a foreword by Doug Scott

Oread Mountaineering Club and Russell, Jean (ed.), *'Climb if You Will': A Commentary on Geoff Hayes*, Rocksport (UK, 1974), with a Scotland section contribution by Doug Scott

Parker, Philip, *Himalaya: The Exploration and Conquest of the Greatest Mountains on Earth*, Conway (London, 2013)

Smythe, Tony, *My Father Frank: Unresting Spirit of Everest*, Vertebrate (Sheffield, 2013), with a foreword by Doug Scott

Sutton, Geoffrey, *Artificial Aids in Mountaineering*, Second Edition 1970, Mountaineering Association with Nicholas Kaye (London, 1970), updated by Doug Scott

Wood, Rob, *Towards the Unknown Mountains*, Ptarmigan Press (Croydon, 1991), with a foreword by Doug Scott

Periodicals and magazines containing articles by or references to Doug Scott

Please see the Notes section of this book for individual article citations.

Adventure; Alpine Journal; Alpine Climbing Group Journal; Alpinist; American Alpine Journal; Appalachia Journal; The Atlantic; BMC Magazine; The British Empire; Cambridge University Mountaineering Club Journal; Canadian Alpine Journal; Ceunant Mountaineering Club Magazine; Climb and More; Climber; Climber and Rambler; Climbers' Club Journal; Climbing; Community Action Nepal Publications; County Climber (Northumbrian MC); The Daily Telegraph; Footless Crow; Fell and Rock Climbing Club Journal; Field and Trek; Global Health and Medicine; Gripped; Gritstone Club Journal; The Guardian; Hard Rock; High; Himalayan Journal; Indian Mountaineer; ISALP; Ladies' Alpine Club Journal; Lancashire Caving and Climbing Clubs Journal; Journal of the Midland Association of Mountaineers; Mountain; Mountain Heritage Trust collections; Mountain Gazette; The New Yorker; The Nottingham Post; The Observer; Oread Mountaineering Club Journal; Peaks, Passes and Glaciers; Pinnacle Club Journal; Rock and Ice Club Journal; Rucksack Club Journal; Scottish Mountaineering Club Journal; The Times; UIAA publications; UKClimbing; The Vulgarian Digest; Wayfarers' Club Journal; The Whole Earth Catalogue; Yorkshire Ramblers' Club Journal

Books relating to Doug Scott's climbing life
and other interests

Abbey, Edward, *Desert Solitaire: A Season in the Wilderness*, William Collins (London, 1968)

Abbot, A.E., *The Number Seven: Its Occult Significance in Human Life*, Emerson Press (London, 1962)

Allan, Sandy, *In Some Lost Place: The First Ascent of Nanga Parbat's Mazeno Ridge*, Vertebrate (Sheffield, 2015)

Alpine Club & Royal Geographical Society and Douglas, Ed (ed.), *Mountaineers*, Dorling Kindersley (London, 2011)

Angell, Shirley, *Pinnacle Club: A History of Women Climbing*, Pinnacle Club (London, 1988)

Armitage, Jill, *Nottingham: A History*, Amberley (Stroud, 2015)

Baird, Patrick D., *The Polar World*, Longmans (London, 1964)

Bartlett, Phil, *The Undiscovered Country*, The Ernest Press (Glasgow, 1993)

Berry, Steve, *Straight Up: Himalayan Tales of the Unexpected*, Vertebrate (Sheffield, 2015)

Bettembourg, Georges, *The White Death*, Reynard House (Seattle, 1981)

Blum, Arlene, *Breaking Trail*, Simon & Schuster (New York, 2006)

Boardman, Peter, *The Shining Mountain*, Arrow Books, Hutchinson (London, 1980)

Bonatti, Walter, *The Mountains of My Life*, Penguin (London, 2001)

Bonington, Chris, *Everest, the Hard Way*, Arrow Books, Hutchinson (London, 1977)

Bonington, Chris, *Quest for Adventure*, Hodder & Stoughton (London, 1981)

Bonington, Chris, *The Everest Years: A Climber's Life*, Coronet Books, Hodder & Stoughton (London, 1986)

Boysen, Martin, *Hanging On: A life inside British Climbing's Golden Age*, Vertebrate (Sheffield, 2014)

Braham, Trevor, *Himalayan Playground*, In Pinn (Glasgow, 2008)

Buchman, Frank, *Remaking the World: The Collected Speeches of Dr Frank Buchman*, Blandford Press (London, 1961)

Burgess, Adrian and Alan, *The Burgess Book of Lies*, The Mountaineers (Seattle, 1994)

Carson, Rachel, *Silent Spring*, Houghton Mifflin (New York, 1962)

Child, Greg, *Thin Air: Encounters in the Himalayas*, Patrick Stephens Ltd (Yeovil, 1998)

Child, Greg, *Mixed Emotions,* The Mountaineers, (Seattle, 1993)

Child, Greg, *Postcards from the Ledge*, The Mountaineers (Seattle, 2000)

Coffey, Maria, *Where the Mountain Casts Its Shadow*, St. Martin's Griffin (New York, 2003)

Cool, Kenton, *One Man's Everest*, Cornerstone (London, 2016)

Craig, Robert W., *Storm and Sorrow in the High Pamirs*, Simon & Schuster (New York, 1980)

David-Neel, Alexandra, *Buddhism: its Doctrines and Methods*, The Bodley Head (Oxford, 1977)

Dickinson, Leo, *Anything is Possible*, Jonathan Cape (London, 1989)

Diemberger, Kurt, *Spirits of the Air*, Hodder & Stoughton (London, 1994)

Drasdo, Harold, 'Margins of Safety', *Alpine Journal*, Alpine Club (London, 1969)

Drasdo, Harold, *The Ordinary Route*, The Ernest Press (Glasgow, 1997)

Drengson, Alan and Inoue, Yuichi, *The Deep Ecology Movement: An Introductory Anthology*, North Atlantic Books (California, 1995)

Elwin, Verrier, *The Tribal World of Verrier Elwin: An Autobiography*, Oxford University Press (Oxford, 1964)

Gallagher, Winifred, 'How We Become What We Are', *The Atlantic* (New York, September 1994)

Gee, Christine and Weare, Garry, *Everest: The View from the Top*, Rider Press (London, 2003)

Gill, Michael, *Edmund Hillary: A Biography*, Vertebrate (Sheffield, 2020)

Godfrey, Bob and Chelton, Dudley, *Climb!*, Routledge (New York, 1980)

Graves, Robert, *White Goddess: A Historical Grammar of Poetic Myth*, Faber & Faber (London, 1948)

Gray, Dennis, *Rope Boy*, Victor Gollancz (London, 1970)

Gray, Dennis, *Mountain Lover*, The Crowood Press (Swindon, 1990)

Hall, Brian, *High Risk*, Sandstone Press (Dingwall, 2022)

Harding, John, *Distant Snows: A Mountaineer's Odyssey*, Bâton Wicks (Macclesfield, 2016)

Harwood, A.C., *The Recovery of Man in Childhood*, imprint unknown (1971)

Haston, Dougal, *In High Places*, Canongate (Edinburgh, 2003)

Hesse, Hermann, *Poems*, Jonathan Cape (London, 1977)

Hinkes, Alan, *8000 metres*, Cicerone, (Milnthorpe, 2013)

Houlding, Leo, *Closer to the Edge: Climbing to the Ends of the Earth*, Headline Publishing (London, 2022)

Howard, Tony, *Treks and Climbs in Wadi Rum, Jordan*, Cicerone (Milnthorpe, 1987)

Isserman, Maurice and Weaver, Stewart, *Fallen Giants*, Yale University Press (New Haven, 2008)

Jitendra, Bothara, S.B., *Improving the Seismic Performance of Stone Masonry Buildings*, Earthquake Engineering Research Institute (Oakland, 2011)

Jung, C.G., *Memories, Dreams, Reflections*, Vintage Books (New York, 1965)

Kapadia, Harish, *Into the Untravelled Himalaya*, Indus Publishing (New Delhi, 2005)

Laski, Marghanita, *The Offshore Island*, Cresset Press (London, 1959)

Lewis, Franklin D., *Rumi: Past and Present, East and West: The Life, Teaching and Poetry of Jalal Al-Din Rumi*, Simon & Schuster (London, 2014)

Liedloff, Jean, *The Continuum Concept*, Penguin (London, 1989)

Longfellow, H.W., *Poetical Works*, Routledge (London, 1877)

Lowe, Jeff, *Ice World*, The Mountaineers (Seattle, 1996)

Macartney-Snape, Tim, *Mountain Adventurer*, Jacaranda Press (Milton, 1992)

Mazeaud, Pierre, *Naked before the Mountain*, Gollancz (London, 1974)

McDonald, Bernadette, *Art of Freedom*, Vertebrate (Sheffield, 2017)

McDonald, Pete, *The Story of the White Hall Centre*, privately published (Dunedin, 2018)

McLewin, Will, *In Monte Viso's Horizon*, The Ernest Press (Glasgow, 1992)

Michener, James, *Centennial*, Corgi (London, 1976)

Milburn, Geoff (ed.) with Walker, Derek and Wilson, Ken, *The First Fifty Years of the British Mountaineering Council*, BMC (Manchester, 1997)

Miller, Lauren De Launay (ed.), *Valley of Giants: Stories from the Women at the Heart of Yosemite Climbing*, The Mountaineers (Seattle, 2022)

Montaigne, Michel de, *Complete Essays*, Penguin Classics (London, 1993)

Moorehead, Catherine, *The K2 Man (and His Molluscs)*, In Pinn (Glasgow, 2013)

Murray, Bill, *The Story of Everest*, J.M. Dent (London, 1953)

Nicolson, Adam, *The Mighty Dead: Why Homer Matters*, William Collins (London, 2014)

Norberg-Hodge, Helena, *Ancient Futures*, Ebury Publishing (London, 2000)

Nunn, Paul, *At the Sharp End*, Unwin Hyman (London, 1988)

Packard, Vance, *The Hidden Persuaders*, Penguin (London, 1962)

Pearson, W. and Utting, G., *Milarepa Health Post; CAN post-Earthquake Reconstruction Report*, canepal.org.uk (Hesket Newmarket, 2016)

Perrin, Jim, *The Villain: The Life of Don Whillans*, Arrow Books (London, 2006)

Porter, John, *One Day as a Tiger*, Vertebrate (Sheffield, 2014)

Pritchard, Paul, *Deep Play*, Bâton Wicks (Macclesfield, 1997)

Rampa, Lobsang, *The Third Eye*, Secker & Warburg (London, 1956)

Rébuffat, Gaston, *Starlight and Storm*, J.M. Dent & Sons Ltd (London, 1956)

Reich, Charles A., *The Greening of America*, Random House (New York, 1970)

Robbins, Royal, *Basic Rockcraft*, La Siesta Press (Los Angeles, 1971)

Robbins, Royal, *Advanced Rockcraft*, La Siesta Press (Los Angeles, 1973)

Roberts, David, *Moments of Doubt and Other Mountaineering Writings*, The Mountaineers (Seattle, 1986)

Sale, Richard, *The Challenge of K2*, Pen & Sword (Barnsley, 2011)

Samet, Matt (ed.), *Vantage Point: Fifty Years of the Best Climbing Stories Ever Told in Climbing Magazine*, Globe Pequot (Connecticut, 2018)

Saunders, Victor, *No Place to Fall*, Hodder & Stoughton (London, 1994)

Saunders, Victor, *Structured Chaos*, Vertebrate (Sheffield, 2021)

Scott, Chic, *Pushing the Limits: The Story of Canadian Mountaineering*, Rocky Mountain Books (Calgary, 2000)

Shatayev, Vladimir, *Degrees of Difficulty*, The Mountaineers (Seattle, 1987)

Shute, Nevil, *On the Beach*, Heinemann (London, 1957)

Sillitoe, Alan, *Saturday Night and Sunday Morning*, W.H. Allen (London, 1958)

Sillitoe, Alan, *Mountains and Caverns: Selected Essays*, W.H. Allen (London, 1975)

Smart, David, *Emilio Comici: Angel of the Dolomites*, Rocky Mountain Books (Calgary, 2020)

Steffen, Will, *Himalayan Dreaming: Australian Mountaineering in the Great Ranges of Asia*, ANU Press (Canberra, 2010)

Stevenson, David, *Warnings against Myself: Meditations on a Life in Climbing*, University of Washington Press (Washington, 2018)

Swenson, Steve, *Karakoram: Climbing through the Kashmir Conflict*, Mountaineers (Seattle, 2017)

Tasker, Joe, *Savage Arena*, Methuen (London, 1982)

Tejada-Flores, Lito, *Games Climbers Play*, Ascent (1967)

Thompson, Simon, *Unjustifiable Risk? The Story of British Climbing*, Cicerone (Milnthorpe, 2010)

Tolkien, J.R.R., *The Lord of the Rings*, George Allen & Unwin, (London, 1954)

Tolstoy, Leo, *War and Peace*, The Russian Messenger (Moscow, 1869)

Tullis, Julie, *Clouds from Both Sides*, Grafton Books, Collins (London, 1987)

Twight, Mark, *Kiss or Kill: Confessions of a Serial Climber*, The Mountaineers (Seattle, 2003)

Viesturs, Ed with Roberts, David, *K2*, Broadway Books (New York, 2009)

Watts, Alan, *Tao: The Watercourse Way*, Pantheon (New York, 1975)

Wilson, Ken (ed.), *The Games Climbers Play*, Bâton Wicks (London, 2006)

Wood, Rob, *At Home in Nature: A Life in Unknown Mountains*, Rocky Mountain Books (Calgary, 1991)

Wordsworth, William, *The Prelude, or, Growth of a Poet's Mind*, Edward Moxon (London, 1850)

Yates, Simon, *The Flame of Adventure*, Vintage (London, 2002)

Yates, Simon, *The Wild Within*, Vertebrate, (Sheffield, 2012)

Yeshe Losal, Rinpoché, *From a Mountain in Tibet*, Penguin Life (London, 2020)

Acknowledgements

My especial thanks to Trish, for her magnificent hospitality and her candour, and for so readily giving me free access to Doug's archive, as well as her and Doug's personal papers.

For maintaining this biographer's morale and for extraordinary help with the text, I would very much like to thank Sandy and Alma Allan, Sir Chris and Lady Bonington, Tut Braithwaite, Greg Child, John Cleare, Dr Jim Duff, Christine Gee, Lindsay Griffin, Steve and Lucie Goodwin, Tom Hornbein, Pamela MacGregor, Bob Pettigrew MBE, Victor Saunders and the Scott family: Brian, Garry, Martha, Rosie, Arran, Euan, Richard – particularly for his genealogical work - and Tena Walton.

I'd very much like to thank Stephen Venables for his enjoyably precise, expertly expressed foreword.

My thanks to Snævarr Guðmunsson for all his detailed work on the complicated Iceland section. And to Mark Bowen for his meticulous help with a wide variety of textual questions. My thanks to Anne Manger for all her work in deciphering and typing Doug's diaries.

David Nightingale worked tirelessly and with the greatest care on vast numbers of photographs; I'm most grateful for all he has done.

A very big thanks to Guy Lee for his work in sorting Doug's photographs and for all his help with the text (plus some excellent stories!).

My thanks to Andrew Simmons at Birlinn for so cheerfully and professionally keeping me on the editorial path of righteousness. My thanks also to Craig Hillsley for his rigorous copy-editing and to the promotions team at Birlinn for their hard work.

I would very much like to thank my Agent, Robert Dudley, for his wise and experienced support.

Doug touched many lives. I'd like to thank all of the following people for their help, so freely and enthusiastically given:

Stein P. Aasheim; Keshab Adhikari; Iain Allan; Dan Ambler (Manchester Gritstone Club); Robert Mads Anderson; Ang Phurba (and son); Ang Tsering; Robin Ashcroft; David Baker; Phil Bartlett; Christine Baxter-Jones; Stuart Beare and Cheryl Wells; Steve Berry; Binod, KC; Mike and Sally Bohling; Chris Brown; Cara Buchan; Adrian and Alan Burgess; Maggie and Patrick Burgess; John Calden;

Dr Robin Campbell; Tomas Carlström; Brian Clarke; Margaret Clennett, Archivist of the Pinnacle Club; Richard Cowper; Frances Daltry; Clive and Sue Davies; Janet Dean; Dhapa Dorje Lama; Leo Dickinson; Professor Hildegard Diemberger; Colin Downer; David Durkan; 'NE'; Neil Edgar; Phil Ershler; Mike Esten; Jim and Marcia Fotheringham; Julian Freeman-Attwood; Jeff and Jennie Frew; Allen Fyffe MBE; Liz Garside; Murari Gautam; Purna Gautam; Ray Gillies; Peter Gillman; Ariane Giobellina; Dennis Gray (and John Appleyard); Ted Grey; Pema Gyalpo; Peter Habeler; Dez Hadlum; Brian Hall; Cathy Harlow (translations from Icelandic); Molly Higgins; Mark Higton; Beth Hodgett, erstwhile AC Librarian; Bob Holmes; Alexander Huber; Pasang Wangchu Hyolmo; Katie Ives; Catriona Jennings; Andy Jess; George Jones; Nick Kekus; Kalpana Khadka; Maina Kharkhi; Steve Komito; Vojciech Kurtyka; Nimala Lamichhane; Angela and Colin Locke; Dr Rob Lorge; Chris Lovell and the BBC Research Dept; Deb Macartney-Snape; Tim Macartney-Snape; Steph Macdonald; Gina Madgett; Jon Maguire; Maureen Mansell; Chris Martin; Elaine Matthews; Bernadette McDonald; Pete McDonald; Richard and Barbara McHardy; Roger Mear; Jamie Mellor; Reinhold Messner; Andrew Moore; Ruth and Gordon Moore; Colin Mortlock; Alan 'Mossy' Moss; Sjur Nesheim; Bikram Neupane; Lyn Noble; Skip Novak; Linda Orritt; Knútur Óskarsson; Ann Oswin; Brian Palmer; Kopila Panta; Andy Parkin; Mike Parsons; Pertemba Sherpa; Mike Poppleston; John Porter; Phil Powell and Sarah Loving; Denise Prior; Jon Punshon; HHJ Alison Raeside; Tom Ramage; Shrijana Ranjeet; Salman Rashid; Steve Razzetti; Steve Read; Mark Richey; Rick Ridgeway; John Roberts; Professor Ritchie Robertson; David Rose; Dr Barney and Rachel Rosedale; Clive and Fiona Rowland; Nazir Sabir; Bob A. Schelfhout-Aubertijn; Professor Mike Searle; Carol Secombe; Alija Shahi; Bob Shaw; Sanjiv Singh; Sonam Dorje Sherpa; Binita Shrestha; Boj Raj Shrestha; Dr Monahon Lol Shrestha; Steve 'Sid' Smith; Dr Claire Souch and Dr Till Pelney; Dick Stroud; Geoff and Barbara Stroud; Julie Summers; Stephen Sustad; Steven Swenson; Andy Syme; Bhai B. Tamang; Mangale Tamang; Pema Tamang; Tej Tamang; John Tasker; Terry Tasker; Peter Thompson; Clive Tully; Helen Urquhart; Glyn Utting; Professor L. Mikel Vause; Björgvin Vigfússon; Eric Vola; Ian Wall; Larry Ware; Bob Wark; Celia Washington; Dr Mike Webster; Susan Webster; Ted Wells; Sally Westmacott; Jonathan White; David 'Wink' Wilkinson; Rob and Laurie Wood; Simon and Jane Yates.

The author gratefully acknowledges the Oread Mountaineering Club's kind permission to reproduce an extract from their 1974 publication *Climb If You Will: A Commentary on Geoff Hayes*.

General Index

Note: Numbers in italics refer to pages on which black-and-white photographs are reproduced

Aasheim, Stein P. 182, 329
Abalakov, Vitaly 131
Aberdonian Kellas Expedition 222
Absalom, David 260
Adhikari, Keshab 260, 261, 329
Afanassieff, Jean 170, 172, 174,175, 176, 177, 199
Aga Khan Rural Support Programme 243
Akester, Roger 74
Allan, Eunice 210
Allan, Iain 124, 329
Allan, Sandy 178, 180, 181, 182, 184, 209, 210, 212, 229, 318n, 319n, 325, 329
Allen, Alison 178, 209, 210, 213
Allen, Rick 177, 178, 180, 181, 209, 213
Allen, Tinsel 43, 44
Alpine Climbing Group (see climbing clubs)
Alpine Club (see climbing clubs)
Alpine Journal 86, 101, 109, 118, 161, 162, 204, 223, 280, 295, 312n, 314n, 315ns, 317n, 318n, 320ns, 324, 326
Altos 181, 242
American Alpine Journal 315n, 318n
Anderson, Robert Mads 213, 329
Ang Dawa, Sherpa 130
Angell, Shirley 61, 325
Ang Phurba, Sherpa 136, 141, 143, 168, 174, 175, 179, 250, 270, 281, 329

Anthoine, Jackie 139
Anthoine, Mo 96, 138, 139, 140, 141, 317n
Armathwaite 231, 289
Ashcroft, Robin 256, 257, 291, 329
Askole 134, 138, 141, 242

Bacon, Chris(py) 207
Bahrabise xxi, 224, 241, 244, 260, 263, 305, Plate 40
Baird, Pat 113, 114, 325
Baker, David 205, 234, 295, 319n, 320n, 321n, 329
Bartlett, Phil 218, 219, 295, 321n, 325, 329
Baslow 28, 42, 43, 97, 157
Bathgate, Dave 130
Baxter, Chris 202
Baxter-Jones, Christine 165, 329
Baxter-Jones, Roger 165, 170, 172, 174, 178, 192, 193
Beagle Channel xxiv, 216,
Beard, Eric 43, 52
Benediktsson, Helgi 194, 196, 205, 206, 207, 208
Berry, Steve 198, 199, 325, 329
Bettembourg, Georges 141, 142, 143, 144, 164, 167, 168, 174, 186, 188, 189, 191, 317n, 325
Bhadur, Bomb 177
Bhutan xxi, 194, 198, 199, 200, 228
Biella, Theses of 235
Big Lottery Fund 247

Birkbeck, Lyn 229
Biven, Peter 39, 311n
Boardman, Peter ix, 135, 141, 142, 143,
    144, 169, 170, 181, 220, 315n,
    316n, 317ns, 325, Plates 19 & 20
Boardman-Tasker Award 275
Bobek, Prof. Hans 82, 313n
Bohling, Mike and Sally 290, 321ns,
    329n
Bolger, Terry 112
Bonatti Pillar 50, 68, 106, 218, 300
Bonatti Route (Grand Capucin) 62, 298
Bonatti, Walter 276, 296, 325
Bonington, Sir Chris ix, 51, 61, 74,
    102, 103, 118, 119, 120, 128, 129,
    130, 133, 134, 135, 136, 138, 139,
    140, 140, 141, 156, 158, 159, 162,
    169, 170, 197, 225, 235, 238, 241,
    246, 251, 257, 265, 266, 272, 275,
    277, 278, 279, 287, 289, 294, 295,
    296, 301, 302, 312n, 316ns,
    321ns, 323, 325, 329, Plate 41
Bonington, Lady (Loreto) 279, 329
Bonington, Wendy 157, 279
Bowen, Mark 183, 214, 217, 218, 219,
    232, 304, 319n, 329
Bowes, Steve 46, 62, 70, 72, 73
Boysen, Martin 118, 119, 120, 135
Braithwaite, Paul (Tut) 116, 117, 118,
    123, 124, 131, 132, 133, 135, 136,
    138, 139, 140, 141, 169, 184, 192,
    212, 214, 266, 279, 291, 294, 239
Brasher, Chris 130, 158
British Mountaineering Council (BMC)
    57, 131, 158, 277, 279, 280, 284,
    285, 286, 287, 288, 309n, 310n,
    321n, 324, 327
Brook, Elaine 118, 192
Brook, Tom 96
Brookes, Colin (Choe) 174, 175,
    176
Brown, Joe 29, 37, 52, 53, 65, 141,
    289, 290, 310ns, 311n, 312n
Bruce, Larry 151, 152, 153, 174, 175,
    176
Burgess, Adrian 165, 318n, 325, 329
Burgess, Derek 56

Burgess, Maggie 148, 199, 200, 229,
    271, 317n, 321n, 329
Burgess, Patrick 271, 329
Burke, Beth 129, 130
Burke, Mick 114, 115, 130, 135, 136,
    139, 273, 315n, 316n

CAFOD 247, 262, 265
Cairngorms xvi, 20, 43, 49, 50, 51, 52,
    80, 113, 164, 250, 299, 300, 311n
Cairngorms (Lochan Buidhe) disaster
    37, 158
Calden, John 156, 161, 317n, 318n,
    329
Carlström, Tomas and Sissel 182, 330
Carrock Fell 289, 306
Carter, Sir David 269
Cheney, Mike 241, 242, 249
Cheverst, William (Bill) 52, 65, 67, 86,
    87, 90, 91, 323
Child, Greg 166, 170, 171, 172, 173,
    177, 178, 187, 188, 189, *190*, 191,
    192, 193, 194, 196, 208, 209, 222,
    223, 318ns, 319n, 323, 325, 329,
    Plate 29
Chile 205, 215, 273, 306, 319n
Chouinard Route (FitzRoy) 212, 304
Chouinard, Yvon 110, 124, 235, 315n
Christchurch (New Zealand) xxii, 151,
    162, 186
Cicerone, publishers 311n, 326, 328
Cleare, John 102–3, 148, 157, 225–6,
    311ns, 314n, 317n, 329
climbing clubs
    Alpine x, 5, 57, 61, 102, 160, 227,
    235, 236, 237, 241, 272, 277,
    285, 286, 309n, 312n, 324, 325,
    326; Alpine Climbing Group 69,
    126, 324; American Alpine 117,
    243; Austrian 46; background and
    history 25–7; Bradford Lads 41,
    310n; French (*Club Alpin Français*)
    70; German (*Deutscher Alpenverein*)
    235; Nottingham Climbers' 1, 30,
    40–3, 46–8, 59, 62, 64–9, 78, 83,
    86, 93, 95, 103, 113, 126, 145,
    157, 173, 295, 313n; Oread 33,

34, 40, 41, 102, 324, 330; Pinnacle
324, 325, 330; Rock and Ice 33,
40, 41, 47, 310n, 324
Community Action Nepal (CAN) xi,
17, 23, 199, 220, 224, 226, 227,
240, 245, 246, 247, 251, 267
'Build Back Better' campaign 262,
263
buildings 244, 248–9, 251–3, 256,
257, 261–2, 263, 266, Plate 39
earthquake 259–67, Plate 38
ethos 243–5
founding 79, 164, 240–3
fundraising 102, 245, 247, 257, 265–
6; auctions 265, 291; Day of the
Dog 257; Everest Stair Challenge
266; lectures 234, 238, 245, 246,
256–7, 266, 290–2; photos and
posters 105, 245, 246, 247, 257;
Stewart Hill Cottage Open Day
245
management 247, 249, 254, 258,
259, 260, 262, 267
Maoists (and insurgency) 251–3,
254, 255
medicine 245, 253–4
policies 255, 261, 263–5
Shramadhan 243, 244, 253, 263
Social Welfare Council 262–3
trustees 246, 247, 249, 251, 252,
260, 267, 296
Community Action Treks (CAT) 130,
240, 247–8, 250, 251, 255, 257,
320n
Covington, Michael 117, 121, 152,
166, 167, 168
Cowper, Richard 179, 180, 209, 210,
214, 224, 230, 318n, 320n, 330
Crew, Peter 53, 312n
Cullen, John 211
Cundy, Malcolm (Pike) 214

Dani 217
Darjeeling 196, 199, 222, 227, 241
Davies, Clive 14, 42, 47, 62, 70, *71*, 73,
77, 79, *94*, 117, 118, 175, 176,
194, 330

Davies, Sue 175, 176, 194, 330
Delhi, New 119, 187, 199, 203, 218,
222
Dickinson, Leo 107, 108, 109, 139,
142, 273, 314n, 321n, 326, 330
Diemberger, Professor Hildegard 257,
330
Diemberger, Kurt 226, 326
Dipendra, Prince 247, 255
Dog and Partridge, Battle of 42
Donini, Jim 276
Downer, Colin 164, 165, 187, 206,
230, 232, 271, 330
Drasdo, Harold 29, 31, 48, 310ns, 326
Duff, Dr James (Jim) 135, 164, 169,
170, 183, 185, 186, 202, 203, 230,
271, 318n, 329
Durkan, David 247, 320n, 323, 330
Dyhrenfurth, Norman 127, 128, 237

Eden Valley 289
Edgar, Neil 245, 246, 330
Efimov, Sergei 179, 213
Egglescliffe School 266
Eiger xviii, 67, 170, 224, 225, 226, 304
Eldorado Springs 150
Elizabeth II, Queen 17, 155, 307n,
314n
English, Mervyn 185, 187, Plate 24
Ershler, Phil 172, 173, 330
Eskdale Outward Bound School 32, 40,
297
Estcourt, Nick 130, 135, 136, 138, 139,
140, 141, 169, 170, 279
Evans, Brian 44, 311n

Fedden, H.R. 82, 313n
Fleming, John 87, 90
Fotheringham, Jim 206, 207, 230,
234, 238, 239, 274, 288, 319n,
330
Fotheringham, Marcia 295, 321n,
330
Fowler, Mick 164, 235
Fox, Roger 244
Freeman-Attwood, Julian 215, 216,
218, 219, 224, 330

Frew, Jeff 246, 250, 330
Fullalove, Jim (Dan Boon) 164, 174, 175
Fyffe, Allen 20, 40, 51, 52, 135, 320n, 330

Gangkhar Puensum 198–9
Gangotri (river, town, glacier) xxi, 186, 187, 188, 302
Garside, Mick 27, 29, 30, 31, 50, 51, 64, 66, 73, 74, 77, 78, *94*
Gaumukh 186, 187, 188
Gautam, Murari 247, 249, 254, 260, 262, 267, 288, 294, 330, Plate 40
Gautam, Purna 249, 252, 256, 259, 320n, 330
Gee, Christine 154, 160, 161, 162, 202, 229, 237, 272, 318n, 326, 329
Geirsson, Jón 205
Geographical Magazine 82
Gers 271
Ghunsa (CAN) xxi, 243, 244, 247, 250, 251, 253, 255, 266, 317n
Ghunsa (Kangchenjunga trek) 142, 317n
Gillies, Ray 34, 42, 48, 50, 52, 62, 64, 67, 70, 73, 75, 77, 87, 88, 91, *94*, 107, 114, 330, Plate 13
Gillman, Peter 107, 314n, 330
Giobellina, Ariane 162, 168, 174, 175, 185, 186, 271, 318ns, 319n, 330
Gippenreiter, Yevgeniy (Eugene) 132, 316n
Glenmore Lodge 20, 40, 49, 158, 230
Godwin-Austen Glacier 173
Godwin-Austen, Henry Haversham 318n
Goodwin, Steve and Lucie 230, 289, 320n, 329
Gorkha, North 241, 243, 244, 259, 263
Graham, Mick 19, 20, 21
Gray, Dennis 40, 41, 42, 43, 74, *94*, 94, 101, 102, 131, 158, 279, 286, 312n, 313n, 326, 330
Grey, Ted 162, 205, 318n, 330
Griffin, Lindsay 200, 201, 202, 218, 219, 220, 229

Guðjónsson, Þorsteinn 205
Guðmunsson, Snævarr 194, 205, 206, 296, 329
Gyaldzen 252, 254

Habeler, Peter 88, 110, 111, 276, 291, 315ns, 317n, 330, Plate 10
Hadlum, Dez 19, 27, 29, 34, 40, 56, 59, *94*, 117, 230, 233, 310n, 320n, 330
Hahn, Dr Kurt 26, 309n
Hall, Brian 167, 168, 169, 174, 175, 176, 265, 318ns, 326, 330
Happer, Mr 29, 80, 85
Haston, Dougal ix, 119, 120, 122, 123, 130, 135, 136, 137, 155, 162, 174, 271, 277, 301, 316n, 324, 326, Plate 16
Hawley, Elizabeth 198, 199
Hayden, Wes 22, 27, 32, 33, 34, 55, 56
Hayes, Geoff 33, 34, 324, 330
Helambu xxi, 244, 246, 252, 271, 306
Hennek, Dennis 107, 108, 110, 114, 115, 116, 118, 121, 126, Plate 13
Herrligkoffer, Dr Karl 127, 128, 130, 241, 284
Hesse, Hermann 100, 149, 161, 317n, 326
Higgins, Molly 99, 121, 132, 148, 149, 150, 151, 152, 153, 174, 175, 176, 317n, 330
Higton, Mark 321n, 330
Hillary, Sir Edmund xiii, 13, 136, 235, 241, 271, 326
'Himalayan Expeditions' 160
Hinkes, Al 177, 178, 179, 326
Hira 253
Holmes, Robert (Bob) 47, 85, 87, 91, 104, 157, 229, 311n, 313n, 314n, 330
Hong Kong 272
Hopkinson, Pip 252
Hornbein, Tom 274, 288, 321n, 324, 329
Howard, Tony 112, 198, 319n, 324, 326
Howell, Baron Dennis 159
Howell, Ian 124
Huber, Alexander 235, 320n, 330

Hunt, Lord ix, 19, 37, 81, 130, 159, 225, 309n, 319n, 320n

Indian Mountaineering Foundation (IMF) 187, 196, 203, 218
Ingoldmells 16
International Porter Protection Group 247
Iran 87, 128, 138, 210, 272, 273
Istanbul 81, 87
Itakura, Professor 95

Jess, Andy 197, 330
John Player's 2, 10, 19, 114, 307n
Jones, George (Yoff) 46, 48, 87, 90, 330

Kambalung Caves 272, 306
Karakoram Highway 179, 194
Karki, Maina 260
Kathmandu xxi, 129, 146, 154, 178, 181, 198, 211, 234, 238, 243, 244, 245, 247, 249, 251, 252, 253, 254, 256, 257, 258, 259, 260, 262, 267, 270, 271, 280, 320n
Kekoo Naoroji Prize 275, 288
Kekus, Nick 146, 181, 182, 203, 204, 238, 314n, 317n, 330
Kemp, Dennis 202
Kendal, Mountain (Film) Festival 257, 294
Khadkha, Kalpana 253
Kharki, Jiban 254
Koch, Phil 114, 115, Plate 13
Komito, Steve 117, 151, 156, 330
Kuen, Felix 128, 129
Kurds 82, 84, 85
Kurtyka, Wojciech (Voytek) 88, 179, 180, 276, 289, 296, 330
Kutumsang 243, 252, 261, 262, 266, 270
Kyrgyzstan xx, 131, 288

Lake Placid xxiii, 272
Lang, Peter 268, 269, 270
Langtang 181, 241, 246, 252, 260, 261, 262, 303, 306
Lauria, Don 110

Lee, Guy 41, 43, 46, 51, 87, 91, 99, 106, 107, 112, 114, 115, 118, 131, 132, 133, 206, 229, 230, 232, 294, 316n, 320n, 329
Lenton 2, 8, 95
Leysin xviii, 271, 287, 306
Lochan Buidhe disaster (see Cairngorms Disaster)
Lock, Andrew 180)
Locke, Angela 246, 275, 290, 321n, 330
London School of Medicine 266
Longland, Sir John (Jack) ix, 26, 30, 86, 158, 308n, 309n
Lorge, Dr Robert (Rob) 245, 250, 253, 254, 255, 258, 260, 294, 330
Loving, Sarah 256, 330
Lowe, Jeff 133, 148
Lukla 130, 167

Macartney-Snape, Tim 172, 173, 203, 231, 318n, 326, 330
Machermo 262, 271
MacInnes, Hamish 51, 128, 135, 238, 317n
MacIntyre, Alex 165, 192, 193, 220, 275, 317n, 319n, 323
Madgett, Gina 153, 154, 231, 317n, 320n, 330
Mahant Maharaj, Swami 162
Mallory, George 67, 236, 309n
Manali 197, 198, 303
Manger, Anne 329
Mansell, Gordon 29, 31, 32, 310n, 311n
Mansell, Maureen 31, 32, 330
Manton, Brian 64
Maria Theresa's 215
Matthews, Elaine 116, 315n, 330
McHardy, Richard and Barbara 184, 330
Meadows, Dan 47, 73
Mear, Roger 211, 212, 220, 221, 330
Melamchigaun 244, 249, 256, 259, 261, 271
Mellor, Jamie 271, 321n, 330
Messner, Reinhold 88, 127, 170, 175, 197, 235, 276, 289, 294, 296, 317n, 330
Milarepa health post 270, 306, 327

Miller, Mark 177, 194, 195, 196

Mingma, Sherpa boy 135

Mitteleggi Hut incident 225–6

Moel Siabod Café 245

Mooney K.C., Terry 174, 175, 177, 195, 196, 220, 249, 250, 251

Moore, Ruth 249, 330

Moores, Paul 212

Morell, Tom 230

Mortimer, Mike 280

Mortlock, Colin 38, 60, 330

Mountain Heritage 40, 324

Mountain magazine 26, 101, 315n, 324

Mountaineering Association 30, 57, 60, 61, 62, 324

Mount Everest Foundation 73–4, 78, 86, 114, 158, 181, 220

Muir, John 112, 276

Muktananda, Swami 162

Mumbai xx, 198, 227, 275, 288, 303, 306

Munros, The 35, 36, 165, 310n

Mustang 250, 257

'NE' 227, 230, 237, 238, 239

Nepal xi, xiv, 17, 23, 91, 113, 142, 148, 151, 155, 174, 181, 185, 192, 199, 204, 205, 211, 224, 238, 240–3, 245, 247, 248, 249, 251, 253, 254, 256, 257, 258, 259, 260, 262, 264, 265, 267, 270–3, 276, 288, 290, 292, 295, 302, 305, 306, 320n; architecture and buildings 271; crafts xi, 245, 257; government 236, 243, 244, 258, 262, 263, 265, 267; map xxi; monarchy 247, 251

Nepalis (see also under individual names) 17, 146, 199, 204, 240, 243, 247, 248, 250, 259, 271, 275, 286

Nesheim, Sjur 182, 183, 305, 330

Nga Temba, Sherpa 179

Nicol, Dave 48, 68, 106, 208

Nightingale, David 291, 321n, 329

Nima Tensing, Sherpa 141, 143, 182

Nobande Sobande Glacier 210

Noble, Lyn 37, 38, 40, 58, 59, 62, 311ns, 312n, 330

Norbu, Sherpa 119

Norris, Andy 177

Nottingham xvi, 1–8, 10, 14, 17, 19, 20, 22, 25, 27, 28, 32, 33, 35, 37, 38, 41, 42, 50, 58, 59, 61, 62, 64, 67, 72, 78, 79, 81, 85, 86, 91, 95, 99, 101, 102, 103, 105, 117, 122, 126, 131, 148, 149, 154, 155, 156, 162, 221, 278, 289, 292, 301, 307n, 308n, 318n, 323, 325

Nottingham Climbers' Club (see under climbing clubs)

Novak, Skip 215, 216, 218, 219, 220, 330

Nunn, Paul 44, 116, 131, 132, 327

Nyalam x, 182, 192

Oelz, Prof Dr 166

Olympic Games 8, 20, 131, 277, 284, 285

Oswin, David and Ann 157, 205, 207, 210, 230, 238, 249, 292, 330

Outdoor Education 25, 29, 30 (see also Eskdale and White Hall)

Outward Bound 25, 26, 156, 309n

Oxford 256, 265, 312n

Palmer, Brian (Henry) 53, 66, 83, 86, 87, 90, 91, 126, 312ns, 330

Palzor, Sonam 203, 204

Parkin, Andy 170, 171, 172, 177, 261, 294, 318n, 330

Parsons, Mike 211, 212, 330

Pasang, Sherpa 174, 175, 223

Pasang Wangchu Hyolmo, Sherpa 252, 330

Patey, Tom 51

Partridge, Keith 265

Pelagic, SS 214, 215, 216

Pellny, Dr Till 264

Perchine, Valeri 179, 213

Pershin (see Perchine)

Pertemba, Sherpa (PT) 135, 136, 167, 218, 271, 294, 316n, 330

Pettigrew, Robert (Bob) 30, 33, 36, 56, 57, 100, 279, 285, 286, 321n, 329

Pinnacle Club (see under Climbing Clubs)

Plas-y-Brenin x

Plymouth College 251
Pohl, Dr Gerda 245, 254
Pokhara 211, 241, 253, 263
Poppleston, Mike (Mick) 21, 37, 58, *94*, 101, 330
Porter, John 234, 279, 319n, 327, 330
Porter, Nigel 211, 249, 250
porters 119, 120, 134, 141, 142, 169, 170, 171, 173, 174, 177, 187, 194, 195, 197, 204, 217, 222, 223, 236, 241, 242, 250, 257, 261, 271
'Porters Progress' 247
Powell, Phil 243, 248, 255, 256, 260, 267, 320ns, 330
Powell, Sarah (see Loving, Sarah)
Prabhu, Sharu (see Scott, Sharavati)
Prescott, Nick 192, 193
Prince Charles (now HM King Charles III) 271
Prior, Denise 266, 330
Punta Arenas xxiv, 211, 212, 215, 216

Radford 2, 7, 8
Rajani 259
Raleigh Bicycles 2, 15, 180
Razzetti, Steve 154, 157, 172, 317n, 330
Read, Steve 39, 42, 44, 47, 48, 70, 71, 107, 311n, 330
Rébuffat, Gaston 59, 74, 133, 301, 313n
Renshaw, Dick 170
Reykjavik xvii, 205, 206, 207, 208, 303, 305
Rheged Centre 238, 257, 290
Richards, Ronnie 134, 135
Richey, Mark 330
Ridgeway, Rick 121, 330
Riley, Tony 169
Robbins, Royal and Liz 109, 314n, 327
Roberts, David 327, 328
Roberts, John 285, 321n, 330
Roberts, Lt Col J. O.M. (Jimmy) 130, 241, 249
Rose, David 200, 201, 202, 228, 330
Rosedale, Dr Barney 129, 130, 257, 330
Rosedale, Rachel 257, 330
Rothschild, Emmy (subs. Freeman-Attwood) 219
Rous, Sir Stanley 159

Rouse, Alan (Al) 165, 167, 168, 170, 171, 172, 199
Rowland, Clive 131, 132, 133, 134, 138, 139, 149, 316n, 330
Rowland, Stephanie 139
Royal Geographical Society 105, 160, 200, 232, 241, 265, 272, 275, 276, 291, 294

Sabir, Nazir 178, 179, 194, 195, 196, 319n, 330
St Petersburg 214
Salutation Inn, The 1, 40, 74
S & S Builders (and building generally) 16, 24, 113, 126–7, 241, 244, 248, 249, 252, 268, 271
Salzburg 272
Samye Ling 16, 113, 227, 230, 237, 238, 239, 319n
Sandhu, Colonel Balwant 119, 187, 218, 219, 222, 223
Saunders, Victor 141, 162, 164, 200, 201, 202, 266, 294, 317n, 318n, 327, 329, Plate 30
Schauer, Robert 181, 182, 203, 210
Scott, Arran 208, 219, 227, *228*, 229, 232, 270, 272, 292, 294, 329, Plate 34
Scott, Dr Brian 3, 7, 13, 16, 17, 18, *23*, 24, 32, 37, 59, *94*, 101, 155, 292, *293*, 307n, 308n, 312n, 329
Scott, Doug Frontispiece, *23, 45, 94, 228*, 293, Plates 13, 15, 17, 22, 27, 32, 34, 35, 40, 41, 42
  accidents in vehicles 20, 49–50, 75, 78, 82, 91, 103–4, 112, 231
  administration, attitudes towards 245, 258
  Alpine Club, presidency of 5, 227, 236–7
  ancestry 4–8
  astrology, interest in 229
  athletic abilities 3, 4, 15, 18, 20, 21, 22, 32, 43
  awards and honours
    academic honours 275–6; CBE 23, 232, 275; no knighthood 162,

237, 275; Piolet d'Or Lifetime 268, 276; RGS Patron's Gold Medal 232, 276

bicycles and cycling 2, 3, 14, 17, 24, 180

birth and birthdays xiii, 13, 26, 28, 177, 188, 193

bolting and pegging 42, 44, 47, 67, 84, 107, 108–9, 117, 166, 171, 235, 236, 284, 288, 289, 315n

British Mountaineering Council (see main entry)

brushes with the law 3, 14, 42, 43, 49, 68, 82, 91, 97, 120, 133

Buddhism 99, 148, 154, 237, 239, 259, 283, 319n, 325

Car Colston farm 32, 37, 56, 103

climbing style 46, 48, 53, 88, 202, 296, 321n

climbs and expeditions (see separate index)

Community Action Nepal (see Community Action Nepal)

Community Action Treks (see Community Action Treks)

comparative religion 84, 237–8

diet (including expedition food) 8, 10, 15, 16, 17, 72, 73, 77, 81, 84, 85, 115, 120, 154, 170, 188, 191, 192, 195, 212, 240, 244, 263, 264, 292, 293; vegetarianism 15, 77, 105, 154, 168, 170, 175, 193, 274, 281

domestic efficiency 105, 268, 273, 293

'Doug's Glamorous Assistants' 291–2

Dovedale Dash (see athletic abilities)

driving 74, 75, 78, 79, 97, 103–4, 116, 156, 206, 230, 231, 297, 291

drugs and smoking 27, 97, 120, 155, 175, 281, 309n

Duke of Edinburgh's Award 25, 33, 37, 309n

education

Cottesmore Secondary Modern 19–21; Lenton Boulevard School 30, 33, 36; Loughborough College 21, 24,

36–7, 38–9, 58, 59; Middleton Primary 18; Mundella Grammar School 21–4; Robert Shaw Primary 18

Elbrus, Mount (see Caucasus)

emotional effect of climbing 56, 58, 106, 111, 157, 259

encounters with wild animals 113, 195–6, 197

Eric Byne campsite 157–8

ethics (including environmental concerns) 3, 69, 111, 112, 113, 114, 147, 157, 161, 162, 171, 209, 217, 218, 225, 227, 235, 236, 243, 265, 268, 270, 276, 284, 296

expedition reports 46, 69–70, 86, 98, 101, 102

family, relations with xiii, 10, 13, 14, 15, 16–7, 18, 20, 22, 24, 32, 37, 55, 86, 101, 126, 155, 244, 270, 292, 308n

films and videos 50, 64, 68, 80, 81, 86, 108, 114, 115, 136, 156–7, 173, 176, 186, 199, 226, 270, 273–4, 315n

final illness 234, 275, 294

funeral & Memorial Services 294

geography, interest in 21, 22, 36, 69, 70

Harlem Globetrotters 18

health xi, 16, 18, 19, 42, 72, 73, 95, 140, 148–9, 180, 206, 208, 224, 233, 237, 257, 268, 274, 288, 312n

heroes 32, 74, 98–9, 131

high altitude tests 165–6, 303

history, interest in xiii, 10–12, 21, 22, 44, 84, 151, 157, 161, 233, 234

hitching 32, 41, 56, 59, 65, 70, 95, 312n

horsemanship 149, 156

houses 2,3, 7, 15, 18, 32, 38, 95, 97, 126, 127, 138, 229, 287

ice and snow caves 29, 123, 125, 137, 139, 143, 144, 168, 171, 175, 181, 205

indigenous peoples, interest in 69, 84, 114, 120, 218, 224, 240, 251, 281
infidelities 95, 97–8, 121, 148, 149, 153, 230, 238, 296
Iran 87, 138, 210, 272–3
Italy, northern 56, 58
Kangchenjunga (book) xi, xiii, 33, 100, 141, 161, 234, 240, 275, 310n, 317n, 323
leadership, attitudes towards 22, 74, 99, 105, 127, 129, 134–5, 241
lectures (see Community Action Nepal)
legacy 246, 285, 295, 296
marriages
　Jan xiv, 24, 72, 79, 93–4, 95, 96, 97, 126, 149, 153, 156, 279, 294; Sharu 148, 224, 229, 230, 279, 294; Trish 268, 270, 279, 287, 294
media, attitudes towards 148, 160, 265, 270, 271, 273, 285
medicine, interest in 79, 105, 241, 245, 250, 281–3, 308n
money, attitudes towards 6, 16, 32, 46, 56, 59, 66, 70, 94, 102, 114, 145, 158, 159, 160, 199, 242, 245, 246–7, 254, 260, 266, 270, 284–5
music, interest in 21, 42–3, 101, 111, 126, 142, 148, 165, 184, 187, 217, 315n
New England 178, 183
'Nomad' period 230
obituaries 268, 294–5
Oetztal Alps (see Ötztal Alps)
opera and ballet, interest in 58, 101, 290
Oread aspirant 40–1
photography 16, 53, 67, 83, 85, 104–5, 111, 136, 142, 148, 154, 156, 157, 162, 323; photographing corpse incident 67
physical character ix, 3, 4, 15, 18, 61, 93, 100, 137, 148–9, 224, 227, 230, 274
political interests 287–8
reading xiii, xiv, 18, 39, 98–101, 109, 119, 142, 144, 161, 241, 290

RGS Gold Medal (see awards and honours)
Romsdal, see Climbs and Expeditions/ Europe/Norway/Troll Wall
rugby ix, 19, 20, 21, 22, 28, 29, 36, 43, 48, 93, 97, 101, 126, 137, 149, 151, 281, 294
S & S Builders (see main list)
Scottish Country Dancing 290
scouting 21, 25, *26*, 27–8, 30, 32, 37, 40, 55
Seven Summits 185, 211, 213, 214, 217, 218, 323
Sezhik Bön Gompa (see Scott/ Climbs and Expeditions/Asia/Targo Ri)
ski-ing 52, 118, 122, 173, 174, 182, 205, 206–7, 233, 287, 305, 306
smoking (see drugs and smoking)
swimming 90–1, 93
Takpa Shiri (see Arunachal Pradesh)
teaching 24, 37, 38, 39, 48–50, 81, 113, 128,
'Third Man' phenomenon 138, 208
trees, interest in 3, 28, 81, 112, 187, 263, 265, 309n
UIAA 235, 236, 242, 265, 272, 273, 276, 280, 284, 288, 290
vegetable gardening 10, 15, 217, 244, 264, 268, 292–3, Plate 42
vegetarianism (see under diet)
vehicles, interest in
　lorries 3, 42, 67, 74, 75, 76, 78, 80, 81, 82, 86, 91, 103, 119, 249; minivans 31, 48, 49, 64, 68, 97, 104, 113, 207, 314n; motorbikes 20, 66, 103–4, 249
voluntary work 155, 243, 268, 291
windfarms 289, Plate 41
writing 27, 37, 64, 99, 101, 102, 113, 150–3, 154, 160, 165, 227, 233–4, 278, 284, 290, 291, 292, 296, 315n
Yugoslavia 37, 55, 56, 58, 69, 81, 87, 311n
Scott, Euan 208, 219, 227, *228*, 229, 232, 270, 272, 292, 294, 329

Scott, Garry 3, 16, *23*, 24, 113, 126,
    155, 244, 292, *293*, 314n, 329
Scott, George 2, 8–17, *9*, 18, 19, 20,
    23, 25, 27, 28, 55
Scott, Janice née Brook 17, 21, 24, 49,
    52, 61, 62, 66, 67, 68, 93–9, 104,
    109, 112, 113, 116, 117, 122, 126,
    130, 134, 135, 148–56, *152*, 160,
    162, 165, 168, 174, 175, 185, 187,
    193, 196, 200, 205, 227, 228, 231–
    2, *282*, 312n, 313ns, 314n, 316n
Scott, Joyce xiii, 2, 3, 7, 8, 10, *11*, 13,
    15, 16, 17, 18, 22, *23*, 55, 64, 86,
    97, 270, 292, 307n
Scott, Dr Martha 117, 150, 151, 155,
    168, 174, 177, 178, 185, 196, 198,
    231, 274, 312n, 329, Plate 22
Scott, Michael 5, 65, 68, 93, 96, 97, 98,
    100, 113, 116, 130, 150, 151, 154,
    156, 172, 173, 174, 175, 178, 181,
    185, 194, 195, 231, *282*, 283, 316n
Scott, Richard 292, *293*, 321n, 329
Scott, Sharavati (Sharu), née Prabhu 17,
    148, 177, 181, 182, 183, 197, 200,
    201, 206, 207, 208, 213, 217, 219,
    224, 225, 226, 227, 228, 229, 230,
    231, 232, 246, 247, 249, 250, 251,
    255, 272, 318n, 319n, Plate 30
Scott, Trish née Blanche 17, 154, 227,
    230, 232, 238, 239, 245, 254, 257,
    258, 259, 260, 268, *269*, 269,
    270, 271–5, 279, 280, 283, 284,
    287–90, 293, 294, 317n, 320ns,
    329, Plate 40
Scott-Ward, Rosie 130, 151, *152*, 155,
    156, 168, 174, 196, 292, 318n,
    329
Seigneur, Yannick 106, 314n
Shah, Gohar 170, 172
Shahi, Alija 240, 330
Sharp, David 280
Shaw, Bob 48, 51, 330
Shawangunks xxiii, 106, 115, 300, 314n
Sherpa(s) (see also under individual
    names) xi, 128, 129, 130, 135,
    141, 166, 175, 179, 226, 240, 241,
    242, 246, 250, 252, 262, 275, 281,
    308n, 320n

'Sherpa Heritage House' 240, 271
Shipton Col 119, 120, 177
Shipton, Eric 32, 98, 124, 149, 285
Shrestha, Bhoj Raj 260, 330
Siddiqui, Rehan 287
Sikkim 143, 199, 218, 305
Sindhupalchowk 252, 260
Singh, Ratan 187
Singh, Sanjeev 260, 330
Smith, Clive 28, 30
Smith, Gordon (Speedy) 131, 132
Smith, Sean 177, 179, 194, 195, 196
Smith, Steve (Sid) 41, 65, 66, 67, 114,
    311n, 312n, 330, Plate 13
Snell's Field 56
Snively, Doug 117, 121, 274
Sofia xix, 270, 306
Solu Khumbu xi, 241, 260
Sonam Dorje, Sherpa 252, 330
Souch, Dr Claire 264, 330
South Africa 272, 306
Sri Lanka xx, 273, 288, 306
Sterney, Terence (Stengun) 28
Stewart Hill Cottage 15, 237, 239, 268,
    271, 311n, 316n, 317ns
Stroud, Geoffrey 32, 33, 37, 39, 55,
    56, 58, 64, 93, *94*, 103, 104, 222,
    311n, 314n, 330
Stroud, Richard 19, 44, 87, 90, 330
'Surgery in Nepal'(SIN) 269
Sustad, Stephen (Steve) 170, 172, 174,
    175, 176, 177, 181, 186, 194,
    196, 203, 204, 214, 257, 319n,
    330
Sutton, Geoffrey 29, 31, 48, 59, 60, 68,
    98, 161, 310n, 324
Swenson, Steve 172, 173, 318n, 328,
    330

Taillac de, family 271
Tamang, Bhai B. 248, 258, 330
Tamang, Mangale 257, 330
Tamang, Mangal Singh (Nima) 181,
    182, 242
Tamang, Saela (Sila) 174, 175, 181
Tamang, Tej Bahadur 247, 250, 330
Tapovan 186, 187, 188
Targo Ri xxi, 224, 225

Tasker, Joe 141, 142, 143, 144, 166, 167, 169, 170, 181, 214, 220, 315n, 317ns, 328, Plate 19, Plate 20
Tasker, John 69, 214, 330
Tasker, Terry 330
Tek, Captain 252, 254
Telendos xix, 288, 306
Temba Lama 262
Tensing, Sherpa Norgay (see Tenzing)
Tenzing, Sherpa Norgay xiii, 13
Terray, Lionel 74, 98, 99, 313n
Terry, Mick 87, 89, 107, 108, 109
Thexton, Pete 170, 171, 172, 206
Thimbu 270, 305
Thimphu 200
Thompson, Peter 45, 47, 52, 106, 311n, 330
Tibesti Mountains (see Scott/Climbs and Expeditions/Africa)
Tibet x, xi, xxi, 16, 21, 120, 188, 192, 199, 205, 217, 237, 238, 245, 252, 328 (see also Scott/Climbs and Expeditions/Asia)
Tighe, Tony 130
Tiso, Graham 130
Torres del Paine 273
Tullis, Julie 226, 328
Turnbull, Dave 285, 287

Unsworth, Walt 159
Upton, Jeff 68, 107, 108, 112
Urquhart, Helen (née Padday) 197, 319n, 330
Uttarkashi xxi, 187
Utting, Glyn 260, 327, 330

Valour in Sport Award 158–60
Venables, Stephen ix-xi, 285, 295, 321n, 329
Vickers, Ken 87, 91
Vulgarian Digest 109, 324

Wall, Ian 257, 258, 280, 320n, 330
Walton, Tena 94, 313n, 314n, 329
Walung xxi, 252, 257, 263, 272, 306
Wark, Bob 48, 49, 50, 84, 311n, 330
Watts, Tony 47, 73, 84, 87, 88, 89, 134

Webster, Dr Michael (Mick) 22, 81, 118, 313n, 330
Webster (later, Holland), Susan 22, 308n, 330
Wells, Ted 108, 112, 330
Wells, Terry 48, 53
West, Martin 248, 255
West Yorkshire Scouts 256
Whillans, Don 10, 29, 33, 44, 46, 52, 53, 58, 61, 65, 74, 127, 128, 129, 170, 172, 186, 187, 188, 192, 278, 310n, 317n, 327
White Hall Outdoor Centre 26, 29, 30, 31, 32, 40, 48, 98, 205, 234, 295, 297, 310ns, 311n, 327
White, Rick 117, 186, 188, 189, 191, 202, Plate 26
Wilkinson, Dave (Wink) 68, 312n, 330
Williams, Jed 243
Wilmott, Tony 107, 109
Wilson, Bob 134
Wilson, Harold 307n
Wilson, Ken 52, 57, 68, 101, 107, 117, 129, 309n, 327, 328
Wollaton
  canal 3, 4, 14, 24; Charlbury Road 2, 3, 7, 18, 32, 38; pit 3, 14; railway line 3, 14; suburb 2, 3, 4, 6, 7, 8, 16, 94; Wollaton Park 3, 7, 18, 20, 38
Wood, Laurie 203, 204, 315n, 330
Wood, Rob 51, 113, 114, 115, 121, 124, 125, 134, 203, 204, 208, 209, 315n, 324, 328, 330, Plate 13, Plate 29
Woolcock, Dave 44
WYG 260, 276

Yacoub, Sir Magdi 253
Yates, Jane 289, 321n, 330
Yates, Simon 177, 202, 209, 210, 289, 321n, 328, 330
Young, Geoffrey Winthrop 68, 161, 233, 308n
Zamok (see Scott, Doug: Fann Mountains)
Zermatt 73, 272

Index of Climbs and Expeditions

Africa
  Atlas Mountains xix, 38, 44, 62, 63,
    69, 70–3, *71*, 74, 84, 95, 101, 289,
    298, 312n, 323; *Kilimanjaro* xix,
    124, 301; *Mount Kenya* xix, 123,
    301; *Tibesti* x, xix, 3, 39, 44, 65,
    69, 70, 73, 74–9, 81, 86, 99, 102,
    299, 314n, 323, Plate 1, Plate 2
Americas
  Aconcagua xxiv, 211–3, 217, 229,
    304, 315n; *Adirondacks* 272;
    Atacama Desert xxiv, 273, 306;
    Baffin Island x, xvii, 22, 51, 101,
    106, 107, 113, 114–8, 131, 145,
    161, 273, 281, 300, 301, Plates
    11–13; *Cascades Range* xxiii, 117,
    300; *Colonel Foster, Mount* xxiii,
    208–9, 303, Plates 28 & 29;
    Denali (Mount McKinley) xxiii,
    118, 122–3, 301, Plate 16; *Estes
    Park* xxiii, 117, 121, 151, 156,
    288, 300, 301; *FitzRoy* xxiv, 212,
    304, 313; *Long's Peak* xxiii, 121,
    301; *Taylor, Mount* 121, 301;
    Tetons xxiii, 116, 301; *Tierra
    del Fuego* xxiv, 215–6, 305;
    Waddington, Mount xxiii, 121,
    124–5, 301, Plate 18; *Yosemite* x,
    xxiii, 52, 54, 102, 106, 108, 110,
    112, 117, 118, 164, 166, 171, 186,
    300, 301, 302, 315ns, 327; BHOS
    110, 300, 315n; El Capitan xxiii,
    110, 111, 113, 117, 150, 186, 300,
    314n; Salathé Wall 54, 109–10,
    145, 300, 315ns, Plate 10; other
    climbs 110, 121, 150, 161, 166

Arctic and Antarctic
  Greenland xvii, 29, 157, 205,
    210–11, 304; *Vinson, Mount* xxiv,
    211–2, 304
Asia
  Afghanistan (see Hindu Kush);
    Ali Ratni Tibba xx, 197, 303;
    Arunachal Pradesh (Takpa Shiri)
    xix, 201, 222–3, 305, 319n, Plate
    36; *Baruntse* 175, 302; *Biacherahi*
    (see Latok); *Broad Peak* 88, 170,
    171, 172, 173, 302; *Chamlang*
    xxi, 173, 175–6, 273, 302;
    Changabang xxi, 118–20, 130,
    133, 145, 301, 315n, 323; *Chombu*
    xxi, 218–9, 305; *Diran* xx, 194–6,
    303; *Drohmo* xxi, 142, 219–21,
    221, 229, 305, Plate 34, Plate 35;
    Everest, Mount ix, x, xi, xiii, xiv, xv,
    xxi, 13, 17, 19, 21, 33, 43, 44, 51,
    67, 106, 116, 117, 120, 122, 124,
    125, 137, 138, 139, 141, 145, 146,
    148, 149, 150, 151, 153, 154, 155,
    157, 160, 161, 162, 166, 167, 168,
    169, 186, 197, 198, 208, 221, 227,
    229, 233, 237, 241, 252, 257, 262,
    265, 266, 273, 275, 277, 280, 291,
    294, 306, 308ns, 317ns, 320, 321,
    323, 324, 325, 326, 327, Plate 14,
    Plate 15; 1972 (Spring) 127–9,
    241, 300; 1972 (Autumn) 129–
    31, 257, 278, 301; 1975 South-
    west Face 133–6, 150, 241, 278,
    301; 1987 North-east ridge 146,
    181–2, 242, 303; *Fann Mountains*
    xx, 91, 213, 304, Plate 3; *Hindu*

Kush xx, 53, 69, 81, 85, 86–91, 91, Plate 5, Plate 6; *Hiunchuli IV (Hanging Glacier Peak)* xxi, 211, 304; *Hunza* xx, 170, 178, 194–6, 303 *Jitchu Drake* xxi, 200–2, 228, 303, Plate 30; *K2* xx, 106, 144, 145, 146, 164, 169, 185, 210, 226, 316n, 318ns, 327, 328; 1978 Expedition 144, 169–70, 278, 279, 302; 1980 151, 170, 186, 302; 1983 Expedition 70–2, 302; 1987 Expedition 154, 155, 172–3, 303; *Kangchenjunga* xi, xiv, xxi, 6, 101, 136, 141–4, 147, 151, 166, 167, 186, 201, 219, 220, 221, *221*, 242, 249, 302, 303, 310n, 311n, Plate 19, Plate 20; *Kangchungtse* xxi, 174, 302; *Karphogang* 171, 302; *Kusum Kangguru* xxi, 144, 146, 166, 167, 302; *Latok Range* 209, 210, 242, 304; *Lobsang Spire* xx, 170, 171, 302, Plate 27; *Makalu* xxi,173, 182, 257, 313n, Plate 22, Plate 23; 1980 Expedition 170, 174, 302; 1984 Expedition 153, 170, 174, 176–7, 302; 1988 Expedition 177–8, 303; *Nanga Parbat* xx, 98, 127, 178, 196, 213; 1985 Expedition 178–9, 303; 1992 Expedition 179, 304; 1993 Expedition 179–80, 304; 1995 Expedition 180–1, 305; *Nuptse* xxi, 144, 156, 166–8, 302, Plate 21; *Ogre, The* (Baintha Brakk) xi, xx, 19, 62, 122, 124, 134, 136, 138–41, *140*, 146, 149, 151, 158, 161, 173, 180, 183, 185, 209, 222, 232,243, 257, 266, 273, 278, 301, 309n, 316n, 320n, 323, Plate 17; *Rimo Group* xx,203, 204, 304; *Russian Pamirs* xx, 89, 120, 121, 122, 128, 131–3, 145, 149, 288, 301; Pik Lenin xx, 132, 301; *Shishapangma* x, xxi, 146, 192–4, 212, 302, 317n, 320n, 323; *Shivling* xxi, 33, 99, 149, 186–92, *190*, 302, 312n, 319n, Plate 25,

Plate 26; *Sosbun Brakk* 122, 134, 149, 150, 301; *Targo Ri* xxi, 224, 305, Plate 37; *Teng Kongma* 220, 305; *Western Ghats* xx, 197–8, 303; *Yaupa* 175, 302

Australasia

Australia xxii, 151, 154, 160, 162, 194, 202–3, 229, 230, 270, 272, 273, 302, 304, 327 *Carstensz Pyramid* xxii, 217, 234, 305, 315n, 323, Plate 33; *Darran Range* xxii, 185, 186, 302, Plate 24

Europe (UK and Ireland)

England Birchen Edge 28, 29, 49, 297; 'Blue Peter' climb 226, 273, 302; Borrowdale xvi, 226, 289, 302; Eden Valley 289; Derwent Valley xvi, 28, 42, 44, 46, 50, 81, 102, 308n, 323; Gordale Scar xvi, 47, 77, 299; Hemlock Stone 4, 24; High Peak xvi, 308n; Kilnsey Crag 41, 46, 123, 299; Kinder Scout xvi, 21, 27, 29, 30, 31, 297, 310n; Malham Cove 46, 47, 299; Scafell Pike area xvi, 33, 47, 297; Wasdale Head 33, 298

Ireland, Northern xvi, 48, 177

Ireland, Republic of xvi, 43, 48, 69

Scotland Am Buachaille xvi, 183, 305 Arran (island) xvi, 21, 31–2, 290, 297, 321n; Beinn Bhan (Applecross) xvi, 165, 303; Ben More (Mull) xvi, 245; Ben Nevis xvi, 25, 36, 50, 51, 80, 164, 298, 302, 311n; Ben Wyvis xvi, 50, 298; Bidean nam Bian xvi, 50–1, 138, 298; Cairngorms 20, 43, 49, 50, 51, 52, 80, 113, 164, 250, 299, 300; Cape Wrath 49; Cuillin xvi, 164, 302; Kintail (Five Sisters) xvi, 33, 35, 164, 298, 302; Mamores xvi, 25, 35, 50, 298, 308n; Old Man of Hoy xvi, 183, 227, 305; Old Man of Stoer xvi, 184, 305; Seana Braigh xvi, 165; Stac Pollaidh xvi, 49, 289, 299, 306; Strone Ulladale xvi, 38, 54, 102,

106–8, 273, 300, 314n, Plate 8;
Suilven xvi, 49, 299; Torridon xvi,
33–5, 187, 298
Wales Beddgelert 30, 297; Clogwyn
Du'r Arddu 52, 299; Gogarth xvi,
52, 53, 102,106, 299; Snowdonia
x, xvi, 10, 30, 37, 40, 41, 52,
63, 65, 94, 103, 297, 298, 299;
Tremadog 227, 303
(Continental Europe)
Bernese Oberland Blüemlisalphorn
xviii, 55, 297; Eiger xviii, 67, 170,
224–6, 304; *Bernina* Piz Palü 68,
300; *Bregaglia* Ago di Sciora xviii,
59, 60, 298; Piz Badile xviii, 59,
60, 298; Pizzi Gemelli 60, 298
Caucasus 214, 305 *Chamonix
Alps* Aiguille de Blaitière 65,
299, 312n; Aiguille de la Nonne
61, 298; Aiguille de l'Évêque
61, 298; Aiguille de l'M 57, 61,
298; Aiguille du Chardonnet 61,
298; Aiguille du Fou 62, 298;
Aiguille du Midi 56, 66, 133, 299,
301; Aiguille du Moine 61, 298;
Aiguille du Peigne 56, 65, 297,
299; Aiguille du Petit Dru 50, 68,
106, 300; Aiguille du Plan 57, 62,
66, 67, 299; Aiguille Mummery
61, 298; Aiguille Ravanel 61, 298;
Cornes du Chamois 62, 298;
Dent du Géant 62, 298; Dent du
Requin xviii, 56, 57, 298; Frêney,
Central pillar of 61, 278; Grand

Capucin 62, 298; Grépon 62; Mer
de Glace xviii, 56, 62, 66, 165,
297; Mont Blanc xviii, 37, 56, 58,
61, 62, 66, 89, 99, 165, 278, 298;
Monte Gruetta xviii, 165, 302;
Montenvers 66, 67; Nantillons
Glacier 62, 95, Vallée Blanche
66; *'Climb for the World' scheme*
224–6; *Dauphiné Alps* xviii, 58–9,
298 *Dolomites* x, xviii, 47, 54,
55, 65, 66, 68, 77, 96, 106, *108*,
109, 162,299, 300, 327 *Iceland*
xvii, 157, 205–208, 230, 296,
303, 304, 305, 319n, 329, Plate
32 *Julian Alps* xviii, 37, 58, 288;
Norway xviii, 112, 178, 182, 288,
300; Hemsedal xviii, 102, 303;
Kvaløya xviii, 183, 305; Lyngen
Alps xviii, 183, 305; Troll Wall
area (Romsdal) xviii, 106, 112,
182, 303, Plate 9 *Ötztal Alps* xviii,
62, 166, 298, 303; *Spain* xviii,
55, 59, 63, 64, 69, 95, 178, 323
Cantabrian Mountains 63, 64,
299; Picos de Europa 63–4, 184,
273, 305; Pyrenees xviii, 64, 104,
113, 155, 29, 300; Sierra Nevada
xviii, 62–3, 70, 73, 95, 298
Middle East
Čilo Daği xix, 38, 39, 69, 79–86,
101, 113, 299, 313ns, 323, Plate
3, Plate 4, Plate 7; *Jordan* (Wadi
Rum) xix, 194, 198, 288, 303,
306, 319n, 326